T0369586

*"The Amazing Iro_
the Invention of the En_

"The Amazing Iroquois" and the Invention of the Empire State

JOHN C. WINTERS

OXFORD
UNIVERSITY PRESS

OXFORD
UNIVERSITY PRESS

Oxford University Press is a department of the University of Oxford. It furthers
the University's objective of excellence in research, scholarship, and education
by publishing worldwide. Oxford is a registered trade mark of Oxford University
Press in the UK and certain other countries.

Published in the United States of America by Oxford University Press
198 Madison Avenue, New York, NY 10016, United States of America.

Library of Congress Cataloging-in-Publication Data
Names: Winters, John C., author.
Title: "The amazing Iroquois" and the invention of the Empire State / John C. Winters.
Description: New York : Oxford University Press, 2023. |
Includes bibliographical references and index.
Identifiers: LCCN 2022042537 (print) | LCCN 2022042538 (ebook) |
ISBN 9780197578223 (hardback) | ISBN 9780197578247 (epub) |
ISBN 9780197578254
Subjects: LCSH: Iroquois Indians—Influence. | New York (State)—
Civilization—Indian influences. | Iroquois Indians—Government relations. |
Seneca Indians—Biography. | Peace—Medals. | Red Jacket,
Seneca chief, approximately 1756–1830. | Parker, Ely Samuel, 1828–1895. |
Converse, Harriet Maxwell, 1836–1903. |
Parker, Arthur C. (Arthur Caswell), 1881–1955. |
Iroquois Indians—History. | Collective memory—New York (State)
Classification: LCC E99.I7 W568 2023 (print) | LCC E99.I7 (ebook) |
DDC 974.7004/9755—dc23/eng/20220912
LC record available at https://lccn.loc.gov/2022042537
LC ebook record available at https://lccn.loc.gov/2022042538

DOI: 10.1093/oso/9780197578223.001.0001

1 3 5 7 9 8 6 4 2
Printed by Sheridan Books, Inc., United States of America

For Julia R. Myers

Contents

Acknowledgments

THIS PROJECT IS an amalgam of the people, places, and experiences that brought me to this moment in my scholarly career. In every chapter I see people I met, books I read, the snippets of insight from colleagues and friends, and the many museums I visited. That makes these acknowledgments an incomplete thought, at best, but for everyone I mention and those that I miss, my thanks for your influence cannot come enthusiastically enough.

To David Waldstreicher. Where to begin? You are a model scholar, writer, and advisor. I have benefitted immeasurably from your brilliance on paper and in person. Thank you for everything. To Andrew Robertson, you have been an ally of mine since I started my academic journey. I am deeply thankful for your professional guidance, your scholarly voice, and your never-ending support. To Camilla Townsend, thank you for your dedication to and invaluable commentary on this project. I aspire to "spin a good yarn" as smoothly, intelligently, and forcefully as you do. To Donna Haverty-Stacke, thank you for helping to mold me into a better educator and for your sage scholarly commentary. To Deborah Gardner, your pioneering work in New York City public history inspired me and our work together exposed me to the real challenges and potential of public history. All of that, whether you knew it or not, influenced this book. To my editor, Susan Ferber, thank you endlessly for your interest in this project and your patience and dedication to it despite a global pandemic. I look forward to the day when we can meet in person. Many thanks go to my friends and reading group of Scott Ackerman, Luke Reynolds, and Krystle Sweda. You kept me honest, on track, and offered comments and editorial advice that strengthened this book considerably. Thanks also to the anonymous readers at Oxford University Press for their insight and suggestions.

More thanks go to the Fred W. Smith National Library for the Study of George Washington, the CUNY Early Research Initiative, and the Graduate

Center whose financial support made this book possible. There were many institutions and people who helped me from a distance and in person at the University of Rochester, the New York State Museum, Library, and Archives, the New-York Historical Society, Cornell University, the University of Virginia, and the Library of Congress.

Special thanks go to those who offered commentary on this project, eased my way through the archives, and whose insights made this book stronger. Thanks to Gwendolyn Saul at the New York State Museum, Joe Stahlman at the Seneca-Iroquois National Museum, Kathryn Murano Santos and Stephanie Ball at the Rochester Museum and Science Center, and Melissa Mead at the University of Rochester. I am also deeply grateful for the project-specific and otherwise general scholarly advice over the years from Marshall Becker, Edward Countryman, Laurence Hauptman, Michael A. McDonnell, and Kandice Watson.

To my dear friend, Scott Ackerman. Thank you for your friendship, insight, and for helping me usher this project through its ups and downs. I could not have done this without you.

To my parents, Don and Lyn. You made this dream possible. To Chuck and Julie. You showed me what was possible. To Katherine, Dan, and Michelle, thank you for everything but particularly for my amazing niece and nephews. They will be great historians one day.

To Maggie. Thank you for your patience, support, and the hours of time you spent helping me work through book problems out loud. Onward to our next adventure—I can't wait.

*"The Amazing Iroquois" and
the Invention of the Empire State*

Introduction

"THE AMAZING IROQUOIS" IN MYTH AND MEMORY

IN NEW YORK'S collective unconscious, the Haudenosaunee, known to many as the Iroquois, are not like other Native Americans. Often, when Americans think of Indigenous history they think of a distant past or of a "vanishing" people. They call to mind old-timey stories of three-masted ships landing on the east coast bearing Pilgrims, or of battlefields filled with musket smoke, tomahawks, and red coats. Or they recall the Hollywood version of the Wild West, where famed actors like John Wayne and Randolph Scott played heroic cowboys defending their homes and families from "savage" war-bonneted Plains Indians while stoics stood by and lamented the loss of their way of life. Even the various names for Indigenous peoples like "Indians," "First Nations," or "Native Americans" seem to convey a distant past, of a "first" but decidedly not modern people.[1]

This imaginary conception of that history subtly shifts, however, when white New Yorkers think of the Haudenosaunee. They are hardly immune from these stereotypes, but that memory also binds them to the conception of a modernizing and forward-looking Empire State. Some may recall the history of the Longhouse, the metaphorical house within which the nations resided. The word Haudenosaunee itself means "people of the longhouse," and within it the Senecas guard the Western Door, the Mohawks the Eastern Door, and between them are the Cayugas, Onongadas, and Oneidas. The Tuscaroras joined the Longhouse as the sixth nation in the early eighteenth century. The Longhouse was also a physical part of daily Haudenosaunee life because they were iconic multiple-family dwellings that could be several hundred feet long and were used for everything from political to religious ceremonies. Today, you can visit a reconstructed Mohawk Iroquois Longhouse at the New York State Museum in Albany, a Seneca Longhouse reconstructed at the Ganondagan Historic Site, or experience the ongoing cultural relevance of this iconic structure at the Iroquois Museum in Howes Cave, New York, whose museum building is modeled on the Longhouse.[2]

Contrast that uniquely Haudenosaunee architecture with the history of the famed "Sky Walkers," those Indigenous steelworkers who built New York City icons like the Empire State Building, the George Washington Bridge, 30 Rockefeller Center, the Chrysler building, and One World Trade Center with Mohawk steel. These steelworkers were an important part of the construction of modern urban skylines throughout the twentieth and into the twenty-first century and became renowned for their supposed fearlessness as they balanced on thin beams hundreds of feet in the air. Meanwhile, Canadian-Iroquois steel plants produced, and still are producing, a sizable proportion of the steel that forms the backbone of skyscrapers in cities across the northeast today. Even if one were to travel out of these cities, a casual observer driving through New York State will notice that the land itself is a living reminder of the Haudenosaunee through its countless Indigenous place names.[3]

Some may recall aspects of Haudenosaunee social and political life that inform our modern conceptions of gender equality. Feminist scholars and political actors, for example, have used the matrilineal Haudenosaunee as models for modern women's rights. New York-based suffrage reformers of the nineteenth century like Elizabeth Cady Stanton drew examples from Haudenosaunee society to emphasize the hypocrisy of America's attitudes toward women's political inequality. Since these women selected national and League leadership, participated in national and League governance, held the keys to naming and kinship, and were expected to voice their political opinions on behalf of their nations, the women's suffrage movement of the nineteenth and twentieth centuries used that aspect of Haudenosaunee cul-ture to draw a stark contrast between New York's own "primitive" Indigenous peoples who granted women political and social rights and the supposedly more "advanced" Anglo-American society who suppressed them.[4]

Those equally politically minded may also think that the United States itself has origins in the philosophy and structure of government established by the League of the Haudenosaunee. This idea was born in the 1970s and 1980s and became what scholars call the Iroquois Influence Thesis. The Thesis claimed that the government of the League served as the model for the US Constitution. But it did not end there. "The character of American democ-racy" itself has evolved from Haudenosaunee culture and politics because their philosophy of government-by-consensus shaped America's vision of its own core democratic principles, and the League governing philosophy also respected individual and local autonomy. The purpose of the Thesis, in that light, was to "grow a more complete, accurate, and honest understanding of the ideas that shaped the character of America." It found a famous adherent in Vine Deloria, Jr., one of the twentieth century's foremost Indigenous intellectuals who was so taken with it that he called its authors the "Rogers and Hammerstein of Indian history." The Thesis created a precedent for those who looked for ways to co-opt aspects of Indigenous life in order to illuminate contemporary American issues. It was an intriguing idea, particularly during the Cold War. Supporters explained that while the Thesis began that effort, "more needs to be done" in order to root the League fully into the United States' founding, "especially if America continues to view itself as a distinct entity set apart from many of the values of Western civilization." After all, as the United States began to tip the scales against the Soviet Union and panned for every ounce of American exceptionalism they could, what could be more homegrown or American than Native America?[5]

These many stories and memories all point to a larger cultural perception of the Iroquois, one that has shed some of the lost-to-time patina that colors how the rest of Native American history is remembered. It is a history that has been remembered as both ancient and modern, alive yet "vanished," and that conveys a moral authority reminiscent of the stereotypical Indigenous "stoic" that speaks to more than the facts of history. That memory has been a useful foil in white America's fight against the regressive impulses of its own society and politics. In that regard, it seems that influential Seneca anthropologist and museologist Arthur C. Parker, himself one of the main purveyors of that memory, was on to something when he titled his 1954 ten-volume unpublished history "The Amazing Iroquois."[6]

Considering this legacy, it is worth asking why the public's memory of the Haudenosaunee is different. Traditionally, the dominant American culture has appropriated the image and history of Native Americans for its own devices. Today, these self-serving metaphors and stereotypes are easy to see and dismiss, and because of that some of the most famous purveyors of these stereotypes are changing their ways. Think of Land-o-Lakes Butter, who in 2020 finally decided to dispense with the Indian maiden from its logo, or the Washington DC football team that, after decades of pressure, abandoned their racist Indian-themed mascot in favor of the Commanders. Unlike these examples, however, the Iroquois have not always occupied the same space as a "charming" or "savage" vestige of the past, but rather have a reputation as an indelible part of New York's progressive democratic culture, as a people who helped make the state's history unique and forward looking. This begs the question: Why have they become a source of Empire State pride when history shows that people across America have long sought to eliminate evidence of Native America's participation in their culture and history entirely?

The answer lies in the fact that these memories were not manufactured by the usual suspects. That is, those white Americans who co-opted Indigenous culture and history for their own ends. Instead, they were influenced and spread by a different set of historical figures: the Haudenosaunee themselves, specifically some of the Senecas' most famous leaders. In that respect, these Senecas were unsung agents in the nineteenth and twentieth century invention of the historical, political, and social conception of the Empire State.[7] They made their own memories, rewrote and represented their peoples' history on their own terms, and then packaged and delivered those stories to New Yorkers who listened to them and often wanted them to be true. These stories continue to be told in museums, classrooms, and popular books. The result of this centuries-long infusion of the Iroquois into New York's history and identity made it possible for New Yorkers to think first of the Haudenosaunee, above all other Native American nations, as the focal point of an effort to find the Indigenous "part of our national soul."[8]

———

"The Amazing Iroquois" traces the long history of this vision of Iroquois exceptionalism. Iroquois exceptionalism is a fusion of New York—and by extension American—exceptionalism and what scholars call "Iroquois supremacy," or the Haudenosaunee's own historic conception of their political history.[9] To find the roots of this idea, this book follows the lives of four related (by blood or by claim) Senecas from the American Revolution to the Cold War: Red Jacket, Ely S. Parker, Harriet Maxwell Converse, and Arthur C. Parker. Each of them was born to or adopted into the Senecas, the largest of the Six Nations in the United States. They also became some of the most famous Native Americans of their generation who, by design or by accident of their celebrity, shaped how the Haudenosaunee and their history are still remembered. Both on their own and with the timely and strategic support of leadership, each of them reminded New Yorkers that the state, its government, its land, and its people had a unique and historic relationship with the Iroquois.

They were assisted in this effort, in large part, by who they were. It mattered to the public that Red Jacket and the Parkers were Seneca, and that Converse was adopted into the Seneca Snipe Clan. As the metaphorical and geographic guardians of the Western Door of the Longhouse, the Senecas constituted the largest national population of Haudenosaunee in the region south and east of Lake Ontario, an area that by the end of the 1820s would become part of the state of New York. Because of the Senecas' relative size and influence among the Six Nations in the United States, when Red Jacket, the Parkers, or Converse spoke, they appeared to be speaking for all the nations. It also mattered that all but Arthur Parker was elected to or given a token title of a national or League chief. Converse, in particular, was given an honorary title as a League chief, a title that held no real political authority but that nevertheless came with the blessings of those Six Nations leaders who supported her. And to be a leader was to be a vital part of Haudenosaunee politics and society. Leaders served as diplomats and carriers of tribal history and were responsible for using "the past to deal with cultural, economic, and political survival."[10] While Converse and Arthur Parker did not hold formal leadership positions, they still played important roles in Seneca society as well as in Six Nations politics. In addition to their influence among the Haudenosaunee, it mattered that they read and spoke English fluently, that all but Red Jacket were Christian (which made them a Seneca minority), and that all after Red Jacket supported degrees of Indian assimilation. White New Yorkers therefore learned about the history of the Haudenosaunee through the lives of four Senecas who were not so Indigenous as to be alien, but who seemed just Indigenous enough to still be considered "authentic."[11]

The key to that contemporary conception of authenticity was kinship. Kinship was "inextricably bound up" with "Iroquois politics and governance" and was central to how individuals understood their place in the world through clan belonging and familial ties.[12] In that light, this book can be read as an extended family story, with each chapter acting like a branch of a family tree. Red Jacket, the Parkers, and even Converse were related to one another in meaningful ways through their real or invented kinship with the family progenitor Red Jacket, their membership in the Wolf or Snipe clans, and their close personal ties to one another. In Converse's case, what mattered more in her experience was how others viewed her kinship. She was an adoptee, and while that mattered a great deal to her and to the Senecas who approved and protected her status in the nation, it mattered more for the outside world who saw her as a genuine and "authentic" kinswoman of the Senecas. Their familial connections, whether real or fictive, also mattered to Haudenosaunee leadership who recognized, elected, and supported each of them, and to those contemporary Americans who viewed them all as famous representatives of

a continuous and unbroken line of ancient and distinguished Seneca heritage. As a result, these four were not only capable of moving through white
spaces and being accepted within them, once there they strategically deployed
their kinship as a weapon, a shield, an authenticator in the eyes of the outside
world, and found or created incentives to deploy Haudenosaunee culture in
moments that mattered.

While Red Jacket, the Parkers, and Converse shaped the memory of an
exceptional Iroquoian history for themselves and the Haudenosaunee on
their own terms, they also used the language and tools of white America to
package and deliver that message to white New Yorkers and those living beyond the Empire State's borders. From the halls of international diplomacy to
popular museum exhibitions, they told Indigenous stories and shared Seneca
perspectives in ways that white Americans would understand and recognize.
An important part of that construction lay in their use and reconceptualization
of the notion of an historic Iroquois empire, one that served as the very
ur memory of Iroquois exceptionalism. That myth of empire, what some
historians have described as a "considerable amount of nonsense," is broadly
attributed to the father of American ethnography, Lewis H. Morgan, and his
landmark 1851 publication *League of the Ho-dé-no-sau-nee*.[13] With the help
of his friend and informant, Ely Parker, Morgan popularized the idea that
the Six Nations were legendary "Romans of the Woods," a "colossal Indian
empire" unmatched in power or presence by any Indian nation "north of the
Aztec monarchy."[14]

As Chapter 1 reveals, however, the myth of Iroquois empire was not invented
by Morgan or Parker alone. It had been percolating among New Yorkers for
decades in large part because Red Jacket and his contemporaries were tireless in reminding the new United States of the Six Nations' historic power.
It became most popular, however, only after the Six Nations ceased to be a
military threat by the time of the War of 1812. In that moment New Yorkers
could publicly, and falsely, claim to have conquered the continent's greatest
Indigenous empire. This was a cornerstone of New York's continuing efforts
to expulse the Haudenosaunee from their land.

Over the next century, with the tending of Red Jacket, the Parkers, and
Converse, this memory of the Iroquois empire grew to encompass many facets
of the Haudenosaunees' political structures and their historic relationship to
New York. That shift changed what New Yorkers considered important in
Haudenosaunee history. Where other Indigenous nations were understood
by white Americans primarily through their unique cultural forms (war bonnets, horses, teepees, etc.), the Haudenosaunee came to be understood just

as much for their political history and relationship to New York State. This not only helped New Yorkers to frame Haudenosaunee history in ways that could adequately respond to their ever-evolving regional anxieties, but it also appealed to the public's patriotic sensibilities as they constantly looked for evidence of their state's exceptional history and found it in the examples provided by their own homegrown Indigenous empire.

That all-encompassing memory of Iroquois empire thus became a useful historical strawman that influenced New York's founding mythology in the nineteenth century and its identity moving forward. It was a Seneca-made memory, albeit one swept up in the "crusader mentality" of American national identity, or the co-opting of select attributes from racial, national, and ethnic "others" in order to recast those pieces into a truly "American" whole. It was, like other myths, a "compressed, simplified, sometimes outright false vision of the past" that was designed to express what New Yorkers wanted their past to look like and what they wanted their future to be. It endured even as they ripped territorial control from the Haudenosaunee through violence, coercion, and fraudulent land sales, a centuries-long process in which "New York built [its] wealth and power by dispossessing and confining the Iroquois."[15] As a result, New Yorkers could still claim to have inherited the land and their state's high economic and political standing in the United States from their Indigenous forebearers who had, they assumed wrongly, "vanished." It was a compelling idea. Indeed, where would the wealthy, powerful, and exceptional Empire State be without the land and unique legacy left behind by the exceptional Iroquois empire?

———

This book is divided into four mini biographies of Red Jacket, Ely Parker, Harriet M. Converse, and Arthur C. Parker.[16] It places each person "in context" to reveal the broader American and "indigenous experience[s] in that era," adding new perspectives to the complex and entangled history of the Haudenosaunee and New York.[17] Each chapter analyzes how each Seneca leader shaped and was shaped by American social and cultural trends, Indigenous and New York politics, Haudenosaunee lifeways, and their own individual desires and motivations.

Chapter 1 looks at Red Jacket, or Sagoyewatha (1750s–1830), a famed orator, tireless advocate of Seneca political and religious sovereignty, and chief who relentlessly pursued peace with the United States. Red Jacket became a leader of the Senecas during the American Revolution and, after the fog of war cleared, his riveting speaking ability and advocacy for peace began to reshape how New Yorkers saw the Haudenosaunee in relation to America's unsure regional hegemony and burgeoning national identity. He spent his life intentionally reminding the United States of his peoples' empire and their historic control over the region, and essential to that end was the medal he received as a gift from George Washington in 1792. Although not intended by the Washington administration to be a symbol of Indigenous nationhood, Red Jacket's political activism transformed the medal from a curious symbol of settler colonialism into an enduring icon of Haudenosaunee sovereignty and identity. That remains the case to this day. By the first decades of the nineteenth century, however, as the balance of power between the Six Nations and the United States in the region changed, Red Jacket's reputation did as well. While he continued to present himself as a symbol of Haudenosaunee imperial sovereignty and power, to the public he had transformed into a conquered man who embodied the fall of the Iroquois empire, a key event that sparked the rise of the Empire State.

Chapter 2 explores the life of Red Jacket's grand-nephew, Ely S. Parker (1828–1895), through the years of Indian Removal, Greater Reconstruction, and the Gilded Age. In deed and reputation, he connected the Haudenosaunee to America's founding moments in the Revolution and the Civil War as well as to New York's historical role in shaping American history. Parker was a chief who effectively inherited Red Jacket's Peace Medal after he saved it from being sold to a museum (it was sold to the Buffalo Museum after his death). With it, on behalf of his people he launched public campaigns to protect Seneca sovereignty during the antebellum expansion of slavery and Indian Removal. Unlike Red Jacket, however, Parker was obsessed with integrating himself into New York and Washington high society and eventually did so. Using these connections, he launched a remarkable public career as a Seneca chief, General Ulysses S. Grant's military secretary during the Civil War, and as the first Indigenous federal Commissioner of Indian Affairs. Despite seeming to abandon his Indigenous heritage, through all of that he took pains to openly embrace and strategically celebrate his Seneca heritage. This mattered not only to contemporaries who read about "Grant's Indian Aid" with fascination, but in the decades after leaving federal service, Parker established himself as an important interpreter and archivist both of the history of the Haudenosaunee and of the legacy of Ulysses S. Grant and the North's victory in the Civil War. Like Red Jacket before him, Parker used the sheer force of his own fame and his knowledge of Haudenosaunee culture and society to bind the memory of the United States' most significant national challenge to the history and culture of the Haudenosaunee. He did this despite the fact that he moved away from his home on the Tonawanda reservation and, over time, was passed over by leadership who selected his siblings to do service for the nation. While Parker never took his responsibilities as chief any less seriously, it was clear that other Haudenosaunee leadership did. To the New York public, however, all of this meant that Parker exemplified the image of a successful assimilated Seneca and proved that the Iroquois were a "civilized" counterpoint to the stereotypical "uncivilized" and anti-American Indian nations of the west.

Harriet Maxwell Converse (1836–1903), an accomplished poet and salvage ethnographer descended from a family of New York Indian traders, befriended Ely Parker in 1881 and, through his sister's sponsorship, was adopted by the Snipe Clan in 1884. From her home in New York City, Converse proved herself to be a talented political operative who became the "chief publicist" of the Haudenosaunee in an era of sweeping political, social, and demographic changes.[18] She was a savvy defender of Haudenosaunee sovereignty against a new federal policy of allotment with a talent for mobilizing public opinion. In return for her service, the Six Nations gifted her Seneca national membership and an honorary title as a League chief, the only time such a title had ever been given to an adopted woman. While the title gave her no authority or real power, it nonetheless helped her to publicly reinforce her reputation as an "authentic" Seneca. With that reputation, she went on to build a vast salvage trading empire based out of her townhouse that removed vast quantities of Haudenosaunee material culture from their control. She and other salvage ethnographers like her participated in the buying and selling of these collections to museums and others who archived, studied, and put those objects on display for the entertainment and edification of Gilded Age and Progressive Era consumers. Converse understood her salvage ethnography as an essential part of her political work defending Iroquois land and history. So if the preservation and protection of Iroquois sovereignty and land was the goal, for Converse that included the preservation of their history and culture. Haudenosaunee leadership was likewise interested in her talents. By granting her national membership and an honorary title as League Chief, they utilized her political savvy and the connections created by her salvage business in their fight against federal and state encroachment. This bargain created a potent public figure who was embraced by both white and Indigenous allies as someone who embodied Iroquois exceptionality. Adding to this was Converse's unique blend of upper-class white femininity, scholarly legitimacy, and "authentic" Seneca-ness which all fused together to turn her into a symbol for a city determined to understand who was truly "American" amid vast immigration and shifting gender norms. Her salvage empire and position as an adoptee and honorary League chief also made her a unique, and therefore exceptional, addition to the ranks of contemporary Gilded Age women who took on the responsibility of preserving Americana by saving historic homes and founding historical societies. As the public watched with fascination, Converse positioned herself as the adoptive caretaker of a new kind of Americana: the politics and history of her "vanished" people. She, like her dear friend Ely Parker, used her personal notoriety to reinforce on her own terms the idea that the Haudenosaunee, since the beginning, were an integral part of New York's history and identity.

Arthur C. Parker (1881–1955), who referred to his biological uncle Ely Parker as "Uncle Ely" and to Converse as "Aunt Hattie," brought together the histories and memories of those who came before and enshrined Iroquois exceptionalism in New Yorkers' collective unconscious through his development of the modern history museum. After Converse introduced him to museum anthropology in New York City, he launched a celebrated career as a public historian and a field-shaping leader of the New York State Museum and Rochester Municipal Museum (now the Rochester Museum of Arts and Sciences). In that capacity, Parker was the one responsible for collecting and interpreting the memories and stories of the Haudenosaunee that grew out of the preceding generations and for strategically incorporating them into influential museum exhibitions, scholarly and popular work on anthropology, archaeology, history, and public parks and signage. Through his emphasis on original anthropological research and a public history philosophy that emphasized community history, Parker used these otherwise colonizing museum spaces to deliver to the public the opposite of what they were expecting: Indigenous perspectives on their own history. Scholars today understand him as an "Indian mediator," a "bridge figure" who fought against universalizing stereotypes while training the white public to resist the "negative stereotypes left over from colonial conquest."[19] He was certainly that, but in a career that unfolded over two world wars, an economic depression, and transformations in national policy regarding Indigenous law and reservations, Parker leveraged his public history not only to make a contemporary statement about stereotypes but also to elevate Indigenous perspectives. This made Iroquois exceptionalism obvious, immutable, and political. It was an experimental effort that was sometimes warped by his own biases, but just as often he elevated Haudenosaunee voices and stories and delivered them to the public unaltered. Building on the work of Red Jacket, Ely Parker, and Converse, Arthur Parker made Iroquois exceptionalism a permanent fixture of the Empire State's progressive intellectual landscape. In many regards, Parker aimed to prove that New York history and culture is in significant ways Haudenosaunee.

The epilogue follows the 2020 repatriation of Red Jacket's Peace Medal from the Buffalo History Museum to the Seneca-Iroquois National Museum. It was, first and foremost, a true homecoming for the Peace Medal, which exists as a symbol of Seneca sovereignty, identity, and history. But it also represents the culmination of the memory work done by Red Jacket, the Parkers, and Converse. In that sense, it is an enduring reminder of the lives of these four who, by making Haudenosaunee perspectives salable to a wider public, did much to shape New Yorkers' collective memory of the Indigenous history of the Empire State and their sense of self. As a museum object, the long saga of the Peace Medal also reveals the important ways that public history has and can shape the public's understanding and memories of their culture, society, and history. Its repatriation to the museum and the Seneca Nation marks only one end to the story of who "owns" this piece of Haudenosaunee history. Moving forward, that story will now be told by the Haudenosaunee themselves. We would all do well to listen.

—·—

While this book highlights only four Seneca lives, the reader will find many other Native American leaders, tribal members, and some even outsiders who better represented the Haudenosaunee for a variety of reasons.[20] Yet Red Jacket, the Parkers, and Converse nevertheless stand out among them because they had a direct and lasting impact on the shape and scope of Iroquois exceptionalism. Their stories reveal how, on behalf of the Six Nations, they carved out a lasting space in New York's historical memory for themselves, their version of Haudenosaunee history, and the ongoing public interpretation of the history and character of the region.

This emphasis on their biographies also helps to reveal how these memory-makers were shaped by the tensions between their own agency and the outside forces that sought to change them. It thus reveals the power of a supposedly "vanished" and colonized community to shape how the outside world sees them, despite the immense outside pressures that sought to eliminate that ability. Much of this took place in the memorials, museums, and varied public history spaces that appear so often in this book. These kinds of spaces are usually regarded as one-sided intellectual arenas where Indigenous history is written by outsiders for Native American peoples, infused with stereotype, and then sealed forever as such in the public's memory. But this book reveals that this process was more complicated because those public spaces and memories were shaped by Seneca individuals who harnessed and reinterpreted the stories shared by the Haudenosaunee themselves. Whether it was Red Jacket and his Peace Medal traveling up and down the east coast to speak to sold-out auditoriums or Arthur Parker elevating Indigenous perspectives in his pioneering public history work, their stories reveal the history of Indigenous peoples who used those very same colonizing tools that sought to erase their people in order to exert real control over how their legacy was received by the public.

This was a complex process, particularly when it came to their ability to combat, or at least deflect, damaging stereotypes. In these moments, the idea of Iroquois exceptionalism tended to reject broader Native American stereotypes to become a subtle kind of antistereotype that defied efforts to universalize Indigenous history and culture. At various times, these four Senecas held themselves and the Haudenosaunee up, or were held up by others, as a people more "civilized" than their "savage" counterparts out west, a stance that challenged the continent-wide and enduring stereotypes of the "vanishing," "ecological," and "noble savage" Indians. These stereotypes collapsed local and regional difference and stereotyped Native Americans as members of a backward people whose very existence was antithetical to a modernizing Euro-American society. The real-life Indigenous peoples in question, however, were neither silent nor accepting of these stereotypes. Many were diverse and savvy interpreters of the dominant culture who adapted to and resisted colonialism on their own terms for their communities.[21]

The Haudenosaunee were a notable part of that group, yet none seem to have noticed that Red Jacket, the Parkers, and Converse wrote these stories and compelled New Yorkers to listen. In that light, this book adds these four to the "canon" of Iroquois history, a list that identifies the anthropologists and scholars, usually white outsiders, whose personalities and perspectives did more to influence the public's understanding of the Haudenosaunee than their actual history and culture. Over three generations, these four imprinted aspects of themselves, their kin, and their own interpretations of Iroquois exceptionalism onto the public's memory. In the process, they helped develop the idea that the New York Haudenosaunee were more "authentic" than the "out-of-the-way" descendant communities in Canada and out west. These are the communities that were forcibly expulsed from New York yet are usually—and incorrectly—deemed less important or relevant than their eastern counterparts.[22] Through the very act of interpreting that history and challenging white America's expectations of what Native Americans should look or act like, these four invited the non-Indigenous public to remember the Haudenosaunee as a unique and progressive people from a unique and progressive state whose history and empire set them apart from the rest of Native America.

All this memory-work was not a straightforward process, nor did it represent a uniform effort to tell Haudenosaunee history on its own terms. Rather, these four collectively took on the complex task of representing the Senecas' contemporary wants and needs, whether they were asked to or not, and made the important decision to distribute those perspectives to the public through outlets that white New Yorkers would understand. This meant that while some Indigenous perspectives were delivered unaltered to the public in impactful and lasting ways, others were shaped to fit public expectations and thus cast the Iroquois as an Indigenous people who mattered less for what they actually did and more because their supposed contributions to white society gave New Yorkers ever more reason to celebrate and build on their own exceptional state and national identity. These entangled memories make up the core tensions that shaped how Iroquois exceptionalism was created, changed, and evolved over time.

In that light, Red Jacket, the Parkers, and Converse were all agents in the invention of the "Empire State." Their legacy and memory-work was immortalized in newspapers, printed public speeches, art and literature, popular memory, and most tangibly and enduringly in the museum exhibitions, parks, and the public memorials they created. By shaping important aspects of the public's historical memory into something that resembled Haudenosaunee conceptions of their own history, they turned their peoples' history into something white New Yorkers would forever remember as *"The Amazing Iroquois."*

I

Red Jacket,
a "Poet Among Politicians"

IN MARCH 1792, George Washington addressed over fifty Haudenosaunee diplomats who gathered in Philadelphia, the nation's capital, to discuss the Six Nations' relationship with the new country, New York and Pennsylvania's illegal land sales, and the eruption of a new war against Indigenous nations in Ohio. Washington, hoping to ensure that the Six Nations would refrain from joining that war, personally welcomed the representatives and Red Jacket, a young Seneca already well known as an orator, who was chosen to represent them. When the summit ended, Washington gifted Red Jacket with an Indian Peace Medal.

The bright silver medal, designed in 1792 by Philadelphia silversmiths, is seven inches tall and five inches wide. Despite its substantial size and weight, it was suspended from a ribbon or leather and worn around the neck. Etched into the front face of the medal is a crudely drawn figure of George Washington sharing a *calumet*, or "peace pipe," with a stylized Native American man who had dropped his hatchet to the ground. Both figures stand on a farm in front of a large tree, and behind them an ox-drawn plow and a modest abode complete the pastoral scene. Engraved underneath the scenic meeting place are the words "George Washington President" and the year "1792"; on the back face of the medal is the official seal of the United States.

Not only is the Peace Medal one of the more interesting places where George Washington's image appears before the turn of the century, but it is a functional relic of early American continental diplomacy. This and other medals like it were exceedingly common throughout Euro-American history. They were part of an ancient European diplomatic custom of giving

FIGURE 1.1 Red Jacket Peace Medal, 1792. Photograph by Hayden Haynes. Seneca-Iroquois National Museum and Onöhsagwë:de' Cultural Center.

medallions to foreign powers as a symbolic gesture of peace, a practice then adopted by the infant United States as an essential aspect of American Indian diplomacy through the turn of the twentieth century. The medal's pastoral design illustrated America's paternalistic desire to assimilate and "civilize" Indians by teaching them an idealized Euro-American lifestyle. This does not mean, however, that Peace Medals were forced upon unwilling recipients. They fit seamlessly into ancient Native gift-giving customs that formed the foundation of continental diplomacy. In sum, they were mutually desirable and valuable gifts. So many were distributed that they were spotted frequently throughout Native America, in American cities and towns, and across the sea. By the 1830s "it was impossible to conduct satisfactory relations with the Indians without medals."[1]

The vast numbers of Indian Peace Medals that were produced and distributed over more than a century begs a question: Why does this medal, the one that became known as the Red Jacket Peace Medal, stand out from the others? The answer lies not only in the likeness of Washington etched into its face, but also in the complicated—and oft-mythologized—memory of its most famous bearer, Red Jacket. No other Indigenous person is so closely associated with a single medal, nor has one medal ever been so closely associated with its owner. Red Jacket, whose people sided with the British during the American Revolution (hence his nickname based on the iconic red coats of British soldiers), received the Peace Medal as a gift from George Washington after the British lost the war. Although this was one of the orator's first major diplomatic meetings with the new US government, he saw the medal as a physical reminder of the United States' obligations to their Iroquois neighbors and recognized the symbolic power that the likeness of the nation's patriarch held in America's public imagination. In the years to come, Red Jacket wore the Peace Medal proudly during each of the fifty public speeches he delivered as one of the Senecas' diplomatic representatives.[2] He strategically wielded it as a reminder to Americans of their obligations to the Six Nations, the Haudenosaunee's historic geopolitical power, and Washington's own regard for that power.

By the turn of the nineteenth century, however, Red Jacket began to lose control of his self-cultivated image as a prominent Iroquoian spokesman and orator. At the same time the Iroquois began to lose land and power, the symbolism of the Peace Medal and Red Jacket's efforts to hold the United States accountable began to shift. Red Jacket's strategic self-association with the father of the nation devolved into evidence of his "friendship" with the president, one that became the stuff of folk legend.[3] The Haudenosaunee's historic power was still remembered, but the immediacy of its threat to New York's borders had diminished. In that environment, the Peace Medal itself became Red Jacket's single most defining feature and almost eclipsed the memory of the orator himself. In all but two of the nearly twenty portraits, statues, and etchings that were completed in his lifetime and throughout the twentieth century, the polished silver medal is immediately recognizable and always sits prominently on his chest, but Red Jacket himself became blurry with stereotype.[4] The Seneca orator slowly became the victim not only of the "vanished" Indian stereotype, but also of the patriotic memory of George Washington and the American Revolution, a person and a rebellion most of the Haudenosaunee fought a war to reject.

This chapter thus explores how Red Jacket cultivated his own memory and how his self-created image gradually shifted as the Senecas' sovereignty was challenged. He entered the political arena between the American Revolution and the turn of the century and remained in politics and in the public eye until his death in 1830. Red Jacket's oratory, a universally well-respected and critical component of Indigenous diplomacy, was the most powerful weapon in his diplomatic arsenal and introduced to the world an anti-American, anti-Christian, and fierce defender of Seneca sovereignty even as his Haudenosaunee peers were sometimes at odds with him and his politics. Although Americans were often on the receiving end of his rhetorical attacks, white audiences outside diplomatic circles over time began to appreciate his oratorical ability, despite his only ever speaking in the Seneca language in public. All contemporary English reprints of his speeches in newspapers and pamphlets were lifted from diplomatic translations, most of which came from two American men who had been abducted and adopted by the Senecas and chose to stay with their captors. Despite that language barrier, however, by the 1820s Red Jacket was filling auditoriums.

The Peace Medal also deserves closer attention. For Americans, the imagery and purpose of the Peace Medal illuminates their desire to "civilize" the Indian and, more realistically, their general inability to do so. The pastoral depictions of an "uncivilized" Indian figure dropping his hatchet in favor of a peaceful and "civilized" plow was intended to send a clear message to Native America about how white Americans thought they should live, but that was not always how it was received. In addition, the Peace Medal was designed to be carried by various Native individuals as a message of US power to places where Anglo-Americans had been unable to reach. Yet the Washington administration realized quickly that these goals were mostly aspirational. The new country was in a fragile state after the Revolution, in terrible debt, possessing a weak federal government, and powerless to stop Britain's blatant violations of the Treaty of Paris ending the war and recognizing it as an independent nation. To make matters worse, the formation of new pan-Indian alliances created potent centers of Indigenous military power to the north and west of New York that the national government, much less the state, was ill-equipped to deal with.[5] Among these powers were the Iroquois, the historic power brokers of the region and a source of existential Anglo-American anxiety. Collectively, these forces "threatened to fragment the nation [George] Washington was building."[6] Red Jacket and his Peace Medal, at least for a time, were a constant reminder of that reality.

In that context, Peace Medals before 1800 were a physical manifestation of America's new Indian policy and one of Washington's varied attempts to stabilize the new nation. They were given to Indigenous leaders with the hope that, through the simple act of wearing them, these individuals would project the administration's message of peace throughout Indian country. In addition, the use of Washington's likeness on the Peace Medals did not simply mimic European diplomatic tradition where a monarch's face was stamped onto diplomatic medals: it was a domestic necessity. Including his face on federal documents and objects was an effort by the administration and the Federalists—Washington's new political party—to tie Americans' ideas about federal authority and postcolonial identity to the living legend of George Washington.[7] In that respect, the medals exemplified how Indian affairs were part of a broad and purposeful development of American national identity.

Red Jacket, who by the turn of the nineteenth century had emerged as an important spokesman for the Haudenosaunee, was also part of that development. He was fiercely critical of the United States, but he also relentlessly pursued peace, an idea reflected in the Haudenosaunee philosophy of *kaswentha*, or "Two Rows," which holds that two culturally distinct people can live alongside one another in relative harmony through the extension of kinship and political consensus that would lead to the elimination of war. This was the principle on which the League of the Haudenosaunee was founded and Red Jacket sought to extend that principle to the new United States.[8] To do this, he followed in his people's footsteps and offered kinship to Americans and supported restoring the Covenant Chain, the historic British and Indian alliance that was established in the late seventeenth century.[9] That message of peace also fueled Red Jacket's rising popularity among the broader American public. For post-Revolutionary New Yorkers and others exhausted by years of imperial conflicts and afraid of ongoing Indian wars, Red Jacket's emphasis on peace helped calm the public's nerves and, in time, amplified his voice beyond the arena of diplomacy.

Between 1800 and the War of 1812, the balance of power between the United States, the Six Nations, and other northern Native American nations had shifted drastically. The US population had expanded in size and geographic reach, and the Haudenosaunee responded in part by ceding a considerable amount of land to protect the core of their sovereign territory. This signaled to many Americans that the great Iroquois empire, much like the other "vanished" indigenous peoples of the region, had finally been defeated, or at least ceased to be a source of geopolitical dread. As a result, Red Jacket became known as the spokesman of the United States' first "conquered" indigenous empire. Likewise, his lifelong resistance to and excoriation of American culture, particularly of Christian missionaries, became a new kind of literary entertainment by Americans who came to enjoy and pity the musings of "eloquent Indians."[10] By the time Red Jacket died in 1830, and while canals and cities carved through places where the Haudenosaunee once held dominion, New Yorkers saw the fall of the Iroquois empire as an essential part of the "inevitable" rise of their Empire State.

Red Jacket was therefore an unlikely person to help a hostile new country shape its national identity. In contrast, the "friendly" Delaware Indian "Saint Tammany" had fought for the Americans during the Revolution and was a heroic American figure "virtually indistinguishable from the average patriot."[11] Red Jacket mattered to New Yorkers because he was not a patriot. When his legacy was slowly rewritten in the first decades of the nineteenth century, New Yorkers, whose state had grown large enough that the threat of the Iroquois had subsided, found in him and his people something unique to New York. His threatening speeches and anticolonial politics eventually transformed into the charming lamentations of America's first "conquered" empire. This was a revision that helped New Yorkers soften the painful memories of a recent and violent past and remember the Haudenosaunee and their place in early American history differently. Here was the birth of Iroquois exceptionalism.

———

Despite how much is known about Red Jacket's political career, his childhood and early life are shrouded in mystery. He was born to the Wolf Clan and his birth name—or at least the oldest one that historians found and contemporaries remembered—was Otetiani, which in English roughly translates to "Always Ready." Historians speculate that he was born in the "1750's, probably 1758, in the Finger Lakes region of what is today New York State."[12] Twenty years later during the American Revolution, he received the nickname "Red Jacket" based on the iconic British military vestment.[13] By the end of the war, he inherited his chieftainship and was given the name Sagoyewatha, which in English translates to "He Keeps Them Awake," or perhaps more accurately, "He Wakes Them Up Early," a name some historians think was given out of respect for his oratorical ability. By his own admission he was a civil chief (domestic affairs) of the Senecas. One biographer suggests that later in life he may have even been chosen to serve as a League chief, one

FIGURE 1.2 *Engraving of Red Jacket based on Robert Weir's 1828 portrait. Sa-go-ye-wat-ha Seneca chief Red Jacket, painted by R. W. Weir; eng'd. by M. J. Danforth,* United States, c. 1830–1880. Library of Congress Prints and Photographs Division, LC-USZ62-128675.

of the fifty elected leaders selected from all the Six Nations who made up the international governing body of the Six Nations Confederacy.[14]

What we know for sure is that Red Jacket's talent for public speaking helped him to ascend through the ranks of Seneca society and politics. Many Indigenous cultures valued oratory highly in cultural and diplomatic contexts, and the Haudenosaunee were no different. But Red Jacket also had an advantage because, when he was a boy, he witnessed true oratorical greatness up close. Based on a story he liked to tell later in life, he had occasion to hear the legendary Mingo orator Logan speak. The young Otetiani had "resolved," in that moment, "to attain if possible, the same high standard of eloquence."[15] Then, after years "playing Logan," Otetiani got the chance to put his talent to use during the American Revolution. As the war raged, his oratory impressed many, and he established himself as one of the Six Nations' most important "defender[s] of Seneca traditions and lands against speculators and missionaries."[16]

For American officials, there is more to Logan's story than how he had inspired a young Seneca to oratorical greatness. For them, Logan's life framed the tension and warfare that defined Otetiani's formative years. Logan was already a recognized leader of the Mingo, but he became well known to Anglo-Americans when his speech "Logan's Lament" was printed in the aftermath Lord Dunmore's War that ravaged the Ohio region in 1774. The war began when Lord Dunmore, the Royal Governor of Virginia, sought to fill a power vacuum left in New York after the death of Sir William Johnson, the British northern Indian Superintendent and friend of the Iroquois who held extensive political sway over the region. Dunmore had long sought to expand British power illegally into the Ohio by leveraging New York's geographic proximity into the region, and Johnson's death gave him the opportunity to act. Dunmore moved an army of "2,000 men" and the Virginia militia to "menace" the Ohio Shawnee and their allies.[17]

The war was bad enough, then Logan's wife's town, like many others, was invaded. His wife and eleven other women and children of his family were brutally murdered by a militia-supplied posse along the Yellow Creek and upper Ohio River. His pregnant sister Koonay was strung up "by the wrists" and then the invaders "sliced her open, impaling the unborn baby on a stake, but spared her two-month-old daughter." This horrifying assault prompted Logan to mobilize his own army. He succeeded in destroying a few colonial towns and, among other Shawnee attacks, caused the mass evacuation of hundreds of colonists back east.[18] Dunmore's War succeeded in throwing the region into chaos. It sparked a bloody fight over Indian land that set colony against colony, colonist against Indian, and resulted in the loss of many lives and the complete collapse of trust between the Ohio nations and the British.

Logan's "Lament," delivered on October 1774 in the aftermath of Dunmore's War, was a grim reminder of a chaotic conflict that put Indigenous land and people at the center of colonial geopolitical politics and memory.[19] Logan explained that, after the murder of his family, he was compelled to gather others to his cause. He set out, "killed many," and after a period of intense violence, he had finally and "fully glutted [his] vengeance." Many Americans rightly understood this speech as a warning. Logan reminded them that when trusts were broken, the Indigenous powers would not sit idly by. But still, there was hope of avoiding war. When tentative offers of peace were extended at the end of 1774, Logan exclaimed that "for my country, I re-joice at the beams of peace."[20]

For the young Otetiani and the Haudenosaunee, "Logan's Lament" told a familiar story. As Lord Dunmore sent his Virginian army into Shawnee country in 1774, Guy Johnson, William Johnson's son and heir, was deeply concerned that the Shawnee would seek an alliance with the Iroquois. If that happened, they would bring the war east. In response, he and other colonial diplomats, including the missionary Samuel Kirkland, scrambled to convince the Six Nations not to mobilize for war. They sent a similar message again one year later when the first shots were fired at Lexington and Concord in April 1775, when they urged Iroquoian nonintervention. The stakes were high because, by their conservative estimates, the Six Nations alone could mobilize an army at least the size of the one Dunmore used to invade Ohio. That kind of military presence could impact and perhaps even turn the tide of war in the region.[21]

Otetiani, much like Logan, earned his reputation during wartime. A young adult at the time of the outbreak of the American Revolution, he was called on to use his skills to represent the Haudenosaunee and the Senecas in their negotiations with the warring Anglo-Americans. At the start of the war, he was a staunch advocate for Iroquois nonintervention, presenting his views at the council fires at Fort Pitt and Albany in 1775 and 1776.[22] As the Oneidas made clear in 1775 in their formal declaration of neutrality to Governor John Trumbull of Connecticut, the Haudenosaunee preferred to let the Americans and British have their own civil war and chose to let these "brothers . . . settle your own disputes betwixt yourselves."[23]

But neutrality would not last. At a two-week long council fire held at Fort Niagara in August and September of 1777, British Colonel John Butler sought to persuade the famed Mohawk Joseph Brant, a long-time British ally and friend of Sir William Johnson, to convince the rest of the Iroquois to join the British in war. Brant was already sympathetic, so Butler sought to close the deal by making lengthy appeals and giving vast sums of money and material gifts to the Mohawks over the course of the summit. This finally convinced Brant and other leaders to ally with the British.[24] Butler also gave Brant a wampum belt that formalized the terms set for their alliance, which Brant then set out to deposit with the Onondagas, the keepers of the Haudenosaunee's diplomatic history. Along the way, he appealed to the varied Haudenosaunee war leaders to join his cause and called for the assembly of a League-wide meeting to discuss the proposed alliance with the British.[25] League consensus was the goal, as it was in all things, but

Brant did not achieve it. The Mohawks, Cayugas, Senecas, and Onondagas all agreed to ally with the British and restore the Covenant Chain, particularly since Butler had promised to respect Iroquois diplomacy and culture by delivering more gifts in the future, but the Oneidas and Tuscaroras did not join them. They sided with the Americans through General Philip Schuyler, who promised to open a trading post at Fort Stanwix for the direct and exclusive benefit of all the Six Nations. They were also impressed after Schuyler reported on the American's surprise victories at Trenton and Princeton.[26]

For a time Otetiani upheld his people's desire to stay neutral, but after the success of Brant's tour, he agreed to follow the majority and ally with the British. He and fellow Seneca leaders Governor Blacksnake, Cornplanter, and Old Smoke were all appointed "war captains" and tasked with mobilizing the Senecas for war. Otetiani would prove to be a "very reluctant warrior," however.[27] While he was a fine political leader and successfully performed his duty as war captain, his peers found much to ridicule when it came to the battlefield. At the Battle of Oriskany in 1777, Otetiani had reportedly fled once the fighting started, though because he "was young and it was his first battle, nothing was done or said to him." Then in 1778, during the Wyoming Valley campaign, in which the British army sought to open a path from the St. Lawrence River to the capital of Philadelphia, Otetiani was reportedly seen hiding well behind his people's battle lines and only occasionally firing his weapon.[28] After these battles, both Joseph Brant and Cornplanter began to call out his cowardice.

His reported cowardice reemerged during the Battle of Newtown, New York, on August 29, 1779, part of an invasion of noncombatant Seneca and Cayuga villages after a Spring attack on an Onondaga village. On orders from General George Washington, Generals James Clinton and John Sullivan invaded the Haudenosaunee with the largest American army assembled by that point in the war. The soldiers were ordered to abandon traditional and rules-based "limited warfare" against the Haudenosaunee, so when they arrived in Newtown, they freely burned houses and farms, killed and captured noncombatants, and desecrated graves. It was an invasion with the goal of extinction. The massive American army caused immense physical damage to farms and houses, torched around forty Seneca villages, and caused thousands to flee to Canada.[29] The invasion forced those few Iroquois who were still neutral to declare themselves new allies of the British. Internally, however, this campaign deepened existing divisions among the four British-allied nations and the American-allied Oneida and Tuscarora. Cornplanter, from that point forward, reviled Washington and gave him the name "Town Destroyer," a name that lives on in infamy.[30]

At Newtown, Otetiani also earned a new nickname: Cow Killer.[31] Even after the Clinton-Sullivan campaign, he still believed that a peaceful relationship with the United States was possible, earning him the derision of his peers. Stories of his cowardly exploits at Newtown, a battle in which the fate of the Senecas seemed to hang in the balance, were circulated widely by his critics. Joseph Brant claimed that Otetiani had selfishly abandoned his post and killed a neighbor's cow to feed his own family. A more dramatic retelling of that story claimed that Otetiani and another Haudenosaunee warrior fled the battle and, while they were hiding, killed a cow. When the two men finally returned after the smoke had cleared, Otetiani claimed that the cow's blood on his weapon was that of an American he had killed in the surrounding fields. Cornplanter also joined the verbal fray. After the battle, he reportedly spoke to Otetiani's wife and told her that he had caught her husband trying to flee after the first shots of the battle were fired. Cornplanter then advised her to "Leave that man—he is a coward!" Yet another "very doubtful" but even more destructive rumor circulated that Red Jacket had had a secret conversation with Sullivan, "Town Killer's" agent of genocide, and promised the general that he would defy his people and his responsibilities as war captain to secure peace and stop the Iroquois' war against the Americans.[32]

Even these serious accusations and Otetiani's reputation for cowardice did not damage the Haudenosaunee leadership's broad appreciation for his political skills or his lineage. They elected him a chief and gave him a new name, Sagoyewatha. By the end of the Revolution, a few British officers at Fort Niagara, in recognition of his service as a scout and army courier for the British, gifted him an officer's jacket and dubbed him "Red Jacket." Even some of his political enemies, in hindsight, recognized his political ability and his fidelity to fulfilling his people's wishes. Governor Blacksnake, a Seneca chief who had also spread rumors of Red Jacket's wartime cowardice, told those same stories decades later but "with a smile" on his face while sitting underneath a portrait of Red Jacket in his home.[33]

After his elevation to Seneca leadership, Red Jacket wasted no time putting his new political position and reputation to work. After the Battle of Yorktown in 1782, the Americans, French, and British met to discuss the terms of British surrender. The Haudenosaunee were not invited to these negotiations, so Red Jacket issued a formal statement that protested the legitimacy of a treaty that would end the war without Indigenous input. Leaving the Six Nations out of the negotiations was egregious not only because the

British would be breaking the ancient Covenant Chain and ignoring the sacrifices the Haudenosaunee had made on their behalf, but also because the British had deliberately misled them with "lies" about their capacity to win the war. Now, as if rubbing salt in the wound, the Crown was "abandoning them 'to be sacrificed or submit to the Americans.'"[34] This feeling of betrayal was echoed by many British-allied Indigenous nations, particularly after word spread that the formal negotiations to end the war were underway in Paris. On September 3, 1783, the Treaty of Paris ended the war without a single Native American delegate present.[35]

Red Jacket's words about being abandoned, it turned out, were prophetic. The intentional absence of Six Nations representation or signatories at the Treaty of Paris made room for the United States to introduce a dubious new concept into their Confederated government's postwar diplomatic lexicon: the so-called "conquest theory." The theory held that because the Iroquois had somehow been "conquered" by the British during the war, they were by right of military victory subordinate to the new United States. Under the logic of the conquest theory, New York Indian agents were ordered by Governor George Clinton at the end of 1783 to "expel most of the ['conquered'] Six Nations" from the state, all except for the allied Oneida and Tuscarora. The theory also supposedly gave the state the authority to take Iroquois land based not on existing law or treaty, but based on colonial charters, some of which were drafted centuries earlier and replaced by new federal laws. The biggest claimant on Iroquois territory under the conquest theory was the state of Massachusetts that, under their vague but sweeping coast-to-coast colonial charter, claimed all Iroquois territory around the Finger Lakes. Not to be left out, New York State used the conquest theory to bolster its own claims to Iroquois territory, as well as to avoid another situation like that in the northeast region of the state where illegal settlers from New England had recently taken over a sparsely populated region, forcibly removed New York officials, and declared themselves the independent republic of Vermont.[36] The conquest theory, in sum, was used broadly by New York to undercut the Iroquois' regional influence, open their land to New York's control and secure its existing borders, and push back against Massachusetts' sweeping territorial claims.

Despite New York and Massachusetts' grand designs, the conquest theory was just that: a theory inspired by a mixture of the historic fear of Iroquois imperial power and the postwar realities of a newly weakened and fractured Six Nations. So, when the Iroquois, New York, and US agents met at Fort Stanwix in 1784 to negotiate a new postwar treaty and draw the new western border of the state and the US, it was obvious from the beginning that the Iroquois would not abide by New York's arbitrary claims to their land. At Fort Stanwix, Joseph Brant became so furious at their claims that he convinced the Mohawk and most of the Six Nations that they, despite the Treaty of Paris betrayal, were better off dealing with the British in Canada. That year, a significant portion of the Haudenosaunee left for the Haldimand Grant in Quebec Province.[37] While this move severed a major part of the Iroquois' military capacity from New York State, it also relocated an important center of Indigenous power (and a vital British ally) out of the orbit of American influence.[38] Red Jacket, the Senecas, and the remaining Haudenosaunee were thus forced to bow to some of New York's demands. But even then, Red Jacket, in a series of speeches remembered decades afterward by the Marquis de Lafayette, kept the Senecas' concessions minimal.[39] They agreed to give up vast tracts of land, but much of it was land they had already traded in an older treaty from 1768. In addition, he offered a vague promise that the Senecas would "subordinate" themselves to the state of New York, a promise that held little weight once George Washington was elected president in 1789 and shifted the locus of Indian diplomacy to the federal government. As historians explain, Fort Stanwix was as good a deal as could be expected for a defeated wartime enemy, particularly after many Haudenosaunee had moved to Canada and left those who remained in New York in a weakened state.[40]

For the United States, the Treaties of Paris and Fort Stanwix "set in motion an array of peoples with competing visions for the continent."[41] Their internal battles, furthermore, "produced" the concept of "the nation."[42] The conquest theory, at least on paper, invited the states to make aggressive and sweeping claims to Indian land. But the angry responses from Indian country to these actions as well as the inability of the federal government to control its constituent parts created new concerns for the new nation. Territorial expansion may have been an important goal for the Confederation government and the many veterans who were promised land after the war as payment for their service, but the national government could not afford to resupply the war-torn northwest and proved unable to offer guidance or protection to those veterans and colonists who migrated there to collect what they were owed. Meanwhile, British officials in Canada were still actively seeking Indian alliances and occupying forts on the American side of the Fort Stanwix border line. As a result, violence between Americans and Indians plagued the borders of the mid-Atlantic states and created a "peculiarly maddening" life for a country desperate for an end to a near-decade of war. This was not only a northwestern problem. Among the indigenous nations of southern trans-Appalachia and the Spanish colonies along the Gulf of Mexico, American instability created new incentives for Indian and Spanish officials to create powerful alliances that excluded the United States entirely.[43] Despite their victory in the American Revolution, the continued survival of the new nation was far from assured.

To make matters more complex, the appearance of new pan-Indian coalitions further threatened American stability and strained their older Indian alliances. These pan-Indian alliances bound together many diverse nations with the express goal of resisting Euro-American colonization. They reinstilled in Americans a fear of Indian war that only fed ongoing border violence.[44] The first of these major coalitions was formed under the Ottawa Pontiac and Delaware prophet Neolin during the Seven Years' War. Their confederacy spread from "Green Bay to the Allegheny River" and "from the straits of Mackinac to the Wabash" in Ohio, and they waged a war that lasted from 1760 to 1764 that almost eliminated the British presence from the region.[45] That memory was still fresh for Americans after their Revolution, and it became even more acute when new pan-Indian alliances formed along America's post-war borders. In 1788, as the states fought over the ratification of their new federal constitution, Joseph Brant was busy building the United Indian Nations (UIN). This new Native American union was formed, in part, to oppose the United States, their Northwest Ordinance of 1787, and Spanish expansion out of Florida and Texas in the deep south.[46] In 1790, one year into George Washington's presidency, a loose multinational confederacy reached critical mass in Ohio along the Auglaize River under the leadership of the Shawnee Little Turtle. The Glaize coalition threatened American interests because a protracted war in Ohio, US officials knew, would spell "destruction [for] the republic."[47] And then in 1807, the Shawnee Tecumseh and his brother, the Prophet Tenskwatawa, formed a pan-Indian coalition that joined together native nations from the Great Lakes to the Gulf of Mexico. The coalition was driven by a religious mandate to remove from Native life all things produced by or traded with Euro-Americans and, ultimately, to remove the invaders themselves.[48] White Americans in this era found themselves in an unstable world.

Indian diplomacy, therefore, was a priority. In 1789, President George Washington took steps to nationalize Indian affairs and bring those problems to heel. With the powers allotted to it by the new US Constitution, Washington's administration set out to form an international policy that was "orderly, national, uplifting, and progressive." An important part of this was to reform Indian policy. To solve the problem of near-constant border violence, the administration took the power to negotiate Indian treaties out of the hands of the individual states and, in so doing, began to treat them as seriously as they would any international treaty. States and private landholders did not stop trying to grab as much Indigenous land as possible, but the federal government made some efforts to curb those efforts and, ultimately, tried to reframe the nation's new Indian policy as one that privileged alliance-building.[49]

In the north, despite the fractures caused by the 1780s conquest theory, the Haudenosaunee's regional influence remained intact. They had, after all, a long legacy of conducting and controlling multinational indigenous diplomacy. Even though the war had fractured their confederacy and severely diminished their military capacity, they remained an important regional player and, perhaps most worryingly for the United States, they were geographically and politically close to the British in Canada. Joseph Brant's clear preference for the British and his postwar successes gaining Canadian support for the UIN left the United States under no illusions that the Canadian Six Nations and the New York Iroquois would not side with the British again if they were forced to choose. As Washington's new Treasury Secretary Alexander Hamilton explained, the Iroquois were not only vital to westward expansion, but the "bare possibility of a war with the six Nations would break up our whole frontier."[50] For America's new national Indian policy to work, they needed Iroquoian trust and compliance.

Their first challenge came during the Tioga Point Council of November 1790 held in northern Pennsylvania. The council was called by the Six Nations to settle a dispute over the murder of two Seneca traders by Pennsylvanians. Red Jacket, speaking on behalf of the gathered chiefs, opened the council with a speech demanding the execution of the murderers. He echoed Logan's speech from more than fifteen years earlier when he explained that "it is natural to look for revenge of Innocent blood." But in this case, the loss of these two men was particularly difficult for the Senecas because they "were very great men" of the "Turtle Tribe," one of "them was a Chief" and the other was descended from chiefs. Red Jacket spoke "from a wounded heart" as he evoked the threat of war and explained that the United States "have stuck the hatchet in our head" not only due to these two murders, but because they were only the latest in a string of killings. "Eleven of us," he explained, had been murdered by Americans since the war ended. It was thus the responsibility "of our great brother, your Governor [of Pennsylvania], who must come to See us" to give the families of the murdered peace and to "brightens [*sic*] the chain of friendship, as it is very rusty." With the allegiance of the Iroquois at stake, Timothy Pickering, the US Indian Agent, promised to do what he asked and to "pull the hatchet from their heads." But Red Jacket was unconvinced. He reminded Pickering of the legacy of William Penn and "the ancient practices of our fathers" who not only promised to pull "the hatchet out of their heads, but bur[y] it. You say you have now pulled the hatchet out of our heads: but you have only cast it behind you; and you may take it up again." He reminded Pickering that "while the hatchet lies unburied, we cannot sit easy on our seats."[51]

By invoking the rusty Covenant Chain and Pennsylvania's own failure to ensure peace, Red Jacket's opening remarks set the tone for a council that would use these threats to gain concessions on issues well beyond the individual murders. One of these issues was a fraudulent treaty signed by the predatory land speculators Oliver Phelps and Nathaniel Gorham. Another was about internal politics when Red Jacket evoked his peer Cornplanter who was, in that moment, in the process of negotiating independently with Pennsylvania for reservation land along the Allegheny River (now the Senecas' Allegany Territory). The inability of the federal government to stop one of its states—not to mention private individuals—from negotiating with Native Americans independently, Red Jacket explained, made the federal government's promise to nationalize and stabilize Indian affairs a hollow one. How could the United States restore the Covenant Chain when they could not even control their own citizens?

Perhaps most worrisome for the American delegates at this summit was the threat of war. Looming over the Tioga Point Council was an ongoing war in the west launched by Little Turtle and his pan-Indian coalition. A few months earlier, Little Turtle's Glaize coalition had won a stunning victory against an American army sent to prevent them from gaining a foothold in Ohio. After the victory, Little Turtle's envoys reached out to Red Jacket and the Senecas in New York, Joseph Brant and the UIN in Canada, and the British in Quebec for supplies and assistance. Not only had the Americans lost a large portion of their standing army to the Glaize coalition, they also worried that the Senecas, their gateway to the west, would side with Little Turtle.

It must have been a relief, then, when Red Jacket reiterated that the Haudenosaunee desired only peace and to "polish the chain of friendship" with the new country. But he tempered that call for peace by explaining that their desires had limits. For one, he pointed out the failures of the Americans who broke with custom by not bringing wampum belts to the council or anything "to [appease] the relatives" of the two murdered Senecas. These were serious diplomatic failings. Second, Red Jacket explained that the delegates in general were making a poor impression on his people. The Americans were not acknowledging Phelps and Gorham as a problem, they kept breaking with tradition and diplomatic protocol by trying to move council locations without Haudenosaunee consent, and they were not stopping traders and squatters from invading Iroquois country (the cause of the murders). Red Jacket's complaints were noted and, with the threat of the Senecas' alliance with the Glaize looming, the gathered American delegates promised to make amends.[52]

Beyond his oratory and political savvy, Red Jacket also exerted diplomatic pressure on the American delegates through distinctly Haudenosaunee means. He learned that one of the attendees was Thomas Morris, son of Robert Morris, the financier of the American Revolution and stakeholder in the first US national bank. As Red Jacket knew, Robert was involved because he had purchased rights to a tract of Seneca land from the Genesee Land Company that year, a tract that was not given up for sale with any consent from the Haudenosaunee. So, Red Jacket sought to make Thomas Morris more amenable to the Senecas' position. Making an ally of Thomas would not only compel him to hesitate to use his family fortune to do the same in the future, but it might also help to make the elder Morris more sympathetic to the Haudenosaunee. To do this, Red Jacket convinced the Seneca clan mothers in attendance to ceremonially adopt Thomas. In the elaborate ceremony that followed, the young Morris was given Red Jacket's childhood name, Otetiani. This strategy may have worked because the land that was purchased by Robert Morris, a tract bounded on the west by Niagara and on the North by Lake Erie, was part of the plot that was returned to the Senecas in the Treaty of Canandaigua in 1794.[53]

With Thomas Morris's public adoption, Red Jacket showcased the power and importance of gender and kinship in Haudenosaunee negotiations and its flexibility as a negotiating tactic against the United States. Morris was not the only target. Timothy Pickering, the official US representative at Tioga Point and future top diplomat assigned to the Iroquois, was also introduced to each of the Seneca women in attendance. They shook his hand and delivered their own grievances to him directly, thereby breaking the relatively orderly and sterile environment of the diplomatic summit. In addition, both Red Jacket and Farmer's Brother, another head Seneca negotiator, also spent time educating Pickering on the nuances of Haudenosaunee diplomacy. They taught him about the practice of gift-giving, a fundamental aspect of Indian diplomacy more broadly, and gestured at offering him Seneca kinship when they gave him the name "Connesauty." This, too, worked. After Tioga Point, Pickering considered himself a friend of Red Jacket's and, at future meetings between the Iroquois and the United States, he privileged Red Jacket's diplomatic voice over others among the Six Nations. Red Jacket was able to skillfully bring together the Haudenosaunees' male-dominated world of political leadership with the female-dominated world of kinship, naming, and adoptions. In these moments, his efforts reflected the diplomatic philosophy that "peace was possible only within a group cemented by consanguinity and a common sense of the moral order."[54] Overall, Red Jacket established himself as an important player in American diplomacy and an ally in their new Indian peace policy. At Tioga Point, the Senecas gained concessions on each of their complaints, including the full payment and annuity from Phelps and Gorham. Red Jacket reciprocated by promising that the Haudenosaunee would not participate in the Glaize coalition's war. He and his peers had proven capable of leveraging their historic regional power, the power of kinship, and the contemporary threat of indigenous war to secure remuneration for their people and peace for the Americans.

The summit at Philadelphia in March 1792, where Red Jacket received his iconic Peace Medal, was another important moment in the Seneca orator's political development. Held just one year after a devastating defeat of Governor Arthur St. Clair's army by Little Turtle and the Glaize coalition, Philadelphia was a part of the Washington administration's "desperate" attempts to secure Iroquoian non-intervention in that war. The president sent Samuel Kirkland, the same missionary who had helped secure the Oneidas' neutrality during the Revolution, to deliver a message to Iroquoian leaders inviting them to the nation's capital. Red Jacket arrived with Kirkland and a large contingent of about fifty representatives and chiefs.[55]

Although the city was well used to the comings and goings of Native Americans who lived in and visited the city, the arrival of Red Jacket and the Haudenosaunee nevertheless created a large public spectacle. This fanfare was due in part to two chiefs, Peter Otsequette and Big Tree, who had died during the journey. When Philadelphians heard the news, they organized a mourning ceremony and funeral procession in their honor. Thus when they arrived at the city, Red Jacket and the delegation found themselves at the head of an "Anglo-Indian parade attended by 10,000 people" that marched through the streets for much of the rest of the day. After the parade, Washington personally greeted the Indigenous diplomats with a formal speech. On the advice of Timothy Pickering, Washington avoided discussing land acquisition, a telling concession respecting the Iroquois' complaints about the administration's poor diplomatic conduct in the past. He introduced Secretary of War Henry Knox and Pickering as chief negotiators for the administration, and he offered a brief description of the commitments the US was willing to make, including gifts, an annuity, and the promise of a lasting peace that would be "founded on the principles of justice and humanity as upon an immoveable rock." After Washington's speech, the gathered Iroquois delegates chose Red Jacket to deliver their formal response on March 31; he served as a principal speaker for the rest of the summit.[56]

As at Fort Stanwix and Tioga Point, Red Jacket used his position to advocate for peace. Throughout the summit, he reminded the American delegates what was at stake when peace fell apart. Red Jacket reiterated Washington's own words of greeting when the president "in effect, observed to us that we . . . were our own proprietors; were freemen and might speak with freedom . . . and Therefore You will hear us patiently while we speak." Once the rules were set, Red Jacket blamed the United States for the war with the Glaize coalition in Ohio, tracing that conflict back to the "disturbance[s]" that still echoed from the civil war between "You and the King of England who are one colour and one blood." That war created this war, not Little Turtle. Red Jacket also invoked the Haudenosaunees' traditional role as the arbiter of regional diplomacy. From Native America's perspective, he made clear, insult had been added to injury when his people, the Ohio nations, and the rest of Indian country were left out of the Treaty of Paris.[57] It was no wonder, then, that Little Turtle preferred war over diplomacy.

Peace, however, was not yet out of reach. While St. Clair's war against the Glaize coalition may have made things irreconcilable between the United States and the Ohio Indians, the Haudenosaunee were still willing to negotiate. Red Jacket reminded the Americans that there was once a time when the "whole Island was shaken and violently agitated" by an Anglo-American war that had "overturned" the internal and external peace of all involved. But "peace is now budding" again between the United States and the Iroquois, and America needed to offer concessions to maintain that peace. Red Jacket then demanded an equitable distribution of annuities and gifts among the Six Nations and proposed that the Americans build a sawmill on Haudenosaunee land for their exclusive use. He explained that these tangible promises would prove Washington was genuine in his intent to create peace that was like "a *rock*, which is *immoveable*" and would also help to bury "in oblivion" all "the evils which have hitherto disturbed our peace." Besides, Red Jacket explained, the British were also very interested in securing an alliance with the Iroquois. If the Americans took peace as seriously as the British "who are by our fireside," they will "soon see all things settled among the Indian-Nations, [and] peace will be Spread far and near."[58]

Despite that pathway to peace, one of the US delegates challenged Red Jacket's claim about American responsibility for the Ohio war. The Seneca orator then pointedly and simply responded *What do you thin(k) is the real cause?* This was met with silence. Not deterred, Timothy Pickering followed that exchange by making a surprising demand: the Iroquois should send warriors to help battle the Glaize coalition. Red Jacket "mocked" Pickering's breach of diplomatic protocol and "ridiculed his assertions of American superiority." The Haudenosaunee had made it clear many times before that they would not be forced into war, particularly by those who were at fault for creating the war in the first place. Pickering backed down, and when the summit closed on April 25, Washington personally chose to give a farewell address, guaranteed the annuity discussed earlier in return for Iroquois neutrality, offered ritual personal condolences for the two chiefs who had died, and gifted the Peace Medal to Red Jacket. These were all important customary gestures as well as an attempt to keep the peace. The Philadelphia council thus proved that the Americans, at least in the short term, would have to negotiate peace on Haudenosaunee terms, regardless of how "subordinate" they thought the Six Nations were. This was not just because of the threat posed by a Six Nations alliance with the Glaize coalition, but because the United States was also interested in maintaining the optics of their nonaggression. Since the new nation was dependent on expansion into Indian land to recoup its wartime losses and impress its European competitors, the Iroquois were central to that end.[59] Catering to them would assist the US in forming alliances with Indian nations, deflect the ire of western Indian nations, and to strengthen them in their continental competition with the British and Spanish.

If appeasing the "Romans of the Woods" was a national imperative for the United States, gift-giving—as Red Jacket often reminded them—was an important part of that strategy. After all, the Haudenosaunee had come to expect that Europeans would offer substantial diplomatic gifts, and they expected the same of the Americans.[60] The US, for its part, mostly complied. Their gifts ranged from wampum strings to steel tools and weapons, but some of the most important objects were the Indian Peace Medals. Washington ordered the first medals to be created by Philadelphia silversmiths and cast by the Department of Treasury in 1789. At first they bore an image of Columbia, Europe's symbolic and feminine personification of the Americas, meeting a generic Indian man in a field. But a redesign in 1792 replaced Columbia with an image of George Washington himself. The President stands smoking a *calumet* with the generic Indian figure who dropped his hatchet (a common Indigenous symbol of war) to the ground, symbolizing how the warlike Indian nations of old had given way to a peaceful and pastoral future with the new nation.

For the Washington administration, the medals were part of a broader effort by the Federalists to expand their nation- and nationalism-building efforts into every corner of federal policy. The party was the chief cultivator of Washington as a "cult" symbol of nationhood, unity, and political stability. Replacing Columbia with Washington was a reference to the supremacy of America's first "republicanized monarch," a natural and comforting symbol for Americans who had spent nearly two decades "smash[ing] the relics of royalty" while searching for their own "human . . . emblem of naturalized aristocracy."[61] His presence on the Peace Medal once again signaled how important Indian affairs were to the new administration.

Following Red Jacket's gift, these Peace Medals were distributed among many Native leaders. Even among the Iroquois his gift was not unique. Farmer's Brother also received one of the 1792 Peace Medals. Contemporaries observed that "so precious did [Farmer's Brother] esteem the gift" that he declared he would "lose it only with his life." Yet as the years wore on, Red Jacket's close affiliation with the Peace Medal eclipsed that of all the other recipients in part because of what his politics and the Medal itself symbolized: peace at a critical moment in American history. Red Jacket proposed a different future than what many Americans saw in the daily realities of imperial wars, Indian war, and the border violence caused by colonization. It was no secret that Red Jacket had a distaste for war, so, from Washington's perspective in 1792, who better than Red Jacket to negotiate with the United States—a country engaged in a losing war with an Indian confederacy in Ohio—on behalf of the Six Nations? With his relentless pursuit of peace and the pacific and pastoral imagery of the Peace Medal itself, these would combine to symbolically pacify the Iroquois in the eyes of land hungry New Yorkers. Even at the highest levels, peace was a clear American priority. After all, in 1793 Henry Knox explained that "the sentiments of the great mass of the Citizens of the United States are adverse in the extreme to an Indian War."[62] The reputation of a sympathetic and war-averse Red Jacket, with Peace Medal in hand, might help Washington smooth over the bumps created by his administration's otherwise flailing Indian policy.

Red Jacket was of course not shy about using Washington's image and desire for peace to his peoples' advantage in Philadelphia and beyond. He used them to negotiate for higher annuities, farm tools, and supplies, all the things that provided the Senecas with the means to maintain their self-sufficiency and their political sovereignty. In addition, he used his American allies like Pickering and, eventually, his association with Washington against his own Iroquoian rivals. In Philadelphia, he had convinced the US delegates to pass over Cornplanter's home at Buffalo Creek while negotiating where to distribute supplies and annuities to the Iroquois. In 1805, Red Jacket spoke in support of the Six Nations in Canada who had voted to depose Joseph Brant for allegedly selling Grand River reservation land for his own benefit and defaulting on his loans. These attacks did not go unanswered, however. In 1802, Cornplanter convinced his brother, Handsome Lake, to accuse Red Jacket of being a witch, a sentence punishable by death. In 1807, another outlandish rumor circulated that Joseph Brant plotted to kill the Seneca orator. After learning about this plot, Red Jacket had "poison[ed]" Brant who then "died very suddenly." This bit of stunning hearsay was added to a six-page report by Peregrine Fitzhugh, Washington's wartime aide-de-camp, to President Thomas Jefferson that primarily discussed the state of Canadian and American frontier diplomacy, Great Lakes trade with the British and Six Nations, and the feasibility of an American invasion of Canada. The murder itself is unsubstantiated, but Brant and Red Jacket's feud was public, fraught, and clearly important to American interests since even a rumor about Red Jacket was worthy of the president's attention.[63]

For the United States, Red Jacket became a vital ally in large part because they had very nearly lost the war against the Glaize coalition. They suffered their first major loss in 1790 and another humiliating defeat and the loss of half of the army a year later. In response, Washington sent a peace envoy under Colonel Thomas Proctor to the Glaize in 1792. The envoy traveled first through Iroquois country where Proctor extended an invitation to Red Jacket to join the American negotiators. Red Jacket agreed to go, donning his Peace Medal, but the mission ground to a halt after British merchants refused—perhaps to aid the Glaize coalition—to charter a boat to take them. Taking advantage of the failure of the American envoy, Little Turtle called for a general pan-Indian council to be held at the Glaize later that year to recruit more nations, including the Six Nations, to its movement. For the United States, peace with anyone but the Senecas proved elusive. Frequent skirmishes and violence were common occurrences between Americans and Native Americans not only in the northwest with the Glaize coalition, but also in the south with the Creek, Cherokee, and Choctaw. Despite this, Washington attempted to raise soldiers from among those southern nations to help fight Little Turtle and his coalition. That effort, unsurprisingly, failed. To make matters worse, in

1794 a local challenge "to the new [American] constitutional order" erupted when farmers in western Pennsylvania rebelled against a whiskey excise tax. The Whiskey Rebellion was finally put down by Washington and the army he personally led, but this showdown again reminded the administration of the necessity of bringing far-flung regions under control.[64] In that chaotic and violent borderland environment, any symbol of control or order like the Peace Medal became invaluable, as did foreign actors like Red Jacket who similarly pushed for peace.

The United States would eventually win the war against the Glaize coalition, but it was not the glorious victory they wanted. To recover from the humiliating losses there, in 1794 Washington sent a better equipped, larger, and more "regularly supplied" army under General Anthony Wayne to Ohio. Wayne "won no decisive victories," but his fort-building and scorched-earth invasion further stalled the coalition, which had already begun to dissolve on its own. The war came to an anticlimactic end after the Shawnee Blue Jacket's small coalition force fell to Wayne's army at Fallen Timbers in August 1794. While this brough the Ohio territory technically under American control and dissolving the Glaize coalition, the costly and grinding war had taken its toll on American control over the west. Considering Red Jacket's intimate knowledge of American diplomacy, he would have been acutely aware of just how tenuous that control was. So when he, Cornplanter, and the Haudenosaunee leadership complained to US officials about land sales made during their war against the Glaize in the Erie Triangle (now Erie County, Pennsylvania), the United States was forced to make extraordinary concessions to them in order to avoid the resumption of war. At a summit held in Canandaigua in October to discuss Erie Triangle land sales, Red Jacket, with the Peace Medal around his neck, and Cornplanter, just off a diplomatic victory securing the Allegany Territory for the Senecas, arrived at the head of 1,500 Haudenosaunee and Ohio Indian men and clan mothers. This show of force reminded Henry Knox of his fear that the Iroquois were fully capable of convincing the Ohio Indians to restart the war, and the head negotiators Israel Chapin and Timothy Pickering agreed. When the summit ended and the Treaty of Canandaigua was signed November 12, the Americans, in exchange for peace, ceded back to the Iroquois vast territories in the Erie Triangle that would become the Cattaraugus and Buffalo Creek reservations.[65]

After Canandaigua, Red Jacket remained at the forefront of Iroquois diplomacy. Between 1794 and 1805, he gave speeches in twenty diplomatic summits and councils, each of which was reprinted in New York newspapers. In that decade, the boundaries of the Cattaraugus, Buffalo Creek, Grand River, and

Cornplanter reservations were established, but the Iroquois' military strength diminished considerably. Red Jacket's general strategy at that point was to out-negotiate American diplomats and, if that failed, to sell peripheral land to protect core Seneca interests. But this tactic became untenable in 1802, the moment of Seneca "rebirth" and the creation of the *Gaiwiio* (Longhouse) religion, when the Great Spirit spoke to Handsome Lake and decreed that the Haudenosaunee sell no more land. Handsome Lake, Cornplanter's brother, had deep "anxieties about the territorial security of the Seneca" and made it a national imperative to cease ceding Iroquois land. At that point, maintaining territorial integrity was as important as resisting encroaching missionaries and white Americans. While Red Jacket was not fully convinced of this new imperative, he nonetheless bowed to the leaderships' support of this new policy.[66]

During this decade the wider American public encountered Red Jacket for the first time. To New Yorkers, a people who were no longer so concerned with pan-Indian coalitions and the border instability those coalitions caused, Red Jacket was an "eloquent Indian," a new type of celebrity in a time when oratory was a widely respected and appreciated skill among Native Americans and Anglo-Americans alike. But that appreciation of oratory was not applied everywhere equally. Particularly when Indigenous oratory was deployed in the protection of their national sovereignty, this was not viewed as a diplomatic skill but as a racial trait. Even the content of these speeches, regardless of any overt political intentions or speechmakers' success, was viewed merely as "proof" of Native America's diminishing power in the face of American expansion. As the fear of northern Indian war dissipated after 1794, New Yorkers were less afraid and more charmed by speeches that spoke of violence, predatory lang hunger, religious oppression, and fraudulent land sales. The public continued to read Red Jacket's brilliant speeches on issues ranging from protecting the Senecas' interests against missionaries and illegal land claims to the problems of a rapidly growing American population, but they were now worried less about the threat of the Iroquois empire and instead focused more on his mastery of Indian eloquence.[67] Without a coalition like the Glaize to rouse the ancient fear of the Iroquois empire, his speeches at the turn of the nineteenth century began to take on the patina of tragedy, even of folksy charm, for New Yorkers who chose to forget the realities of the past decade.

What set Red Jacket apart from other indigenous orators in this environment was his sheer talent. Historians know that Red Jacket was an exceptional orator because contemporaries said so and because his language tends to speak for itself, but he was also an exceptional performer. He had a keen wit, a masterful control of irony, and a strategically applied a scathing sense of humor. Depending on his audience and needs, he was able to speak alternately from the perspective of the conquered or the conqueror. In addition, he was an engaging persona. With his Peace Medal prominently displayed across his chest at every public appearance, Red Jacket was a charismatic showman who created an "effect [that] was riveting." His oratory, when combined with the "armory of his capacious intellect" and performative talent, provided him with "weapons of forensic warfare" which he used to protect Seneca country and, in the process, dazzle the Euro-American literary public. Although he seemed to exemplify the quintessential eloquent Indian, Red Jacket also defied that typecasting by choosing to speak in public exclusively in the Seneca language. The English translations of his speeches were often done by his long-time interpreters, Jasper Parish and Horatio Jones, American men who were captured in their teens (likely during the Revolution) by the Senecas but who chose to remain with their captors for the rest of their lives. When they translated for Red Jacket, they respected his orders and refused to dress up his speeches "to fit the romanticized expectations that literary audiences had for Indian Speech." Red Jacket was known to joke in and speak fluent English, but his insistence on making the Seneca language public helped him to cultivate a consistent Indigenous presence that supported Haudenosaunee sovereignty. Despite outsider's efforts to confine his oratory to that of a folksy "vanished" Indian, his language remained a rhetorical barrier against Anglo-American cultural influence. In that environment, Red Jacket proved to be a true "poet among politicians."[68]

White literary audiences and American Indian agents were not the only ones listening. The Federalist and Republican partisan presses of New York in the 1790s, papers born of self-interested political "Hook and Snivey"—or "trickery and deceit"—found their own value in Red Jacket's speeches. This partisan wrangling over Iroquois politics occurred in an era when President Thomas Jefferson, newly elected in 1800, and the Republican party in New York and nation-wide began to abandon the policies of national centralization established by Washington to survive the nation's infancy and instead "insisted" on a "minimal and cheap" national government. This included dramatic decreases in military spending and domestic expenses, but no austerity measures applied when it came to fueling the expansion of the United States westward into Indian territory. Take, for example, the 1803 Louisiana Purchase that nearly doubled the territory claimed by the United States, the new federal energies dedicated to the expansion of slavery, and the abandonment of the Federalists' gestures toward limiting American expansion into Indian country. After the Jefferson's election and the so-called "Revolution of 1800," George Washington's efforts to bring back British-like policies to control America's illegal territorial expansion into Indigenous land was replaced with Jefferson's effort to flatly "coerce Indians to make massive [land] cessions."[69] This was a moment when helping American farmers, slaveholders, and land speculators invade Indian country outside of wartime became a national priority.

One of the speeches that captured intense partisan attention was Red Jacket's 1802 pretrial public defense of Stiff Armed George, a Seneca man convicted by a New York court of murdering a white man, John Hewitt, near Buffalo Creek. The Senecas, who understood their sovereignty to include the ability to dispense their own law and justice on the reservation, hid Stiff Armed George from the state. When a New York court sought George's arrest, Red Jacket spoke in his defense, claiming not only that George was reportedly drunk at the time and had only accidentally killed Hewitt, but also that the Senecas had different laws when it came to "crime committed in liquor" versus one "committed coolly and deliberately." George's case allowed Red Jacket to tie the fact of the murder to Haudenosaunee politics more broadly, much like he did at Tioga Point. Through the unfair treatment of George, Red Jacket evoked the tense relationship between the Six Nations and the United States and reminded them that the Haudenosaunee had signed no treaty "with the state of New-York." The New York court thus erred in using a nonexistent treaty to demand that the Senecas abide by the state's law and hand George over. This was a legal fiction that both undercut federal authority in conducting Indian affairs and echoed the conquest theory. If it was embraced, there would be much broader repercussions for Iroquois sovereignty.[70]

In addition to making a federal case out of New York's claims of a separate treaty with the Haudenosaunee, Red Jacket used George's pre-trial defense to protest one person in particular: Jefferson's new Iroquois Superintendent (the chief diplomat assigned to the Haudenosaunee), Captain Callender Irvine. To the Iroquois, Irvine was a pale imitation of the well-liked Superintendent he replaced, Captain Israel Chapin, a Federalist appointed by John Adams. In Red Jacket's retelling, George's drunkenness was symptomatic of Irvine's corruption. He had stolen annuities, made trade deals to enrich himself, and had illegally sold off Seneca land. In addition, Red Jacket explained that the Haudenosaunee had "long complained" to the federal governments that Irvine, who chose to live in the Geneseo Valley two hundred miles away, was far too distant to listen to their complaints in the first place. Under Irvine, the Senecas had "no Guardian—no Protector—no one [who] is now authorized to receive us" to settle grievances exactly like George's. Irvine's lack of presence damaged the diplomatic trust that had been building between the Iroquois and the United States ever since "you were under the government of Great-Britain." A competent Superintendent, on the other hand, would have the "power to settle offenses of [George's] kind" and alleviate any problems. Red Jacket then compared Jefferson's poor choice in Superintendent to the standard set by "General WASHINGTON" who "told us that we had formed a chain of friendship which was bright" when he promised that the "United States would be equally willing to brighten it, if rusted by any means." Even "President ADAMS," Jefferson's predecessor and political rival, had offered "satisfactory redress" to Seneca complaints in the past. When they did, "peace and harmony was restored." As Irvine showed, the federal government had not only failed in their duties to keep peace with the Iroquois, but the current administration also seemed to turn a blind eye to the legacy of the nation's own patriarch. Red Jacket reminded those gathered for his speech that "we are independent of the State of New York" and are not, in any way, under its law, and if Jefferson, the "President of the United States[,] is called a Great Man, possessing of great power," can he "not even control the laws of this state" or "appoint a Commissioner" with the Haudenosaunees' consultation "on the subject" as was always done before? This only proved that Jefferson's current Indian policy was failing.[71]

This speech, not surprisingly, caught the attention of the influential Republican newspaper *The Hudson Bee*, an important player in the "strenuous electioneering" that garnered public support for Jefferson's election. The *Bee* expressed their "astonishment at the enormity of the late fabrication said to be a speech of *Red Jacket*," which they claimed was an elaborate Federalist conspiracy, a "fabrication" filled with "gross and numerous distortions" intended to undermine Republican rule. Other Republican papers struck a similar tone in discussing the speech and even fell back on the familiar trope of Indians as a people who could only speak broken and barely coherent English. In their view, the speech could not have been Red Jacket's because the language was simply too good to have come from an Indigenous person.[72]

In Red Jacket's case, his words were described as so "singular and so different from the *Indian* mode of *talking*" that the speech could have been written by none other than Israel Chapin himself. The former Superintendent was the true "evil genius who delights in mischief," masterminded this elaborate Federalist "farce," and stoked the flames of "party spirit for the purpose

of alarming the public, and exciting the fears of women and children."
Interestingly, the Republican press was not entirely wrong in their complaints
that someone had created a vast conspiracy. But as it turned out, it was not
the Federalists, Chapin, or Red Jacket who had done so, but their own Henry
Dearborn, Jefferson's Secretary of War, who first claimed that Red Jacket's
speech was false.[73]

The partisan misuse of Red Jacket's 1802 speech cut both ways. For the
Federalist *New York Gazette*, Red Jacket was stuffed into an ill-fitting costume of an ignorant Indian who reflected the Republican's own ignorance
back on them. The *Gazette* sarcastically explained that in order for the
Republican's interpretation of Red Jacket's defense of Stiff Armed George
to make sense, one simply had to deploy the Jeffersonian's favorite "time
saving device"—which was to read nothing and thus know nothing at all—
to reach the conspiratorial conclusions the Republican press did. Only
then, once someone willingly sank himself into ignorance, would he agree
with the Republicans that "Mr. Jefferson is a very charitable man" who legally and morally "dispenses with all laws" as he sees fit. After all, even "Red
Jacket, the chief of the Seneca nation, seems to think that the President"
has that authority, particularly after Jefferson fined the corrupted Irvine
for stealing Iroquois annuity money, only to turn around and return the
fine right back to him.[74]

The Federalist press also got ahold of another of Red Jacket's speeches in
March 1803 during Stiff Armed George's trial. A number of papers reprinted
Red Jacket's speech verbatim in which he used the trial and George's subsequent acquittal to expose the hypocrisy of those who blamed George for the
murder and, even worse, "had powerful temptations" to cast him in "an un-
favorable light." The Americans who blamed George did this to instill doubt
on the character of George and the Haudenosaunee more broadly in order
to bury their own history of "impunity with which the white men had, in
various influences, committed murders on the Indians" with no recourse.
George's trial, in that sense, was about more than one man. It was a whole-
sale rejection of the US's predatory expansion into Indian land and of the
new administration's Indian policy that had dismantled the two previous
administrations' relatively "friendly dispositions" with the Iroquois. To make
matters worse, Red Jacket, who presumably wore the Peace Medal while in
court, explained that not only was the United States breaking its promises to
the Haudenosaunee, but slandering him, Stiff Armed George, and by extension the Iroquois' sovereignty was an assault on the very legacy and memory
of George Washington.[75]

Red Jacket would also go on to become a renowned figure in literary circles in the years following Stiff Armed George's trial. In 1805, he delivered a scathing speech to a Reverend Jacob Cram of the Massachusetts Missionary Society who proposed the establishment of a new Baptist mission at Buffalo Creek. At the Senecas' council fire called to discuss Cram's proposal, Red Jacket fumed about the long history of white people who were given so much by the Haudenosaunee but never reciprocated and only ever desired more. He reminded Cram of the their long and fraught history with New York, a history in which the Six Nations had been "so often deceived by the white people" that trust was, at best, difficult to earn. But the oldest and deepest problem was the fact that the Great Spirit did not give the Haudenosaunee a "religion written in a book." If, as Cram argued, there is only one way to worship, only one true religion that must be taught in a mission church, "why do you white people differ so much about it? Why not all agree, as you can all read the book?" Cram's church, in that sense, was simply another in a long line of selfish demands by white Americans. After all, "You have our country, but are not satisfied; [now] you want to force your religion upon us." The Haudenosaunee, he concluded, "do not wish to destroy your religion, or take it from you. We only want to enjoy our own." When the council came to an end and Red Jacket approached to shake his hand, Cram refused, rose sharply from his seat, and "replied that he could not take them by the hand; that there was no fellowship between the religion of God and the works of the devil." Red Jacket and his delegation simply smiled and walked away. Cram was suitably shamed and later came back to apologize for his rudeness, but his mission was never built.[76]

This speech resonated with New Yorkers when it was first published in 1808. For many observers, it was not just another moment when Red Jacket had proven himself to be a model "eloquent Indian," but was a declaration of Haudenosaunee religious independence, one that reflected the experiences of well-known populist evangelical preachers who traveled the state and country and who likewise rejected established religion's authority and orthodoxy. In other words, Red Jacket's rejection of Cram resonated with the state's own regional and religious pride. For New Yorkers, the Senecas' speech openly and unequivocally rejected the influence of established Christian religion, as did those itinerant evangelical preachers. But it was also a rejection of the missionary from Massachusetts, part of a cultural rallying cry in which New Yorkers sought out ways to disrupt New England's lofty claims to their "region's superior Christianity" by celebrating their own unique religious practice.[77] In that moment, Red Jacket's defense of

Haudenosaunee religion supported New Yorkers' own religious independence and unorthodoxy.

In 1811, two more of Red Jacket's speeches that struck a similar tone were printed in a pamphlet titled *Native Eloquence.* These became his most reprinted and popular speeches. The first was a response to the Reverend John Alexander who, like Cram, was criticized for proposing the construction of a Christian mission in Seneca country. Red Jacket expressed his peoples' frustrations at the "Great numbers of black coats" that were "amongst the Indians," and who with their "sweet voices" and "smiling faces, have offered to teach them the religion of the white people." To illustrate why this was a bad thing, Red Jacket pointed eastward to New England Indian communities, at "Our brethren" there, who took up Christianity. The result? "They are a divided people—we are united—they quarrel about religion—we live in love and friendship—they drink strong water—have learnt how to cheat—and to practice all the vices of white men, which disgrace Indians." Christianity, he explained, teaches only the bad and none of the supposed good promised by American society. "Brother," he continued, "if you are our well wisher, keep away and do not disturb us . . . forms of worship are indifferent to the Great Spirit . . . we like our religion and do not want another." Red Jacket then drew a comparison between good and bad Christianity. The Quakers, for example, "council us," give "us plows, and show us how to use them. They tell us we are accountable beings, but do not say we must change our religion. We are satisfied with what they do" because they do not pressure the Haudenosaunee to leave their land or change.[78] Alexander was simply another in a long line of predatory outsiders.

The second speech struck a similar tone. It also identified a new threat, the Ogden Land Company (formed in 1810), which would come to be one of the biggest threats to Iroquois territorial sovereignty for generations to come. This speech was delivered in response to John Richardson, an agent of the Ogden Land Company, who had recently attempted to separate Haudenosaunee families from their land through private deals and the retroactive sale of the land returned at Canandaigua. In that speech, Red Jacket made a moral stand against the corrupted and "crooked manner" that the Ogden Land Company used to claim Seneca territory and who egregiously demanded the Haudenosaunee be removed from New York State entirely. Ogden had not only failed to "walk . . . in the straight path pointed out by the great Council of your nation," the company had "no writings" from the President to back up their bogus land claims. Red Jacket also tore into the legal logic of Richardson's claim. "You tell us your employers have purchased of the Council of Yorkers [the New York State Legislature] a right to buy our lands," but this cannot be as "the lands do not belong to the Yorkers; they are ours" given "by the Great Spirit." Besides, there simply was no extra to give. The Iroquois had already sold much to the state and so retained only what they needed to live on. Red Jacket also used Richardson to speak to an issue that cut to the heart of Indian removal: "If we move off into a distant country, towards the setting sun," he explained, the Haudenosaunee would become "foreigners, and strangers" in a strange land and would be "despised by the red as well as the white men, and we should soon be surrounded by the white men" who would "kill our game, come upon our lands, and try to get them from us." Nothing would change, despite the "sweet voices and smiling faces" of the Ogden Land Company and the hollow promises of Americans that "assure us of their love and that they will not cheat us." In the end, "Indians must take care of themselves, and not trust either in your people or in the king's children [in Canada]." The Ogden Land Company was already in the process of becoming the biggest private threat to the Senecas' sovereignty, but to New Yorkers who only read this speech, it became an origin story of a Native American nemesis, a thrilling dramatization of the newest threats facing the Haudenosaunee and, by extension, all the "vanished" Indians in the east.[79]

The popularity of *Native Eloquence*, due to its engaging combination of local pride and a villainous origin story, speaks to a shift in New Yorkers' perception of the Iroquois over the preceding decades and how that change manifested on the eve of the War of 1812. This was an important aspect of early Iroquois exceptionalism. Reviewers of *Native Eloquence* captured this shift when they explained that Red Jacket's speeches are no longer interesting as "confidential or important 'State Papers,'" but were mostly intriguing as "literary curiosities" that showcased his ideas on "Indian rights" and his rejection of "black coats," or missionaries.[80] What mattered to an interested public in 1811 was less the threat of the Iroquois empire at war than the relatable and eloquent stories about a people defending themselves against foreign invaders. They saw the Iroquois not as an ancient and threatening imperial power, but as a sympathetic partner in a broader struggle for sovereignty. This shift in thinking was made possible because the Six Nations, as well as other northern Indian nations, had for more than fifteen years ceased to be a significant military threat to New York. In addition, the United States itself was a far larger, more populous, and more stable country than it was in the 1790s. Even though American diplomats still worried that the Shawnee Tecumseh (at war in Indiana by 1811) was actively seeking an alliance with the Iroquois which raised concerns about an Iroquois-British treaty and a broader pan-Indian alliance, for many New Yorkers, the existential threat of Iroquoian war was no longer so troubling.[81]

That diminished public fear did not mean that American diplomats took the Iroquois any less seriously. Red Jacket continued to visit his contacts in Washington, where he again became the comforting face of Iroquois diplomacy and neutrality to a country preparing for war. He gave three speeches in 1810–1812 that promised to maintain the Covenant Chain with the United States and nine wartime and postwar speeches that fulfilled other Iroquoian goals. In the spring, summer, and fall of 1811, in response to the violence in Indiana between the pan-Indian coalition of Tecumseh and the Prophet Tenkswatawa and the American and local forces commanded by William Henry Harrison, Red Jacket was already in Washington declaring the Six Nations' neutrality in the conflict. Then, in the early stages of the War of 1812, Red Jacket pushed for Haudenosaunee neutrality, even if the Six Nations were eventually forced to side with the Americans in 1814 after the Indian allies of the British threatened Iroquois country.[82] As he had during both the Revolution and the Glaize War, Red Jacket played a peaceful diplomatic role and demanded concessions in return for Haudenosaunee neutrality, and was listened to and respected by his American allies.

Red Jacket's international political responsibilities may not have changed; however, the way most Americans remembered the Haudenosaunee had. Few in that era captured this shift as cogently as DeWitt Clinton, an ardent advocate of Indian removal and one of the country's greatest spokesmen for an American continental empire. The son of the New York governor during the American Revolution, George Clinton, Dewitt also served as governor of New York and mayor of New York City, a presidential candidate, and became best known for public projects like the Erie Canal and establishing his intellectual credentials by shaping "New York City's most illustrious civic institutions."[83] He embodied the idea that the 1810s and 1820s were the "start of an expansive new era" in American "nationalistic sentiment" when the United States was still an "open-ended experiment." Clinton was also a student of Iroquois history. For a man who in policy and rhetoric believed so strongly in the glorious future of the Empire State, Clinton's conception of how Indigenous history fit into New York's conception of self are important and revealing. To be clear, his work was not some proto-decolonized effort to celebrate the history of the Iroquois. But he embodied how New Yorkers would have implicitly understood the Iroquois as an important part of their own history. Two of Clinton's major speeches help to illuminate that line of thinking. The first, *Discourse Delivered Before the New-York Historical Society*, was delivered to the New-York Historical Society in 1811 and offers important insights into how New Yorkers saw the Iroquois fitting into the future of the United States, and of the country's resultant place in the world. The second was delivered to the Literary and Philosophical Society of New York in 1814.[84]

In Clinton's speech delivered to the New-York Historical Society in 1811, around the same time Tecumseh formed his confederacy and the Napoleonic Wars had engulfed Europe, he reminded his audience that, in those uncertain times, to know a country's history is to understand its national purpose and its people's potential. He prompted his audience to take a wide look at history and to "trace up our ancestry to as high and as remote a source as possible" through the two "most interesting departments of human knowledge . . . Biography and History." Doing that, he reasoned, leads inevitably to the history of the "red man" of New York, the first inhabitants of the land. Here one would find the Iroquois, a people whose history and society revealed the extraordinary "energies of the human character," which New Yorkers, by inhabiting the same land, also shared.[85]

In Clinton's mind, to know the history of the Haudenosaunee was to know the history of New York. The Six Nations "have occupied the same territory before us" and, "although [they are] not connected with us in any other respect," students of history are "small in their capacity for improvement" if they do not "advance in wisdom and in virtue, from contemplating the state and the history of the people who occupied this country before the man of Europe." After all, he explained, the rise of New York State filled the vacuum left behind by the Iroquois, the "Romans of this western world" and a "federal republic" who conquered the "greatest body of the most fertile lands in North America." But eventually, as the publishers of *Native Eloquence* suggested, they "vanished" in the face of inevitable white progress. This was a fundamentally important part of Clinton's belief in Indian removal, and in a meandering address he mused on the many disconnected and often stereotypical theories for that declension. He blamed this on their peculiar style of war, low birth rates, the adoption of European clothes unsuited for their own climates, abuse of alcohol, lack of civilization, and most significantly, their susceptibility to European disease.[86]

Despite the imaginary declension of the Iroquois, Clinton also understood them to be a self-evidently exceptional people and, by geographic and historical association, so were New Yorkers. He highlighted that exceptionality through a brief biographical sketch of a few different Iroquois figures like Joseph Brant, Cornplanter, and Red Jacket. To bring these people to life,

Clinton referenced Red Jacket's 1802 speech to the assembled Six Nations where the Seneca orator defended himself against Handsome Lake's accusation of witchcraft. This, Clinton explained, was evidence of the extraordinary power of Red Jacket's uniquely Iroquoian oratorical ability, one that separated the Six Nations from other Indian nations. So great was his talent that the "iron brow of [Iroquois] superstition relented under the magic of his eloquence." Red Jacket had easily swatted away the charges of witchcraft and thus proved that the Iroquois, a "barbarous" people, could be swayed by the power of oratory, a God-given talent of a "minister of the Almighty." Clinton then expanded his application of Iroquoian genius to another familiar orator, Logan. Lest others claim that Logan, and not Red Jacket, was the "most splendid exhibition of Indian eloquence . . . let it be remembered that Logan was a Mingo chief," the second son of a Cayuga chief, so he "belonged to the Confederates" even if he did not "live in their patrimonial territory."[87] In Clinton's mind, Red Jacket, Logan and their contemporaries were living proof that the Iroquois were exceptional.

Framing Iroquois history as something of the past while also claiming its influence on the present was a delicate balancing act. Giving too much credit to the Haudenosaunee (and Native Americans broadly) and its living legends would mean confronting and confounding the myth of the "vanishing" Indian. So on one hand, Red Jacket was a living representative of New York's exceptionalism and a reminder of the land's innate capacity to create greatness. But on the other hand, beyond a few individual examples, the Iroquois were broadly regarded as a people of the past, a myth that reflected New Yorkers' buried anxieties about the violence and injustices that accompanied America's not-so-distant wars and expansions into Iroquois country and westward.

That anxiety, and the simultaneous efforts to bury the history that caused that anxiety, were essential to Clinton's broader theories of the founding of New York State. In his theories on the ancient history of New York, he explained that the Iroquois were not the first but the second evolution of Native peoples in the region. As proof, he pointed to the ancient ruins of many Iroquois towns and palisaded "forts" that dotted the New York landscape. The forts, he hypothesized, were built by a different breed of Indian, some advanced race that long preceded the Haudenosaunee. But at some point in history, Asia suddenly "discharged its inhabitants" who traveled to the Americas where they conquered the fort builders. These newcomers were the true ancestors of Red Jacket and the Iroquois empire, a group that only turned back the clock, so to speak, on the ancient's development. This explained why the Iroquois were somehow both a "primitive" tribal people but also produced individuals with world-class genius like Red Jacket, Joseph Brant, Logan, and others. It was a remarkable—and remarkably incorrect— theory, especially considering that multiple Senecas had told Clinton directly that their ancestors had built the forts before they were rendered obsolete with the formation of the Confederacy in the 1400s. But Clinton was unconvinced. It must have been some other ancient race who built them because he couldn't believe that the Iroquois could possibly have had the society-wide agricultural support to maintain such a vast population to need such infrastructure.[88] Though meandering, this theory was Clinton's way of showcasing New York's exceptionality. The first race of New Yorkers was certainly advanced, and the conquering Asiatic race was not. But over time, the natural environment and the legacy of that advanced ancient race, implanted some measure of greatness into its new inhabitants and their descendants, the Iroquois. New York State, then, was only the latest to inherit that place-based exceptionality.

Clinton's musings on that ancient migration and the origins of New York State revealed his deeper, and potentially cataclysmic, fear for the future of the United States. That worry reveals how he saw empire, New York's historic mistreatment of the Haudenosaunee, and Euro-Americans' mistreatment of Native Americans generally as entangled and formative in American history. At its heart, Clinton explained that American predatory land grabs and the spread of disease had so severely impacted the Iroquois that the cosmic moral scale was out of balance. If this was not corrected, the United States would eventually suffer the same fate as the advanced pre-Iroquoian race when some other "transcendent genius" would rise and "rally the barbarous nations of Asia, under the standard of a mighty empire." Then, "after subverting the neighboring despotisms of the old world," this leader would "bend his course toward European America." They would conquer the continent, and then "the destinies of our country may then be decided on the waters of the Missouri, or on the banks of Lake Superior." This monstrous enemy would take revenge on the United States for "the injuries we have inflicted on her (Native American) sons," and they would usher in a "new, a long, and a gloomy night of gothic darkness [that] will set in upon mankind." If that happened, "the wide-spread ruins of our cloud-capp'd towers, of our solemn temples, and of our magnificent cities" will become the objects of their study, just as Clinton and others studied the ancient ruins of the Iroquois and Indigenous mound builders.[89]

As evident from Clinton's speeches, he did not merely "admire" the Iroquois, as some scholars suggest. To him, their history and society framed his very understanding of New York exceptionalism and its place in the world, the rise and fall of empires, and the United States' place in that history. This sheds new light on his 1814 address *Introductory Discourse Delivered Before the Literary and Philosophical Society of New York*. Clinton delivered this "admired" 120-page speech that took a wide-ranging look at "the progress of the sciences in America," including geology, ethnography, philosophy, and the evolution of learned societies in the United States. Clinton believed that the advancement of these fields was of vital national importance, so it is revealing that he, an avowed supporter of Indian removal, also mentioned the Indigenous people who played a role in the creation and discovery of American scientific knowledge. Just as Red Jacket and the Iroquois were essential to understanding New York's history, so were the many long-forgotten Indigenous people across the continent who served as guides for naturalists and Euro-American explorers, held critical knowledge of shy or extinct animal species, revealed the extent to which historic and modern diseases spread among human populations, and were themselves living subjects for the study of ancient human societies. Clinton did not give much credit to these individuals nor did he bother to provide most of their names, but their presence in his work is nonetheless telling. If he believed that American science was a symbol of nationhood and served as a rejection of "the accusations which are brought against our country by the literati of Europe" about Americans' ignorance and mental degradation, then Native Americans, regardless of how vanished Americans wished them to be, were part of that project.[90]

Clinton's inherent understanding of the importance of Native American history reframes how the New Yorkers of his time understood the Iroquois' place in the creation of the Empire State. Historians explain that the "origin of the term [Empire State] is shrouded in mystery," but most agree that it started to see widespread use around the 1810s.[91] Several elements of New York society have inspired that nickname. First, the Erie Canal was planned and partly built in this decade. The canal would make New York a truly "Atlantic and western state" and, once completed in 1825, Clinton's secretary Charles Glidden Haines declared that "New York . . . is now an empire." Second, New York, for the very first time, surpassed Virginia in population and economic productivity. The state had achieved the "highest rank for population and wealth" in these years and, as a result, "substituted the 'Empire State' for the 'Old Dominion' in its standing in the Union." Finally, as this chapter and Clinton's speeches reveal, the memory of the Iroquois empire and the ancestral land they inhabited was another important part of New York's conception of its own history and legacy. Even if the inventor of the term "Empire State" may "remain unknown," that matters less than how it was understood at the time: as an amalgam of New York's industrial energy, economic su-premacy, and homegrown Indigenous empire.[92]

But as Red Jacket's postwar life made clear, the three elements that shaped the Empire State were strange bedfellows indeed. The forces arrayed against the Haudenosaunee were enormous, in large part because their land was directly in the path of the as-yet unconstructed Erie Canal. The canal was epic in scale and promised to become a vital connection between New York City and the new city of Buffalo, the "Holy Grail of lake commerce." The construction of the canal started in 1817 and quickly created a "lake effect" that exploded economic development in the region. This resulted in a vast increase in the white population who flooded the area for work, which put even more pressure on the Haudenosaunee. In that environment, they not only faced loss from the New Yorkers and New Englanders who built the canal, but also faced new pressures as the brand-new cities Syracuse, Utica, Rochester, and Buffalo were created to support its commerce. The Haudenosaunee, politically and demographically, were clearly "on the de-fensive." When the canal opened October 26, 1825 to huge fanfare, it was celebrated as a distinctly New York project that carried "nationalizing" im-portance. DeWitt Clinton, as Governor of New York State, participated in the opening ceremonies in Buffalo. As a massive crowd gathered to watch the first ships launch, Clinton, the force behind the Erie Canal's construc-tion and completion, stood waving to them from the deck of the *Seneca Chief*, the boat leading the ceremonial flotilla on its ten-day journey to the Atlantic Ocean.[93]

Red Jacket, still the Senecas' most visible defender, occupied the same media landscape as the Erie Canal. Newspapers knew that Red Jacket's de-fense of his people against the canal's encroachment "will be read with in-terest." Despite the long odds, Red Jacket was remarkably successful in his politics during those years. He built what historians call the "Red Jacket Legacy" wherein their sovereignty and "any of the current legal rights of the Haudenosaunee, upon which they have sued for land claims owed to them by the state, are based on treaties negotiated" in this period. Newspapers followed him on this journey and on his diplomatic trips to Albany, Buffalo, and Washington, and New Yorkers watched with interest as he spoke at dip-lomatic councils, gave invited speeches, and met with private land companies, state representatives, Congressmen, and Presidents James Monroe and John Quincy Adams.[94]

Red Jacket became a captivating celebrity figure. In the 1810s–1820s, he traveled the east coast giving speeches exclusively in the Seneca language,

FIGURE 1.3 Engraving of Dewitt Clinton mingling the waters of Lake Erie with the Atlantic Ocean. The Miriam and Ira D. Wallach Division of Art, Prints, and Photographs: Print Collection, The New York Public Library. New York Public Library Digital Collections. https://digitalcollections.nypl.org/items/510d47d9-7f5e-a3d9-e040-e00a18064a99.

appearing in public "in his full Indian costume" wearing the "Washington medal," and well into in his seventies still held himself with "the fine carriage which the Chieftain still gallantly sustained." In 1823, he met former President James Monroe and arrived at "the legislative chambers, during the session of two houses . . . dressed in a deer skin frock coat and pantaloons, and wore a large silver medal suspended at his breast, which had been presented to him by General Washington." In these meetings and others, Red Jacket gained a reputation as one "increasingly unwilling to yield any additional territory." Despite his no-compromises negotiating, all marveled at his "gentlemanly comport." Those who had occasion to informally converse with him reported on his ability to "speak the English language with correctness and fluency" and were impressed by his "consummate skill and adroitness" in negotiating, a talent which "prove[d] him to be in politics what Tecumseh was in war." Red Jacket's reputation was such that, by the 1820s, he began to receive invitations to speak to public audiences. His first solicited public speech was in 1822 at "The Academy" in Palmyra, New York. With his Peace Medal around his neck, he gave a speech in the Seneca language about familiar topics like the dangers of white land hunger, the American's betrayal of George Washington's legacy and of his promises to the Haudenosaunee, and the Senecas' rejection of missionary influences. Owing to the language barrier that the translator apparently had difficulty overcoming, his "native eloquence and rhetorical powers could only be guessed at, from his manner and appearance." But that seemed not to matter to the audience, however, because the venue "was almost instantly filled with an attentive auditory."[95]

His celebrity even spread abroad. In November 1823, at a "Fancy Ball" attended by "1,475" people at St. Peter's Church in Liverpool, England, American navy officer Major William Gamble grabbed the city's attention when he masqueraded as Red Jacket, "Chief of the Seneca Indians," one of the handful of "Americans" represented in costume at the ball. Even after Red Jacket passed away in 1830, his reputation as an orator continued to resonate overseas. In 1849, a Dublin newspaper advertised the fantastic impersonations and lectures of the traveling performer Mr. Charles Whitney, who had "spared neither time nor expense" in assembling the finest theatrical presentation of "Renowned Transatlantic Orators—Eccentricities of Hoosiers—[and] the *unique* Eloquence of the Red Men of the Forest!" This cavalcade of all things American included Whitney's impersonations of people like John Randolph "the impersonation of sarcasm," Henry Clay "the orator of refined genius," John C. Calhoun "the polished statesman," Patrick Henry the "incarnation of revolutionary zeal," King Phillip "the last of the Pocanokets," and "The Seneca Chief, Sa-go-ye-wat-ha ('He keeps them awake'), or Red Jacket" who needed no introduction.[96]

Behind Red Jacket the celebrity, of course, was the man and his never-ending fight against the daily realities of settler colonial invasion. In the age of the Erie Canal, the Senecas had lost the Genesee Reservation and substantial portions of the Buffalo Creek and Tonawanda reservations. They also were forced to cede areas in Buffalo in 1837-1842. Red Jacket was also continually frustrated in his efforts to protect whatever land was left from an internal group, the "individualistic" Christianized Seneca minority faction, who insisted on negotiating separately with outsiders and without the approval of the Senecas in council. In one consequential case, these Christianized leaders met privately with the Ogden Land Company and signed a treaty on behalf of all the Haudenosaunee, which ceded the Gardeau Reservation on the Genesee River to New York in 1823. This sale, in addition to parting with even more land, in violation of Handsome Lake's teachings, resulted in a series of conversations between representatives of the United States and the Christianized faction leaders about ways to circumvent Red Jacket's negotiating authority altogether. During that the process, Red Jacket earned the enmity of Thomas McKenney, the head of the new Office of Indian Affairs in the US Department of War, who publicly declared Red Jacket an illegitimate leader. Then in 1826–1827, McKenney and the Ogden Land Company held meetings with Young King and Pollard, two of the Christianized faction leaders who signed a fraudulent treaty that would have caused the complete cession of Seneca land and forced the Haudenosaunees' removal to Green Bay in the Wisconsin territory. The betrayal of the Christianized chiefs showed Red Jacket and his allies the devastating influence of Christianity on the Senecas, a lesson reinforced when his own family fell prey to the religion. His son, "Jonathan Jacket," in 1820 married "Yee-ah-weeb," a Christian woman from the Cattaraugus reservation, and they became the first couple "solemnized in this tribe according to the Christian Institution." Red Jacket's second wife also supposedly converted to Christianity, as did the rest of Red Jacket's children, and he was so incensed that he temporarily separated from his wife over this.[97]

Despite these setbacks, Red Jacket continued to relentlessly champion the Senecas' territorial integrity. After months of negotiations and with the legal assistance of the Society of Friends, Red Jacket forced Young King to concede that the 1827 treaty was fraudulent. This hard and bitter fight against a powerful internal rival, however, took its toll. Red Jacket briefly had his chieftainship revoked from 1827–1828, a shocking development that was even reprinted in the London newspaper *Examiner*. He was only reinstated after appealing to leadership and to the Senecas' Quaker allies, who in turn convinced President John Quincy Adams to order an investigation into the fake treaty. That investigation, with the Quakers' help, found that the treaty was indeed fraudulent. Despite Red Jacket's legal and moral victory, Young King and his Christianized faction had proven that they held substantial political power. To prevent such internal fractures from ever again destabilizing Seneca leadership so completely, Red Jacket chose to negotiate with them. He would listen to the small but clearly influential group, and so adopted a strategy of reconciliation.[98]

In that new spirit of reconciliation, Red Jacket took one final diplomatic trip. From January to April 1829, while he was in his mid to late seventies, Red Jacket launched a lecture and celebrity tour along the east coast. The tour was his last attempt to lay the groundwork for a new relationship with the notorious Indian hater and incoming president, Andrew Jackson. The public flocked to hear this living legend. While in Albany on his way to Washington to meet Jackson at the White House, Red Jacket delivered a speech to a large audience at a museum. Many in the room were friends and supporters of the new president who did not appreciate Red Jacket's perspective on Jackson, a man he had publicly "compared" to George Washington and found wanting. Red Jacket spent the rest of his days in similar venues trying to establish a new relationship with the United States when he died on January 20, 1830. His Peace Medal and position as chief were inherited by his nephew, Jimmy Johnson.[99]

Red Jacket's famed eloquence and the material legacy of his Peace Medal lived on as an enduring symbol of New York's early history. As such, Red Jacket became a subject of interest for artists and writers. He sat for or was the subject of interpretation by artists and ethnographers from 1807 to 1891, including George Catlin, Henry Inman, Charles Bird King, C.G. Childs, John Lee Mathies, John Mix Stanley, F.O.C. Darley, Seth Eastman, C. Burt, Robert W. Weir, Baroness Hyde de Neuville, James G.C. Hamilton, and the silhouette artist Perot (Joseph Sansom).[100]

A fundamental aspect of all but one of these artworks was the physical object of the Peace Medal. It served as a visual anchor that kept the shapeshifting memory of Red Jacket rooted in place and time. He was depicted variously as a stoic, a warrior, and a Wild Westerner. In literature, he was a Scotsman, patriot, and a revolutionary. Yet the Peace Medal remained the sole constant. It embodied Red Jacket's ties to the American Revolution and to George Washington, even as the details of his life were rewritten as each generation passed. As the shape-shifting memory of Red Jacket suggests, the historical realities of the famed orator ceased to matter as much as the memory of the Iroquois empire's role in the creation of the United States.

The conspicuous presence of the Peace Medal reveals the staying power of that symbol. This was important not only because it bound the memory of the Haudenosaunee to the American Revolution, but because it was Red Jacket himself who insisted on wearing and showcasing the medal. This was evident in the creation of the most important depiction of Red Jacket; the 1828 portrait by Robert W. Weir (found at the beginning of this chapter). This portrait inspired those that followed. Red Jacket posed for the portrait in the artist's New York City studio and is portrayed standing in a rocky field representing Seneca country. With *gustoweh* in hand and the Peace Medal around his neck, he leans on a hatchet which may represent the one given to him by George Washington in 1792. Importantly, Red Jacket curated this image by "dress[ing] himself in the costume he deemed most appropriate to his character." While posing in Weir's studio, "When his medal appeared complete, [Red Jacket] addressed his interpreter, accompanied by striking gestures; and when his noble front was finished, he sprang from his seat with great alacrity, and seizing the artist by the hand, exclaimed, with great energy, 'Good! good!'"[101] This iconic visage of Red Jacket and his Peace Medal, one that set the tone for every portrait afterward, was at his own insistence.

For some, however, Weir's portrait proved insufficient for those attracted not to realism but to fiction. For those people, the "popular idea of Red Jacket" was based on an 1836 poem by Fitz-Greene Halleck. The poem was titled *Red Jacket. A Chief of the Indian Tribes, The Tuscaroras. On Looking at his Portrait by Weir.* It presented Red Jacket as a "warrior as well as an orator" which was a stereotype inspired by the novelist James Fenimore Cooper who popularized the "noble savage" archetype in *The Leatherstocking Tales.*[102] Halleck's poem is told from the first person where he stands next to Cooper and the ghost of Red Jacket, the "King of Tuscarora," while all three contemplated Weir's portrait "In all its medalled, fringed, and beaded glory." At the core of this image was Halleck's perception of Red Jacket, a man who captured a certain kind of Americana when he did "boast that we, the Democratic, Outrival Europe, even in our Kings!" His oratory revealed a man who possessed "The monarch mind, the mystery of commanding, The birth-hour gift, the art Napoleon." But he was also a warrior covered with scars, bore weapons, and had a quick-to-violence disposition. He was thus torn between "Hope—that thy wrongs, may be by the Great Spirit Remembered and revenged, when thou art gone;" and "Sorrow—that none are left thee to inherit Thy name, thy fame, thy passions, and thy throne!"[103] That perception of Red Jacket as an orator and a warrior influenced others. Twenty years after Halleck's poem, Felix O.C. Darley, a popular illustrator whose semi-realistic portrayals of American folk heroes "Invent[ed] the American Past," rejected the memory of Red Jacket's oratory entirely. He created an image of Red Jacket whose hair was bound in a feathered mohawk and who wore a "blanket," fringed pants, and who toted a rifle "on the war path." The martial memory of Red Jacket, however, did not win the day. An 1866 edition of *Harper's New Monthly Magazine* critiqued Darley's depiction of Red Jacket saying that it, and Halleck's poem, bore no resemblance to the real Red Jacket of history. One need only to look at his nephew, Ely S. Parker, to see Red Jacket's legacy was that of a statesman—not a warrior.[104] The memory of the exceptional Iroquois thus helped to protect his memory from being fully enveloped by the far more popular images of the Wild West and the "savage" Indian stereotypes.

Perhaps the most important and enduring interpreters of Red Jacket, one who showcased the orator and rejected the warrior all while reinforcing the memory of the Iroquois empire, was William Leete Stone, Red Jacket's first biographer. Stone set the tone of Haudenosaunee history for decades with his 1841 *The Life and Times of Red Jacket or Sa-go-ye-wa-tha*, part of a multi-volume biographical series. He aimed to do a few things with these volumes. First, in his life of Joseph Brant, he set out to write a "previously unwritten

RED JACKET (BY DARLEY).

FIGURE 1.4 Red Jacket engraving by F. O. C. Darley. "The Red Jacket Medal,"
Harper's New Monthly Magazine 32, 1865–1866, 324.

border history of the American Revolution." In the future volumes on William
Johnson, he planned a sweeping history of the Iroquois Confederacy, the first
Euro-American attempt to collate and record the history of the Confederacy
not as a political or imperial report, but as actual history. Finally, his Red
Jacket volume set out to explore the so-called "end" of Iroquois history
through the life and times of an orator "most familiar to the American ear,"
whose life was bracketed on one end by the American Revolution and on the
other by the Iroquois in New York being forced to sign a new Constitution
in 1838 that supposedly signaled the death of the Six Nations and the Great
League of Peace. What is striking is why Stone thought Red Jacket and his
contemporaries were such a critical part of the history of early America and
New York: he was genuinely interested in better understanding the broad
implications of the Haudenosaunee on early American history. In other
words, Stone, like Clinton before him, proposed that indigenous history is

early American and New York history. Just as Red Jacket's importance was self-evident, so was the Iroquois empire's historical importance during the American Revolution and the formation of the Empire State.[105]

In 1852, George Copway, the famed Ojibwe missionary and ethnographer, traveled to Buffalo to deliver a lecture on Native American culture. As he neared the city, he took a detour after learning from a local that the gravesite of legendary orator Red Jacket was nearby in the Cattaraugus Reservation. When Copway arrived at the gravesite, he was incensed at the condition in which he found Red Jacket's modest headstone and the graveyard. Determined to do something, Copway reserved part of his lecture time to appeal to the Buffalo public to save the remains of one of Iroquois country's most important leaders. The audience rallied behind him and promised action, but Copway was unwilling to wait. Just after he finished his lectures, he enlisted the help of a local businessman Wheeler Hotchkiss, who lived next to the cemetery, and a local undertaker named Farwell. Together, they dug up Red Jacket's bones. Copway placed the remains in a four-foot-long red cedar box and quietly relocated Red Jacket to Hotchkiss' locked basement.[106]

The deed did not go unnoticed. Several local Cattaraugus Senecas including "Moses Stevenson, Thomas Jemison, Daniel Two-Guns, and others" saw Copway's grave robbery and were furious. Mere hours after Red Jacket's remains were taken to the basement, Stevenson and Two-Guns had gathered a posse of Senecas and other "excited sympathizers" to storm Hotchkiss' home. With a "menacing attitude" they demanded that the grave robbers return Red Jacket's remains to his people. Copway reluctantly complied. After the posse reclaimed the remains, the story becomes less clear. Some said that the remains were "secreted" away for years among many Seneca houses and was thus cared for collectively by the community. Others, however, heard that Red Jacket's casket was brought immediately to the home of Ruth Stevens, his stepdaughter. According to Ely S. Parker, Stevens had either kept the red cedar casket containing his remains in a room in her home or, most likely, reburied his remains on her property. What we do know is that, in the early 1880s, Red Jacket's remains came into the possession of a Reverend Asher Wright who donated them to the Buffalo Historical Society. In 1884, the Historical Society reinterred Red Jacket and other contemporary leaders in a lavish ceremony in their remains were escorted by six hearses and an impressive "cortége of seventy-five carriages." The memorial caravan was filled with

Haudenosaunee leaders, descendants of the reinterred, and other New York dignitaries and their families. To top it all off, the design for a new statue of Red Jacket, one that still stands over his grave today, was unveiled. The well-attended ceremony was widely covered in newspapers and, for one observer, marked the "last public manifestation of the dignity and nobleness of the Senecas."[107]

During that lavish celebration of Red Jacket's legacy, he was laid to rest in the same complicated place within New York's memory in which he lived. The Haudenosaunee mourners attending his reburial, for one, defied the vanishing Indian myth. The new city of Buffalo, his final resting place, was built on Seneca land that was colonized by the Empire State. Even the Buffalo public's enthusiastic response to Copway's call to protect Red Jacket's remains—and the extraordinary lengths a few of them were willing to go to achieve that end—reflected New Yorker's ongoing and heartfelt connection to Red Jacket's memory and the role he played in the state and America's founding.

For generations of Haudenosaunee and New Yorkers to come, the memory of Red Jacket, his Peace Medal, and the Indigenous empire he represented would become an intellectual and cultural touchstone for understanding the relationship between Native America and the New York's founding moments. This understanding turned into a nostalgia for an exceptional Iroquois narrative that not only masked the hard realities of Red Jacket's life, but that also belied the ongoing struggles of the Haudenosaunee who continued to navigate clashing internal allegiances, grapple with the painful realities of colonialism, and fight to protect their sovereignty and history. Few embodied that complexity better than Red Jacket's nephew, Ely S. Parker.

2

Ely S. Parker,
the "Last Grand Sachem"

ON APRIL 9, 1865, Union General Ulysses S. Grant and Confederate General Robert E. Lee met in the small town of Appomattox Court House, Virginia, to discuss the Confederate Army's terms of surrender in the Civil War. When Lee and his entourage arrived, Lee was introduced to each of Grant's staff and shook each man's hand in turn. But when he came to Lieutenant Colonel Ely S. Parker, Grant's military secretary, Lee noticed "his swarthy figure" and hesitated. Did Grant "have a negro" on his personal staff? If so, "onlookers feared," that might have been enough of a "gratuitous affront" to end the negotiations "immediately." Whatever Lee thought in that moment, however, he quickly recovered his composure, shook Parker's hand, and the negotiations began. After the terms of surrender were set, Parker himself transcribed the articles of surrender and the document was signed. As the gathered men got up to leave, Lee approached the young Lieutenant Colonel with some final words: "I am glad to see one real American here," he said. Parker waited a beat and then simply replied, "we are all Americans."[1]

This anecdote has a long history. It first appeared in print in Horace Porter's 1888 four volume series, *Battles and Leaders of the Civil War*. Like Parker, Porter was an officer under Grant's command and was in the room to witness the Confederate army's surrender. Since Porter's retelling, it has been repeated by academic and public historians alike. Some focus on Lee's reaction to Parker's race and connect it to its obvious cause: the brutal war fought over slavery and its lasting impact on the American racial consciousness. Others bring the two halves of the story together and interrogate the notion of a nonwhite person as a "full" or "real American," a powerful metaphor that helps to frame understandings of American nationhood, citizenship, and the memory of the Civil War itself. More recently, Parker's participation in this moment has called attention to the complex Indigenous and Western history of what had always been conceived of as a black and white, northern versus southern war.[2]

But within this well-known story is another issue that has long gone unnoticed: the "real American" half of it was not part of Porter's original story. This is not to say that historians have not recognized that other aspects of the story might also be apocryphal. Even Horace Porter himself admitted that he could not truly know what Lee was thinking when the Confederate general hesitated to shake Parker's hand. The problem is that the "real American" comment was a late addition by Ely Parker's nephew and biographer, Arthur C. Parker. There is no extant record of this language being used at Appomattox, in the postwar years, or throughout the first two decades of the twentieth century. Ely Parker himself never mentioned it in his unfinished autobiography. The phrase only appears after the 1919 publication of Arthur's biography, *The Life of Ely S. Parker*, and was based on Arthur's memories of kitchen table conversations with family members and Ely's dear friend, Harriet Maxwell Converse. What is more, Arthur also claimed that the "real American" exchange was not even conducted in front of the gathered dignitaries but was instead part of a private side conversation between Ely Parker and Robert E. Lee while the two men supposedly had their backs turned to Grant and the others in the room. The exchange, if it occurred, was never meant to be public.[3]

What is missed when this story is taken at face value without closer inspection of the "real American" exchange is the Indigenous spin that Arthur Parker infused into his uncle's epochal wartime experience. By the time *The Life of Ely S. Parker* was published, the story of Appomattox already had a stable and singular meaning: that Lee initially thought Ely Parker was black. This made sense within a society focused on the black and white divide in the years after the collapse of Reconstruction as Americans grappled with the realities of a Jim Crow America. Newspapers also reflected that interpretation, so Porter's story remained mostly unchanged through the 1930s and during the evolution and popularization of the Lost Cause myth. Perhaps most famously, Douglas Southall Freeman, the Pulitzer Prize–winning historian and an important proponent of the Lost Cause, spread the racial dimensions of these stories when he cited Porter's story in his 1934–1935 *R.E. Lee: A Biography*. Decades later in 1959, the phrase "real American" appeared in Burke Davis's popular history, *To Appomattox*.[4]

Arthur Parker's intervention, then, did not disturb the memory of Appomattox, nor of the meeting between Ely S. Parker and Robert E. Lee, so much as seek to return a missing piece of to it. Arthur was a savvy interpreter of Haudenosaunee history who looked for ways to integrate a nonthreatening Iroquois exceptionalism into American history, so this subtle injection of an Indigenous memory from one of the Senecas' most famous sons was designed to fit into a story that held singular meaning for a people seeking to learn about the Civil War through the lens of a divided Jim Crow America. While the exchange did not truly catch on until the 1950s because it was relegated to "history's shadow" like many other aspects of Indigenous history, Arthur Parker was on to something.[5] The language of a "real American" was a reminder to Americans that Native Americans, and most importantly the Haudenosaunee, were active participants in the country's formative moments.

This chapter thus explores how Ely S. Parker, by design and by accident of his celebrity, built on his grand-uncle Red Jacket's legacy and sought to remind Americans that the Haudenosaunee were always an important part of their national history. Whereas Red Jacket's self-built legacy was later spun by outsiders as a parochial story rooted in New York, Parker exercised more control over his own public narrative. He gained attention and respect as an Army Colonel, Adjutant General, and US Commissioner of Indian Affairs and leveraged his "authenticity" as an elected leader among the Haudenosaunee. Over time, he established himself as the face of Iroquois country. This self-definition and general acceptance by white America was possible in part because Parker lived in an era where the locus of the so-called "Indian problem" had moved westward. As the spaces Native Americans filled in the American mind and the physical world changed shape and shrank as the century wore on, there always seemed to be room for an assimilated and patriotic Indian like Parker, a man historians describe as "draw[ing] power from Indianness and Americanness in combination."[6] Unlike Red Jacket, Parker put his service to country and Seneca-ness together to form an acceptable, if somewhat unorthodox, Indigenous interpretation of New York society and history.

A major part of Parker's influence within white America came from his relentless quest for acceptance among New York and Washington, DC high society. Unlike Red Jacket who sought to leverage the American public's interest in him for his own diplomatic and strategic use, Parker fully embraced assimilation and relished life among American elites. He left behind his Tonawanda Reservation home and lived variously in Washington, Connecticut, and New York City. He proved early on to be a savvy political actor and a capable defender of Iroquois sovereignty, but his ongoing belief in assimilation and obsession with the trappings of white high society were largely unpopular among most Haudenosaunee. Other leaders, including a few of his brothers and his sister Caroline who never moved away from Tonawanda, were more important than Ely in protecting the Senecas' sovereignty long-term and in resisting the encroachment of predatory missionaries, their schools, and land speculators.[7]

Parker's interest in white high society, however, did not mean that he was immune from the animus directed at Native American peoples. Throughout his life, he was tarred by damaging stereotypes and those who questioned his motives and whether he belonged in American society. Despite those criticisms, by the end of his life he was heralded by the non-Iroquois press as one of the greatest representatives of his people and, importantly, as a true American.

That fame is attributable to his remarkable political career as a Seneca chief, a Lieutenant Colonel and Adjutant General in the US Army, and the Commissioner of Indian Affairs. This chapter acknowledges the importance of these career successes, but it mostly focuses on the spaces in between them where Parker's identity, his popularity, and ability to reinforce specific historical and political narratives bound the history and memory of the Haudenosaunee to the United States before, during, and after the Civil War. These moments were most visible during his military and government service and his public appearances. These were important moments where Parker found reasons to infuse his conception of Haudenosaunee history and culture, and not least their exceptionality, into America's evolving antebellum and postbellum self-identity. His ability to sell his message of Iroquois exceptionalism benefited from the mid-nineteenth century's expansion and standardization of the newspaper infrastructure. As a result, people across the country were able to read mostly uniform accounts of Ely Parker's extraordinary life in the many articles published across state and local newspapers that were then repeated well beyond the borders of New York and Washington.[8] Readers across the country learned about his people's patriotism, his meaningful friendships with famed Americans like Lewis H. Morgan and Ulysses S. Grant, how the northeastern Haudenosaunee were connected to larger national issues concerning slavery and the west, and even about his important work in retirement with the New York Police Department.

In the end, the mutually reinforcing reputations of Parker the Seneca chief and Parker the American Patriot afforded him a visible platform from which to comment on American society. By virtue of his actions, celebrity, and example, he continued what Red Jacket had begun and reminded the public of the Haudenosaunee's long and consequential relationship with New York and the United States.

Ely Samuel Parker was born Ha-sa-no-an-da on the Tonawanda Reservation near the town of Pembroke, New York, in 1828. His English name was an invention of the family, a tradition that began with his father, Jo-no-es-sto-wa, and his two brothers who fought alongside the Americans during the War of 1812. After the war, the three brothers decided to take the surname "Parker" from a British officer who was supposedly adopted during the war by the Senecas. Jo-no-es-sto-wa, who gave himself the name William Parker, was a farmer and Seneca chief, a man of purportedly great physical presence

FIGURE 2.1 Photograph of Ely S. Parker, c.1860–1865. Brady National Photographic Art Gallery. National Archives and Records Administration, photo no. 528267.

and generosity. In the early 1820s, he received a marriage proposal from Ga-ont-gwut-twus, or Elizabeth Johnson, the daughter of the Six Nations chief Jimmy Johnson and grandniece of Red Jacket. William spent one year in pre-marital residence with Elizabeth in her mother's home on the Tonawanda Reservation where he worked to prove himself "a successful son-in-law." After they wed, William and Elizabeth moved out of the Johnson matriarch's home and onto their own farm. During the 1830s, they had seven children, one girl and six boys, all of whom were raised in the orbit of the Baptist mission and educated at the mission school.[9]

Born in 1828, Ha-sa-no-an-da was their fourth child. The Parkers lived "in relative comfort" as farmers and traders, but most importantly they were a po-litical family with a unique heritage. His father was a chief of the Wolf Clan and a son of Handsome Lake, and his mother was a clan mother and grand-niece of Red Jacket who Ha-sa-no-an-da was taught to call "grandfather." His parents, carrying on the tradition that William and his brothers started, gave their newborn son a second, English name. They named him "Ely" (rhyming with *freely*) after the local Baptist minister Ely Stone, a man Ely would re-member "very well." At some point years later, Ely, like his siblings before him, created his own complete English name. In keeping with Euro-American tra-dition he adopted his father's surname, Parker, but also took his uncle's name, Samuel, as his middle name.[10] Even before he became a teenager, Ha-sa-no-an-da had transformed himself into Ely S. Parker.

He came of age when Americans sought to solve the "Indian Problem" with a brutal sequence of so-called Indian Removal policies. The "problem," as the country saw it, was that desirable land was occupied by Indigenous people and it seemed, as the nineteenth century wore on and Red Jacket's time faded into the past, that "the Enlightenment dream that transformed Indians would remain on lands east of the Mississippi by adopting white ways was gradually abandoned." To solve that "problem," beginning with the elec-tion of Andrew Jackson in 1828 and continuing through the 1830s and 1840s, coordinated federal expulsion policies helped the United States colonize the entirety of the land mass east of the Mississippi River. As a result, the US gov-ernment launched an unprecedented state-sponsored project with the express purpose of eliminating their Indigenous neighbors through forced disposses-sion. The motivations for this project ranged widely. Some believed that it would somehow save Indigenous peoples from uncontrollable white expan-sion, while others blatantly called to "ethnically cleanse" American land to make way for the expansion of the government, its industry, its farmers, and its slaves. That project was also ingrained in the American consciousness since

Indian affairs shaped how Americans understood Manifest Destiny. In the 1820s through the early 1850s, for example, half of the presidential candidates had confronted Native Americans either on the battlefield or through actively seeking their expulsion through federal policy. Parker was thus born into a world in which the expulsion of Native Americans was an essential component of America's westward ambitions and its attitude toward Indian country.[11]

The Haudenosaunee, the most populous Indigenous nation in New York, were at the center of the state's removal efforts. When Parker was ten years old, the Senecas were once again under assault from a familiar enemy: the Ogden Land Company. Riding the momentum generated by the nation's expansionist fervor, the Ogden Company began a project in 1836 to force the Senecas to sign a treaty agreeing to cede all their rights to all their land. Ogden Company President Joseph Ogden and the local federal Iroquois agent, James Stryker, worked for two years to secure by illicit and overtly threatening means more than eighty Seneca signatures. They claimed to have gotten most of the signatures, and on January 15, 1838, the Ogden Company and the New York State Legislature approved the treaty and presented it to the US Senate. The final draft declared the company's exclusive right to purchase all four Iroquois reservations and for the Iroquois to voluntarily leave New York in five years' time. The treaty was, not surprisingly, "largely an imposed agreement that merely satisfied the interests" of Ogden and the state government.[12]

The Senecas mounted a strong defense. They submitted to the New York State Legislature a body of evidence compiled by the inheritor of Handsome Lake's religious leadership mantle and Red Jacket's Peace Medal, chief Jimmy Johnson, which proved that the treaty was fraudulent. Johnson, among others, had known about the scheme all along and submitted ample witness testimonies that the two men had used illegal coercion and "deceit" to get the signatures. Johnson also enlisted outside help. According to a Quaker Society of Friends anticorruption report compiled for 1838 and published in 1840, they found evidence that the Ogden Company had staged sham "elections" of "chiefs," used financial bribes to secure "16 of 81" signatures, and through intimidation and violent coercion secured the rest.[13] This defense, however, did not convince the legislature, and the Treaty of Buffalo Creek was approved and sent to Congress.

Owing to the momentum of national Indian removal, the Buffalo Creek treaty was approved by the Senate. While the Senecas' defense was compelling, and even President Martin van Buren expressed reservations, it came down to a tie breaking vote cast by Vice President Richard M. Johnson, a famed Indian

fighter and politician whose political legacy was built on his family's colonization of Kentucky and the claim that he fired the shot that killed Tecumseh in
1815. The treaty approved by the Senate nullified Haudenosaunee claims to all
four of their reservations and the land around Green Bay.[14] In return, the Six
Nations would receive a 1,824,000-acre Kansas reservation they would share
with the Stockbridge Nation of Long Island and the Munsee of Wisconsin.
The Haudenosaunee had five years to evacuate their homeland and move to
Kansas.

Jimmy Johnson, his Seneca coalition, and their Quaker allies fought in
federal court for four years to challenge that fraudulent treaty. Their unyielding resistance succeeded, to a point, in May 20, 1842 with the signing
of the so-called Compromise(d) Treaty. Signed at a Six Nations council at
Buffalo Creek, this new treaty did not annul the 1838 treaty, but "allow[ed]
for the return or repurchase of lands by the Iroquois." In other words, the
Iroquois could buy back their land from the federal government before the
Ogden Company could intervene. What made this treaty "compromised"
was the major concession won by the Ogden Company: the treaty allowed
for the Senecas to repurchase their Allegany and Cattaraugus reservations,
but not the Buffalo Creek or the Tonawanda reservations. Senecas there were
still being removed to Kansas and their land put up for public auction.[15]

Despite this half-victory, the Senecas would continue to fight the Buffalo
Creek treaty over the next fifteen years with the help of a savvy political actor,
Ely Parker. But first, Parker needed to grow up. At ten years of age in 1838, the
same year the first fraudulent Buffalo Creek treaty was signed, Ely was out of
the country visiting a family member in the Seneca settlement of Grand River,
Canada. Why he left home when just barely out of Ely Stone's mission school
is debated. Some historians argue that Parker was sent there (presumably) by
his family to "perfect his woodcraft," though why he could not have done this
at Tonawanda is unclear. Parker's nephew and first biographer Arthur Parker,
however, believed that Ely, even at such a young age, had somehow sensed
the national disturbance that the Ogden Company had caused and asked his
parents to leave. He "did not," Arthur explained, "wish to stay in a country
where confusion, deceit and trickery existed."[16]

Regardless of the reasons for his absence, Parker only stayed in Grand
River for three years and heard from a distance what was happening in
Tonawanda. During those years, he met with family members of his uncle
Samuel's wife, traveled the province while working alongside Canadian
Iroquois traders, frequented the local British military base, and perfected
his woodcraft. Parker presumably learned a great deal about Native life and

coexistence with Anglo-Americans, but historians pinpoint one event that particularly shaped his early life. While traveling to London, Ontario, shortly before returning to New York, a teenage Parker was accosted by a few British soldiers from "a provincial regiment." The soldiers teased him for his inability to understand English and mocked the fact that he was Native American. He remembered that as a moment that "galled him" and he vowed to never again be so humiliated. His solution was to attend a white school. In 1843, with his family's financial assistance, Parker enrolled at the Yates Academy in Orleans County. With "no Indian companionship," he spent the next two years learning English and received a thorough classical Western education that included training in Greek, Latin, literature, and arithmetic.[17]

As the only Seneca and nonwhite student, Parker was something of a spectacle at Yates. He struggled with English early on but grew to be a fine orator whose "deep, full voice" filled auditoriums. He also showed talent as a long-distance runner and competed with a friend from Tonawanda, John Steeprock, in international meets held in Buffalo. To the locals who watched the growth of this young Seneca, his achievements did not compensate for his obvious racial differences. This prejudice unfolded in dramatic fashion during his courtship of a young white woman named Mary, the daughter of "one of the most aristocratic families" in the area. Residents of the town of Yates came out in droves just to see Parker and Mary together. Neither her parents nor friends approved of their relationship, and that pressure may have proven too much for Parker to bear. Parker withdrew from Yates in the fall of 1845 and transferred the following year to the more prestigious Cayuga Academy in Aurora, New York, far away from Mary.[18]

Among the Iroquois, Parker also stood out. His talent as an orator, his command of English, and his access and connections to white communities were increasingly regarded as potentially useful weapons in their fight against Ogden. While enrolled at Yates, Parker was "put to work as an interpreter" and as a diplomatic envoy. He was brought into service as a runner, or a lower tier of diplomats who were required to be fast moving (literally) and fast thinking. Runners were trusted with the expansive authority to "summon councils, convey intelligence from nation to nation, and warn of impending danger." As a runner, Parker made multiple trips to Albany, Washington, DC, and each of the Haudenosaunee reservations in New York and Canada on behalf of the new (as of 1839) Seneca chief John Blacksmith and the Six Nations. Parker was an important part of the political strategy to protect Tonawanda. In the post-Compromised Treaty years, the Senecas, under the leadership of Blacksmith, had adopted a sweeping anti-removal strategy that combined outsourced legal help and advocacy with unbending local non-compliance. The goal was to avoid expulsion to Kansas and preserve the land while their people fought in court. Although Blacksmith's strategies delayed efforts on the ground, they failed to fully change minds in Washington. In 1845, Secretary of War James M. Porter ordered the Tonawanda Senecas to comply with the Compromised Treaty and reminded them that they must "leave their homes . . . by April 1, 1846" and remove to Kansas.[19]

Given the high stakes of the Tonawanda's resistance strategy, Parker's role as runner and translator from 1844 to 1848 was vital in establishing a good relationship with the public and the state and federal governments. While some among the Senecas were "suspicious" of Parker's growing comfort with Albany and Washington high society, most were supportive. He was, for one thing, an effective in-person and on-paper translator for Blacksmith and the Six Nations leadership. As a sixteen-year-old, one of his first official tasks was to translate and sign an official statement to President Tyler in 1844. Parker proved to be capable of moving easily between Seneca and white society. He wore suits, spoke fluent English, and made friends as he worked. In recognition of his ability, in 1846 Parker was entrusted with leading a cohort to the nation's capital to meet with James K. Polk and to speak with Indian agents and congressmen. This trip was the latest in Blacksmith's pressure campaign, and part of Parker's visit to Washington was to remind the United States of the Six Nations' historic and continued friendship. To do this, Parker was lent a familiar symbol to carry with him—the Red Jacket Peace Medal—to remind officials of the historic friendship between the United States and the Haudenosaunee.[20]

Parker, wearing a suit and the Peace Medal, cut a striking figure. His arrival coincided with the visit of a delegation of fifty or so headmen from the "Texas-Mexico border," a group that came most likely to discuss the geopolitical fallout of the Mexican American War that ended the previous year. This delegation, as Parker reported to his childhood friend and Cayuga Academy classmate Reuben Warren, "shook up city life" because of their "wild" appearance. Parker was aghast that they wore "very little clothing to cover their bodies" with "all kinds of brass rings and beads and shells."[21] His own clothing not only signaled the Senecas' relative level of "civility," but he knew the Peace Medal was a reminder of the long-standing US relationship with the Six Nations. Parker therefore understood how powerful expressions of physical difference were. He was still, clearly, Seneca, but was also an assimilated Indian representing a "civilized" nation. He was not "wild," but a living reminder of the exceptional imperial Iroquois that William Stone discussed in his histories just a few years earlier. In addition, he, unlike the Westerners, sought belonging in white society. Parker learned in these years to value the connections, friendships, and lifestyle that elite white society offered. He took pride in his Seneca-ness which he valued as highly his American-ness. And Americans, for the most part, took him at face value. This Washington trip was the first time that Parker arrived in full public view as a paragon of an assimilated Native American and a representative of the exceptional Iroquois.

As he made friends and contacts in high places, Parker's exposure to American society had two consequences. First, he was able to find and recruit people who were able to help the Tonawanda Senecas in their battle against removal. Second, he became attracted to life in high society and, over time, would begin to physically distance himself from Iroquois country. While he explicitly projected his Seneca-ness in important moments, he made the

FIGURE 2.2 Photograph of Ely S. Parker, c. 1840s. The Western Reserve Historical Society, Cleveland, Ohio.

choice to integrate fully into American life. This was evident in Parker's relationship to the lawyer and famed ethnographer, Lewis H. Morgan. The young
Seneca became Morgan's primary source of information and insight into
Iroquois country, and he invited Morgan to meet extended Parker family. Ely,
and especially Caroline, shaped what Morgan collected, studied, and understood about all things Seneca. Morgan also briefly served as a legal representative of the Senecas in 1844. After years of access to the Parker family, Morgan
published his field-shaping 1851 ethnography *League of the Ho-de-no-sau-nee*
which established him as the United States' premier ethnographer.[22]

But this relationship was not as one sided as it seems. Parker personally
and professionally benefited from his association with Morgan's social circle
and his ethnographic interests. Parker's influence on Morgan's research for
League also established the young Seneca as an "Indian who attained distinction in the larger American society." It was an early example of how he
identified himself in public as an "Iroquois Indian," a distinction that reinforced Morgan's assumptions that the Haudenosaunee were different from
other Indigenous peoples and uniquely bound to New York.[23] In addition,
Morgan gave Parker access to New Yorkers of privilege and enabled him to
expand his social network and connections.

While they would remain friends for the rest of their lives, the 1840s and
50s were formative and mutually beneficial years for both Parker and Morgan.
Initially, Morgan found Parker while working as a lawyer in Aurora and following the ongoing saga of the two Buffalo Creek treaties. He had always
had an interest in the Iroquois and decided that the best way to satisfy his
curiosity was to write an article about them. In April of 1844, he learned that
a Tonawanda delegation headed by John Blacksmith was on the road from
Tonawanda to Albany to meet with the governor and state legislature. The
amateur ethnographer immediately left for Albany and followed Blacksmith
into a local bookstore. What he did not expect to find there was Blacksmith's
bright young translator, Ely Parker. The two immediately took a "strong
liking" to one another. Over the next week, Parker helped set up interviews
with the Tonawanda delegation and offered to serve as translator. This was
such a fruitful trip that Morgan was able to publish his first article about
the Iroquois five months later. From then on, he was a regular visitor to the
Parkers' home on the Tonawanda reservation, paid Ely and Caroline's tuitions
at the Cayuga Academy, and considered the Parkers "the most talented Indian
family of the Iroquois stock." Through Parker, Morgan had accumulated vast
quantities of Haudenosaunee material culture, much of which he donated to
the New York State Museum in 1851.[24]

In that time, Parker worked just as hard to integrate himself into Morgan's high-society circles. He joined Morgan's social club and ethnographic *salon*, the Grand Order of the Iroquois, an organization founded in 1842 that was dedicated to "studying. . . the structure and principles of the ancient League [of the Iroquois]." The organization attracted New York's elite from across the state and was thus the perfect setting for a talented and ambitious young man looking to expand his connections. Parker's influence on the Grand Order was felt early on when he inspired its leadership to change its administrative organization based on his knowledge of the structure of the Six Nations confederacy and its leadership. The Grand Order then transformed itself into a loose copy of the Six Nations where members were organized by region into nations, nations were subdivided into clans, clans were overseen by *sachems* (or chiefs), and all *sachems* were given made-up ceremonial "Indian names" and, while in session, dressed up in "Indian costume."[25]

Fellow members included a few other Iroquois (who Parker may have brought with him), scholars like William Leete Stone and Henry Rowe Schoolcraft, members of the clergy, military veterans, scientists like Charles Talbot Porter, and other elites from across the state. An assimilationist society, the Grand Order explored ways to solve the "Indian problem" through education, Christianization, and demographic assimilation. The Grand Order learned through Parker what was at stake in the Tonawanda Senecas' fight for sovereignty in the 1840s and were even willing to leverage Order resources to help "defeat the crooked schemes" of the Ogden "land sharks." For Parker, membership in this organization instilled in him a general fascination with the "mystery and pageantry" of secret societies. In 1847, presumably with the sponsorship or at least the support of Morgan and others in the Grand Order, Parker was inducted into Batavia Lodge 88 of the Freemasons and became a lifelong member.[26] By 1847, Parker had deeply embedded himself among northern New York's high society.

In the meantime, he began to grow his own reputation as an expert on all things Iroquoian. His knowledge of Haudenosaunee religion was so extensive that Morgan, who dedicated *League* to Parker, recognized his contributions as "one of the most interesting portions of the work." Relatedly, Parker's political position and scholarly reputation made him a one-man authenticator of Seneca material culture and an interpreter of cultural meaning. He built a small collection of his own, and in the late 1840s tried his hand at publishing. His first and only ethnographic publication was an account of a Six Nations council held at Tonawanda that was published in the *New York Evening Post* on October 1847. Despite it being his first piece, the editors were so impressed by the article written in "Mr. Parker's own very neat and legible manuscript" that they printed in the paper "without alteration of a comma, capital letter or word." The editors made a point to comment on the fact that "it is quite seldom that an article sent us for publication is written and punctuated with so much accuracy," much less one written by an Indian.[27] By this point, his talent and expertise were attracting notice outside Tonawanda.

Despite his busy political and social schedule, Parker was determined to find a career that would both help Tonawanda and impress his new white friends. After returning from his 1846 trip to Washington, he apprenticed himself at the law practice of W. P. Angel in Ellicottville, New York. Angel was the New York Indian subagent, and Parker clerked there for him for three years while he read law under the mentorship of Angel, a man deeply knowledgeable about Indian affairs. His future as a lawyer looked promising, but Parker would soon learn a valuable lesson in the limitations of Indian participation in American life. In mid-to-late 1848, when he applied to practice law in New York, he was denied a license by the courts because he was not a US citizen. Parker was devastated. His professional rejection disillusioned him about the balance he thought he had struck between the legal limitations of living as a Native American in the United States and the friendly acceptance New York high society gave him. After that, Morgan recommended that Parker put his Cayuga Academy education to work and try his hand at engineering, a colonial enterprise that had helped build the Empire State. He accepted Morgan's help and, by 1849, relocated to the town of Nunda where he cleared trees for the Genesee Valley Canal. After shadowing the engineer in Nunda, he moved to Rochester (where Morgan lived) to begin work as a canal engineer full time.[28]

These career moves shaped the rest of Parker's life. When he had accepted the clerkship at Angel's law firm, he had also moved off the Tonawanda reservation and given up most of his responsibilities as a runner. Then at the end of 1848, Parker learned that he had not been chosen by the Tonawanda leadership to represent them during their most recent trips to Albany and Washington. Instead, they chose his brother Nicholson to represent them in their fight against Ogden and the looming forced expulsion to Kansas. The Seneca council had also initially nominated Ely as the official US interpreter for the New York Indian sub-agency in 1850, but they ended up renominating Peter Wilson, the incumbent interpreter, to fill that role. Having physically distanced himself from Tonawanda, Parker was no longer able to serve in his previous capacity. Even though he would eventually buy property near his family's home, he would never again live among the Senecas.[29]

Even at a distance, however, Parker remained dedicated to the Tonawanda cause. For the Senecas, his past service, his connections in New York and Washington, and his hereditary ties to Red Jacket, Handsome Lake, and his father's chieftainship ensured that he would remain an important figure in Haudenosaunee politics. When Jimmy Johnson passed away in 1851, Parker, the "educated man of fine talents and exemplary habits," was approved to inherit his title as a "Sachem of the Six Nations" and given a new name, "Do-ne-ho-ga-wa" or "Open Door." That same year, Parker's career took a turn when he was promoted to Assistant State Engineer for Canals.[30]

Despite his new professional responsibilities, as a new chief Parker remained involved in Tonawanda politics for the next decade, a time when the resistance strategy of John Blacksmith would eventually prevail in the Senecas' "heroic battle against removal." The non-compliance strategy had stalled state and federal momentum, and the Iroquois enjoyed a series of critical legal victories won by their new lawyer, John H. Martindale of Batavia. Even though much of their reservation land, nearly thirteen thousand acres, had already been sold off or illegally occupied by squatters and land speculators, they continued their assault against the Ogden case in Washington. In multiple visits to Washington and Albany by Parker and other Tonawanda diplomats, the Senecas put intense pressure on Congress, governors, and presidents to reject the Ogden Company's claims. Another old ally, the Society of Friends, led multiple inquiries and sent reports to Congress to prove the Senecas' claims of Ogden Land Company corruption.[31]

From his office in Rochester, Parker was frequently called on by the Six Nations and Martindale to be the lawyer's conduit to the Iroquois. He was involved in conveying information, demands, and letters from the Six Nations to Martindale's office in Washington where the lawyer would go on to win an appellate court case in 1852 and a Supreme Court victory in 1856. The Blacksmith case, heard by the highest federal court, resulted in the near nullification of the Compromise(d) Treaty. Parker's influence did not stop there. After Franklin Pierce was elected President in 1852, Parker was called upon to speak on behalf of the Tonawanda Senecas. He had supported Pierce, an advocate of removal, on the campaign trail purely in opposition to Millard Filmore who served as legal counsel for the Ogden Land Company. Parker thus leveraged his campaign support to gain an audience with the new president. Similarly, from 1852 to 1853 he wrote letters on behalf of the Tonawanda to New York Governor Horatio Seymour, a man who thought of Parker as the main "representative of the ancient confederacy of the Six Nations."[32]

One of Parker's final official acts concerning the preservation of Iroquois sovereignty occurred in 1857 when he, his brother Nicholson in Washington, and sister Caroline in Tonawanda worked with a Seneca diplomatic corps and John Martindale to negotiate a new treaty. The resulting Tonawanda-Federal Treaty of 1857 ceded the Tonawanda Senecas' claims to Kansas, preserved what reservation land was left in New York, and held the Tonawanda reservation in federal trust. During these negotiations, Parker was keenly aware of the outside forces in Washington that could help the Tonawandas' case. He made it clear to federal officials that, since the passage of the 1854 Kansas-Nebraska Act had opened those territories to American settlement, the Seneca land in question was worth far more to the federal government than the remaining reservation land in New York. This argument added an unexpected political incentive to their negotiations. Parker had, once again, proven his worth at a critical moment in Tonawanda history. While the following years would see more challenges to the Tonawanda Senecas' sovereignty, by 1857 Parker had helped them eliminate their oldest private enemy and protect their sovereignty.[33]

Meanwhile, his engineering career took a Western turn. In March of 1857, he was appointed by the US Department of Treasury as Superintendent of Construction for a customs house and hospital in Galena, Illinois. At the same time, he got involved in the local and Chicago Masonic Orders and achieved some acclaim as an eloquent speaker at Masonic events and a gentlemen of standing and "Grand Orator" in the Order. Professionally, his intellect and capacity for solving political and bureaucratic problems turned him into a capable and popular government administrator. When the cornerstone of the Galena Customs House was laid in April 15, 1858 after a series of delays caused by construction problems and his trips to New York and Washington on Tonawanda business, "both the Masonic Order and the Galena Brass Band came to assist in the celebration." Parker was then asked to consult on the construction of a hospital in Galena and another customs house in Dubuque, Iowa, seventeen miles away. With the successful and timely completion of these projects, Parker had "gained the respect" of locals and federal officials.[34]

But that acceptance did not come easily. For some, Parker's Seneca-ness mattered more than his oversight of infrastructure essential to the region's wellness. When Parker made trips back to Tonawanda for his duties as chief and annual vacations, some saw him as a "Chief of the Six Nations" who, once he left the city, "divest[ed] himself of the habiliments of civilization." Parker, the able Superintendent and a Mason in good standing, became a "portly . . . half-and-half [looking] Indian" with "long straight hair" and a "copper complexion," an uncivilized man who made himself fat off "turtle soup." But at least, a newspaper reported, his transformation "generally does not present any appearance suggestive of tomahawks and scalping knives."[35] In these moments, the public saw a man literally shed the trappings of polite society to reveal the uncivilized Indian underneath.

Amid this scathing stereotyping, Parker nevertheless sought ways to use his Seneca-ness to shape his own narrative. For example, in a well-publicized speech to the Chicago Convention of Masons in September of 1859, Parker offered his perspectives on assimilation, the popular myth of the vanishing Indian, and the importance of his ties to Red Jacket and his people's ties to the United States. At the Mason's dinner gala, the "full-blooded . . . Grandson of Red Jacket" and "last remaining" chief of a "noble race" praised the Masons' tolerance and acceptance of his racial background. He evoked Red Jacket who, the apocryphal story went, near the end of his life asked "Where shall I go when the last of my race shall have gone forever? Where shall I find home and sympathy when our last council fire is extinguished?" Parker found an answer when he "knocked at the door" of the Masons to see if "the white race will recognize me, as they had my ancestors, when we were strong and the white men weak." What he found there was a "Christian brotherhood" and "companionship beneath the royal arch," a group of "valiant sir knights willing to shield me here without regard to race or nation."[36]

Parker also explained to his Chicago audience that, by accepting him as a member, the Masons had proven that the "Indian race" would live on in Americans' collective memory. Through education, an enlightened pursuit that was of value to the Masons, Americans could make sense of the fact that Indigenous history *was* American history. After all, Native America lived on "in the names of your lakes and rivers, your towns and cities," and "call[ed] up memories" of peoples "otherwise forgotten." After explaining this, he removed "the wampum from his neck and drew from his bosom a large massive medal, in oval form . . . and passed it around the tables." He explained that this was Red Jacket's Peace Medal, the physical reminder of his office as chief, of Parker's familial ties to him, and of that fateful moment when "your nation was in its infancy" and the Haudenosaunee stood alongside them.[37] This speech was also a not-so-subtle reminder that the Haudenosaunee, despite the myth of the vanishing Indian that Parker himself had helped perpetuate through his actions, were still here and were exceptional.

Parker's career up to this point sheds some light on his important decision to join the Union Army at the outbreak of the Civil War. But it was not, in hindsight, a foregone conclusion that he would. After all, historians claim that most Senecas had little interest or stake in the "causes" that drove the United States to war, and Parker, like most of the Haudenosaunee, was not a US citizen and therefore was twice denied a commission as an army engineer. So why did he persist?[38]

Part of that is explained by his service to the Tonawanda which suggests that he was aware of the national debates over slavery. In his service as a runner and chief, he made many visits in the 1840s-1850s to Washington where political discussion was dominated by slavery and the sectional fissures it caused. These experiences imprinted on him what good government could do to overcome national problems, so it was not a surprise when he encountered the new Republican party, a political party formed in the 1850s who believed that the creation and cultivation of an "efficient and impartial [federal] bureaucracy," one established in defiance of corruption and slavery, was a force for good. Parker also experienced this in the decades prior. In his home state, the Free Soil Party of the 1840s fused with prominent antislavery Whigs like New York Senator William Seward to help create a national antislavery coalition. As Parker traveled to the state and national capitals, he moved among those politicians who were part of the Whig and later Republican strategy to "install antislavery men in the seats of federal power."[39] The Blacksmith case of 1852, in which Parker served as the interlocuter to the Tonawanda, was argued before the same Court that five years later heard the Dred Scott case. While there is no record of exactly who Parker met every step of the way, it is very unlikely that a politically interested man who saw the value of good government and invested in every opportunity to integrate into American society did not know a great deal about those issues and picked a side.

As Parker would know well, abolitionism and antislavery politics had also been part of New York's political culture for decades. New York City was the site of the nation's first "black nationalist celebration" on July 5, 1800, which celebrated the state's gradual emancipation law. African Americans and abolitionist leaders in New York and Philadelphia declared January 1, 1808, the start of an annual "National Jubilee" when Congress banned the country's participation in the African Slave Trade. In addition, newspapers like the *Freedman's Journal* allowed Americans to "hear unmediated and distinct black voices" for the first time. The *Freedom's Journal* had "perhaps several thousand reading at least parts of each weekly issue" and was reaching residents of a state that was also home to antislavery organizations like the New York Manumission Society and the American Colonization Society. Parker, a man who perpetually sought out social organizations, became a member of the Rochester Athenium and Mechanics Association in 1856, an organization with a library where members enjoyed access to "most major newspapers of eastern cities" and invited guest speakers like abolitionists Susan B. Anthony, Oliver Wendell Holmes, and Frederick Douglass.[40]

In addition, the debate over the Senecas' forced exodus to Kansas happened alongside America's colonization west of the Mississippi River and the debates over the future of slavery in those territories. While Parker served as runner and chief, the territories of Kansas and Oklahoma had already received more than forty thousand survivors of the brutal Indian expulsion policies of Jackson's administration, a stream of exiles that would continue under his successor, Martin van Buren. This opened the door to the massive expansion of slavery into the Deep South and established the foundation for slavery's growth in those territories. After 1854 and the passage of the Kansas-Nebraska Act, Kansas exploded in a multi-year and bloody conflict that would determine the future of slavery in the territory. Bleeding Kansas was the dominant subject of newspapers throughout the country, and significantly, in Tonawanda. In 1856, the Commissioner of Indian Affairs Andrew Manypenny reported that the Senecas were caught in the middle of Kansans' war over slavery. In his report on the negligence of the new territorial Governor Andrew H. Reeder, who was unable to control the many "whites, caught up in the sectional conflict over slavery," Manypenny expressed his worry about how the conflict was perpetuating and deepening the long history of theft and violence that had plagued the Senecas who had settled in Kansas since 1838.[41] Parker would have realized that the Haudenosaunee, despite what his people may have thought, had a stake in the expansion of slavery because of the way it imperiled the nation.

The final reason Parker joined the war connects to Galena. After his appointment to construct the Customs House and hospital in 1857, he had formed a close friendship with a West Point graduate, retired army officer, and local tannery clerk named Ulysses S. Grant. The two men enjoyed "long 'talks'" while both lived in the city and attended Masonic meetings together. Parker, who in 1854 had briefly been a Captain in the New York militia, likely had much to say to Grant about matters of war. Parker had also become close friends in Galena with John Aaron Rawlins, a "champion" of the pro-slavery Democrat Stephen Douglas and a Democratic Party elector for Illinois in the presidential election of 1860. Yet despite Grant and Rawlins' deep political differences, President Abraham Lincoln's call for volunteers appealed to them equally and they both joined the US army.[42]

Parker, however, did not follow his friends to Washington. Instead, he returned briefly to Tonawanda before setting out for Albany where, as Red

Jacket and many other Haudenosaunee leaders had during the War of 1812, he personally sought a military commission from Governor Edwin D. Morgan. Despite his proven engineering ability and his militia rank of Captain, he was denied a commission because he was not a citizen of the United States. Though dejected, Parker learned that John Martindale, a West Point graduate himself, was commissioned as a Brigadier General and military commander of the District of Columbia in September of 1861. Parker thus left Albany for Washington to appeal to Martindale who connected Parker to other federal officials. While there, Parker personally made his case "for the non-slave holding interest" in October 1861 to Secretary of State William Seward who, like Governor Morgan, turned Parker down. It was a "white man's war," Seward explained, and while he thought that the Iroquois were "by no means savages," they are nevertheless "neither regarded as citizens nor recognized as foreigner." In that respect, "naturalization is forbidden to them, and they can be endowed with the privileges of citizenship only by special act of the Legislature."[43]

Parker was not alone in trying and failing to enlist. Haudenosaunee men from across the state had flocked to recruiting offices the moment the war began. Their reasons for joining the war varied and were not a matter of simple "patriotism," despite what army recruiters thought. For them, choosing to serve in an American war was a complicated choice. For some, war validated positions of leadership. For others, it was a matter of family legacy for those whose ancestors fought in the Revolution and the War of 1812. Some families were patriotic, but mostly they thought the South's rebellion a travesty of "Devilism and Rebelism" and understood wartime service to be a generally honorable act.[44]

Whatever their reasons for enlisting, the Haudenosaunee were nevertheless turned away. Parker only learned about the scale of the problem after he returned home after his embarrassing rejection by Seward. Not only were the men from the reservations being turned away, he learned that his brother, Isaac Newton Parker, had suffered a similar fate in Buffalo. Men were even being removed from existing regiments retroactively on "account of their being Indians." So Parker tried another approach and petitioned for citizenship but that was rejected as well. All were growing frustrated, so he and the Tuscarora Cornelius C. Cusick started a campaign to petition members of Congress and the New York legislature to change the laws barring the Haudenosaunee from service. After six months of a relentless and multifront campaign to convince the state to accept Iroquois volunteers, the state changed their enlistment rules. In March 1862, New York recruiting offices were ordered to "accept Indian recruits" so Parker, Cusick, and others immediately set out to raise volunteers. Despite their past rejections, the Iroquois' desire to serve had not diminished and, by the end of the war, 517 had joined the army (of over 3,700 Iroquois living in New York's reservations).[45]

On May 25, 1863, Parker was commissioned as "assistant adjutant general of volunteers with the rank of captain" and ordered to serve "on the staff of General Smith, now at Vicksburg [Mississippi]." His "departure was made the occasion of a meeting of the Council House of the Tonawanda Reservation" where the other chiefs gave him their blessings. Captain Parker was first sent to Illinois, where he left by steamship for Vicksburg. He arrived on July 7, after the battle for the city had been won by General Grant and the Union army. At camp, Parker reconnected with General Grant and, on Grant's order, he was reassigned as an engineer for the Seventh Division, Seventeenth Army Corps. The following summer, General Grant made Parker his secretary, a position Parker held through the Confederate's surrender at Appomattox, and was promoted by the end of the war to Lieutenant Colonel.[46]

During and after the war, Parker's Seneca-ness shaped his perspectives on the conflict. When he wrote back to Tonawanda from the battlefield, his views on the war-torn South were seen through an Iroquoian lens. Days before the Union Army's occupation of Chattanooga, Tennessee, Parker wrote a long letter to his sister about the upcoming battle. He anticipated that the Union Army would "thrash them soundly," but he also noticed the condition the local economy and the formerly enslaved people. "Throughout the entire South," he explained to Caroline, "as far as I have seen" the "country people do not live as well or as comfortable as the Tonawanda Indians." Stationed in Tennessee, the "ancient homes of the Cherokee," Parker also marveled that he was quartered a mere "twelve miles" from the historic home of the Cherokee chief and Confederate ally, John Ross. Cherokee country was littered with abandoned buildings and people left in the wake of the fleeing Confederate army. The southern "white trash" left behind could "hardly speak the English language" and hung on to the naive belief that their army would come back to save them. The former slaves of the region lived precariously in the deserted homes of the wealthy. Those who flocked to Union lines were "of course . . . with us and are our servants for pay" as the Union army fulfilled its wartime campaign of military emancipation, but most simply salvaged "fine rosewood and mahogany furniture [that] now forms the ornaments of negro cabins." Even the "fine dresses that white ladies once bedecked themselves with" now "hang shabbily upon the ungainly figure of some huge, dilapidated negro wench." Indeed, "any Indian house is better and more comfortable and cleaner" than what he witnessed among black and white people inhabiting the ancestral home of the Cherokees.[47]

Parker was also well known in the army as "Grant's Indian aid," and that was how he was introduced to the public after the end of the war. When he had the opportunity to publicly demonstrate his patriotism and service, he did so in a way that leveraged that nickname to showcase his Seneca heritage. An important part of this was his strategic deployment of Red Jacket's Peace Medal. In the months before and after Appomattox, newspapers followed Grant's "Indian Aid" on campaign and then on Grant's victory tour across the country. Parker, as early as 1864, was introduced to the public as a patriot of the "purest blood of the Iroquois" and the grand-nephew of "the famous Red Jacket." After the war ended, the papers explained that Parker was "of course . . . officially present at the surrender of Gen. Lee," but what people may not know was that, even during the war, Captain Parker "carried with him the great silver medal presented to [Red Jacket] by Washington in 1792." As Grant's victory tour entourage arrived in Washington on April 13, Grant and Parker were personally congratulated by President Lincoln. In a meeting scheduled hours before Lincoln was to leave for a play at Ford's Theater, Captain Parker "showed this medal to the late President, and spoke feelingly of the associations it represents."[48]

Even without the medal, Grant's "Indian aid" was always on public display. A month after the meeting with Lincoln, the "huge . . . dusky-faced" officer was in full view of thousands as he marched next to Grant at the head of a grand military parade in Washington called by President Andrew Johnson to celebrate the end of the war. Such parades were held across the country, often accompanied by other celebratory events. At the prestigious Astor House in New York City, Parker, the "Head Chief of the Six Nations," gave the diners a chance to hold the Peace Medal. And for two full months after that, Parker and his Peace Medal traveled across the east coast with General Grant on his national victory tour. In that time, the Seneca chief and army officer established himself as a true American in a fractured postwar moment where "memories" of the war "remained . . . problematic."[49] He and the Peace Medal were living reminders to Americans that the Haudenosaunee were a key part of the Union's victory and, more broadly, a part of American history.

Soon after the victory tour ended, President Johnson assigned Parker to serve as a liaison between the United States and the Native American nations of the west. Under the direction of D. N. Cooley, Commissioner of Indian Affairs, Parker was assigned "to negotiate under the instructions of the Secretary of the Interior" and try to help calm the sporadic violence that erupted between Native nations, white settlers, and the US Army. Others on his team included the Quaker Thomas Wistar, Brigadier General W. S. Harney, General Alfred Sully, and Superintendent of Southern Indian Affairs Elijah Sells. They aimed to "harness" the federal government's "postwar reformist spirit and direct it to Indian affairs" or, at the very least, take "a moment to stop and question Indian confinement" to reservations.[50]

The team's first assignment was to negotiate a postwar peace at an Indian council at Fort Smith, Arkansas, in the final months of 1865. At Fort Smith, Parker and his fellow diplomats participated in a council of Wyandots, Shawnees, Osages, Quapaws, Kansas-based Senecas, Cherokees, Creeks, Seminoles, Choctaws, Chickasaws, Wichitas, and Comanches. The American commission was given the full authority to negotiate on behalf of the federal government with the gathered tribes and those who had, by siding with the Confederacy, lost their claim to all previous treaties with the United States. At Fort Smith, "in spite of the bitter infighting between loyalist and rebel factions" among the gathered nations, the treaty confined all the Indigenous peoples to reservations in Kansas and Indian Territory (Oklahoma), enforced the demilitarization of the Confederate-allied Indian nations and demanded their written statements of loyalty to the United States, and set in motion the outlawing of slavery among all Indian nations. Holding that position for almost two years, Parker would play an important role in trying to secure peace among the Indigenous nations of the west.[51]

In these negotiations, his civilized Seneca-ness relative to the Westerners' "incivility" was notable. As the *Philadelphia Inquirer* reported, the chief of the "Tonawanda band of Senecas" and Grant's "Indian aid" offered "immediate assurance to the Indian Delegates at the Council" of the federal government's sincerity in their "friendship." Parker was a "civilized" Indian "of much culture as well as native intellect" and held "a lively interest in the advancement of his people, of whatever tribe." Parker essentially had two jobs. One was as an army officer and diplomat, and the other was as a civilized Seneca who set an example for the gathered Native American diplomats, many of whom, a report detailed, were not just "uncivilized" but not even "full blooded . . . red men of the forest." Many showed a "strong intermixture of white, and a lesser of negro blood being very apparent." Some, like Parker, "seated themselves quietly on benches, after the manner of orderly American citizens," but many others "bore every emblem of the wild Indian of the past." These so-called "blanket Indians" sat in "contradistinction to those who have adopted the garb and habits of civilized life." Parker's Seneca-ness was recognized by some of the Native American delegates who appreciated the fact that "the United States

have seen fit to include a member of an Indian tribe with its commissioners."
At Fort Smith, Parker became the face of US attempts to gain the "loyal[ty]"
of Indian country and set an example of Native civility that all could follow.[52]

His next assignment, which he conducted from May through July 1867,
was to investigate the December 1866 massacre of eighty US soldiers at
Fort Phil Kearney (in what today is northeastern Wyoming). Known as
the Fetterman Fight or Fetterman Massacre, Parker met with the "Lakota,
Cheyenne, and other Indians along the Missouri River in Nebraska and the
Montana territory" to calm tensions and negotiate a peace. He resisted calls
for revenge from the army and the other US delegates, and instead sued for
a mutually beneficial peace, supporting measures that would grow reservation economies and stabilize local politics to ensure such a massacre could
not happen again. He knew that a federally ensured peace process had the
potential to bring peace and mutual prosperity as well as open the door to
future assimilation.[53]

Amid his work in the West, Parker occasionally visited Tonawanda. On
one visit in September 1866, he delivered a highly publicized speech at the
Tonawanda's annual Green Corn Festival in Orleans County, New York.
An "unusually large audience" came to hear Parker, the "grand-son of
the celebrated Indian Chief, Red Jacket, and a member of Gen. Grant's
staff," speak for the first time after the war at an event hosted by "the
Senecas, the proudest of the Six Nations, and the leading people of the
great Iroquois League" who "once covered and owned all of Western New-
York." According to the national newspaper coverage, the "Grand Sachem"
Parker focused on what was most important to his work in the west: peace
and assimilation. He reiterated the familiar selective assimilationist rhetoric about "advancing Indians in education, agriculture, mechanics, and
all the arts of civilization" while simultaneously "shun[ning] the vices of
the white man." The speech was, in that respect, unremarkable in its content. Where his hour-long speech diverged from assimilationist orthodoxy was that it was delivered entirely in the Seneca language. The *Buffalo
Express* reported that, although the speech proved "beyond our compre-
hension ... from the way it was received by his auditors, we were convinced
that it was eloquent and instructive." Tellingly, the paper's interpretation
of what Parker said came from "those who understand" the language, so
any translation was filtered through another Seneca.[54] Parker's Green Corn
speech not only showcased his Indian-ness, it forced non-Indian media
and audiences to pay attention to his people's culture translated through
its own intermediaries.

While doing government work, Parker continued to correspond with the Six Nations and his sister in Tonawanda, kept apprised of western Indian politics, and, after Grant was elected president in 1868, was appointed US Commissioner of Indian Affairs. The country's first Indigenous Commissioner took office April 26, 1869. Parker was aligned with the Republican administration's reformers who were filled with "optimism" as they "attempt[ed] to improve [government] efficiency." Grant himself brought a certain energy to Indian affairs because he "sympathized with the plight of Indians" and saw the West as more than a place for white expansion: it was the seedbed for future Indian citizenship. But that political inclusion broke in some ways with popular will, which impacted the political career of his new Commissioner. Parker proved during his short tenure to support policies that rejected the ideas of those "reformers" who were "less concerned about the Indians' dignity and self-determination than their submissiveness and conformity."[55] In that sense, while he agreed with the majority of federal officials that Indian confinement to reservations led to economic and political conformity and the suppression of their wild and warlike predilections, he also believed that these were matters over which Indigenous peoples themselves should have some control.

Parker's appointment gave his political allies confidence because they knew that this "grand-nephew of Red-Jacket" would "see the 'Indian ring,'" a nickname for the widespread corruption and nepotism among federal Indian superintendents of the Office of Indian Affairs, "broken up." It also helped that, among the Haudenosaunee and the "people in Western New York," the "chief of the Seneca nation" was beloved "irrespective of party." Parker's appointment came at an important moment in American Indian affairs because by the end of the war, "Americans wanted Indians out of their way, but it was not clear how that should be accomplished." If only because of his reputation, he offered the office stability, expertise, and a clear model of assimilation. While some doubt lingered as to whether he could be appointed to the position because he was not a US citizen, he was nevertheless approved by the Senate.[56]

Parker attempted to reform the Office of Indian Affairs (OIA) in several ways. He and Grant sought a reformed Indian policy that prioritized peace between Indian country and Washington. With the assistance of the new Board of Indian Commissioners (BIC), a new oversight commission proposed by Parker that held appropriations power, he advocated for reforms in Indian country that he had long wanted for the Haudenosaunee: citizenship, Christianization, and gradual assimilation but on Indigenous peoples' own terms. Importantly, he also set the tone for anticorruption in the agency's activities. In a June 3 circular letter to Indian Superintendents across the country, Parker informed his colleagues that, in the spirit of creating a "humane and wise" Indian policy, the office would undergo an internal review to root out corruption and inefficiencies. The letter also explained that the OIA would honor all standing treaty obligations, "collect the Indians and locate them in permanent abodes upon reservations," and provide "reasonable appropriations" to the reservations to help people transition and assimilate.[57]

Despite his best efforts, however, Parker's tenure as Commissioner of Indian Affairs was short lived. The OIA's new policy for the US government to respect all treaties as written and remove the Indian commissioners from the political realm would, in part, require moving the OIA from the Department of State to the Department of War and stocking the Indian agency with trusted army officers, Quakers, and proven Indian advocates like Parker. This plan, however, suffered setbacks that impacted Parker's position. William Welsh, the first chairman of the BIC and a deeply suspicious person, accused Parker of fraud. In January 1871, after Parker returned from a trip to the Missouri River to survey the Native nations in the Dakotas, Welsh learned that he had signed an emergency contract to a shipping company to transport "Indian goods to points on the Missouri river, principally for the Sioux of Dakotah." Welsh claimed that this was done without the approval of the BIC, and by extension Congress, and so it must have been a plot by Parker for the sole financial benefit of the company and himself.[58]

Parker defended his actions. First, he explained that the money in question was allocated one month before he went on the trip, so he had not squeezed more from Congress. Besides, even if it had cost more, the financial consequences of the contract were negligible compared to the preservation of the peace policy. After all, peace was only possible if the western nations were confined to reservations, and that deeply unpopular policy was salable only if the government supplied the provisions they had promised in treaties. Parker circled back and argued that this new contract in fact fit within the existing treaty between the Sioux and the United States and, if the supply lines stopped, Indian nations everywhere "would abandon their agencies and at once resume their nomadic habits, taking from citizens whenever they might fancy and inaugurating war if deemed to their advantage." The failure to "continue the supplies" would force the western nations to "commence depredating." Calling on the memory of the Civil War and the long-held fears of Indian war, Parker suggested that abandoning peace by not taking drastic action would "perhaps inaugurate a general Indian war."[59]

His self-defense and Congress's investigation that found him innocent did not prove sufficient to clear his name, however. Welsh's initial accusation had started an avalanche of public accusations, dragging Parker into larger partisan battles over Grant's administration. Some aimed their ire at the new BIC who they thought had relegated the position of Commissioner to a mere "clerk of the board of Indian commissioners," a problem that critics claimed had forced Parker into a position of "ambigu[ity]" and left him no choice but to be corrupted. Others targeted Parker's Seneca-ness directly as the country's racial animosities colored the debate over his corruption. The problem, as they saw it, was that he was chosen by Grant because of his race. Despite his experience as chief, Lieutenant Colonel, Indian agent, and his management of the OIA, critics argued that the "Indian chief had not yet distinguished himself much as head of the Indian bureau." Any number of "pale-faces" would have done better, they believed, and "we are not sorry" that Parker, "finding the position 'anomalous,' has seen fit to hand in his resignation." Parker finally succumbed to the intense political pressure and stepped down on June 29, 1871, after just two years in office.[60]

The accusations hurt him deeply. After his resignation, Parker removed himself from public life. While in Washington, he invested in various businesses and in the stock market, making a small fortune through a carpet company. He may have also been an early investor in John D. Rockefeller's Standard Oil Company. His financial success allowed him and his wife Minnie Sackett to move out of the capital later in 1871 to the "white man's heaven" of Fairfield, Connecticut, where their only child, Maud Theresa Parker, was born in 1878. From there the Parkers led, at least for a time, a charmed life. The town was connected by rail to Wall Street, where Parker spent his working hours building a successful career as a private investor in the stock market. He maintained contact with the Tonawanda Reservation and agreed to board his niece Minnie, Nic's daughter, while Nic served as the Tonawanda's official interpreter in Washington. Minnie found life in Fairfield difficult, however, and she returned home after less than a year. Yet the stock market could be fickle. In September 1873, Parker and many other investors lost much of their fortunes in the collapse of the financial firm Jay Cooke and Company. Despite their losses, the Parkers were able to keep their mansion in Fairfield and, with what they had left, purchased a second home on West 42nd Street in New York City as their primary residence. After they moved to the city, Parker's friend William F. Smith, then on the Board of Commissioners for the New York City Police Department (NYPD), appointed the unemployed Parker as a clerk on September 30, 1876.[61]

Parker spent the rest of his days in his office in the Department of Repairs and Supplies at NYPD headquarters at 300 Mulberry Street. His clerkship was quite unlike his previous careers. He was still the colonel and the chief in public memory, but he was no longer a changemaker or even a man of much political relevance. Parker worked in a job with little recognition or authority, and he seemed to be overworked and thus took "very little satisfaction" from his job. He also fell ill multiple times and watched his extended family members die. Yet during these years he also met the woman who would become his closest friend, Harriet Maxwell Converse. Their relationship sparked in her an interest in Haudenosaunee history.[62]

But if Parker is seen simply as a low-level clerk who lacked the power of his former positions, this misses the things he did inside and outside his professional duties at the NYPD. From the 1880s until his death on August 30, 1895, he was involved in public projects and events that were important in his efforts to fuse the history and memory of the Iroquois and the United States together. By deed and reputation, and regardless of his profession, Parker remained the most famous living representative of the Haudenosaunee. In addition, his work at the NYPD and his relationship with Converse attracted Indigenous visitors from Iroquoia and around the country to the city to meet the famous chief. Parker was also a visible and integral part of the preservation of the memory of the Civil War. He became an active member of the New York Grand Army of the Republic, a veterans association formed in 1866, and served as one of the caretakers of the legacy of Ulysses S. Grant.[63] It was in New York City, during the supposed drudgery of retirement, where Parker set out in earnest to build his and his peoples' legacy.

A major part of his work on shaping Iroquois exceptionalism was the memorialization of the life of his uncle, Red Jacket. Parker played an important role in his reinterment in the Forest Lawn Cemetery in Buffalo on October 4, 1884. To prepare for that moment, he carefully authenticated Red Jacket's remains as well as the ten other Haudenosaunee Revolutionary-era heroes buried with him. Parker worked closely with the secretary and former president of the Buffalo Historical Society, William Cullen Bryant, to ensure that the "survivors and families of the departed chiefs" were all consulted about the authenticity of the bones and that the Historical Society was given permission to reinter them. On the day of the reburial, the remains of the honored dead were transported from their temporary holding places at the Buffalo Historical Society by six hearses and an impressive "cortége of seventy-five carriages" to the cemetery.[64]

As the event planner and master of ceremonies, Parker oversaw the creation of the Red Jacket Burial Plot at the main entrance to Forest Lawn. Men and women from Six Nations reservations in New York and Canada volunteered as an honor guard, and Parker and Converse sat among "scores" of Haudenosaunee, other Native Americans, and white visitors who came to remember and pay their respects to one of the most famous Iroquois men in history. The day-long ceremony began with speeches in the Seneca language by Parker and his brother Nicholson. Other speakers included William Cullen Bryant, the Cayuga chief James Jemison, the Seneca Reverend Z. L. Jemison, and the Tuscarora chief and Parker's brother-in-law John Mountpleasant. They honored those interred like Cornplanter's brother Farmer's Brother, Young King, Little Billy (who escorted George Washington to Fort Duquesne during the French and Indian War), and Governor Blacksnake. This illustrious reburial, in the view of one commentator, marked the "last public manifestation of the dignity and nobleness of the Senecas," but that clearly downplayed the ongoing activities of the dozens of Haudenosaunee people in attendance and the many speeches given in the Seneca language.[65]

The Buffalo Historical Society, the primary fundraiser and administrator of the reburial, planned for a memorial statue to honor the Red Jacket Burial Plot. Fundraising responsibilities were given to Converse, and in 1890, when she had received "several substantial pledges to the monument fund," Parker followed that by unveiling his own statue design to the Historical Society and the public. In collaboration with New York artist James Edward Kelly, who also designed a bust of Parker wearing Red Jacket's Peace Medal in 1895, Parker designed a bronze statue of a dying tree clinging by its roots to a large stone boulder. It would be enormous in scale at twenty-six feet tall with a circular base twelve feet in diameter. The memorial would honor the "undisputed monarchs of the forest" who had long ago extended "peace, friendship, and hospitality to the forerunners" of modern Americans.[66]

The tree- and boulder-centric design conveyed Haudenosaunee history and lifeways, celebrating Red Jacket's memory on Seneca terms. The statue would include bronze tablets representing each of their clan totems, as well as various historical scenes from Red Jacket's life. The dying tree, which one newspaper interpreted as a "remembrance" of Red Jacket's apocryphal last words in which he compared himself to a "blasted hemlock," could also be a representation of the Great Tree of Peace, the international law created by Deganawideh long ago that bound the Six Nations Confederacy together in peace. The boulder, an allegory evoking George Washington's promise to the Senecas in 1792 of a peace "founded on the principles of justice and humanity

FIGURE 2.3 Bust of Ely S. Parker by James E. Kelly, 1895.
Rochester Museum & Science Center, Rochester, NY.

as upon an immoveable rock," was supported by "four bronze turtles" that
represented "the Indian belief that the earth is a great place supported by
turtles."[67]

Parker may have created something unorthodox, but he understood what
was at stake in the design. Red Jacket's monument would help to shape how
future generations saw the Haudenosaunee, their history, and their most famous orator. The tree and boulder did not simply portray Red Jacket as an
"aged tree" who represented the "ending or death of the Iroquois Confederacy,"
the narrative white audiences were used to hearing, but spoke directly to
Haudenosaunee audiences by incorporating aspects of their cosmology, social structure, and political history.[68] The memorial may have looked as if it
perpetuated the widely held myth of the vanishing Indian, but it simultaneously celebrated Seneca resilience on the Haudenosaunees' own terms.

The memorial committee, however, thought Parker's design was ugly. The Buffalo Historical Society and the memorial funders deemed it "horrid and grotesque" and quite simply too "unorthodox" to fund to completion. That claim revealed the committee's deeper rejection of the Senecas' own symbols and memory, even if it was presented by the authentic Seneca voice of Ely Parker, one of the Historical Society's friends and an American hero. In their minds, the statue did not properly glorify the myth of the "vanished Indian" and thus did not truly represent the memory of the "Last of the Seneca." Instead, the Buffalo Historical Society turned to Ohio artist James G.C. Hamilton, who borrowed from the Historical Society's original plans and proposed a much more traditional and generic Greek-revival sculpture that looked remarkably similar to the 1882 statue of George Washington at Federal Hall in New York City. This new statue was approved in 1890 and erected the same year, though it did not receive a formal public dedication until 1892. At the top of the memorial stands an 8.5-foot-tall bronze statue of Red Jacket wearing a cloak draped around his left arm, a pose reminiscent of classical Roman sculpture, while his right-hand gestures with open palm toward the western horizon.[69] James Hamilton's statue proved that there was not much interest in promoting a Seneca-specific claim to Red Jacket's memory, not when Americans could claim him on their own terms.

Of course, hanging prominently around the neck of the statue of "heroic size" was the Peace Medal. It was the most recognizable attribute of Red Jacket, one that recalled the memory of George Washington and the creation of the United States. Red Jacket's left hand holds a silver-gilded tomahawk pipe, another gift from Washington. The tallest object in the cemetery and visible from a busy Buffalo thoroughfare, the statue stands atop a hexagonal stone base where each side represents the Six Nations of the Iroquois Confederacy. Prominently displayed is the nameplate "Red Jacket, Sa-go-ye-wat-ha (He-Keeps-Them-Awake): Died at Buffalo Creek January 20, 1830, Aged 78 Years." Below the nameplate is a telling sampling of Red Jacket's last words:

> When I am gone and my warnings are no longer needed, the craft and avarice of the white man will prevail. My heart fails me when I think of my people, so soon to be scattered and forgotten.[70]

These carefully chosen words reflected his nickname, "The Last of the Senecas."[71]

Despite the Historical Society overruling Parker's memorial vision, his proposal was eventually brought to life. A statue of similar design was erected

FIGURE 2.4 State of Red Jacket by James G.C. Hamilton, 1890.
Photograph by Bill Coughlin. Historical Markers Database.

by the Waterloo Library and Historical Society in 1891 to mark Red Jacket's
birthplace in Canoga, New York, an area famous for being the crossroads of
Sullivan's 1779 brutal invasion of the Haudenosaunee. Thomas M. Howell of
Canandaigua, a friend of the Waterloo Historical Society, had interviewed
several chiefs as well as Parker himself about Red Jacket and the memorial
before its dedication. The project artists, W & J Littlejohn of Seneca Falls,
explained that the "old sycamore" depicted in the memorial supposedly once
stood over the "wigwam" of Red Jacket's birthplace. Parker's fingerprints
are all over this statue, not least because it was unveiled to a large crowd on
October 13 by John Jacket (Red Jacket's grandson), Nicholson Parker, and his
granddaughter Bethia May Parker, who spoke at the opening ceremonies.[72]

Elsewhere in retirement, Parker also began to revive his old ethnographic
and political interests in the history and lifeways of his people. He advised

FIGURE 2.5 Red Jacket's Birth Site Monument. Photograph by Bryan Olson. Historical Markers Database.

those who reached out to him for perspectives on Indigenous history, fact-checked for publishers, and continued to speak at Masonic functions on the history of the Six Nations. His connections to the Haudenosaunee and Native America broadly were also more practical. From his office at 300 Mulberry Street, he assisted Harriet M. Converse with the operation of the Indian Colony of New York City, a space for Indigenous residents and visitors in New York City who came for work, leisure, or tourism.[73]

His relationship with urban Indians did not stop at the Hudson River. In May 1892, he made an extraordinary claim on behalf of the Haudenosaunee on "a plot of ground in Philadelphia." The "'wampum lot,' as it is locally known," was a small plot of land "fifteen feet three inches by forty-seven feet in area" located in an alley behind the thirty-year-old Chamber of Commerce building at "Second and Gothic streets" (today on Second Street between

Walnut and Chestnut Streets). Parker went to Philadelphia and claimed the lot with a wampum belt that, for the Haudenosaunee, served as the original deed for the plot. The plot and the belt were gifts from Pennsylvania governor John Penn, grandson of William Penn, to the Six Nations generations ago. The original deal was struck sometime before the Seven Years' War between the Mohawk leader Hendrick Peters Theyanoguin and Governor John Penn to "cement the friendship formed" between the Six Nations and Pennsylvania government "and [to] create a tie for future treaties." At the time, Penn thought it prudent to secure a political relationship with the "all-powerful Indian tribe known as the Iroquois."[74]

Penn hoped the Wampum Lot would "forever after" serve as a place to "erect a tent of state and smoke the calumet and make treaties." For their part, the Penn family made efforts to protect the land by building a fence and wings of the family home around it to create physical barriers to entry. But as a result, when the new Chamber of Commerce building was built in 1867, the Wampum Lot had remained unused for more than a century. The city government, unable to buy the property outright because of the Iroquois' ownership of it, instead encircled it fully and, "by right of adverse possession," claimed it and turned it into a driveway. When Parker, the "greatest of [the Iroquois'] great men," arrived in the city in 1892 bearing the Haudenosaunees' legitimate "title to property," he found the Wampum Lot under city ownership. His "conference" with Charles Knecht, the former president of the Chamber of Commerce, revealed what actions the city had taken to colonize the lot. Knecht explained that while "no title could be obtained to the property" because the "wampum belt established a proprietary right given by the Commonwealth," technically the city had not actually built upon it and so was still respecting that right. They had, therefore, found a way to use it as city property while also maintaining its status as "exempted . . . from taxation" and "conferred forever" upon the occupant. With the Wampum Lot gone, the city shed its last remnant of Penn's "peaceable" Indian legacy.[75]

Parker's claim on the Wampum Lot at that moment was no accident. At the same Parker visited Philadelphia the Haudenosaunee, with the tireless help of Harriet Maxwell Converse, fought a public battle against Albany and Washington who sought once again to remove them from their land. For someone with his long political experience and the ability to create publicity, he knew that laying claim to an extremely valuable section of one of the oldest and most well-established American cities would connect the Haudenosaunee and their politics to the memory of the seat of the myth of Penn's Peaceable Kingdom, the place where George Washington first gave Red Jacket the Peace

Medal, and the historic home of American independence. Whether the claim on the Wampum Lot was Parker's idea or another unique part of Converse and the Six Nations' broad campaign to garner public support and protect Haudenosaunee sovereignty in the 1890s, it was a bold public statement that mirrored his ongoing efforts to remind the public of the Iroquois' exceptionality and central place in American history.

Parker also had a hand in the preservation of New Yorkers' Civil War memory. Like many others with a vested interest in preserving and shaping the memory of the war, Parker collected and archived wartime ephemera and "artifacts" that would one day "wind up in museums, monuments, imaginative literature, history books, and commemorative occasions." Parker also actively participated in the Grand Army of the Republic (which created the national holiday of Memorial Day) and in a similar group called the Military Order of the Loyal Legion, marched in annual public ceremonial "musters" in Syracuse, and attended many popular memorial dinners honoring Grant's legacy hosted by fellow veterans Horace Porter and William T. Sherman. But Parker, as one of the most famous Indigenous people in the country and as Grant's military secretary, offered a unique perspective on the war. As such, he contributed to a "recollection series," an assortment of written statements, artwork, and portraits that offered "some noble reminiscence" of Grant that "prove[d] his genius" as a warrior and statesman. Parker's recollections of what happened at Appomattox, in particular, inspired a painting by Thomas Nast who was commissioned in 1894 to complete "a large picture of Lee's surrender to Grant." Titled "Peace in Union," this remains one of the famous images of the iconic meeting at Appomattox, a painting truly monumental in scale at "14 feet long, ten feet high," and featured "ten full length figures" that included Grant, Lee, Rawlins, and Parker, "all formerly residents of Galena."[76]

Parker was also active in the Grant Monument Association, an organization dedicated to fundraising and planning for a public monument in honor of Ulysses S. Grant. Parker's greatest contribution to the Association was at a dinner at the Waldorf Astoria on April 27, 1893, in honor of what would have been Grant's 71st birthday. In front of a crowd of 150 donors and close friends of the general from across the world, the Seneca chief gave a speech to the assembled guests and gave them each a "souvenir," his own personal narrative of the events at Appomattox, that they received in thanks for their attendance and financial generosity. The souvenir was truly unique because it was drawn from Parker's personal wartime correspondence and document collection. It "consist[ed] of a pamphlet, bound in leather, containing Gen. Parker's narrative of the circumstances of the surrender of the army of northern Virginia

FIGURE 2.6 "Peace in Union" by Thomas Nast, 1894. Galena-Jo Daviess County Historical Society.

to Gen. Grant by Gen. Robert E. Lee, and the correspondence between the two generals preceding the surrender." The "Indian Colonel" was not only at Appomattox and transcribed the terms of surrender, he claimed to have sent the "famous telegram" that Grant dictated to Parker to notify President Lincoln of Robert E. Lee's surrender. Along with each souvenir was a rare image from his private collection of "the original draft in the handwriting of Grant of the terms of surrender of Lee's army." The souvenirs and his speech were, as he explained to the donors, his own special "memorial" to Grant's legacy. By the end of the evening, Parker announced that they had raised $400,000 for the memorial to date and were two-thirds of the way toward their goal. Parker would not live to see the monument dedicated in Riverside Park in 1897, but he and his personal archive gave Association donors a living memory of Appomattox.[77]

Parker also memorialized the Civil War through Indigenous stories. At the 1891 dedication of the 42nd New York Infantry memorial at Gettysburg, Pennsylvania, he spoke in honor of the "brave deeds" of the volunteer "Tammany" regiment who fought at the battle of Gettysburg in 1863. The unveiling ceremony included speeches by officers and veterans of the battle, even of a Colonel John R. Fellows, "an ex-officer in the confederate army," for a large crowd of veterans and their families. Parker, like the other speakers, first celebrated the bravery and virtue of the Tammany regiment. These were soldiers who went to war "to maintain the integrity of the American Flag and the right that it alone should float over" the United States. The brave 42nd held back an "invasion" of "this free state by a hostile army whose avowed object was the dissolution of the Union you were seeking to preserve, and which strove to perpetuate the institution of human slavery which your success would abolish and destroy forever." The monument, therefore, was in honor of the "memory of your comrades whose dust mingles with the dust of this ground."[78]

Parker was also careful to tie their patriotism and sacrifice to the legacy of the regiment's namesake, Tammany, the famous Delaware Indian chief. A veteran of the "Revolutionary War" and ally of the new United States, a leader with "no equal" whose "enthusiastic admirers among the whites dubbed him . . . the Patron Saint of America." He was "a member of the Delaware," a people that Parker explained "enjoyed liberty in its largest and most liberal sense," yet were also a people in "a perpetual state of war" until they were "broken and the people subjugated by the more powerful and proud Iroquois of New York." The history of Delaware wars and violence stopped only after the Iroquois conquered them, but, for Parker, the Delaware served as a reminder of the contemporary "Indian problem." He explained that the problems facing Native America at the end of the nineteenth century were precisely those that Tammany and his people fought and struggled against in the eighteenth century, namely, the corrupted and the hollow platitudes of Americans and Christian missionaries who promised "peace on earth and good will toward men" but delivered neither.[79]

Then, Parker returned to Tammany himself. Despite belonging to "this doomed race," he was a brave and "wise councellor (sic)" who had "every good and noble qualification that a human being may possess." Tammany's "memory was ever reverenced among his people" and is "still perpetuated among the whites" by the work of the Society of St. Tammany who maintained the Democratic party's headquarters in a building in New York City dubbed Tammany Hall. To Parker, the Delaware chief was a reminder that "all true and honest patriots" must understand and know both Native American and Euro-American history. All patriots should learn "thoroughly the history of his country from its discovery and settlement onward," all of which connected the multiple colonial wars with "aborigines" to the recent war which freed "four millions of slaves" and created a new class of "citizens equal with you." Parker ended his speech with a poem about Tammany that reminded his audience that Native Americans, in war and peace, in friendship and animosity, were, are, and will be a part of America's founding moments: "With him let every generous patriot vie, To live in freedom or with honor die."[80]

This rousing speech was designed to prove to white Americans the long-standing patriotism of Indian peoples and to make space for Parker to talk about the "Indian Problem," but his invocation of Tammany also delivered a more focused message: that the Iroquois themselves were a historically "civilizing" force. Their conquest of the Delawares in the early eighteenth century saved them from perpetual internal war and from being "made women" by the French and English colonies. Stories sprang up in English diplomatic circles that the Delaware were given a new and masculine purpose as the now-nephews and allies of the Six Nations. These were stories actively spread by the Iroquois. Despite what seemed to be a mutually beneficial relationship, the Iroquois often denied the Delawares political agency and ignored the diplomatic realities of the Delawares' historic and "masculine" resistance to European invasion. The Iroquois League created similar fictional diplomatic stories about other nations in the effort to expand the Tree of Peace, exert control over the region, and create new buffers between their country and the European invaders.[81] For Parker speaking to the Tammany Regiment in 1891, he was invoking the Iroquois' own diplomatic mythology to remind the American public of his people's historic imperial power and make the new claim that the Haudenosaunee brought civilization to the Indian world.

Four years after his speech to the Tammany regiment, Parker, who still clerked at the NYPD, passed away at the home of his friends Arthur and Josephine Brown in Fairfield, Connecticut, on August 30, 1895. For a few days before after his death, the "Last Sachem" lay in an open casket in full army dress uniform in the Brown's parlor. There, mourners came to pay their respects. Minnie and Maud Parker, Harriet Converse, members of the Grand Army of the Republic and the Loyal Legion, the Masons, and the Society of Colonial Wars all attended and laid in his casket medals from each of their orders. Clergy from the Episcopal church paid their respects, and many veterans he had served with during the Civil War arrived in full military dress. Some left elaborate floral arrangements in various shapes and sizes from a cross to the shape of a door, the symbol of Parker's role as a chief of the Senecas, the "keeper[s] of the western door of the Longhouse."[82]

Seated among these well-wishers was a slightly more conspicuous group. "Six full-blooded Indians, silent and stern," formed an honor guard around his open casket for as long as mourners came to visit. These six men were occasionally joined by three Haudenosaunee women who were seen laying and removing a succession of wampum strings and belts over his body.

While mourners came and went and offered their sympathies to Minnie (and presumably Maud) and Harriet Converse, the three women kept busy "disput[ing] in occasional whispers . . . who should be the successor of the dead sachem and receive the beads" as well as his name, Do-ne-ho-ga-wa. After the three days in the Brown's parlor, Parker's remains were interred in a Fairfield cemetery and then, two years later in 1897, with Minnie's permission, his remains were moved again to the Forest Lawn Cemetery in the Red Jacket Burial Plot. The Haudenosaunee women's conversations about "succession" at the Brown's house continued through these reburials. When the casket was ready to be lowered into the ground at Forest Lawn, one of the women placed "an Indian pipe" into it and then a "great American flag" was draped over the top. At the last minute, one of the women approached the casket, lifted the edge of the flag, and pulled "strings of wampum" out from underneath it and handed it to the eldest woman of the group. Ten months later in July 1896, the Haudenosaunee held a Condolence Ceremony "to choose a new chief." There, Thomas Jefferson Poudry was chosen as a new "Grand Sachem" and given the name Do-ne-ha-ga-wa, "the Indian name of General Parker."[83]

Even as mourners flocked to say goodbye to the "Last Grand Sachem of the Iroquois" and, by extension, the supposedly vanished Iroquois, the Haudenosaunee women in attendance presented a different reality. The various strings and belts of wampum that lay across the uniformed body bedecked with medals and military honors impressed on those in attendance that Ely Parker's Seneca-ness and patriotism were one and the same. Even the sale of his estate one year later by Minnie sent a similar message. Although Parker's belongings were sold because Minnie struggled financially despite her very modest widow's pension, she also—if only subconsciously—continued

FIGURE 2.7 Reinterment of Ely S. Parker in the Red Jacket Burial Plot, 1897. The Buffalo History Museum.

to link Parker, the Haudenosaunee, and American patriotism together. In the advertisements selling his estate, Minnie showcased her husband's original letter in Grant's handwriting of Lee's terms of surrender which sold for "$2,000," as well as the Peace Medal, a "part of the history of this country," that was sold to the Buffalo Historical Society. These were sold as part of Ely Parker's collection which included a "library . . . which is rich in the field of Indian history," and an ethnographic collection which contained "some personal belongings of historical value."[84]

Years later, Parker's legacy was celebrated once again. At the Forest Lawn cemetery in Buffalo, a new headstone for Parker was unveiled in 1905. That ceremony was attended by hundreds of attendees from the G.A.R., the Loyal Legion, and the Buffalo Historical Society who all gathered around the towering statue of Red Jacket to remember the late chief and Colonel. Parker was, as an ex-editor of the *Philadelphia Inquirer* described, "not as much as a typical Indian as a splendid savage." He was an exemplar of what Indians were supposed to be and, for that, the author would forever remember the "last sachem of the Senecas."[85]

On December 21, 2000, the Assistant Secretary of Indian Affairs Kevin Gover dedicated the Bureau of Indian Affair's (BIA) new "Ely S. Parker Building" in Reston, Virginia. The dedication ceremony was attended by more than one hundred people, including officials from the US Department of the Interior, the BIA, representatives of the architectural firm who designed the building, a Wolf Clan mother, a runner of the Tonawanda Senecas, and a lineal descendant of Ely S. Parker who was also a Heron Clan mother of the Cayuga Nation. In his keynote address, Gover highlighted the historic importance and legacy of the "former warrior and Commissioner of Indian Affairs." He noted that Parker was the first Indigenous person to hold that office and spoke briefly about his two-year term at the OIA. Importantly, he emphasized the "paradox" of Parker's identity as a Seneca who also believed in assimilation.[86]

As Gover explained, that paradox did not stop him from protecting Native Americans. Parker sought to protect Native treaty rights and "to eliminate widespread corruption," a mission that came at a steep cost to his "personal reputation and political career." After the keynote, the runner Norman Hill (or Taa-Wonyas) gave a "thanksgiving blessing" in the Seneca language to mark the occasion, which the Wolf Clan mother Evelyn Jonathan (or Einjhonesh) translated into English. As a final testament to Parker's legacy, it was noted during the ceremony how rare an honor it was for an individual to have a building named after him. Gover then "pondered" if Parker, as an assimilated Indian and thus a "paradox," would appreciate the fact that his legacy was bound to a notoriously unpopular department that he had ultimately failed to change?[87]

Probably. Parker was, after all, a firm believer in the power of a just and powerful federal government to change Native American life for the better, even if he himself was not able to implement those changes. What he would not have understood quite as well was Gover's comment on the paradoxical nature of his being an assimilated Indian. Parker thought that assimilation was the solution to the "Indian problem" and spent years integrating himself into elite white society and proving to the public that the exceptional histories of the Iroquois and the United States were indeed compatible. In addition, his reputation and acceptance by white America shielded him and, he hoped, his people from the worst impulses of a society and a government that by the end of the nineteenth century proved violently intolerant of difference.

Gover's twenty-first-century moral judgment about Parker's life casts the nineteenth-century Seneca chief as morally ambiguous at best and inherently wrong at worst in his actions. But this assumption only buries the nuances of Parker's life, not to mention those of many other assimilated Indians. It contends that Parker, a man born to Seneca leadership, could not have been as "authentic" as others because he was assimilated and therefore insulated from the problems many of his kin faced. How then do we interpret the actions of a man who chose, in defiance of his own desire to integrate into white society, to speak publicly in his own people's language at their events? What about the chief and runner who worked until his death to shape how Americans remembered the history and legacy of his people long after he permanently left Iroquois country? Or what about the man who took his responsibilities to protect Haudenosaunee and broader Native American sovereignty seriously, even if in hindsight his approach proved flawed? Applying this logic, is Iroquois history something that Parker and his family were not a part of simply because of their associations with the United States?

Of course not. Therein lies the problem with flat portrayals of assimilated peoples as a historical "paradox." There is no question that people like Parker often regurgitated what white audiences wanted to hear, often for their own benefit, but a more critical analysis of Parker's life reveals a far more complex history. He was indeed assimilated, in fact he took steps to ensure that happened, but by speaking on the colonizer's own terms in their own language, he was also able to shape public opinion about the Iroquois in surprisingly sensitive ways, even if that was not always his intention. These moments made Haudenosaunee culture and history more palatable to an otherwise dismissive white culture that sought only Indigenous erasure and, at times, cultural cooptation. By design and by accident of his celebrity, Parker's relationship to assimilation influenced the way future generations of New Yorkers remembered the Iroquois, even if they forgot that it was the Iroquois themselves who had popularized aspects of their own history and told those stories on their own terms.

The person Ely Parker entrusted most with writing that history was his dear friend, Harriet Maxwell Converse, who trumpeted her vison of Iroquois exceptionalism while simultaneously claiming that they were a "vanished" people. As Parker knew well, New Yorkers were as willing as ever to listen to that message.

3

Harriet Maxwell Converse, "The Woman Who Works for the Indians"

IN PREPARATION FOR the October 1884 reburial of Red Jacket at the Forest Lawn Cemetery (the same reburial organized by Ely Parker), Harriet Maxwell Converse, a brand-new Seneca adoptee and an accomplished poet, composed a poem dedicated to Red Jacket, the "Last of the Seneca."[1] The epic titled *The Ho-De'-No-Sau-Nee: The Confederacy of the Iroquois* captured Converse's conception of the faded glory of the Haudenosaunee, an echo of the popular mythology of the "vanished" Indian, a trope popularized in Red Jacket's time and reinforced during the Indian Wars that raged less than a decade before his reburial. As the last stanza put it,

> *Will no faithful stone, recording-*
> *In the Monumental Glory*
> *Of its pale historic marble-*
> *All the bravery of their birthright,*
> *Lift unto the gaze of ages*
> *All their storied power and honor?*
> *Will their legends and traditions*
> *Go untuned in songs of nations?*
> *Or, enshrouded in a darkness,*
> *In their natal earth embosomed,*
> *Will, in sorrow, all this people,*
> *In dim sepulcher to oblivion*
> *And to silence yield their names?*[2]

Unlike her contemporaries who were willing to let Native Americans fade into historical obscurity, Converse looked beyond the Iroquois' supposed disappearance to ask: Who will preserve their history and legacy? Will their "songs and traditions" go "untuned"? Will their "bravery and birthright" go unrecorded in the "Monumental Glory" of time-honored histories carved in marble? Will the American people "to silence yield their names"?

Converse dedicated the end of her life to answering those questions, and her efforts revealed the extent to which public perception, both Haudenosaunee and not, influenced the evolution of Iroquois exceptionalism. Beginning with that poem and continuing until her death in 1903, Americans read in newspapers about Converse's remarkable Seneca life. They witnessed her political career and how her friends, colleagues, and even some among the Haudenosaunee themselves endorsed everything from her adoption to her receiving an honorary title in 1891 as a League chief in return for her tireless defense of Seneca land and sovereignty in court and in the public arena. In addition, she had a successful career in salvage ethnography, a term used to describe the predatory practices of people who made their livings and built their academic reputations on the acquisition (in some cases by dubious means), study, and sale of Indigenous material and oral culture.[3] To the public, Converse was not only an "authentic" Indian because of her adoption and honorary title, but her salvage also meant that she was a full-fledged expert on the Iroquois. To those who believed that the Iroquois needed "saving," who better than Converse to ensure that their names were not "yielded to silence"?

Ely S. Parker introduced Converse to his family and the Senecas after the two met in 1881. Over the next few years she grew so close to him and his extended family that his sister, Caroline Parker Mountpleasant, sponsored her adoption into the Seneca Snipe Clan in 1884. Once Converse was adopted, the combination of her "authenticity" and expertise on all things Haudenosaunee, not to mention her great skill in the written word, turned her into a celebrity among New Yorkers. The Parkers' influence gave Converse access to the highest levels of Indigenous society, which she used to expand her salvage activity. Over time, her fellow salvage ethnographers and other scholars participated in her ever-expanding salvaging empire to advance their own careers.

Converse thus contributed to the long history of salvage ethnographers participating in Indigenous cultural genocide. She believed that Haudenosaunee history and culture was an archivable thing in desperate need of saving but that her adoptive people seemed incapable of doing it themselves. So she dedicated herself to preserving and protecting their "vanishing" history. She eventually amassed and displayed a vast collection in her townhouse-turned-ethnography museum. Most of the cultural damage was incurred when she oversaw the transfer of vast stores of Haudenosaunee material culture to museums and private collectors. Converse became such a prominent voice among salvage ethnographers that she convinced her adopted peoples' leadership to give—and New York State to take—physical and legal ownership of all their wampum belts, the very objects that contained the political history of the Iroquois empire. This transfer gave meaningful contemporary weight to the memory of Iroquois exceptionalism.

She believed that the act of salvage was an essential part of her broader political strategy to protect Seneca sovereignty. Today this dualism appears paradoxical, but to Converse and some of her contemporaries (including Ely and Arthur Parker) it was not. With the vocal approval of key members of Haudenosaunee leadership who endowed her with honorary political titles, Converse spent two decades lending her considerable writing and administrative talents to the defense of their sovereignty against a new development in federal Indian policy: allotment. The goal of allotment, a policy that took brutal shape in the infamous 1887 Dawes General Allotment Act and in subsequent assimilation efforts, was to sever Native Americans from the land by undercutting their land rights and eliminating tribal sovereignty, all of which would ultimately destroy their cultures. This was joined by assimilation policies that were intended, as Carlisle Indian School founder Colonel Richard Henry Pratt infamously explained, to "release" Indians from "tribal relations" and bring them into civilized society by "kill[ing] the Indian" to "save the man" inside.[4] Allotment made room for groups like the Friends of the Indian who moved into those dismantled reservation spaces to educate, assimilate, and erase Indigenous cultures. As New York elected officials eagerly threw themselves into allotment fervor through the turn of the twentieth century, Converse committed herself to the legal and public defense of the Six Nations.

Therein lies the core of Converse's complex life. While she salvaged everything in sight, she did so as adopted kin and political ally. She was celebrated and reinforced by powerful allies—white and Haudenosaunee both. This was, on the part of Six Nations leadership, strategic. After all, once adopted she suddenly had a personal stake in the future of the Haudenosaunee. This even manifested in her salvage when she held certain cultural secrets away from the public eye, a fact that could not have been lost on her Seneca adopters who utilized her political talents to defend against allotment. She was not alone in this. As ethnographers today explain, Indigenous peoples adopted ethnographers due to a range of reasons from "pity or genuine affection to pragmatic calculation." Regardless of those motivations, a close personal connection between adopter and adoptee was a prerequisite.[5] It would therefore be a mistake to let the cultural damage she did diminish the immediate need for and contemporary seriousness of Converse's adoption and the bonds that were created on both sides in that moment. Of course not everyone agreed with the decision to let her get so close to the Haudenosaunee, but she was nevertheless publicly vetted and defended by leadership at strategic moments in their fight against allotment.

These forces came together in 1891 when, in return for her political service, the Seneca leadership gave her a membership in the Seneca Nation and the title of an honorary League chief, a representative to the Six Nations League.[6] These titles, the highest honors given to any adoptee, carried no real political authority and were granted only under extreme political circumstances, but the outside world did not understand that, nor did Converse or her supporters do anything to correct their misunderstanding. It certainly helped that Ely reinforced the authenticity of her kinship and leadership. To the non-Indigenous public, Converse was reborn in 1891 as an authentic white chief, a woman who was one of the most sought-after Indian experts in the country.

Historians have since called Converse the "chief publicist" of the Haudenosaunee, a "trusted advisor and advocate, challenging racial and cultural slurs and defending their civil and treaty rights, traditional Longhouse religious practices, their lands, and their governments." In 1908, her first biographer and protégé Arthur C. Parker praised her unique political career and dedication to her people. Historians and biographers since have been interested in Converse's politics and the ways in which she was influenced by her friend, Ely Parker.[7] What those narratives often miss, and what was so essential to her contributions to Iroquois exceptionalism, was how she herself controlled that narrative through how she viewed her kinship, politics, and salvage ethnography not as disparate aspects of her life, but as one and the same. She was colonial kin, a salvage ethnographer and adopted (and protected) Seneca, who saw no tension between the two. As key members of Haudenosaunee leadership and the white public agreed, she was both a salvage ethnographer dedicated to studying Iroquoian history by taking culture out of their control and an adopted kinswoman whose salvage ethnography and resultant fame made her a powerful political ally in the fight to protect Haudenosaunee laws, traditions, and memory.

Converse spent this period of her life in Manhattan and was adopted by the Senecas during a time when the so-called Wild West, an image of Americana invented by advertising studios in New York City and perpetuated across the world in elaborate theater productions, had collapsed America's perception of Native Americans into the mono-lithic stereotype of a war-bonneted and rifle-toting plains Indian. To New Yorkers, Converse put a familiar, local, exceptional face on what they would otherwise regard as an alien and dangerous people. She set an ex-ample for New Yorkers seeking racial stability in an interracial city and represented American exceptionalism and superiority amid the influx of vast numbers of foreign immigrants.[8] She was not alone in this. As the famed historian Henry Adams explained, the city's elite at the end of the nineteenth century were similarly creating their own identities on an is-land that had "become America's technological showplace, its communica-tions and information capital, its financial center," and had even created a "new type of man—a man with ten times the endurance, energy, will and mind of the old types." This energy was embodied by New York's powerful new cohort of Gilded Age industrialists who took on a near "mythical sig-nificance" as they flocked to Manhattan in the last half of the nineteenth century and disproportionately shaped local and national culture, politics, and the international economy.[9] In this environment, Converse and the Haudenosaunee she claimed to represent were eagerly embraced as yet an-other exceptional example of an exceptional people in an exceptional city.

Part of that exceptionality was reinforced by who Harriet Converse was. In the Gilded Age and Progressive Era, American women began participating in new and important ways with the national political, social, and intellectual landscapes. As public battles raged over women's suffrage, "New Women," and temperance, New Yorkers took particular interest in Converse. Even though she remained mostly silent on the issues concerning women's national polit-ical rights, she nevertheless benefitted from the public conversation about white women's new status in the economy and in politics. These shifting gender norms also affected how quickly the public embraced her as an expert on the Iroquois. This manifested most obviously in the transformation of her townhouse in New York City into an ethnographic *salon* that attracted the greatest anthropological and museological men of her day. These people vis-ited Converse to marvel at her vast collection of Indigenous material culture and ephemera, and to speak to the various Indigenous peoples who called on her. In that respect, Converse presented a unique twist on the work of middle- and upper-class women, most famously represented by groups like the Mount Vernon Ladies' Association, who created space for themselves within the male-dominated scholarly world by taking on the responsibility of preserving and protecting Americana, historic homes, and other national cultural resources.[10]

There was also a practical political dimension to her salvage. Salvage ethnographers often believed that robbing Indigenous peoples of their history and culture was for their benefit, and Converse was certainly in that camp. But there were also telling moments where she viewed the state itself as having a vital mission to protect Haudenosaunee history even as it actively attempted to subvert their sovereignty. For Converse, this understanding culminated in her support of the infamous cession of the Six Nations' wampum belts—the material archive of their geopolitical legacy—to the official ownership and care of New York State in 1898. In doing so, she had done her duty as colonial kin to "save" her adopted peoples' history. In her mind, who better than the Empire State itself to protect the legacy of its home-grown Indigenous empire?

None of these aspects of her life, however destructive or hypocritical, were lost on the Haudenosaunee. The public's perception of her mattered a great deal to the Six Nations leadership, who knew well the value and the risks of accepting outside help. Converse's Seneca life, in that sense, helps to illuminate an important facet of their varied defenses against illegal land seizures and legislative attacks on their sovereignty. Historians of the twentieth century Civil Rights era make a useful comparison to illustrate that strategy. They explain that Indigenous civil rights leaders brought on white people to help defend their communities from outside threats because it was clear that "whatever the strategies and tactics" they used, "given Native Americans' relative demographic insignificance, they all realized they could not do it alone. Non-Indians had to be reckoned with, educated, and enlisted. In short, the support and even active participation of sympathetic non-Indian people proved essential to any possible reform."[11] Converse, a well-connected and well-to-do woman who was also the best friend of the Senecas' most famous living son, was an obvious choice for this role.

Converse's life illuminates just how much public perception and the production of history mattered in the making of Iroquois exceptionalism. If Red Jacket had proven that exceptionality by example and Ely Parker through his inheritance, patriotism, and fame, Converse did it by popularizing a specific and limited image of Haudenosaunee "authenticity" amidst allotment, the myths of the Wild West, the realities of immigration, and the new role women played in American society. Ely and Arthur Parker both did much to protect her legacy (and theirs) and to remind New Yorkers that she was one of the Senecas' most famous daughters, adopted or not. Key contemporaries,

Haudenosaunee and white alike, also proved ready to reinforce and reinterpret this for their own ends. Converse's depictions of her own Seneca life helped to make indigeneity acceptable, even desirable, to New Yorkers who struggled to define their own national and cultural identity amid massive urban demographic change. While her story echoes the all-too-common narratives of those who claimed belonging and coopted Native American culture for their own ends, it also reveals how that very cooptation and adoptive kinship was utilized, and occasionally protected, by Haudenosaunee leadership who strategically deployed her in their fight against allotment.

Harriet Maxwell was born in Elmira, New York, in 1836 to a family that formed part of the lengthy chain of elite families who emigrated from Scotland and settled mostly in the Carolinas, Virginia, and Massachusetts after the English Civil War. The Maxwell family hailed from Cavaerlerock Castle, southeast of the town of Dumphries. Converse's great-grandfather, Alexander Maxwell, and his wife in 1770 set out for the British North American colonies following

FIGURE 3.1 Portrait of Harriet Maxwell Converse. *Myths and Legends of the New York State Iroquois*, 1908, 14.

the Seven Years' War. Shortly after they embarked, a violent storm halted their progress, and the ship was forced to stop in Patrick, Ireland.[12]

Converse's grandfather Guy Maxwell was born in Patrick, and two years later in 1772 the family once again set sail for North America. The family settled first in Carlisle, Pennsylvania, but shortly after left for Martinsburg, Virginia (now in West Virginia), a century-old enclave for Scottish migrants to North America. Guy eventually left for Milton, Pennsylvania, after his appointment as Pennsylvania's Justice of the Peace in 1788. Guy would leave his position in the Pennsylvania state government in 1794 to run a trading post in Seneca Country. His family, including a new son, Thomas Maxwell, moved to a house on the Chemung River located in a town we today call Elmira, New York. Thomas grew up at the trading post, and this was where he was reportedly adopted into the Seneca Wolf Clan, Red Jacket and Ely S. Parker's clan, at the turn of the nineteenth century. He later "fought with all the traditional ardor of a Scottish American" in the War of 1812.[13]

More than twenty years after the war, Harriet arrived as the youngest of Thomas' seven children. The details of her early life are not well known, but her biographers would later suggest that she "inherited" her obsession with Iroquois history and culture through her father, a "friend and favorite" of the local Senecas. By the 1860s, she had established herself as a published journalist and talented poet. The critics of the *New York Independent* thought "at least one" of her poems was "worthy of Keats." In 1860, Harriet married her second husband Franklin Converse, "father of the banjo," who gained fame as a musician and, with her financial assistance, wrote the banjo's staple instructional book. Frank himself was no stranger to Indian Country. Before he met Harriet, he had reportedly become a "great favorite of the Indians" of Illinois while traveling the region with a music group out of Chicago. Harriet and Frank would eventually move from White Plains, New York, to their new townhouse in New York City where they would spend the rest of their lives.[14]

In 1881, Harriet Converse met Ely S. Parker. Under his tutelage and devoted friendship that strengthened after he and his family moved from Connecticut to Manhattan, Converse's familial interest in Iroquois history and culture became a full-blown personal and intellectual obsession. Despite the fact that he never had time to write himself, Parker was regarded by Lewis H. Morgan and the following generation of anthropologists and "Indianologists" to be the foremost expert on Iroquois society and history. Through his family and political connections to leadership, he provided Converse with an elite insider's perspective on Seneca life, religion, customs, and politics. She was a quick study, ingratiated herself with Parker's family, and after a few years was adopted into the Seneca Snipe clan on the recommendation and with the sponsorship of Ely's sister, Caroline, and her husband, the Tuscarora chief John Mountpleasant. Converse's adoption meant that she had become kin and a cousin of the Parkers.[15]

Converse's adoption into the Snipe Clan came at a moment when the popular perception of Native Americans and Indian country was almost monolithically Western. The image of a mythologized Wild West dominated white American's popular understanding of Indian history, and it was used to determine Indigenous peoples' place within the industrialized postwar nation. The public's conception of Native Americans was, in large measure, rooted in the memories and dramatized stories of Indian violence and "savagery" that grew out of the Indian Wars of the 1860s–1880s.[16] As Ely Parker experienced while serving as Commissioner of Indian Affairs, the violence caused by the US Army in their enforcement of federal reservation policies highlighted the urgency of solving what many in the government saw as the "Indian problem." The government's solutions included allotment, citizenship, forced accultura-tion, and industrial education, all of which was written into law at the federal and local level and enforced at the tip of a bayonet. Americans, just as they had after the Civil War, saw the violence inherent in their racially redemp-tive promise of teaching Indians "civilization" and were only too happy to forget the realities of the Indian Wars. It was easier, therefore, to elide that violence and ignore the human and cultural toll these policies took in favor of a mythologized drama in which Americans' duty was to save the continent's "barbarous" Indigenous children from themselves.

For Americans, that mythology took visceral form as an immensely pop-ular form of middle class entertainment called Wild West shows. Starting in the 1860s, these shows, predominant among them Buffalo Bill's Wild West Show, brought the mythology of the Wild West to the country and the world. They revolved around familiar themes of "Race violence, manhood, and the home" and featured theater pieces that "thrilled" audiences who were riveted to stories of "white men ward[ing] off 'savage' dangers to the home in order to advance civilization." One of the most popular of these stories was "Attacks on the Settler's Cabin" in which a rough and ready man and his nuclear pio-neer family held back a tide of barbaric Indian invaders who sought to destroy his orderly homestead. The primary audience of these shows were urban and middle-class easterners, people from New York and other major eastern cities whose ticket sales fueled the growth of this form of popular entertainment. Given the distance between the audience and the subject matter, the Wild West Show producers felt free to stretch the truth and dramatize as they saw fit because, in most cases, viewers were mostly ignorant of the realities of the land, economies, and peoples who actually lived out west. The Wild West Shows dramatized violence as the means by which civilization triumphed over barbarism and, over decades, turned "violence against all savages, be they Indians or immigrants," from merely a regional "necess[ity]" during the Indian Wars into "a hallowed American tradition." These shows, rooted in those images of casual and thrilling violence, were so popular that, by 1906, the Western genre had become the "dominant subject of American drama."[17]

It was not violence alone that drew crowds, but also the fact that Wild West Shows were creative and performative masterpieces. Remarkably diverse corps of actors gave audiences the chance to come face-to-face with a controlled image of a multiracial America. The audience wept at the tragic romanticism of doomed warrior-leaders like the Chiricahua Apache Geronimo and the Lakota Sitting Bull. They took a patronizing liking to the industrious Chinese worker, jeered the Mexican "racial degenerates" and the archetypical "savage" Indians, pitied the occasional "noble savage" who lost his homeland, and laughed at and sang along with black minstrels. The producers of Wild West Shows spared no expense putting on these performances. Audiences jumped at the sound of rifles and smelled the burning gunpowder from cannons, felt the thundering of hooves from dozens of live horsemen performing in mock battles set at Little Big Horn and Wounded Knee, and watched well-known actors and real-life frontiersman perform the epic of Hiawatha or fight against the Mexican army at the Alamo.[18]

Urban Americans saw these Wild West stories through the lens of the ongoing problems they faced in their own neighborhoods. The dramatized tale of civilized men facing down non-white "uncivilized" invaders fit easily into contemporary Americans' belief in Anglo-America's social, political, racial, economic, and technological superiority, which informed their views on the waves of immigrants arriving on their shores from Europe and Asia. For those living in New York City, like Converse, the "simmering" problems of late nineteenth century immigration were reflected in its astounding impact on the city that, as historians explain, "seemed about to collapse into a cacophony of inharmonious differences." The Wild West Shows offered some order to the chaos in the form of a comforting story of American civilization triumphing over barbarity. World's Fairs delivered a similar message during massive multiweek public spectacles that offered white Americans "visible proof" of a rigid global racial hierarchy dominated by Anglo-Americans. Celebrating the enormous power of the modern Euro-American industrial economy, the Fairs contrasted this by creating ethnographic villages that were populated by other races and people. In the famed 1893 Columbian World's Exposition in Chicago, for example, the ethnography division, headed by the famed anthropologist Frederick Ward Putnam, hired natives and "primitives" from around the world to live in mock villages for the duration of the fair to "entertain, titillate, and educate," as well as make a handsome profit from selling "commercialized exoticism."[19]

That manufactured battle between civilization versus savagery, indeed in the notion that there was some global hierarchy of races, was evident in Converse's own perception of Native America. Her scrapbook contained news clippings about the Crow, the Mille Lacs, the Ottawa, and individuals like Sitting Bull who all fell to the might of the US Army and to what reporters called their own "wretched conditions." She also followed Indian policy at the highest levels of government, as indicated by her clippings from Indian Commissioner J. D. C. Atkins in 1886 who advocated for the "Removal of All Extreme Western Indians."[20] In addition to her interest in policy, Converse the salvage ethnographer was involved in some capacity with the 1901 Pan-American Exposition in Buffalo, New York, through her friend, Frederick Putnam, who had also organized the Columbian Exposition. She even had a hand in a Wild West–style show as she supported the career of Edward Cornplanter, a Christian Seneca convert to *Gaiwiio* who, at various times in the 1890s, performed in Wild West companies from the famous *Flaming Arrow* national tour show and eventually created his own Red Jacket Tour Company.[21]

These activities, however, do not square with what Converse encountered in or wrote about Iroquois country. She told New Yorkers that her people were not a stereotypically Western, uncivilized, and violent type, but rather an exceptional people apart from the rest of Native America. Part of her understanding of that exceptionality manifested in her desire to connect herself to Red Jacket. After she was adopted into the Seneca Snipe clan, she inaccurately claimed that she had been adopted into the same clan as Red Jacket, revealing that her understanding of kinship ties was somewhat twisted. As Arthur C. Parker explained in Converse's posthumously published *Myths and Legends of the New York Iroquois*, Red Jacket was a member of the Wolf Clan of which Converse's father Thomas—not Harriet—was supposedly adopted decades earlier. There was a connection there, Parker acknowledged, but more relevant for Converse was the fact that the Snipe Clan were the ancestors of Red Jacket's stepdaughter, Ruth Stevens, the caretaker of the orator's remains before their interment at Forest Lawn Cemetery. In other words, Converse's adoption made her a descendant of Red Jacket's wife's kin, not Red Jacket or his maternal line.[22]

Converse's attempts to get closer to Red Jacket's legacy and claim it as evidence of Iroquois (and her own) exceptionality was not entirely unexpected. After all, Red Jacket was, even in the 1880s, an outstanding example of Iroquois "natural dignity and suavity," a man of heroic status who "lived and died a patriotic Indian," and was of the same bloodline as her dear friend Ely's family. Converse had even saved a physical piece of the Seneca orator when she took flowers "from the casket which contained the remains of Red Jacket" to preserve in her scrapbook.[23] Through kinship and through physical objects, Converse sought to move herself closer to Red Jacket, the "Last of the Seneca," an enduring symbol of Iroquois exceptionalism.

Another way that Converse understood Iroquois exceptionality was through her adoption and elevation in the political ranks of the historic—but now, she thought, "vanished"—Six Nations Confederacy. When Converse was first adopted in 1884, she inaccurately explained that, decades before her adoption, some "old tribal customs [had been] abolished" but they were "dusted off" in preparation for her adoption. She said the same thing about the Condolence ceremony in 1891 where she became a member of the Seneca nation in a "forgotten rite [that] would be reproduced" from ancient memory specifically for her. Later that year, when Six Nations League chief Daniel La Forte in a "special council" declared her an "honorary member" of the League, she did not claim responsibility for the revival of any ceremonies but still saw herself as the newest representative of the "expiring" Iroquois Confederacy, an historic empire that once held "subjugating power" that "dictated war and peace" in the region. She explained that the Six Nations were a "military alliance once courted by the crowns of France and England" and a "proud sovereignty whose lordly patrimony" once dominated other Indigenous nations from the Hudson River to the Great Lakes. Threaded throughout her language of dead people, customs, and ancient history was Converse's own understanding of the Iroquois as a group of living and breathing people who were, in large measure, defined by their past as a grand empire central to the rise of the Empire State's dominion that had since "vanished." Even her use of Ely Parker's language in *Myths* reflected this thinking. She received a letter from Parker after she was given the honorary title of League chief in which he praised the "honors . . . showered upon (Converse) by the remnants" of the Iroquois, the "simple but honest hearted children of our ancient forest" who gave her membership in their empire that, as "empty and shadowy though they may be," was an honor she rightly deserved.[24]

Perhaps the most important way that she interpreted Iroquois exceptionality was through salvaging the material and oral history of the "grand Indian empire."[25] After her adoption, she became ever more fascinated and inspired by their "laws and customs" and "marveled at their wonderous national vitality (and) their endurance." Converse visited every Haudenosaunee reservation in New York and Canada at least once, perhaps even visiting each once per year. On her visits she claimed to be "showered" with gifts by strangers wherever she went which sparked in her a love of collecting material culture. By the 1890s, she had accumulated so much that she had "probably the finest private collection" of Haudenosaunee and "Indian relics in the world, including a full set of wampum belts." Converse's lifetime of collecting, for some observers, proved that she truly "loved" her people. Others, like Ely Parker, praised her salvage as having true educational and cultural value. In a glowing letter that she included in the introduction of her 1892 "The Historic Iroquois Indians" lecture series, Parker commented that by the late 1880s Converse had collected and done so much work on Iroquois culture that she had become *the best informed woman* on Indian lore in America!" Similarly, Daniel G. Brinton, an archaeologist and president of the Association for the Advancement of Science, praised her "highly appreciated" work on the Iroquois, claiming that it "will increase interest in the study of Indianology."[26]

Converse was hardly alone in her impulse to preserve aspects of American culture, which by the end of the nineteenth century was regarded as a middle- and upper-class feminine venture. The women involved in these efforts "took particular pride in demonstrating their patriotism" through the creation of preservation societies like the Mount Vernon Ladies' Association and the Ladies' Hermitage Association. Through her salvage of Haudenosaunee culture, Converse joined the ranks of many women in New York, Boston, and Philadelphia who collected American art and objects and were therefore regarded as "the patrons of tradition and Americana."[27] Leveraging the social and intellectual acceptability of women's participation in historic preservation, Converse took that a step further and converted her townhouse on West 20th Street into an ethnographic museum and *salon*, both of which were well attended and well received by the most prominent anthropologists and intellectuals of the period.

Converse's transformation of her home into a hub of the city's intellectual life combined two contemporary trends. The home was still considered a private space, but more and more middle- and upper-class women were participating in a new "design trend" of displaying various foreign items and artistic motifs for the enjoyment of their visitors. This trend reflected the individual's own taste, of course, but it was made possible by America's growing global economic interconnectedness and, for many, demonstrated women's active participation in that economy. The second trend touched on the traditionally "masculine" act of collecting itself. More and more women were collecting foreign objects for the more masculine goal of "solidity," or the notion that displaying their collections demonstrated an appreciation of the items' educational or financial value rather than just visual appeal. Converse's creation of a public education-oriented gallery in her own home reflected these trends, but hers was no ordinary home display. These objects made up one of the greatest private collections of Indigenous material culture in the city, and the participants in Converse's *salon* were among the greatest minds in ethnography and museology including Ely and Arthur Parker; *Puck* magazine owner, cartoonist, and future Seneca adoptee Joseph (Udo) Keppler; Columbia University and the American Museum of Natural History (AMNH) anthropologist Franz Boas; famed ornithologist and naturalist Frank Chapman; archaeologist of the AMNH and future director of the Southwest Museum Mark Harrington; and the anthropologist of the Peabody Museum at Harvard University and the AMNH, Frederick Putnam.[28]

As the centerpiece of New York's Indian Colony, her home also offered Indigenous visitors to the city a refuge from "the hurley-burley" of New York's busy streets and provided them with supplies if they needed assistance.[29] Newspapers reported that the colonists themselves, some of whom visited her townhouse and attended the *salon*, were industrious and hard working. For New Yorkers, these were an entirely different racial group than immigrants who were characterized by their pauperism, mental deficiencies, greed, criminal activity, and alcoholism.

As the leader of the Colony, Converse was a highly desirable guide for those outsiders planning visits to Iroquois country. For example, Converse in 1886 agreed to escort the State Indian Agent Thomas D. Green and ex-Utica Mayor C.W. Hutchinson to the Onondagas. There, the two men were introduced to "head pagans" like Oneida League chief Daniel LaFort, the "leader" of the Christianized Indians "Jarius Pierce," the local celebrity "Aunt Cynthia Farrar" who spent her small fortune to purchase land back for Haudenosaunee debtors, and the 107 year old "Aunt Dinah," the last living person in the United States to collect a pension from the War of 1812. For her guests, these sorties into the reservations combined visiting the proud and "civilized" Haudenosaunee with a calming reprieve from the racial and class tensions in the city caused by the ongoing waves of immigration. To Converse, she held up the Haudenosaunee as the best of what historians of this era have defined as "conceivable aliens," or people who were clearly not white but also not as bad as most immigrants.[30] The Iroquois were seen as first Americans, not strange or inconceivable foreigners, and were therefore understood by some to be worthy of societal and racial redemption.

Converse's notion that the Haudenosaunee were a unique and civilized people was part of an ongoing but deeply flawed social reform movement that was best observed in an organization called the Friends of the Indian. The Friends were an influential group of men and women who established the Lake Mohonk Conference, held every year at Lake Mohonk, New York, from 1883 to 1916. They met to argue and discuss policy solutions to several social and political topics, one of the major ones being how best to assimilate Native Americans into American society. They correctly diagnosed severe problems in Indian legislation and in the reservation system, and to fix them they "proclaim(ed) themselves 'the conscience of the American people on the Indian question.'" In the Friends' view, Indigenous voices were sublimated to outsiders who were driven by the belief that "the Indians' own judgment could not be trusted."[31] The only chance society had to save Indians and their memory from a corrupted federal system, not to mention to clear their tribal land for "progress," was to absorb them into the American population by educating and Christianizing them in order to transform them into proper members of a civilized nation. This, however, required the elimination of their social, cultural, economic, and religious traditions, as well as the severance of people from their land, which ultimately meant the elimination of the reservation system and their sovereign political rights.

It proved to be a powerful and popular idea. The Friend's campaign to eliminate tribes' claims to resource-rich land eventually inspired the passage of the federal General Allotment Act of February 8, 1887, more popularly known as the Dawes Act, which had significant consequences throughout Indian country. Written by Henry Dawes, a Senator from Massachusetts and Friend of the Indian, the Act gave the US president the authority to order that reservations "be surveyed, or resurveyed if necessary, and to allot the lands in said reservation in severalty to any Indian located thereon." The Dawes Act allotted each Native American family member a diminishing amount of property (starting with the male head of household and moving down to children) carved from the reservation whole. By allotting land to individuals, supplanting Indian political authority, and placing the authority of this process under the Secretary of the Interior, the Dawes Act eliminated the political authority and independence of tribal governments. In the West, allotment was used as a wedge to separate Native peoples from their land by predatory federal, state, and local officials, as well as private companies and speculators.[32]

The Dawes Act was also inspired by the recent memory of the Indian Wars. The violent resistance of Indigenous nations to the Army's brutal dispossessions and murders provided ample evidence to the United States that the power of Native American nations must be weakened. The Dawes Act decentralized and destabilized them, threatening "cultural genocide by forced integration." Yet contemporary Progressive reformers and Friends rejoiced and "proclaimed (it) the equivalent of the Magna Carta, the Declaration of Independence, and the Emancipation Proclamation all rolled into one." It would, they claimed, save Indigenous peoples from extinction by incorporating them into "civilized" society. From 1887 to 1900, 150 million acres of reservation territory across the continent dwindled to 77 million as Friends, private investors, land speculators, and mining companies pounced on seized Indigenous land.[33]

The Dawes Act did not, however, apply in the same way to the Senecas in New York. The reservations were deemed a self-governed area protected by treaties and private property rights and was therefore "explicit[ly] exempt[ed]" from allotment. New York State knew this, so the legislature wasted little time trying to find ways to apply the Act to these reservations. In 1888, a special committee of the New York State legislature was formed and chaired by Assemblyman J. S. Whipple of Cattaraugus to investigate how New York tribal governments allotted their land to their members, to test the legitimacy of both Indian title to the land and the claims of Ogden Company "and any other companies or organizations or individuals," and to review in full the treaties signed between the state, the federal government, and New York's "Indians therein." The committee concluded in February 1889 that despite the Senecas' relatively protected sovereign status, New York could legally replace the current reservations with an allotment system that recreated the conditions of the Dawes Act.[34]

Converse responded to this. She attempted to prove, through her own personal experience, Haudenosaunee exceptionality, making her efforts to discredit the Whipple Report her first real political test as an adopted Seneca. After the Report was published, she reached out to her extensive contacts and found among them a kindred spirit and a man who would prove to be a valuable ally in the coming political battles: Joseph Keppler Jr., the son of the German-born founder and cartoonist of the famous *Puck* magazine. Keppler was well-known among politicians in New York and Washington as an accomplished political cartoonist who gained fame through his scathing critiques of corporate monopolies and US imperialism abroad. He was also on the board of the West Shore and Buffalo Railway and served as the Tonawanda

Reservation's point of contact with the railroad, giving him some experience with Haudenosaunee politics. On Converse's urging, Keppler stepped into the fight to discredit the Whipple Report and, a few years later, was effective enough that he was given the Senecas' power of attorney to negotiate on their behalf in Washington DC. In return for his service to the Senecas, Keppler was adopted in 1898. Converse later in life even suggested that Keppler would "take her place" among the Senecas as an honorary League chief after she died.[35]

The Senecas' fight took on new urgency in 1891 when J.S. Whipple authored an eponymously named bill that translated the report's language into legislation. The new Whipple bill would subject the Senecas to the Dawes Act and force citizenship on the Haudenosaunee. Through Converse, the Six Nations were able to respond to the State Legislature as one. In June 1891, a Seneca man named Ska-na-wah-deh, the Seneca chief and "Speaker of the Fire Keepers" John Buck, and the Secretary of the Six Nations Council at the Ohsweken Council House in Onondaga Josiah Hill, requested that Converse deliver to Congress a wampum belt that included the joint statement of the Six Nations protesting the bill. They also entrusted her with petitioning the state legislature and the governor, a trust which paid off when Governor David B. Hill refused to sign the Whipple bill due in part to Converse's representation of the Haudenosaunee and her conveyance of Iroquois public opinion to the wider New York public. In recognition of her efforts, the Senecas at a Condolence ceremony in September granted her the name "Gaiiwanoh, or 'Our Watcher'" and elevated her to Seneca national membership. Later that year, she was further recognized with a new honorary title as a Six Nations League chief.[36]

Converse saw herself as a new member of Six Nations political leadership, and this made her more sensitive to other nonlegislative issues that threatened them. She took a broad and critical look at what exactly New Yorkers understood about the Haudenosaunee. Public opinion helped convince Governor Hill not to sign the Whipple bill, so she realized how important it was to more clearly define what Iroquois "authenticity" meant to as wide a public as possible. Central to that effort was identifying who, exactly, was kin—truly adopted—as opposed to merely a "friend" of the Haudenosaunee. The public mostly knew about naming, or informal and sometimes invented ceremonies in which a person was given an "Indian Name" but not actually adopted. As the Whipple fights unfolded, Converse suggested to the Haudenosaunee that a public discussion clarifying what naming meant—or didn't mean—should be included as part of major public festival occasions like the seasonal Green Corn Dance held in Buffalo in 1902.[37]

Converse focused energy on naming in large part because she was sensitive to how her own reputation was being used and misused in public forums. In the Spring 1893 edition of the *Journal of American Folklore*, Converse responded to a letter to the editor from Sara L. Lee, a reader from Boston, about Iroquoian history, naming, and belonging. This all took place in the "Scrap Book" section of the journal, an interactive section that Converse knew had the power to promote potentially destructive myth-building, particularly given readers' tendency to send in charming anecdotes about ages past and the people left behind by modernity like "Negro superstition concerning the violin" and Christopher Columbus' belief that Friday was an unlucky day. In the "Scrap Book," Converse responded to Lee's original letter which sought to correct a newspaper article that Converse had published focusing on women "firsts" in Native America. Lee took issue with the claim that Converse herself was the first white woman ever to be adopted into the Haudenosaunee. Before that claim could become "settled error," Lee reminded the *Journal* readership of a "Mrs. Ermine A. Smith," a woman she claimed was the "first white woman adopted by a tribe of the Six Nations [the Tuscarora]" in 1880.[38] This mattered to Lee because it was Smith, not Converse who was adopted five years later, who was first.

Lee foregrounded the issue of gender and expertise when Smith, a real first, was recognized by none other the influential ethnographer Horatio Hale as a woman whose pursuit of "studies in Indianology . . . *alone* would make any *man* famous." Lee praised Smith's unyielding pursuit of knowledge and charity in Iroquois country, a strenuous effort that eventually endangered her health. Such was Smith's devotion that, despite her declining health, she continued to spend sporadic "years" living among the Iroquois. Lee ended her letter with a nod to the pioneering spirit of these kinds of women and other firsts, even mentioning Converse herself, when she conceded that "too much honor cannot be paid to Mrs. Smith, Mrs. Converse, and other women who are devoting their energies to the Christian work of helping Indians."[39]

In her rebuttal to Lee's letter, Converse explained that Lee was an example of the many who fundamentally misunderstood the critical nuances of adoptions and kinship and, by extension, mischaracterized not only who counted as an Iroquoian first, but more importantly missed the finer points of Haudenosaunee-granted "authenticity." In a lengthy response, Converse clarified for the *Journal's* audience that Lee did not know about the "various degrees of induction" into Haudenosaunee familial and political networks.

She outlined five distinct levels of adoption ranging from "a name given" at the lowest and most informal level (and the "most common" because of the simple "friendliness" of a Haudenosaunee person who gave an outsider a name and so "adopted" them) to the highest level of a "league adoption" when a person becomes a "member of *all* the six tribes." Among the Iroquois, name adoptions of "foreigners" were quite "common" for "white men and women," many of whom had been embraced by families and clans since the eighteenth century but never actually entered a Haudenosaunee kinship network in any formal capacity. So, while Smith's adoption was relatively uncommon because she entered the Tuscarora at the third level of a family or "clan adoption," she did not compare to what Converse understood as her adoption one level higher into the Seneca "*tribe*," much less her honorary title of League chief, a political elevation "so rare in occurrence" that it "immediately becomes history."[40]

"Firsts" like these mattered to Converse and her contemporaries. As historians have explained, the desire to find firsts reflected society's need to construct a national mythology that variously Anglicized a diverse nation, helped them to discover an exceptional history, helped individuals to make a profit, satisfied one's desire to "fool the experts," and collectively created a national narrative that legitimized American's own curated historical understanding of themselves in order to soothe their social anxieties. Converse's response to Lee's letter was her attempt not only to claim legitimate Iroquoian political authority (of which she had none), but also to bind her legacy to the legendary Seneca captive Mary Jemison, a woman many New Yorkers regarded as a true first. Converse described Jemison as an English New York colonist who was taken captive "during the Revolutionary War" at thirteen years of age, was later "inducted into the Seneca Nation," and became "the first" woman to be adopted into one of the Six Nations. Calling on Jemison's memory was a strategic move because Jemison, like Red Jacket, was a well-known patriotic figure and an object of American folklore whose captivity narrative was wildly popular in its day and at the end of the nineteenth century. When it was published in 1824, the *Narrative of the Life of Mary Jemison* was one of only four American publications (alongside James Fenimore Cooper's *Leatherstocking Tales* series) that sold more than 100,000 copies in the first three years of publication in Europe and the United States.[41]

In the context of the Indian Wars and the Wild West, Converse's evocation of Jemison was swept up in the drama of warfare and violence because Jemison's was not just an autobiography from America's founding moments, but a dramatic and engaging captivity narrative. This genre combined the taboo of racial mixing with the romanticism of a "savage" capture to create a dramatic story that pitted civilization against savagery, male against female, and white against red. The stories themselves often elided the very real violence experienced by captives as well as those who had been "redeemed" back into Anglo-American society, but that was hardly the point.[42] The violence of captivity and the captive's voluntary rejection of Euro-American society had a dark voyeuristic tone that captivated Euro-American audiences for generations. Converse, of course, was a far cry from a captive, but by positioning herself with Jemison as one of the two most famous white women in history to be formally adopted into one of the Six Nations, she was able to harness the allure of the myth of captivity. Converse leveraged what many New Yorkers understood as her peaceful ascension to the upper echelons of Haudenosaunee society and politics and spun it as yet another piece of evidence to be used against those who saw the Iroquois as no different than their violent brethren of the West.

Beyond Converse's discussion of historic Indigenous women, she generally did not speak about issues relevant to American women in the 1890s. Instead, her public discussions of women were primarily used to educate the public on Iroquois exceptionality when compared to other Indigenous tribes. Still, although Converse never wrote about suffrage, prohibition, or women's expanded economic, societal, and political roles, women in the suffrage movement used her incredible political career as proof of women's political potential. They, in other words, coopted Converse's false narrative about her own Seneca life, particularly her honorary title of League chief, a distinction that others highlighted along with her membership in organizations like the New York Women's Press Club, the American Authors Guild, and the Buffalo Historical Society.[43]

In contrast to how other women saw her, Converse's own perspectives on women were less clear. In her pamphlet "How I Became a Seneca Indian," she does not dwell long on the role of women in adoptions or elections, though she does mention them. While she was clearly willing to tie herself to Red Jacket and Mary Jemison, she was less willing to reveal the vital role women played in her adoption. Still, the pamphlet in most respects is a fascinating and telling first-person perspective of Converse's adoption ceremony. She begins by describing the invitation to join the Snipe from "the Seneca Chief Tho-no-se-wa and his wife." The nameless "wife" was Caroline Parker Mountpleasant, a close friend and the first Seneca person Converse met when Ely brought her to the Tonawanda reservation in 1881. Converse's description of the adoption ceremony included many Senecas dressed in "old-time costumes" and, of the four types of people she saw and described in the crowd, two groups were women, one was a group of children of no specific gender, and the last was of "young chieftains." Once the public adoption ceremony was announced, "elderly Indian women" began preparing for a feast. Beyond this, however, Converse gave relatively little analytical space in her writing to women's roles in Iroquois government. She referenced the fact that Haudenosaunee "women have a voice in the councils," but not what that means. In her description of the 1891 Condolence Ceremony where she received her name "Ya-ie-wa-noh, or 'Our Watcher,'" she described being "seated between two aged matrons who acted as my sponsors, assuming the responsibility of my nomination." Clan mothers were responsible for sponsoring tribal leadership, though Converse did not attribute any agency to them, nor did she mention that these Clan mothers were also responsible for selecting the potential leaders who the men would then vote on. Yet she still noticed that these "matrons" escorted her to her seat as a "guardian" of the eastern door of the symbolic Longhouse, a political act that carried symbolic meaning.[44]

Converse did, however, offer one unique and telling thought about women in contemporary Haudenosaunee society. She generally described their society as a primarily agricultural one, although ceded that some did live in "the primitive way." In general, her description of men did not challenge the stereotype of the Indian "stoic." The men were "of fine physique, broad-shouldered, deep-chested," as tall as "pines," and all possessed a "quiet dignity." But women were an exception. They did not live in the "primitive way" as the stereotypical "squaws" of the Wild West did, but kept "elegant" homes and were "usually well educated, are amiable, domestic, industrious, presiding over their tastefully furnished houses with an undefinable grace and an ease that seems born to their people."[45] Through these women, Converse chose to reveal an exceptional Iroquois existence that was quite different than what many expected to find in the rest of Native America. Her descriptions also revealed an aspect of reservation life often ignored by reformers, politicians, and Friends who sought out and even manufactured stories of poverty and backwardness among Indigenous peoples to legitimize and valorize their humanitarian work.

Converse's limited exposure to reservation life also reveals a bias in what she saw and who she met in her travels. Her close friendship with Parker ensured that she spent most of her time with Christian leadership and relatively wealthy families, and her own social background primed her to find and visit those who were most like herself. When Converse described their homes as she might any of her white neighbors', she exposed the Haudenosaunee—a people that many regarded as "foreign"—as living, decorating, and thinking in ways that were immediately recognizable to non-Indigenous readers. In so doing, she once again described a markedly different people than those Western Plains Indian tribes popularized by Wild West Shows and more like the Gilded Age elite. Historians have understood Americans at the end of the nineteenth century as generally seeking "authentic" Indians "obsessively" because they were examples of a people "far outside the temporal bounds of modern society," but Converse, in this case, did the opposite.[16] She sought out like elements of her own life in Haudenosaunee culture in order to fit them squarely within the American mainstream.

In that light, historians have missed some important aspects of her writing on gender in her sole published ethnographic volume, *Myths and Legends of the New York Iroquois* (1908). At first glance, Converse's language on women's rights in *Myths* is direct and pointed, and it drew a clear bridge between the Haudenosaunee and the women's suffrage movement. Under the section titled "Women's Rights Among the Iroquois," for example, she introduced the reader to an Indian people who "generations before the coming of the palefaces to this country" created a political system wherein the " 'mother' or women's rights should be included in the law and be forever protected." *Myths* also explained that the Haudenosaunee were matrilineal, so children do not inherit the father's property or title. Instead, the Haudenosaunee inherit their titles, property, and kinship ties through their mothers and grandmothers. Women, as *Myths* explained, were also arbiters of political and religious ceremonies. Clan mothers retained the exclusive power to grant family names and leadership titles to "reliable" men of her family to replace a family member who had passed away or was removed from office with a vote that included the clan mothers. Women were even keepers of " 'Chief's belts,' " or the important records tracing the lineages to determine who was eligible for election to political office. Without these women-owned belts, "no attention was paid to any nomination unless confirmed by these wampum belts." What was more, women's "legal rights were never interfered with" as her "civil claims" were considered "sacred." Clearly, Converse's language in *Myths* is much stronger than her other comments on Iroquois women in any regard.[47] *Myths*, therefore, represents more of the political mindset of Arthur Parker, Converse's protégé and editor of the volume, than Converse's own thoughts. It was published posthumously by Parker, and it is not a stretch to see how he may well have buttressed her limited interest in women's roles in Haudenosaunee society and American women's fight for political rights, much in the same way that he invented his Uncle Ely's "real American" comment at Appomattox at the end of the Civil War.

Myths, a collection of Converse's essays and ethnographic analyses, also points to her most important contribution to preserving and protecting the memory of the Haudenosaunee: her salvage ethnography. She was one of many archaeologists and ethnologists of the time who stole, bought, or traded in Indian material culture without regard for tribal need or much care for their cultural practices, and who profited directly from the removal of "prehistoric" material culture from Native American hands.[48] As predatory as this practice was, Converse and her contemporaries nevertheless saw her collecting as central to her identity as an adopted kin who was fighting to protect Seneca sovereignty and to prevent Haudenosaunee history itself from disappearing. After her adoption in 1884, she spent considerable time transcribing Iroquois oral histories and mythology, writing about their secret societies, and collecting and preserving vast stores of their material culture. Following her supposed elevation to Haudenosaunee leadership in 1891, Converse was able to amass huge collections of historic and culturally significant materials and donated, sold, or traded them through her *salon* and elsewhere to museums and other private collections.

Soon after her honorary appointment as a League chief, she had taken so much that she was widely regarded as one of the most important contacts for salvage ethnographers seeking to collect and study Haudenosaunee culture. She and her *salon* became the nexus of an economic network that catered to collectors and museums looking to buy and trade culturally and politically significant—and sometimes insignificant—objects from the Haudenosaunee and other Native Americans in the name of scientific exploration and profit. Of the many items she bought and sold, one of the more prized commodities she traded in was wampum. Wampum belts, individual beads, and strings were used to keep a record of international councils, economic exchanges, and diplomacy, and once they appeared in Converse's trade network they were quickly sold to the highest bidder. Converse also salvaged *hadu:wi*, misnamed "false face" masks. These were particularly sought-after objects due to their highly sensitive and secretive spiritual use, but also because collectors and museum curators used these masks' alien and sometimes frightening visages as the perfect centerpiece or capstone to a Native American history exhibit. "Mrs. Converse" was known to have bought a "number" of "real old (masks)" over the years and from these, reproductions were made and provided to other museums, which itself became a lucrative subbusiness of salvage ethnography and continued for decades after she had passed away. The masks' rarity and sensitivity would suggest there were not many to go around, yet Converse managed to collect and sell so many different masks between 1881 and 1903 that, in the New York State Museum alone, 100 of them had survived the 1911 Albany capital fire that all but destroyed multiple other collections.[49]

Converse's salvage interests were not limited to unique Haudenosaunee political or cultural items, either. At her townhouse in Manhattan, she displayed a "Jackson" Indian Peace Medal, a knife and leather scabbard, tobacco pouches supposedly owned by Red Jacket, beads, blankets, a "tomahawk" that she used "as a paperweight," and a "war-dance drum" she used "for a waste-basket." She also displayed curios that ranged from paddles supposedly filled with "small pox germs, yellow fever, etc." to transcriptions she or others took of Haudenosaunee oral histories and mythologies. Many of these items were sold from in her townhouse after she passed away to museums or Frederick Putnam. Famously, Converse had also acquired the largest collection of Haudenosaunee silver brooches ever collected, which she donated to the New York State Museum in her father's honor. The collection was originally held by the "pagan wife" of Red Jacket, but since each of the ninety-four items were inherited and traded over decades "across the Six Nations," individual provenance was unknown. The collection included brooches of Algonquin origin, which her descendants claimed were taken from a "captive in the old age." Most important to her was a silver brooch given to Red Jacket after he was, she inaccurately claimed, inducted into the Freemasons. Her collecting over the decade was so vast, her sales and donations to museums so great, that Melville Dewey, Secretary of the Board of Regents for the State University of New York and the creator of the eponymous library classification system, argued that she was singularly responsible for "building up" the New York State Museum's "new Indian museum." The museum staff gave ger an "Indian name," "The Woman Who Works for the Indians," and she was made an "honorary member of the University staff as the Indians so wisely have made you a chief among them." Due to the extraordinary growth and size of their new collections due to Converse's contributions, Dewey drafted a bill in 1896 on behalf of the Board of Regents for the State Legislature to create a new ethnography department within the museum.[50]

While Converse saw her salvage as a reflection of her political responsibilities to the Six Nations, there was an obvious tension between her academic enterprises and her personal commitment to protecting the memory and heritage of her adoptive people. In some ways, her kinship skewed what she chose to make public. For example, in an article in 1892 in the St. Louis newspaper *The Republic*, she described the history and traditions of

FIGURE 3.2 Photograph of Iroquois silver brooches donated to the New York State Museum by H. M. Converse. *Myths and Legends of the New York State Iroquois*, 1908, Plate 5.

the Iroquoian medicine society called "Ne-gar-na-gar-ah," a secret society of healers of which Converse was a member. Claiming that she had the blessing of the members of the society (highly doubtful), she publicized information about this secret society of healers, its history, and the "deeply religious spirit" that motivated its members. Yet she carefully rejected outsider's claims that the society used "pagan profanities," a clear sign of an "uncivilized" people, in its work healing the community. To make the secret society more palatable to an American audience, she refused to elaborate on certain details to protect the more sensitive practices and, significantly, drew comparisons between the Society and Christianity in order to make it appear even less "uncivilized."[51]

In 1897, Converse's salvage and her brand of cultural and political protectionism came together at a crucial moment in Six Nations politics when she raised the question of who, exactly, was responsible for preserving and protecting their history. She laid out the problem in a memorial published in *The Buffalo Examiner* in 1897 on the death of Thomas Webster, a Seneca of the Snipe clan who for sixty years was the "Ho-no-we-na-to," or "he who holds the wampum" for the Confederacy. Converse explained that in his capacity as Keeper and interpreter of history and law, Webster had unilateral control over the Six Nations' wampum archives, a job that was "imperative, his office absolute and important." No one questioned the interpretation of the Keeper. But once he passed away, Haudenosaunee leadership found that many of the belts he was responsible for were missing. Converse despaired that, with his death, any memory of those belts vanished and so a piece of Six Nations history and diplomacy were forever lost. In response, she issued a desperate plea to the public for help: "It would be poetical and retributive justice if all who possess any relics of these once magnificent people would donate them to the State of New-York, there to be seen and forever preserved as memorials of the Confederacy of the Iroquois."[52]

She made the case that her adoptive people were literally dying, losing their history, and it was up to the state to preserve their legacy. The transfer of these belts from the Onondagas to New York was about more than cultural preservation. Not only were they an integral part of historic Haudenosaunee diplomacy with Europeans, the belts were (and are) an official Indigenous state record. Converse's belief that New York needed to both own and protect that aspect of Iroquoian sovereignty shows that she felt that New York State was the appropriate and obvious authority to archive and protect the belts. As anthropologist William N. Fenton explained more than eighty years later in response to an attempt by the Onondagas in 1971 to repatriate the belts, "Wampum" was a vital Iroquois material and political legacy "as American as apple pie, the log cabin, and the splint basket." It thus deserves to be protected "for all of the people" of America, but only by those best qualified.[53] For Converse, this meant that New York State was best suited to preserve that history.

If the Iroquois empire had given life to the Empire State, then the formal transfer of the Six Nations' political legacy to New York State signaled the latest event in that historic inheritance. But as much as Converse thought this was a natural choice, the cession of vital collections of Native American heritage to state governments—not to private museums or collectors—was an uncommon occurrence in the 1890s. The idea that a state government had a responsibility to preserve its own history only became widespread during the New Deal in the 1930s. Then, the state governments became the default

repository for similar types of collections and further developed a vested interest in preserving their own state histories. In Converse's time, the general
assumption was that private money—not public resources—would fund the
preservation and maintenance of historical collections and, as Ely Parker experienced, raise monuments and memorials. There was some public-private
cooperation, particularly at the federal level, but those were the exceptions.
When it came to state-level preservation, museums like the New York State
Museum would buy and trade somewhat in ethnographic and historic
collections, but governments and their affiliates were mostly engaged with
the creation of parks and public open spaces.[54] In other words, the state was
most interested in landscapes rather than archives.

For Converse, however, who better than the Empire State, the inheritor of the land, legacy, and exceptional history of the Iroquois empire, to
own and protect their diplomatic history? In 1898, she had convinced the
Onondagas to make that transfer, but how she did that is not entirely clear.
Perhaps, as Converse herself said, the belts truly were disappearing and, despite the Haudenosaunees' best efforts, they simply could not staunch the
flow so they had no choice but to cede control to the state. Or perhaps, as
Arthur Parker claimed, it was "Largely through Mrs. Converse's influence"
and urging that the Onondagas eventually voted to transfer ownership of the
belts to New York State regardless of their capacity to keep and preserve them.
Whichever it was, the Onondaga called a meeting of the Six Nations in 1898
and voted to cede the wampum belts to the State Museum which had promised to "safely keep forever all wampums of the Onondaga nation" and the Six
Nations. On June 29, 1898, the transfer was formalized when the belts were
delivered from "the Six Nations' archives into the keeping of the State." From
then on, the Director of the State Museum would be the "Official Custodian
of Records and Wampum Keeper of the Six Nations of the Iroquois of
New York," notable since the title and responsibility of "wampum keeper of
the Onondaga Nation" had only ever been held by elected Onondagas. The
ceremony marking the transfer was a spectacle. It was open to the public, and
railroads offered discounted tickets for New Yorkers to attend this "special
excursion" and witness the most "powerful Indian confederacy of America"
transfer its political legacy to New York State.[55]

Barely one year after Converse had "saved" Iroquois political history by
taking it from them, she was once again thrust back into her role as an honorary League chief to fight against allotment. Between 1899 and her death
in November 1903, she travelled frequently between New York City and
Washington, DC, on behalf of the Six Nations in their opposition to the 1900

Ryan bill and the 1902 Vreeland bill. On the Ryan bill, William H. Ryan, a Congressman from Buffalo, continued what the state legislature had begun eight years earlier in the Whipple bill and drafted a new one to force allotment and, crucially, citizenship on the Iroquois. The bill passed the House, and as it sat in the Senate, Converse moved quickly to rally the public against it. She was the conduit through which members of the Seneca Nation sent letters related to the Ryan bill to federal officials, she nominated Joseph Keppler to serve as the Senecas' legal representative in Washington, and she managed the travel and lodging for the official Seneca delegation from the Allegany reservation who arrived to "read aloud" the letters on the floor of the Senate.[56]

Converse's politicking may have made it look to DC like the Senecas were all on the same page, but things were less certain among their leadership. While none among the Haudenosaunee were in favor of allotment outright, some like William G. Hoag, the recently elected President of the Seneca Nation, assumed the inevitability of the bill's success and planned for that eventuality. Hoag was a contested figure. Regarded by critics as a "halfbreed," he was seen as one of the few Senecas to have the "advantage & ability to cope with a white-man('s government)" and, as such, was considered part of a greedy and corrupted Seneca political machine who would only enrich themselves from allotment. Hoag's critics claimed that his cronies had fraudulently "elected themselves" and, once in office, would "hold the reigns of our govt" for "25 years." In that time, they would take "every dollar belonging to our nation" for their benefit. Hoag fought back against these accusations. He claimed they were illegitimate because they stemmed from the Onondaga chief Andrew John's personal vendetta against him. Hoag argued that John's "followers" were few and had little power, yet John's attacks proved potent enough that Hoag spent time publicly belittling John and even lashed out at Converse for not acting in good faith.[57]

Concerned with the political infighting at home and the general state of the Senecas' case in the capitol, Converse sought out alternative perspectives on the problem of Indian citizenship as the Ryan bill sat in the Senate. Perhaps she, like Hoag, feared that allotment would succeed and wanted to prepare for that eventuality. This would do much to explain her insistence that the Onondagas transfer their wampum belts to New York State and the state alone. For perspective on the Ryan bill, Converse reached out across the St. Lawrence River to E. D. Lannon in the office of the Canadian Commissioner of Indian Affairs in Brantford, Ontario, to ask about his experience with Indian citizenship. Lannon explained that Indians in his province had been given citizenship and the right to vote locally through the citizenship

Franchise Provincial Act of 1885, an act that was designed to accompany the 1885 Federal Franchise Act that gave Canadian Indians the franchise in national elections. That Federal Franchise Act, however, was repealed in 1898 because it was deemed poorly applied to Natives throughout Canada and, in Lannon's experience, was particularly problematic for the Six Nations. The issue was that Canada's Indigenous population "occupied land of their own" in the different Provinces, a legal distinction at odds with the attempt to bring Native land under the control of the "Federal Government."[58] Echoing Converse's worry about the future of her own adoptive people, Lannon explained that citizenship forced Canada's Six Nations into a tricky middle ground legal status where most federal law simply did not apply to them because of provincial laws despite the fact that they were, at least on paper, national citizens.

Lannon also addressed the impact of the right to vote on Canada's Indigenous population. They had the franchise for a little more than a decade, but Lannon explained that it had a "bad effect" on them due to the widespread governmental corruption and mismanagement of Indian resources despite the supposed protections that national citizenship and voting rights allowed. National politicians often "falsely reported" on important information relevant to the governance and resources of the Indigenous nations, and even the Provincial governments who "control(ed) their affairs, were abusing their trust and squandering their money." Among the Six Nations in particular, there was a widespread loss of confidence and a "general dissatisfaction." In addition, voting in national elections "in no way interfered with their properties" or "money" even though the Federal government held them in trust, a problem primarily due to the Six Nations' unique relationship to the Provincial governments. Lannon made it clear that, regardless of their national citizenship and voting rights, the Haudenosaunee were "in no way supported by the (Federal) Government." They could only vote for "a candidate in the Federal House," but this was a worthless proposition as there was little incentive to do so. The Canadian Iroquois were, in sum, "in the same position as if the Franchise was not extended to him." Converse heard similar messages from the Seneca C. H. Abrams of the Tonawanda Reservation. Abrams echoed Lannon's conclusions and wrote to Converse in 1901 asking her to resist the Ryan bill for fear that President Roosevelt "will work against us Indians and make us become citizens."[59]

They were devastated, then, when the Ryan bill became federal law in February 1901. While the citizenship requirements in early drafts were lifted, it still included incentives for the Iroquois to voluntarily become citizens and therefore make themselves subject to American law, a move that would open the door fully to allotment. To make matters worse, shortly after Ryan's legislative victory, Edward B. Vreeland, a representative from Cattaraugus, introduced a "noxious bill" in January 1902 that revived the Ogden Company's dead and near century-old claim to the Tonawanda Reservation. This time, unlike the Whipple or the Ryan bills, Vreeland's language considered the matters of citizenship and allotment settled. This bill pursued a different goal: a $3,000,000 settlement to be paid by the Senecas to "extinguish . . . the claim of the Ogden Land Company" once and for all. The Vreeland bill was, as Joseph Keppler reported from Washington and Converse herself confronted when she arrived a month after it was introduced to the House, an illegitimate and blatant land grab and a crass attempt to "swindle" the Senecas out of money. Local news confirmed this. Andrew John reported to Converse that A.W. Ferrin, the white New York Indian Agent of the Allegany Reservation, had spoken out publicly in favor of the bill in an article published in the *Cattaraugus Republican*. In normal situations this was not unexpected from federal officials, but the problem went deeper. As John noted, Section Four of the bill outlined future processes for seizing Iroquois land after the $3,000,000 settlement was paid. This was problematic because both Ferrin and Vreeland would benefit personally from land sales since they had recently both "got a lease for oil purposes from the Indian Council by his trickery." The bill, quite clearly, was a "scheme" invented by Vreeland to "get himself and his white people . . . a clear title of these Indian lands."[60]

Beyond the bill's clear bias, Converse received word that Vreeland was deploying old Ogden Land Company tactics to cajole individual Senecas into signing a petition in support of the bill. Edward Cornplanter reported that Vreeland supporters were "buying" petition signatures from Senecas living on reservations in support of the bill. These people were, in effect, being taken advantage of and signing themselves up to be allotted. In response, Converse assembled a team of Arthur C. Parker and his close friend and colleague, Mark R. Harrington, to go to Washington to protest these nefarious tactics in the Senate but they were "driven away" when they attempted to speak against the bill. Seeking a different tack, John sent Converse the Six Nations' joint statement protesting the bill and encouraged her to publish the statement in Washington and New York newspapers to galvanize public support.[61]

Despite the hardships, Converse and her Seneca delegation held firm. She risked the "fury" of Senators when she sought out financial support to assist other Haudenosaunee individuals and groups who came to Washington to protest the Vreeland bill. When Congress attempted to delay a vote to force these newly arrived Senecas to leave the Capitol building, she, Parker, and Harrington waited out their vote. In addition, Converse made great efforts to appeal directly to New Yorkers through newspapers. She distributed the formal protests of the Six Nations in council, even sending in the language of an anonymous Seneca person, "and a pagan at that," whose "very strong document" she hoped would galvanize Haudenosaunee and white supporters. Arthur Parker would later marvel at her ability to reach the Washington and New York public and her succinct and eloquent explanations of Seneca perspectives through her "many able letters in opposition" that she had printed in the media. Their efforts worked; in 1904, the Vreeland bill was defeated.[62]

Though Converse's efforts in DC may have seemed unimpeachable among the Haudenosaunee, that was not true for everyone. On July 19, 1903, just four months before she passed away, an unnamed person lodged a formal complaint against her to the Seneca Nation. It claimed Converse had smuggled illegal alcohol into the Tonawanda Reservation. This was a serious and morally significant claim. Not only did the *Gaiwiio* religion ban alcoholic drinks, but when New York extended the Seneca Nation of Indian's jurisdiction over the Tonawanda, Cattaraugus, and Oil Spring reservations in 1842, the state incorporated in that law the Senecas' own demands that the sale and importation of liquor into Iroquois country be banned. Despite this attack on her, Converse had the full support of Seneca leadership. From "their Long Homes" in Newtown, New York, a General Meeting of the Seneca Indians declared the charges spurious. They declared that to think that she "in any way or by any means thought to introduce intoxicating drink among [us] is a most malicious fabrication and slander, and that, to the contrary, it is well known by our people that she has ever and in all occasions advocated the principles of temperance among us." At the end of her long and contentious Seneca life, Converse and her legacy were protected by Haudenosaunee leadership.[63]

Just two years after Harriet Maxwell Converse participated in Red Jacket's reinterment ceremony, a different memorial service took place across the river in Brantford, Canada. A monument honoring Red Jacket's contemporary and political nemesis, the Mohawk chief Joseph Brant, was unveiled to a Canadian and American audience of thousands on October 13, 1886. The nine-foot-tall monument was wrapped in two large Union Jacks and, once unveiled, revealed a life-like statue of the Mohawk statesman that stood atop a two-tiered base of stone quarried in England. The base was adorned with detailed depictions of other Iroquois figures and their "trophies," including tomahawks, furs, and lacrosse sticks. Scenes from Brant's life were immortalized in bronze friezes on the bottom tier. Brant's monument, in all its red, white, and blue glory, formed the backdrop for speakers who addressed an audience of Canadians, Americans, representatives of western Native Nations, and the Lieutenant Governor of Ontario, John Beverly Robinson. One of the speakers, Allen Cleghorn, a Mohawk chief and president of the Brant Memorial Association, described the Haudenosaunee during the American Revolution as a people "determined to sink or swim with the English" and credited Brant with providing "the means of ultimately saving to Britain half of this American continent." Chief A.G. Smith of the Canadian Six Nations took this sentiment a step further when he expressed hope that the memorial would ensure that the Haudenosaunee continue to "be ever loyal to the British Crown." To show that his speech "came from the heart," he publicly gifted a wampum belt to the artist who created the monument, Percy Wood, so that all in attendance would remember the occasion, symbolism, and promise.[64]

To Converse, however, the scene at Brantford was that from "a land of strangers."[65] She knew from Red Jacket and Parker, not to mention her own work, that the Six Nations played an important role in the founding of the United States, but the cloyingly patriotic scene at Brant's memorial was at odds with her own knowledge of the Six Nations' relationship with Canada and of the New York Senecas' relationship with the United States. Her view of the ceremony was colored by the fact that she had long assumed that the Haudenosaunee were already a "vanished" people who were incapable of protecting their own history or culture. In her mind, the Canadians erred deeply in trying to coopt all the Six Nations into helping build a brighter national future because, as she had tried to prove time and again, Anglo-America's efforts to protect the history and memory of the Iroquois were better spent reaching out to communities not in political partnership, but to encourage them to give their culture and history over to the state before they disappeared completely. Unlike the forward-looking scene in Brantford, Converse was far more comfortable with Red Jacket's New York ceremony, which both physically and metaphorically looked away from present-day politics and the contemporary "vanished" Indian toward a mythological Haudenosaunee past—a mythology that her own salvage ethnography had helped to create and that further cast the New York Haudenosaunee, not the Canadian, as the real and "authentic" Iroquois.

But as her protégé Arthur C. Parker would reveal, Converse was short-sighted in that regard. Parker, unlike his "Aunt Hattie" who dedicated her life as colonial kin to taking away the culture of those she deemed to be a people of the past, knew that the real value of the memory of the Haudenosaunee lay in the interpretation of the past for use in the present and the future.

4

Arthur C. Parker and "The Amazing Iroquois"

IN 1991 DAVID HURST THOMAS, the renowned archaeologist at the AMNH, won an award from the Society for American Archaeology (SAA) named after the famed Seneca museologist, Arthur C. Parker. He thought little of the award's namesake at the time. But nine years later, he was asked to write an afterword for a new scholarly book that interrogated the complex relationships between Native Americans and archaeologists. It was then that Thomas learned that Parker was not only the founding president of the SAA, he was something of a rarity in his time: a Native American who was also an archaeologist. While reflecting on Parker's career, Thomas asked a critical question that used Parker to get to the heart of the tension between the anthropologists and archaeologists who seek to study Indigenous cultures, and Native American peoples themselves, who seek to protect their culture from them: "Who Is Arthur C. Parker, Anyway?"[1]

Many have tried to answer. William N. Fenton, the dean of Iroquois Studies who got his first archaeological job working under Arthur Parker in the 1930s, suggested in 1981 that he was "the most distinguished Indian savant of his generation," a racially mixed man at home on "either side of the buckskin curtain."[2] More recently, an important part of understanding Parker's mixed-race identity is to recognize that he was a practitioner of "indigenous archaeology," the term for Native American–descended archaeologists who can "exist in a sort of heterotopia ourselves . . . in that our work within archaeology is viewed by some Natives as an act of treason and by others as an act of revolution."[3] Parker certainly fit that description. As early as 1903, a teenage Parker placed himself at the forefront of a revolution in New York archaeology and anthropology by helping break ground for the first time in his peoples' reservations for the AMNH in New York City. His personal knowledge and connections also provided him with access to insider Indigenous knowledge that, in turn, led his archaeological team to new and fruitful dig sites, where vast quantities of sensitive material culture could be taken from Iroquois country and stored in far-away repositories. Parker's archaeological successes, if not always his cultural sensitivity, established him at an early age as a pioneering expert on his peoples' culture and history. As time went on, his work inspired ongoing anthropological interest in the history and culture of the Indigenous peoples of New York State.

His fieldwork, however, lasted only a few years. For the rest of his career he was a pioneering voice in what today is called public history, a field that encompasses museums, various types of public and digital historical programming, and parks and memorials. This chapter therefore answers Thomas' question not by emphasizing Parker the archaeologist, but Parker the public historian. From his first museum exhibition job in 1904 until the day he died on January 1, 1955, Parker's influences extended well beyond the intellectual contributions he made after excavating the Haudenosaunee reservations. Among many other achievements, Parker oversaw the creation of a new Division of Archaeology and Ethnology in the New York State Museum (1906); served as the Director of the Rochester Municipal Museum (1924); authored hundreds of newspaper and journal articles; penned books, including three novels and histories for children; cofounded the Society of American Indians in 1911; served as Vice President of the American Association of Museums for twelve years; oversaw the Works Progress Administration's New York Indian Arts Project; and in retirement wrote the most important but unpublished series on Haudenosaunee ethnohistory that no one has read, "The Amazing Iroquois."[4]

Despite this extraordinary intellectual profile, scholars nevertheless tend to study Parker mostly in the context of his Indigenous identity and his short archaeological career. Perhaps this is because the idea that Parker's public history was scholarship at all seems incomprehensible, given that archaeology in his time was newly considered a legitimate and recognized scholarly field yet Parker did not receive a doctorate or teach at a university. When given the choice to pursue a PhD at Columbia or continue to train at the AMNH, Parker abandoned conventional wisdom and chose to train in the museum. Yet it is also true that until his death in 1955, Parker proclaimed himself a museologist (a term he invented) in addition to archaeologist and anthropologist, and he would dedicate his career to bringing these fields together under one roof. He indeed inhabited two worlds, one Indian and the other white, one "authentic" and the other academic, but brought it all under the umbrella of his museums.[5]

As a result, Parker established himself as one of the most important interpreters of Haudenosaunee history in his generation and profoundly impacted how the public engaged with that history. In many ways, he leveraged his museology to reinforce his own conception of Iroquois exceptionalism and combined that with the voices of the Haudenosaunee themselves. If examining Red Jacket, Ely S. Parker, and Harriet M. Converse reveals the many ways they entangled Iroquois exceptionalism and American history in the public mind, then Arthur C. Parker was the one who organized them into a coherent package and showcased how exceptional Haudenosaunee history—not just "Indian" history broadly—truly was.

Parker did this in large part by turning his museums into scholarly research institutions dedicated to educating the public about the exceptional Haudenosaunee by using their own stories and voices. He expanded and reinforced this message in newspapers, public history sites, and parks across the state, and in traditional published scholarship. All of this created an Indigenous generated narrative that stayed remarkably consistent during two World Wars, the Great Depression, and the beginning of the Cold War. At the same time, Parker shaped what history museums and public history would look like in the future. He experimented with experiential learning, wrote the manual on the ethical and efficacious running of history museums, and moved beyond other museums in his field as "the loci of the anthropological discipline" to being "social and community institutions centrally concerned with popular education and leisure."[6] In that respect, he is the father of the modern history museum, a revision that was in no small way influenced by his conception of his peoples' exceptional history.

Part of what made Parker such a potent public historian was his politics. An assimilationist, he was like his Uncle Ely in his confidence that there was a place for Indigenous peoples in American society and culture, writ large. But Parker approached that idea by immortalizing in exhibitions, parks, and writing what many regarded as the opposite notion: that the Haudenosaunee were a people apart from the rest of Native America. It was their very exceptionality that spoke to their capacity for assimilation. This chapter thus builds on histories that point to people of the era who broke with convention by talking about Indians in culturally specific ways, rather than in broad stereotypes, like Parker and his contemporary, the Dakota Sioux anthropologist Dr. Charles Eastman. They were transforming what the public knew about Native America by using culturally relevant descriptors rather than nonculturally relevant ones, like how all Indians wore Plains "costumes." Parker and others were part of a new group of Indigenous peoples of this era who listened to their own elders "rather than non-Indian stereotypes."[7]

Parker certainly attempted to impress his anthropologist peers with this, but he did so in large part by infusing that message into his public history practice. He "played Indian" to advance his career, but also made real and public efforts to create meaningful spaces for—and to defend Haudenosaunee perspectives on—their own history and culture, even if this diminished him in the eyes of his peers. This was an early, if incomplete, form of decolonized public history. For Parker, Iroquois exceptionalism and identity was not just a career-building tool, it guided his public history and politics. Over time, he successfully reframed and reinforced New Yorker's conception of the historic Iroquois empire according to the Haudenosaunee's own standards. This revised the public's mental image of the empire's enlightened and excep-tional descendants, all of which then flowed back into the anthropological community.

Parker finished what his ancestors, including Harriet Maxwell Converse, who he called Aunt Hattie, had begun: he bound the popular memory of his peoples' history to that of New York's. He reframed the Haudenosaunee not as a vanished or conquered people, as his massive ten-volume unpublished retirement project, "The Amazing Iroquois," offered, but as a truly unique people with an enduring legacy. Parker did much to make the Iroquois a household name in New York through his museum's educational authority and, as a Seneca public figure and scholar, he contributed greatly to the on-going public and scholarly interest in the Haudenosaunee. He had a lasting impact on why the Iroquois are a household American name today, even if Parker himself is largely ignored as a serious interpreter of that history.

———

Arthur Caswell Parker was born in 1881 on the Cattaraugus Seneca Reservation to a prominent mixed-race family. His Anglo-American mother, Geneva Hortenese Griswold, was descended from eighteenth-century Connecticut missionaries and served as a teacher on the Cattaraugus and Tonawanda reservations. Geneva met Frederick Parker, Ely Parker's brother, while he worked as a local station agent on the New York Central Railroad. Because of the Parker family's patrilineal ties to the Wolf clan, Arthur and his two siblings had no claim to a birthright membership into the matrilineal Senecas.[8]

GA-WA-SO-WA-NEH
Arthur C. Parker

FIGURE 4.1 Photograph of Arthur C. Parker. *American Indian Freemasonry*, Buffalo Consistory, 1919, 2.

The Parker family lived in relative affluence. The family home was part of an area in Cattaraugus where a Seneca Christian minority population formed the "nucleus" of an assimilated neighborhood surrounded by the far more populous and so-called " 'pagan' or 'longhouse' homes." In that environment, Arthur's family were exemplars of what historians call the "structural model" of assimilation, in that they were part of a community where many of their immediate neighbors seemed to willingly embrace American citizenship, worship at the Church, and speak English as their primary language. Arthur eventually left Cattaraugus to attend the coeducational Centenary Collegiate Institute in Hackettstown, New Jersey, and in 1899 moved to Dickenson Seminary in Williamsport, Pennsylvania, where he began what he thought was a life in the clergy. While at school, he soon discovered a deep interest in archaeology. In his time off from coursework at the seminary, he attended sessions of his Aunt Hattie's *salon* in New York City. There he met many high-profile intellectuals, connected with his Uncle Ely, and was introduced to Haudenosaunee and other Indigenous men and women. The young and curious Parker also took those opportunities to visit Frederic Ward Putnam's anthropology division at the nearby AMNH and his Peabody Museum at Harvard University.[9]

Parker clearly enjoyed this rich intellectual environment. Putnam, a man ever on the hunt for young intellectual talent, was suitably impressed by the young Seneca, and in 1899 gave Parker an archaeological internship at the AMNH. Parker left the seminary and, until 1902, worked at the AMNH under the direction of Mark Harrington on digs from Long Island to the St. Lawrence Valley. When offered a chance to join a dig on the Cattaraugus Reservation in 1903, the same year Parker was adopted into the Bear Clan and given the "free name" (or uninherited name) Gáwasowaneh, or "Big Snowsnake," he leaped at the opportunity to return home and was able to provide crucial insights about Cattaraugus for the archaeological team. This dig, among others conducted under the auspices of the AMNH, established Parker as a serious archaeologist working for a premier American research institution. Yet it put him at odds with Senecas living on the reservation who balked at the team's successes digging up and removing their ancestors' remains and material culture for study. Parker would eventually try to strike a balance between scientific study and a more nuanced respect for his peoples' culture, but in these early years he indiscriminately dug and salvaged "ancient Iroquois sites in western New York" and, in the process, established himself as an "authority" on the Haudenosaunee.[10]

Putnam then encouraged the promising young Seneca archaeologist to enroll in a doctoral program at Columbia University to study under his colleague, Franz Boas. Parker took a few classes with the eminent scholar and there had his first exposure to the rigorous, if still relatively new, world of academic anthropology. His decision about whether to pursue a PhD or not would prove to be a formative one. Graduate degree programs in anthropology did not yet exist at most universities, but archaeologists and anthropologists like Putnam and Boas had sought for years to formalize and professionalize the study of anthropology through university training. By the time Parker had to make his choice, these programs had already mostly replaced museum apprenticeships as the standard for training professional anthropologists and archaeologists.[11]

Despite his mentor's pressure and Boas' outstanding academic reputation, Parker chose museums. Considering academia's predominance and clear advantages at the time, scholars disagree on the reasons why he made what looked like a career-stunting choice. William Fenton claimed in 1968 that Parker did this out of sheer impatience. He supposedly found the long academic training time "impractical" and preferred the shorter "congenial and informal tutorials of Professor Putnam." This was a decision, Fenton concluded, that "haunt[ed]" Parker's career because "it was an achievement that he very much coveted and envied in others," but would not attain himself (and then only in an honorary capacity) until 1940. Other scholars argue that Parker, in fact, "could not know for sure in the early 1900s that anthropology had decisively entered a new professionalized phase." Even so, he still made the wrong choice because by choosing museums he had "invested his future . . . with an ambiguity from which it never completely recovered." Besides, he was far too eager to "get ahead quickly with a marriage and a career" and a PhD would do much to delay that life goal. He did, in fact, marry an Abenaki woman Beulah Tahamont or "Dark Cloud" in 1904 as he was making this career-shaping decision.[12]

Some scholars, however, give Parker more credit. They argue that his decision was about more than simple expediency, and they defy the notion that he had somehow misread the academic environment when both Putnam and Boas were pushing him in that direction. They find that Parker's choice mostly hung on Putnam's own belief in and study of cultural evolution, a theory that held that societies had set stages of evolution through which every human society ascends on its way to civilization. Progress, therefore, was societal as well as technological and thus could explain the contemporary "Indian problem." Because Parker was a lifelong assimilationist, historians read backward from his later career decades later to suggest that he, in 1904, had naturally gravitated toward Putnam because his theory would have had a more immediate impact on American Indian legislation. In other words, compared with Boas' competing theories that made the "Indian problem" academic rather than political, Putnam's world seemed more practical for Parker's career prospects and offered him a better chance to make a positive societal impact for his people. This difference, and the fact that the "ordered confines of the museum" and its resources were immediately available to Parker in the moment, made his choice clear.[13]

This last explanation is somewhat more compelling than the others, but they all ignore an obvious and vital part of Parker's intellectual makeup: his early interest in museums. His Aunt Hattie's museum and the AMNH shaped his perspectives on science and the culture of scholarship, but museums also made his ongoing and future interventions in scholarship and politics possible. Parker was from an early age not only interested in museums, but personally and professionally invested in museums' educational and scholarly potential, as well as their demonstrated importance to society.[14]

We see this in Parker's first professional museum experience in 1904, the same year he was at career crossroads, at the brand-new Hotel Astor in New York City. He was offered the chance to curate the New York section of the hotel's Indian Hall, home of the American Grill Room.[15] The Indian Hall and Grill Room, designed by the German restaurateur William C. Muschenheim, was one of the many high-end amenities offered at the new Hotel Astor, a $7 million project. The hotel's lavish interior décor featured the art and themes of world cultures from the German Renaissance to the "mysteries of China," ancient civilizations, and classical European style and architecture.

But it was the Indian Hall that commanded attention as the "most picturesque room of its kind in the country." Because it surrounded diners in "things American," to one writer of *The Washington Post* it was a welcome reprieve from the "endless duplications" of the *ancien régime* and the stale reproductions of New York's many "Dutch cafes." The objects displayed on the walls were culled from Indigenous peoples hailing from every corner of the continent. Arranged in a primarily geographic orientation around the room, the exhibition presented to diners a mosaic of continental cultures and an exploration of the conquered Indigenous peoples of North America. During and after meals, guests enjoyed perusing exhibitions of Inuit hunting and fishing spears, Shoshone beadwork, cultural artifacts taken from the "American small boy[s] favorite" the Comanche, and the material culture of other Natives of the Great Plains, California, and the southwest.[16]

The Indian Hall gave Parker his first taste of museum work leading a curatorial team. His work was an example of retail ethnography, or the exhibition of Indigenous material culture for the express purpose of offering wealthy consumers an "authentic" foreign encounter as part of a dynamic shopping experience. Newspapers even emphasized the stories of guests who claimed to have personal connections to the items on display. The Indian Hall, in that sense, blurred the lines between education, entertainment, and lived experience. In January 1905, a guest named Captain Jack Crawford had a particularly close connection to an item in the exhibition. Decades earlier, Crawford had served in the US Army in Arizona when it was sent in response to the 1871 massacre of 150 women and children at an Apache settlement near Camp Grant in the Aravaipa canyon by a local coalition of Anglo-Americans as well as some Mexican Americans and Tohono O'odham. Crawford thus fancied himself the resident Indian expert among his friends dining at the Grill Room. While commenting on the various items on display, he caught sight of the "brilliant feathers" of a war bonnet on the wall. He got up from his table to take a closer look and, after the inspection, rushed back to the table to report that "that is the very bonnet I took from an Apache chief

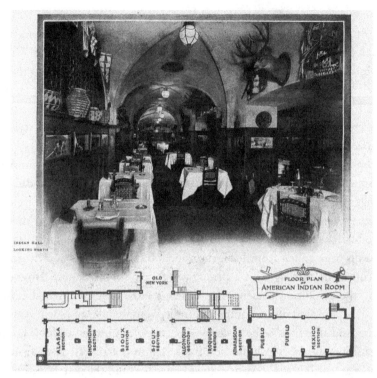

FIGURE 4.2 Photograph of the Indian Hall in the Hotel Astor. *Hotel Astor, Indian Hall* (New York: Malcolm & Hayes, c. 1908). Image from the author's collection.

when I was with Gen. Crook in his campaign against the Indians. I sent it to Mrs. [Harriet] Converse twenty-five years ago."[17] Not just for this diner, the Indian Hall and Grill Room transported all its visitors to a bygone era that disassociated "conquered" Indigenous peoples from contemporary life.

Through his work on the Indian Hall, Parker was expanding his professional network. While working on the New York section, he reached out to Putnam, now his mentor, to request pieces of the Peabody Museum's collection to supplement the "photographs" he had already requested from the AMNH and the Smithsonian's Department of Ethnology. Parker's correspondance caught the attention of Andrew S. Draper, the new Commissioner of Education for New York State, whose department oversaw the New York State Museum in Albany. Impressed with Parker's archaeology and his work on the high-profile Indian Hall, Draper offered Parker a position overseeing the Department of Ethnography and Archaeology as it transitioned to its new home near the capital building. Parker accepted the job and set out to transform the State

Museum into a full-fledged research institution. Importantly, he worked to re-focus the museum's scattered ethnography collection on the Haudenosaunee and other Indigenous nations in New York. Central to his vision was that the museum would conduct its own archaeological and anthropological field-work and build its own local collection.[18]

Only two months into Parker's tenure, however, he learned that the new Director of the Division of Science, John M. Clarke, the "Wampum Keeper of the Six Nations," was resistant to Parker's ambitions. Clarke denied Parker's first grant application to fund an archaeological dig at Cattaraugus on the grounds that the proposal did not include plans sell the "relics" they found to recoup the cost of the dig. Instead, Clarke suggested, Parker should buy "relics" from elsewhere because it was cheaper. This did not sit well with the new Curator. Parker vented his frustration in letters to Putnam and expressed "disgust" at museums that claimed to do their own scholarship but, in truth, only collected strange and exciting-looking artifacts to put on dis-play regardless of their educational and scholarly value. Parker believed that ethnography and history museums, like the natural history exhibitions of his beloved AMNH, should be sites of public exploration, education, and knowledge creation. The so-called "scientific institutions" that spent precious funding merely "hunting" for "curiosities" were unworthy of the name. This philosophy would culminate in his 1935 field-shaping *A Manual for History Museums* where he explained that in a history museum, "if there is talent, time and text, there certainly should be some contribution to knowledge." A good museum's purpose was clear: "Rewriting and restating a generally known story of a community is not research."[19]

To make matters worse, Parker found that the State Museum had never conducted its own archaeological dig. And while Clarke professed to support the museum and Parker's efforts to right that imbalance, he ultimately proved unwilling to devote the resources to hire someone or issue grants to support that scientific vision. Parker complained to Commissioner Draper who only responded in noncommittal language that "gathering and preserving state traditions, folk lore, implements, or anything else related to New York tribes" is certainly of value. To Parker, Draper's vague response was as hollow as Clarke's promises. In October 1904, seven months after he started working at the State Museum, Parker was again venting to Putnam. Not only did the museum seem to lack the will to be a true research institution, but he also learned that they were planning on selling the collections they did have in-cluding "choice Seneca material" and other objects that were "very hard to du-plicate" to the AMNH. The AMNH will then have culled even more "from

N.Y. state, if they take my few specimens." Backed into a corner, Parker asked Putnam if the Peabody would intervene on his behalf and help him to "have the memory of my people preserved in tangible form."[20]

In Albany, Parker was learning valuable lessons about the realities of running a museum department. His transformative vision clashed with the State Museum's continuation of business as usual, and he was fighting an uphill battle to create a research institution. Still, Parker knew that the implementation of his vision was essential to creating a good public museum because, in addition to benefiting the scientific and educational mission of museums, original scholarship was fundamental in fighting back against cultural forgeries in an era when material culture "counterfeits are in vogue."[21]

By April 1906, his tireless efforts had finally begun to bear fruit. The twenty-five-year-old archaeologist gave himself a new and unofficial title, New York State Archaeologist, that advertised his scholarly ambitions for the State Museum. Then in June, Parker successfully applied for funding to launch archaeological digs in Erie and Chautauqua Counties. His most successful dig was at the Ripley Site in Chautauqua, which moved forward despite the state's grant being so insufficient that Parker bought much of the equipment himself. His team found two "undiscovered" villages, one a pre–Six Nations Erie village, and hundreds of graves. The Ripley dig established Parker as an influential archaeologist in his own right. For the State Museum, it produced "several thousand specimens" including an amazingly well-preserved Erie woman's hand banded with copper bracelets and rings. It marked "the first successful effort to obtain a collection wholly by the research method" in the country. The Ripley dig also opened New York's Indigenous history to future archaeological study. Decades later, William Fenton would describe it as "a Landmark in the history of American archaeology because it represents one of the first attempts to describe the complete excavation of a large site and then interpret the results as a description of local culture."[22]

Central to the success of the dig was Parker's relationship with the reservation. As State Archaeologist, he expended considerable effort expanding his network of local informants who made his archaeological exploits possible. After all, as he knew well, long-buried sites unknown to archaeologists were sometimes known to the Haudenosaunee. So good was he at finding these sites that, to this day, when such "discoveries" are made they are called "Parker Sites." Of particular value to Parker was his relationship with the leadership of the Newtown Longhouse at Cattaraugus where he attended many ceremonies and festivals over the years. He also formed a professional relationship with important informants like the Tuscarora-Onondaga Albert Cusick, a hereditary chief turned Episcopal minister who was an historian of his people. Parker commissioned projects like Cusick's wax cylinder recordings of Haudenosaunee songs, dances, and other public or secret Haudenosaunee spiritual rituals, all things that anthropologists assumed "younger Indians" would not know or might change and were therefore worthy of preservation and archiving. Because of his network of Iroquois informants like Cusick, Parker could confidently declare to Putnam that the State Museum had "purpose" and could become an institution "of standing among museums."[23]

Part of that growth was in the production of new scholarly publications and increased public outreach. In 1908, Parker edited and published Harriet Maxwell Converse's *Myths and Legends of the New York State Iroquois*, a book that included Converse's ethnographic analyses and a collection of relevant letters, documents, and images of objects in the State Museum's collection. He also published accounts of Haudenosaunee history in local newspapers. His work post-Ripley brought him the support of famous ethnographers like William Beauchamp, a well-known amateur ethnographer, and William Henry Holmes, Chief of the Bureau of American Ethnology at the Smithsonian, both of whom endorsed Parker's biography of Ely S. Parker, which was published in 1919. Parker also integrated his family's history into the museum by publicizing events such as the transfer of a wampum belt and Red Jacket's Peace Medal to his Uncle Ely in 1852, a moment that designated him the "Keeper of the Western Door" of the Longhouse and the last "sentinel-sachem of a crumbling empire." Through his office at the New York State Museum, Parker offered the public an interpretation of the long legacy of the Haudenosaunee empire and Red Jacket through his uncle, a Civil War hero and model of assimilation, both of whom were guardians of the Six Nations and lifelong patriots of the United States.[24]

On site at the museum, Parker leveraged his growing reputation to propose a new and vitally important exhibition, the Iroquois Indian Group dioramas. This was a years-long project, much like his building of the ethnography division, and was ambitious in terms of its scale, content, his insistence on ethnographic accuracy and historical focus on the Haudenosaunee, and its existence outside of a natural history museum. Funding limitations for this project, however, again got in the way of his plans. The State Legislature in 1908 had agreed to fund only traditional small-scale "transitory specials" and "pageants" in the museum and generally refused to entertain what Parker pitched as a "lasting exhibit which for years to come would form a valuable educational feature." To get around this problem, Director Clarke, now on board with Parker's vision, began soliciting private donations for this project.

He reached out to his political and personal contacts to solicit donations and ultimately succeeded in raising "$15,000" from a "Mrs. F.F. Thompson, of Canandaigua, a daughter of ex-Governor Myron H. Clark" to begin work.[25]

In large part, what drove such interest and generosity from donors was Parker's own enthusiasm for the project and his insistence on ethnographic accuracy. He publicized that the dioramas "will become the most remarkable ethnological exhibit in America, if not the world." He was not far off in his assessment. The wax figures that would populate the dioramas were not the generic models of Indigenous peoples found in contemporary (and modern) natural history museums; they were wax "life casts" of real contemporary Haudenosaunee men and women living on the New York and Canadian reservations. In Parker's sweeping plan, these wax figures acted out an all-encompassing history of "hunting and forest life, house and home life, warfare and war customs, agriculture and food preparations, the arts and industries, ceremonies, and a council scene showing the use of wampum belts." The dioramas would also use "every art known to the artist and theatrical expert" to build the most lifelike and captivating displays possible. Parker's "frequent trips" to reservations to find models exposed him to Haudenosaunee artisans, many of them women, who were hired to create the authentic clothing and tools on display. These included Julia Crouse or "Drooping Flower," a matron of the Seneca Turtle Clan, to create the historically accurate dresses. Two other Seneca women also made costumes for the project, Alice M. Shongo and her daughter, Maude Hurd. Parker also sourced locally for artistic talent. David C. Lithgo, a renowned Albany artist trained in Europe, created the scenic background images. Caspar Mayer, another Albany artist, made the life casts. The sole nonlocal was Henri Marchand, an award-winning French sculptor, who created the wax figures. With all of that talent on board, Parker explained that the dioramas would both attract public interest and "serve as a fitting memorial to a people who have done much for us—and whom we have never thanked."[26]

The dioramas, known as the Iroquois Indian (or Life) Groups, were dazzling in their realism and scale. They offered, as one reviewer put it, a "magic window" into the historic world of the Haudenosaunee. Planned and built from 1906 to 1917, they were exhibited at the State Museum until the 1970s. When the first of the dioramas premiered in 1909, critics expressed admiration that they were already "Known Across the Seas" and were "believed to be the most authentic exhibit in the world of the life of any single race." The main hallways of the museum building were designated for the exclusive use of the Iroquois Indian Groups, with each group contained in an area

FIGURE 4.3 Photograph of "Council of the Turtle Clan" from the Iroquois Indian Group dioramas. Exhibition Catalogue *The People of the Longhouse: A Guide to the Iroquois Indian Groups in the New York State Museum* (Albany, NY: The New York State Museum, 1960). Image from the author's collection.

at least twenty-five feet wide, fifteen feet deep, and twenty feet high. They were, truly, theatrical pieces. The glass was manufactured without framing or seams to avoid breaking immersion, and the lighting in the room gave visitors the impression that they had been transported back in time to a real place surrounded by real people. The background paintings were photo-realistic and curved from end-to-end, enveloping the viewer in the space where the edges blurred seamlessly into the foreground. One particularly large diorama measured an impressive eighteen feet tall and more than fifty feet wide. The settings ranged from a palisaded Seneca fort to women farming maize in a field. While the scenes were diverse and scattered over time, Parker explained that, when taken together, they defied stereotypes of the Haudenosaunee as "a wild, tent-dwelling people" akin to the popular stereotypes of Plains Indians. Instead, they showed the Iroquois as a "race well on the way to civilization" and living in their "celebrated 'long houses,' in a community." The dioramas, he continued, rejected a faulty history that was "written by their enemies" who portrayed the Iroquois as a vanished and primitive people "far behind in civilization."[27]

The stunning realism and popularity of the dioramas also gave Parker an intellectual platform from which to address the scholars in his field whom he criticized for writing only for themselves and avoiding interactions with the public. He explained that it was "not enough that the specialist should know and should have written a series of monographs" for other experts, because without active intervention on the part of the scholar, history museums "too often become morgues" where collections go to be seen but not heard. This was a problem for Parker because "in the widest sense of the term, 'museum' includes the universe," so museum curators have a social responsibility to make their research accessible and meaningful to a public audience. As he explained a decade later, museums and their collections, as exemplified by the Iroquois Indian Group dioramas, should be more than a "'consultive library of objects.'" They should be true "public museum[s]" where people go not merely to "*consult*" on the history of the Iroquois, but to be immersed in a history and anthropology that will cultivate a genuine "*interest*" in a subject "without effort or fatigue."[28] The dioramas satisfied this directive.

They also challenged what the public thought they knew of New York's Indigenous history by using their historical narrative to send a contemporary political message. The dioramas, when coupled with numerous newspaper articles and public speeches written and delivered by Parker, reinforced two themes near and dear to his heart: women's rights and the Iroquoian origins of Anglo-America. For women's rights, Parker tied the ongoing suffrage movement to the Haudenosaunees' matrilineal society. A supporter of women's suffrage, he had an academic as well as a political motivation to compare the social and cosmological roles that Haudenosaunee women played *vis á vis* American women. In the dioramas, Parker explained how and why women were portrayed doing field labor, and in one scene were even shown intervening to save a prisoner of war's life in order to adopt him. Haudenosaunee women, Parker explained through the dioramas, held "significant" influence and "power" and enjoyed an important political and social "sphere of influence." He made the significance of this historical truth clear by explaining that "we savages" are more democratic and enlightened than the so-called "civilized" American people because "our women" are true "political actors." The Haudenosaunee only learned that "it was wrong to treat our women humanely and give them political rights until we got an insight into civilization—and we are quite surprised."[29]

Parker rarely missed an opportunity to explain how the Haudenosaunee, long before the "pale faces . . . invaded" and with only their "wampum-woven laws," had declared that "women's rights should be embodied therein and protected forever!" He wondered aloud that as "modern American women stands . . . pleading for her political rights, does she ever stop to consider that the barbarian red woman that lived in the forests of New York state five hundred years ago, had far more political rights and enjoyed a much wider liberty than the twentieth century woman of civilization?" As his dioramas show, Parker used his museum spaces to advocate for women's participation in politics, the workplace, and higher education. Indeed, in 1943, he was recognized and honored by Keuka College, a women's college, with an honorary doctorate of humane letters for his "long work in assisting women to find better places in the world of education and administration."[30]

The dioramas also created a space for real Seneca women's voices to be heard in the state capital. The women Parker hired to create the clothing and tools for the dioramas used their proximity to the state government and Parker's reputation to comment on the issues facing Iroquois country. For example, while visiting Albany to talk to Parker about her work on the dioramas, dressmaker Drooping Flower convinced him to introduce her to Governor John A. Dix. In the meeting with the governor and reporters that followed, she raised the issue of the "out of date and extremely harmful" treatment of children and families on the Cattaraugus Reservation. She thought that, if the Senecas were forced to live like New Yorkers, then they should be protected like New Yorkers. In this way, Parker did double duty as an educator and as a conduit through which Haudenosaunee voices made themselves heard. It was therefore likely that when he published Harriet Converse's *Myths and Legends of the New York Iroquois*, it was he, not Converse, who unequivocally declared that "as the woman of today stands advocate and petitioner of her own cause, should she not offer an oblation of gratitude to the memory of the Iroquois Indian who called the earth his 'mighty mother' and who, through a sense of justice, rendered to the mothers of his people the rights maternal, political, social, civil, religious and of the land!"[31]

The second theme reinforced by Parker in the dioramas was that the Haudenosaunee had made vital historical contributions to Anglo-America's contemporary continental supremacy. Central to this was the myth of the Iroquois empire, to which Parker added an element he knew held widespread popular appeal: American patriotism. Parker explained that the dioramas honored the history of an Indigenous empire that was "the master type Indians of the continent" who made "no small measure" of contributions "to civilization." Even more, they were the people who "saved this area for English speakers" through their resistance to French invasion. Inspired by his own long familial legacy of patriotism, he predicted the Iroquois Influence Thesis of the 1970s–1980s when he explained that the Iroquois empire was the first to suggest a "union of colonies as early as 1755," and that the Six Nations helped to ensure American independence in 1812 when its men and women enlisted alongside Americans to fight against the British. From Red Jacket to Lafayette's Tuscarora confidant, Nicholas Cusick, Parker explained that "You can't beat these people for Patriotism."[32]

He thought that the Iroquois' unique patriotism and historical precedent could teach Americans a lesson about their own social problems, too.
To make this case, Parker pointed to a "civil war" that erupted in 1909 among
Canadian Iroquois between a younger generation of "warriors" and an older
generation of civil chiefs. The "warriors" supported the "overthrow" of the
"oldest established government on the continent" for a new constitutional
system, while the civil chiefs wanted to avoid the fate of their southern
New York Iroquois brothers who were "pampered, pauperized and cheated by
turns until they are demoralized and dependent." Parker sided with the civil
chiefs. As he explained after his 1910 visit to the Canadian Six Nations, the
Haudenosaunee under a traditional government were still "one of the most
progressive nations in the world." The "so-called savages" in Canada who still
lived under "Hiawatha's" government formed centuries ago had established
a pension system, a home for orphans, free medical care, a national hospital,
and Iroquois-run schools "in opposition to white's opinions on the subject."[33]
The dioramas reflected an ingrained Haudenosaunee progressivism, Parker
explained, and set an example for Americans who should aspire to real and
contemporary Iroquoian successes because they had once "saved" America
and, by way of example, could do so again.

Despite the high rhetoric that surrounded the creation of the dioramas, it
was soon after the first set were finished and displayed in 1909 that Parker's
ambitions would, literally, go up in flames. The Capitol Fire of March 1911 in
Albany ripped through the capitol building, much of the city, and the new educational buildings, taking with it all of the Ethnography and Archaeological
collections except those from the Ripley dig, selections of Lewis Henry
Morgan's collection, Converse's collection of silver brooches, the wampum
belts under Director Clarke's care that were stored in a separate facility, and
the recently finished dioramas that were being stored in a separate section of
the building. The sheer scale of this tragedy was immense for the museum
staff, but they did not stand idly by. Parker himself, using his Uncle Ely's
Cornplanter pipe-tomahawk as his "fire axe and mascot," spent hours running in and out of the burning buildings to save as much of the ethnography
collection he could. Despite his efforts, of the $30,000 value of the State
Museum's collections which included its foundational gift of "relics" that
Lewis H. Morgan donated decades earlier, only $1,500 survived. Clarke, the
wampum keeper, admitted that, if belts in the State's possession had burned,
he would "never be able to look an Iroquois Indian in the face again." Parker,
who "risked his life to save the collections," was devastated by the loss and fell
ill for weeks.[34]

FIGURE 4.4 Photograph of a hallway containing the burnt remnants of anthropological displays on the fourth floor of the Education Building in the aftermath of the Albany Capitol Fire of 1911. Corridor on the Fourth Floor—Capitol Fire. Unidentified photographer. 1911, gelatin silver photographic print, h. 9 1/4″ × w. 7 7/16″ (photograph); h. 10″ × w. 8″ (card). Albany Institute of History & Art Library, Ser 3/93, DI 152.

Not one to be deterred for long, however, he began to rebuild the museum and, at the same time, entered the arena of national politics. In 1911, he founded and became a central figure in the Society of American Indians (SAI), an organization staffed mostly by Indigenous peoples from across the continent. As the SAI's first Secretary, editor of the monthly *American Indian Magazine*, and the organization's president in 1917, he expanded his network of contacts throughout the country. In his various capacities, he led the development of every stage of the SAI's growth, which included the establishment of a legal division that assisted individuals and tribes in petitioning the

Bureau of Indian Affairs (BIA, the department that replaced the Office of Indian Affairs), the creation of an annual conference and quarterly journal, and a national campaign of public outreach.

Service in the SAI sharpened Parker's assimilationist instincts. At its core, the Society was founded to promote Indian assimilation in response to the rampant abuses and corruption of the BIA. This thinking was rooted in the recognition that the "Indian problem" was a historic and ongoing national American political problem. Parker wrote that poverty, corruption, and predatory land-hunger that targeted reservations "does not affect the Indian alone nor have its origins on Indian reservations alone." The failure of Indian legislation and American attitudes toward Native Americans "penetrate to the very bottom of our economic system" when "*crooked business concerns*" and "*dishonest citizens*" are allowed unfettered access to reservations. To fix it, the country needed to address the "major portion of our problem" which "is a white man's problem and concerns itself with the moral education of white men." By making this claim, Parker was responding to concerns similar to those voiced by his contemporary, W. E. B. Du Bois. Du Bois saw the major problem of the twentieth century as the black and white color line, but that was only possible after a century of forgetting Native American history and people.[35] Parker, in part, sought to remedy that forgetting. With his input, the SAI demanded a policy-driven reversal of predatory racial thinking and erasure as the only solution to advancing Indigenous society and sovereignty.

Parker's thinking on Native American rights at the SAI, however, was a jarring, mismatched combination of the well-established paternalism of Indian policies pushed by social progressives and Friends of the Indian of the 1890s and a genuine faith in Native America's promise and potential to save a corrupted American society. This tension, however, seemed like not much tension at all because Parker had a keen eye for audience and could deftly blur the two together. In a speech he delivered at the first conference of the SAI in October 1911, he embraced the common notion that in the pre-Columbian era, few Native Americans north of Mexico "were above the first stages of barbarism and some were pure savages." And yet, he explained, the Indigenous people of that era were also "subtle enough" to see the benefit of the European's material "advantage" and to adopt what made their own societies better. This assertion of intellectual flexibility and social adaptability proved to Parker that people were influenced by environmental factors, not racial "difference in capacity," as Franz Boas was then arguing outside the political arena. Taking this notion a step further, Parker placed blame on Americans themselves for the failure of Native America to catch up. "Progress," he explained, "can not be made any faster than the majority or their ruling element are willing to make it." No person can remain apart and distinct in an "abnormal position" and then be expected to "compete on an equal footing with the dominant race."[36] This balance of social Darwinism, the scholarship that sought to disprove theories of a global racial and social hierarchy, and a scathing critique of American society and government had the breadth and nuance to speak to a national American and Indian audience at the same time.

For Parker, the key to the project of racial leveling was education. He assumed the familiar stance of people like his friend, Carlisle Indian School founder and fellow SAI member Richard H. Pratt, when he argued that education was fundamental to teaching "independent action, of a pride that would lead to self-help," and that it would create a "clamor" for the "abolition of special laws that permitted the practice of tribal customs not consistent with modern progress." The laws he was referencing were those passed after the Dawes Act of 1887 that dissolved traditional tribal cultural practices, such as the Ghost Dance. Parker asked who, exactly, was responsible for the educational institutions that would teach Native Americans self-help and white people tolerance? Not the "pseudo-philanthropist" who only worked through "egotism and avarice," nor missionaries who have limited training and "prescribed [religious] functions" of their schools. It was the "government and the state" who were responsible. After all, if the government can create "experiment stations" growing vegetables and raising cattle, it can certainly "establish industrial and social betterment stations among a people to whom this country owes a great debt."[37]

Eventually, Parker's argument that education played a vital role in ensuring Indian uplift while allowing them to maintain their self-identity became SAI policy. In the months leading up to its 1911 conference, he was the organization's biggest cheerleader in New York and likely was the source of an influential *New York Tribune* article that described the SAI as "Looking for an Indian Booker T. Washington to Lead Their People," which presented Parker's argument that Indian education was crucial to American equality and freedom. In his conference speech, he framed education as the cornerstone of the SAI's policies of Indian advancement because civilization itself "is a matter of evolution. It is not bred over night or even in a century." Education and enlightenment were the clear first steps in the achievement of cultural assimilation. President William Howard Taft turned down Parker's invitation to speak at the 1912 conference, but he agreed with the State Archaeologist that his educated peers are doing the right thing and are "awaking to the realization of their duty" to help others. Taft went further and agreed that the problems Parker outlined were not problems of the Native American "race, but more those affecting him as an individual" and, most importantly, as a "potential citizen."[38]

Beyond his stance on education, Parker convinced the SAI to find and publicize the exceptional histories of the various peoples that composed vast Native America. In the SAI Constitution, which he and Reverend Sherman Coolidge, the Society's first president, jointly wrote in 1912, there is evidence of Parker's scholarly understanding of Indigenous history. The Constitution presented two core functions of the SAI that were clearly tied to Parker's work and what the dioramas represented at the State Museum. In one, the SAI was tasked with creating an Indigenous "bureau of information" to track "publicity and statistics" to get the most accurate information on Native nations. In the other, the SAI would establish a national education plan to "present in a just light a true history of the race, to preserve its records, and to emulate its distinguishing virtues." Thus, Parker focused on picking apart and understanding the nuances affecting the United States and Native America. To achieve this, as the chair of the SAI's education committee he created and executed a plan for an American Indian Day (AID) which by 1916 was adopted by states, local governments, and Indian agencies across the country. After AID passed in New York in May 1916, a public celebration was held in Central Park, with an invocation of the day given by the Onondaga Chief Jesse Lyons at the Hotel Astor. AID gained further national exposure in 1946 when the US Senate voted, but did not pass, a bill that would have declared AID a national holiday.[39]

Soon, however, Parker began to see institutional cracks forming among the members of the SAI. The organization's membership was composed of "primarily middle-class Indians" and governed entirely by Native Americans. Leadership had toyed with the idea of limiting its membership only to federally registered members of tribal nations, but influential outsiders rejected those limitations. Richard Pratt in 1913 complained to Professor Fayette A. McKenzie, another non-Native member of the group, that the focus on Indigenous-only membership made him feel like "half a member." Pratt and others complained that they had no recognition in the organization and that their opinions were overlooked. They were not alone in this complaint. Even Indigenous members of the SAI complained that the leadership was unrepresentative, particularly when it came to the "viciously impractical policy" of hosting their conference in cities, hotels, and universities, places that were far away from reservations and inaccessible to the very people it proposed to help.[40]

In addition to the SAI-wide problems, Parker's own leadership and claims to represent the Haudenosaunee were attacked on a few fronts. In all likelihood, he saw this coming. From the beginning of his service to the SAI, he was concerned that his support of US citizenship for Native Americans was inimical to his own people's active rejection of citizenship over the past "60 years." How could he have credibility if his ideas did not match the Haudenosaunees'? To make matter worse, the SAI had proven incapable of creating a functioning legal aid division to handle the sheer number of complaints flooding in from all corners of the country. Parker found himself alone in dealing with these issues, especially given that the leadership's constant internal battles prompted the departure of influential leaders like the Yavapai doctor and activist Charles Montezuma. These issues compounded Parker's struggles to single-handedly run the SAI journal, outreach campaign, and legal aid division. After six years of active involvement, he eventually lost faith in the organization and parted ways with it in 1918. He left the SAI with the opposite belief he held when founding it: it was impossible for a pan-Indian organization to create an "intertribal consensus" that could solve the Indian problem once and for all.[41]

Parker's departure from the SAI is regarded by historians as proof that he was forced out because his one-size-fits-all assimilationist ideas clashed with what Indigenous peoples continent-wide wanted when they called for tribal independence, a reformed relationship with American society, and the protection of their unique cultures, languages, and religions. His ideas about assimilation clashed with those realities, certainly, but as his museology makes clear, that was not his only motivation. Parker was convinced that the Haudenosaunee had an exceptional history and culture, so even as he used the State Museum to distribute AID literature he continued to showcase the history of the relative civility of the Haudenosaunee, their densely populated historical settlements, their "extensive continental trade," and their possession of "Considerable Artistic Instinct Even in the Early Days."[42] In that light, Parker's faith in the SAI collapsed not only because assimilation seemed impossible nationwide, but also because he, like the others who left, recognized that one organization could not harness the uniqueness of every nation and culture in Native America.

Regardless, the SAI had enabled him to develop a national platform which he used to argue the idea that the Iroquois empire had jumpstarted continental civilization long before Europeans invaded North America. The Six Nations were, he explained, "founded" long before European contact "on the doctrine of group welfare." Talented individuals were offered honorary positions within the governing bodies of the Six Nations, and women could initiate "proposition and demand action" and even "nullify a national or confederate decree." The Haudenosaunee, he said, also respected individual rights, took care of orphans and the aged, adopted the people they conquered, and, unlike the shamanistic stereotype of the ecological Indian, believed in a single creator. He made the case that the historic Six Nations were so well-governed and stable that "without European interference [they] would have erected an aboriginal empire of no mean magnitude." To prove this, he pointed to his own archaeological and ethnographic work to show how, before 1492, the Iroquois "War Machine" had broken the "Eries and Attiwandaronk [or Neutral]" nations to become the predominant Native power and society in the Northeast. At the moment of European contact, the Six Nations were the best and strongest evolution of American society. As an exceptional "Seneca by birth," the State Archaeologist deemed himself in a unique position to tell this history of the "highly cultured Iroquois."[43]

Alongside that history of Haudenosaunee supremacy, Parker continued to reject the popular Plains Indian–style Wild West stereotypes that had taken hold of New Yorkers' popular imagination. He took aim, for example, at a beloved and highly publicized New York state tradition: the annual Iroquoian "adoptions" of outsiders and politicians by the Tonawanda Senecas in their fall "corn festival" in Rochester. Parker explained that this event—where the adoptees were given fake war bonnets—was merely a "Wild West type" performance. He informed the public and past recipients that his people saw this event as "a ridiculous farce" in which the they "have made much of a joke out of the mock adoption ceremonies." The Senecas had twisted what the public assumed was an "authentic" Indian ceremony for their own ends. It was not a somber and spiritual occasion, as many white observers believed, but rather one that "cause[d] violent laughter on the part of the redmen and women" involved in it.[44]

These moments reveal Parker's desire to privilege and elevate his people's voices not just for his own sake, but for the the sake of the Haudenosaunee as well. He did this also while defending his scholarly work on Haudenosaunee historical and cultural perspectives. In 1916, the Tuscarora scholar Dr. J. N. B. Hewitt, an anthropologist for the US Bureau of Ethnology at the Smithsonian Institution, and the anthropologist Dr. A. A. Goldenweiser, both negatively reviewed Parker's *The Constitution of the Five Nations*, citing its ethnographic inaccuracy. Parker responded to these criticisms by suggesting that these well-regarded and senior scholars had missed the point of his work. If they had simply "read the introduction," they would have seen that Parker's

Constitution was not some top-down reinterpretation, but an oral retelling of the "Dekanawida legend" by Seth Newhouse, "a Mohawk who has expended a large amount of time and given the subject a lengthy study." This oral history, given entirely in the Mohawk language, was carefully translated by a team lead by Parker's friend Albert Cusick and his team of ethnographers Horatio Hale and William Beauchamp. Parker's work was an oral history, delivered and translated by two Haudenosaunee men, and all done in the way that the Haudenosaunee themselves would recognize. Parker also reminded Hewitt and Goldenweiser that there was a second version of the legend published in his *Constitution* that offered the story from the perspective of the sitting Six Nations Council members who "reviewed and corrected" the legend themselves. Parker ensured that, by taking these steps, the "original orthography was retained."[45]

In that sense, Parker rightly found the criticism of his "compilation of native documents . . . gratuitous." It was, after all, an account many times vetted by various Haudenosaunee parties at multiple levels. Parker also felt that Hewitt and Goldenweiser's tone was strangely personal because there were important cultural and political nuances of the Haudenosaunee languages that English could not quite capture and, by deriding it as being written "in clumsy, stilted English, involved and lacking in force of expression," they had again missed the point. Hewitt's English translations may have read better, Parker admitted, but that was because Hewitt added his own literary flourishes that were not in the Haudenosaunee sources. Under the guise of artistic license, Hewitt had warped these stories to suit his own needs. This was a problem because while faithfully translated oral stories may look "clumsy" on the page to some people, Parker had no desire to "alter their writings, even for the sake of presenting them as I personally desired to see them." It was clear that Hewitt was not taking these voices seriously on their own terms, and Parker resented scholars who disregarded the work of contemporary Haudenosaunee peoples, particularly those who served their communities be preserving their heritage and history. These included the wampum belts so excoriated by Hewitt and others "may be regarded as [genuine] even though not made during the days of Dekanawida."[46] Parker was mounting a defense of Haudenosaunee oral history and tradition against scholarly expertise that was highly unusual for an ethnographer of his time.

He continued that thought by critiquing the methods employed by Hewitt and his networks of informants. Parker again criticized the Smithsonian ethnographer for "directing the minds of his informants" which "no doubt, as he himself suggests, has contributed largely to their store of ancient lore."

In other words, the stories were Hewitt's, not the Haudenosaunees'. Hewitt had therefore given his scholarship an artificial but no less "enormous advantage" because he was "previously instructing for a period of years his native informants" on how to speak and what to say. This problem was illuminated in the writing itself because "no translation or presentation in English can gracefully and fluently express the Iroquoian idiom," and so the beautiful retellings of Hewitt's "literal translation" only "robs the native thought of much of its meaning and emphasis." The problem, quite clearly, was that the "'facts' so collected [by Hewitt] seem like re-importations; in other words, like telling one's informants what to say and how to say it."[47] His fellow scholar's manipulation of Indigenous voices hurt not just scholarship, but the Haudenosaunee people and their history.

While Parker was defending the Haudenosaunee on paper, the Senecas were being dragged back into the public eye in other ways. In 1917 the newly formed State Police were called in to assist with the containment of a smallpox outbreak in the Cattaraugus Reservation. The outbreak highlighted both real and manufactured problems in the reservation health system, poor relief, and it drew attention to the generally depressed conditions in Cattaraugus. To combat that image of the Senecas as a poor and suffering people, Parker sought to tie their history to contemporary politics and patriotism. He found the perfect opportunity when he was appointed to the state Draft Commission after the United States entered the Great War on April 6, 1917. His official duties were to recruit men from across the Six Nations for the army, but he also found that a good number had already crossed the border and joined Canadian army regiments even before the United States joined the war. Interpreting this as proof of a deep and underlying patriotism, Parker reported that, like the Haudenosaunee, Indigenous communities from across the continent had voluntarily spent $4 million to buy war bonds, doubled their typical cattle output for the war effort, and dedicated the lives of a fifth of their young men of fighting age to the cause.[48]

Parker's glowing reports of his peoples' patriotism also illuminated their objections to being considered "aliens." After canvassing New York reservations for the draft board, Parker reported that the Senecas resented the term "alien" on registration questionnaires. They felt that it was both an inaccurate and an offensive term because of their unique legal status within the state. In a letter to F. S. Hutchinson at the Office of the Adjutant General, Parker advised him that, although the Provost Marshall ordered that wards of the government could not be drafted, the questionnaires still required that "aliens and Indians are required or asked to register" whether or not they were citizens. Parker explained that the Haudenosaunee saw this forced draft and the term "alien" as further attacks on their sovereignty because the Six Nations "are in a state of treaty relation with the United States and the State of New York" and are recognized as "nations" with certain rights going back to the Treaty of Fort Stanwix of 1784. They are distinctly not "aliens." This term, which Parker reasoned may well have been a typo on the draft forms, nevertheless besmirched the national pride of the Iroquois by associating them with non-Americans. As he reported to a New York newspaper, the Haudenosaunee were rightly "incensed over the name 'alien'" because they were by treaty obligation and legal precedent independent nations. And many, like Parker himself, were proud citizens. The Iroquois, he made clear, were "real Americans."[49]

Parker meant that quite literally. As a member of the draft board, he urged all the Haudenosaunee to comply with the Selective Service law and to fight on behalf of the United States. It was, he reasoned, their patriotic "duty" as potential citizens. Even if one wanted to claim exemption as a "non-citizen Indian," he advised them in July 1918 to "protect yourself as a loyal American" and complete the registration form. However, Parker's public efforts to persuade them to enlist was mostly for show. Arthur H. Dretader, the Clerk of the Seneca Nation, reported the same month that all men of legal age had already registered for the draft, so a special registration drive was unnecessary. The Onondagas also reported two days later that all men ages 21–31 had registered for the draft a full year earlier in June 1917.[50]

Parker's efforts to sign up his people for the draft may have been unnecessary, but they did have an impact. The presence of the Draft Board among the Haudenosaunee meant that, for the first time, all men of fighting age and their families were added to the state's census records. A detailed census investigation increased the state's administrative presence in the reservations and offered state lawmakers yet another chance to bring the sovereign nations under Albany's control. This manifested in the 1919 Machold bill which, after it passed, established the New York State Indian Commission (SIC). The SIC was designed to oversee all Indian affairs in the state, much like the Office of Indian Affairs at the federal level. Parker was selected to serve as secretary of the commission and, in that capacity, had access to state politics for years to come. Throughout—and perhaps despite—this administrative invasion, Parker continued to bolster the narrative of Haudenosaunee patriotism while chipping away at broader Indian stereotypes. Positioning himself as a representative of the Senecas and the state, Parker spoke from a position of authority when he explained that the Haudenosaunee did not volunteer to fight because of their "bloodlust," but because they were the "only real Americans" who put their lives on the line to see that "the world may be made nearer what it ought to be."[51]

As Parker knew well, the New York draft drive, the smallpox outbreak, and the creation of SIC were all linked to national conversations about Native American citizenship. In 1920, a federal citizenship drive was passed in Congress that extended the option of citizenship to all Indigenous nations based on an up or down majority vote on each reservation. Four years later, universal citizenship was forced on Native Americans after the passage of the Carter bill, or the Indian Citizenship Act of 1924. In between those landmark years, Parker actively pushed for New York Indians to become citizens. He was helped in that effort in July 1920 by New York Governor Al Smith who gave instructions to the SIC to assemble a team under Edward A. Everett to find new legal pathways to further subsume the Iroquois reservations under the state government. The result was the formation of the Everett Commission, a three-person task force of Attorney General Charles D. Newton, Dr. R.W. Hill from the State Board of Charities, and Arthur Parker. Parker, on hearing rumors that universal Indian citizenship was making its way through Congress, set out to convince his people that "the Indians and whites must work and prepare for this end." The majority of the Six Nations in council disagreed, however, and became one of only a handful of Indigenous communities across the country who voted to reject US citizenship in May 1920. Undeterred, the Indian Welfare Society (IWS), an altruistic volunteer group established to help uplift New York's Native American population, tried again that November, but the leadership doubled down on their previous decision.[52]

Despite Parker's failure to convince his people of the virtues of US citizenship, he did find a personal silver lining. At a meeting of the IWS at the end of 1920, he was able to turn the table on a new and damning rumor that threatened his standing among the Haudenosaunee. The rumor held that the Everett Commission, while on a tour of the reservations that summer, had tried to trick the people they met into independently registering for citizenship without consulting tribal leaders. The rumor turned out to be false, but it threatened to damage Parker's character and scuttle the Commission's efforts. In a scheduled speech to the IWS, Parker blamed the spread of the damning rumors on "show Indians," or those morally corrupted Indigenous and white cultural appropriators who donned war bonnets and nontraditional clothing in public in order to "look" more Indian and who, in the process, sold themselves out to an ignorant white audience. These impostors eroded Haudenosaunee cultural heritage while miseducating the public about their life and culture. In that sense, they were just as "guilty" as "the whites" in perpetrating "this fraud" and in "sell[ing] their own self-respect and the respect of their nation for a few dollars, thereby deceiving the public and putting their people to shame." Parker advised that the Haudenosaunee should band together and speak as one to resist this incursion into Iroquois country and "wear the gustoweh and not Sioux war bonnet" or else their politics, "ceremonies[,] and religious beliefs be . . . cheapened."[53]

That speech has been seen by historians as the moment when, "from this point onward," Parker used his racial background to further his own career. But this was far from a new strategy. Even if he did deploy his identity as a weapon, it was not always to further his own career. From the beginning, he proved willing to elevate the unique aspects of his people's culture and history even if it put him at odds with his peers. The speech becomes even less of a turning point considering that Parker had aimed his words directly at his main political opponent at the IWS meeting, Chief Jesse Lyons of the Onondaga. Lyons, a staunch opponent of assimilation and an orator widely regarded as "the modern Red Jacket," was scheduled to speak at the meeting, but likely to Parker's delight, was photographed wearing, of all things, a war bonnet.[54] Parker's speech, then, was less the sign of a new political strategy and more about his practiced ability to wield his knowledge about his peoples' exceptional history to establish himself as a guardian of Haudenosaunee culture who, in this case, was a better cultural and historical protectionist than Lyons, a chief who actually represented the Six Nations.

From 1920 to 1924, the year that Parker left the State Museum to become Director of the Rochester Municipal Museum, his reputation continued to grow, yielding accolades and invitations to advise on various public projects. In 1922, he received his first honorary graduate degree, a Master of Science from the University of Rochester, which celebrated his pioneering work in New York archaeology nearly two decades earlier. The same year, while working on a book project on the history of the State Museum, Parker was contacted by Governor Nathan Miller's office with a formal request from William de Leftwich Dodge, the artist contracted to create a new mural for the state capital building. Dodge typically had few qualms about taking artistic liberties with Native American stereotypes, but in this case felt compelled to reach out to Parker for guidance on "proper costuming, et cetera" for the "New York Indian['s]" for inclusion in the murals that would grace the rotunda. Then in 1923, Parker gained the attention of the US Secretary of the Interior Hubert Work who appointed him as a regional representative to the Advisory Council for the BIA.[55]

In 1923, Parker proposed the creation of a state park at Indian Falls in Genesee County, an area nearby the Tonawanda Reservation. He reached out to Robert Moses, New York's influential parks administrator, and received positive feedback from him and Fred B. Parker, a legislator from Batavia, and Albert Moot, the President of the New York State Association. The proposal for the new state park included plans to build a Haudenosaunee-focused exhibition space where the "the legendary spirit that attaches to this spot" would be interpreted. To help keep that spirit alive, Parker planned a restoration of his Uncle Ely's historic homestead that would be staffed by tour guides trained to talk about the "Senecas, [the] original owners, who live at Tonawanda nearby."[56]

As Parker began work on the park, the *Albany Knickerbocker Press* in December asked him to comment on that project and the history and future of the state's capitol region. Taking advantage of the opportunity to explore the meaning and importance of Iroquoian land, the "famed ethnologist" offered a "new prophecy of [the] districts growth, tracing [its] upward climb to [a] peerless center of American industry and culture." Parker explained that Albany was well-suited for the future because of its incredible past. In the colonial era, Albany was an agricultural and trade center of the region that attracted the Dutch, French, and English. Yet despite the Europeans' superior technology, Parker explained, they nevertheless continued to grow crops and trade "the same way Indians always have." The region was, after all, a "crossroads" of civilization well before Europeans landed on North American shores and, throughout its history from the "Mahikans" to the Mohawk, it was a hub of economic activity. To Parker, that past would inform the areas future. Looking fifty years ahead, Parker, much like DeWitt Clinton a century earlier, predicted that the region's Indigenous foundations would allow it to bloom into a center of innovation and industry. It would become the perfect home for a contented populace living in beautiful communities, all nestled in the shadow of the "Eastern Doorway of the ancient Long House." Parker's vision, however, would not entirely come to pass. His Indigenous park at Indian Falls, part of Albany's grand future, fell through due to budgetary constraints in 1926.[57]

The failure of the Indian Falls project only reinforced Parker's sense of the importance of preserving and reinterpreting Haudenosaunee history beyond the borders of a reservation, the covers of a book, or the walls of a museum. In October of 1925, he, then a trustee of the New York State Historical Association, got involved in the reinterpretation planning of the popular Letchworth State Park which had opened in 1906 on Seneca land. The

Letchworth project was far more ambitious than the Indian Falls project. To prevent its being deemed a similar financial failure, Parker modeled it on the institutional partnerships that already existed between the AMNH and the Palisades Interstate Park, as well as the State Museum and the Allegany State Park.[58] These partnerships benefited the natural history museums, which utilized the raw natural materials provided by the parks, and the parks likewise benefited from the financial stability of the museums. Parker envisioned a similar arrangement for Letchworth and the Rochester Municipal Museum, where as director he enjoyed control over the allocation of its institutional resources and the intellectual energy of its staff.

The Letchworth plan would expand the existing facilities and refocus them on the interpretation of local history and New York-specific flora. Parker simultaneously proposed a vast reinterpretation of the museum and a redirection of the library to focus on local topics. Such a transformation would have immense social and educational value because, as he explained, the lay public thought about history "entirely from the local and, consciously or otherwise, the vital value of the museum and its possibilities has no adequate appreciation."[59] Parker understood that the best way to educate people about why history mattered was through connecting with their own personal life and on-site experiences.[60]

To promote that experiential learning, the Letchworth expansion would feature the construction of a new "Indian village." This village would be life-sized and include a historic palisaded *castle*, complete with storage buildings, a "substantial bark house," and a working farm where native plants would be harvested with traditional agricultural techniques. The village would also board a real Seneca family who would "live there under aboriginal conditions and cultivate the garden," and so bring to life a history "which will be easily grasped by the most casual visitor." Authenticity and historical accuracy were essential. This thinking, however, was a marked departure from what the National Park Service (NPS), the biggest first-person interpretation developer, expected from its Native American employees and boarders. For decades, national parks had allowed Indigenous people to live in the parks with limited autonomy on the condition that they maintain and interpret (as docents) the history of the park while wearing stereotypical Indian "costumes" in public. The Sierra Miwok living in the Yosemite National Park, for example, were forced to wear culturally incorrect feathered headdresses and "buckskin" while speaking with visitors. The Native interpreters were paid to take pictures posing alone or with a family, and their housing was contingent on them hosting public pageants called "Indian Field Days" where a panel of Native employees would judge the homemade Indian "costumes" submitted and worn by white visitors. Parker's vision for Letchworth, a project "designed for [the] single purpose" of reflecting local historical and ethnological accuracy, offered something quite different with its village and family "ethnologically consistent" with a real Seneca village.[61]

Just three months into the initial planning phase, Parker learned that a rival proposal was making its way through the State Museum: another Indian village designed by an E. W. Countryman in the Allegany State Park. He was concerned that Countryman's village would sap Letchworth's funding, but he also saw it as a battle between two competing memories of the Haudenosaunee. Parker and Charles Adams, a colleague at the New York State Museum, leveled many critiques at Countryman's plan, above all that the proposed village was like those found at turn-of-the-century World's Fairs that collapsed cultures from all corners of the continent into a single circus-like "side show." Parker and Adams knew that this was what most people expected a Native American history exhibition to look like, but they believed that the village would be just another "trashy city amusement" like the Wild West Show and its spin-offs that were found "so frequent in and about some of the city parks and resorts."[62]

Countryman's proposal, in their eyes, sacrificed scholarly rigor and ethnographic and historical accuracy for entertainment and spectacle. Visitors to the Allegany Indian village would meander without guidance through space and time as they encountered a "Navajo Logan," a Chippewa Lodge, a nondescript "Sweat House," and a "Haida and Siwash House," among others. The village's random assortment of Indigenous architectural forms would knit together "miscellaneous exhibits" that told a chaotic story "not native to New York State." Countryman's plan was eventually dropped, but the news was tempered when the Indian village section of Parker's own plans were also rejected. Still, Parker and Adams ultimately succeeded in scuttling a historically damaging park, as well as in getting funding for the reinterpretation of the existing Letchworth museum and arboretum that, at least, focused solely on state and local history and the history of the Haudenosaunee.[63]

During the period from 1929 to 1945, when Parker served as Director of the Rochester Museum, he was highly productive and "mature[d]" as a museologist. He standardized his museum's public educational material, made research of collections the museum's core function, designed exhibitions to be visitor-centric and experiential, proposed changes to museums nationwide that would standardize language and administrative procedures, and taught museum leaders that their "service" to the public should be the primary component of their job description. Throughout all of this, Rochester gave Parker an intellectual home where he was not constantly limited in what he could do or work on.[64] He had come a long way. The State Museum had taught him about museum administration, the SAI had shown him the pitfalls in believing in a national pan-Indian movement, the war had taught him to sell his people's history to American audiences in ways they would understand and eagerly engage with, and his experience with parks proved how powerful, and potentially damaging, nonexperts were when they misinterpreted Native American history. These were lessons he brought to the Municipal Museum.

One of Parker's top institutional priorities was to develop the city with his museum as a focal point. As the Municipal Museum looked to expand in 1926 and courted donors to help it move to a new central facility downtown, Parker advertised his grand designs for its future. The current museum had "Outgrown [its] Quarters" and, as the city would expand and industrialize over the next decade, he proposed that the "Museum should be [a] Central Building in [the new] Civic Center Plan." It would become a publicly accessible educational institution "set like a jewel within a golden circlet" of the new, prosperous Rochester. As the city looked toward its industrial future, Parker warned that "a city without a museum is an amnesia victim."[65] The Municipal Museum would help secure Rochester's future as a thriving cultural and social space.

As cities around the country went through similar periods of industrial expansion, Parker explained that museums, public pillars of social and educational development, needed trained and dedicated curators, "museist[s]" who could provide their cities with the appropriate guidance. With the stakes of running a successful museum so high, Parker criticized other institutions that, far too often, "cop[ied] the faults" of others and hired fake "museum men." These people were not professionals; they merely donned "the guise of an unfamiliar profession" and damaged their institutions and the cities that trusted them. The primary problem they caused was that, under their leadership, museums would accept random collections and interpret them with little knowledge of curatorial best practices, much less history. Like Countryman's Allegany Park proposal, this disturbingly widespread practice did nothing but confuse history with trivia. Once that happened, "the muses miserably perish" as museums devolved into mere cabinets of curiosities, becoming concerned solely with satisfying a donor's "ego" and turning into dusty monuments to a collector's vanity. The museum world needed an institution like the American Association of Museums (of which Parker was a member), founded in 1906, to universalize museum best practices, set guidelines for employees, and offer critical guidance on how museums can and should reject unrelated or trivial donations that only warped institutional missions, funding, and focus. Without training, these amateur curators have only "the whiskers of a Polish musician and the fingers of a Parisian sculptor, but he fails to produce the harmonies of either," and history itself suffers.[66]

Parker's museological vision extended well beyond Rochester. In 1935, he published *A Manual for History Museums*, the first American methodological volume of its kind for museums. Intended for museum professionals, it set administrative and curatorial standards that created the blueprint for history museums ever since. It covered topics like how to start an institutional advancement department, the management of collections, proper exhibition lighting techniques, and drafting the perfect institutional mission statement. As historians explain, Parker's volume has become so deeply embedded in modern museum "common knowledge" that it is "easy to overlook" the book's importance to modern museology. With this book and his editorship of the journal of the American Association of Museums, Parker by the 1920s had established himself as one of the country's premier museologists, a category and name he invented.[67]

When it came to where the museum fit in American life, an important part of his thinking was in the capacity of museums to engage the public in history and scholarship, a mission that transcended concerns about their economic solvency. He explained to the Rochester Chamber of Commerce in June 1929 that museums were the fastest growing institutions in America. That was a dubious claim, but he used it to make his real point: that their educational value was of the utmost social importance. A month before the stock market crash that triggered the Great Depression, Parker wrote about the Municipal Museum's recent acquisition of a circa 1829 New York "Old Country Store." Installed as a period room, the Country Store was a place of importance to local "social history, of culture," and a site-specific exhibition that anticipated Henry Ford's Greenfield Village, which opened in 1933. The period-accurate shelves, items for sale, "dressed figures" that inhabited the store, and even the artificial country store smell piped into the building, all invited the public to truly experience a moment in time and better understand why it mattered. Parker used this example to show that the Municipal Museum was financially stable despite the depression, but even more, that museums generally were vital because they provided the city with a "quick and effective means of educating its masses." Museums provided the public with an education, as well as a sense of local pride, that transcended temporary economic circumstances because they had long-term social and cultural consequences.[68]

In Parker's museological vision, a museum and museologist's responsibilities did not stop at its front doors. In 1933, Parker found an opportunity to memorialize one of his family's ancestors far away from Rochester on the shores of Keuka Lake. He proposed the installment of plaque and monument that would mark the location of the historic home of Red Jacket's mother, the birthplace of America's "greatest" orator and the home of a woman "well-respected by locals." At the end of the year, in front of a crowd of locals and government officials, Parker's daughter Bertha and a local girl from the Tonawanda Reservation unveiled the memorial. When it came to memorials, he was careful to support only those he thought worthy. When called in to review other historical markers pitched to the New York State Historical Association by various community members, he critiqued those that were not well planned or thought out, particularly ones based on Native American history. Without a firm foundation in scholarship, he warned, these rogue public lies would create a permanent network of misinformation that threated to do "great harm" because they "seized upon most of the old theories and traditions now looked upon as doubtful and false."[69]

Just such a memorial was pitched in 1935. Parker negatively reviewed the application for a marker on Onondaga history that was to be placed on the Syracuse-Oswego state highway. It was submitted by a local Syracuse member of the Sons of the American Revolution (SAR), Frank Decker, who had also chaired his own share of historical marker committees. In his application, Decker, despite having "no special knowledge as to the history of our native Onondaga Indians," nevertheless felt qualified to create a plaque on Haudenosaunee history because he was "greatly interested" in their history "from boyhood." Parker, a past board member of the Historical Association, intervened to correct a number of factual errors in Decker's proposal, as well as his clear lack of knowledge about the size and scale of the Iroquois empire he was attempting to memorialize.[70] The sign was never created.

In addition to his museology, Parker remained a renowned expert on the Haudenosaunee who published multiple books and dozens of historical, archaeological, and anthropological papers. From 1934–1935, he served on the Committee on State Archaeological Surveys for the American Research Council, and he was elected a member of the Society of University Indians of America. As an established expert on the Haudenosaunee, he continued to field questions from authors and state agencies on their history and cultural practices. In another convergeance with his Aunt Hattie's work, in 1935, the Pennsylvania Department of Public Instruction asked him to fact-check Converse's findings on the Iroquoian origins of Groundhog Day in

FIGURE 4.5 Photograph of a monument commemorating
Red Jacket's boyhood home and his mother's burial place on
the western banks of Keuka Lake, New York. Photograph by
author.

preparation for their celebrations. Parker's authority on the Haudenosaunee
was also recognized internationally. Dr. I. N. Vinikov, Chief of the Department
of the Most Primitive Peoples in the USSR's Academy of Science, singled
out Parker as the only person who could advise his department on the history of the Haudenosaunee and asked him to compose a 10,000 word essay
synthesizing important scholarship published since Morgan's *League*. In
his response, Parker pointed to anthropologists of the past such as Erminie
Smith and modern studies by the US Bureau of Ethnology, particularly those
of J. N. B. Hewitt, Mark Harrington, and Jeremiah Curtain, who published
a book on Seneca Folk Tales in 1908. Parker made it clear to Vinikov, however, in a comment that echoed his past critique of Hewitt and Goldenweiser,

that the Haudenosaunee themselves "tell the Dekanawideh epic differently" than non-Iroquoian scholars, and that subtle variations on this story existed among each of the Six Nations. Parker advised him to abandon a one-size-fits-all approach to that history, and even hinted at the inaccuracy of the anthropological method of upstreaming, or the practice of looking for cultural "authenticity" only in things that had never changed. After all, the history of the Haudenosaunee was still evolving and "it appears that culture patterns, social traits and language, far from being inalterable are in a constant state of flux with aboriginal peoples, notwithstanding strong taboos against innovation."[71] Many scholars, he warned, were uninterested in understanding the Haudenosaunee on their own terms.

To the outside world Parker may have been a recognized authority on the Haudenosaunee, but his reputation among them was less clear. Central to this was his outspoken support of John Collier, President Franklin Roosevelt's new Commissioner of the BIA, with whom he maintained a friendly correspondence for years. Collier was the mastermind behind the 1934 Indian Reorganization Act (IRA), more commonly known as the Indian New Deal, which dismantled the devastating 1887 Dawes Allotment Act and ensured some measure of self-government for most reservations. For most Native nations this was a positive legal change, but the Haudenosaunee saw it differently. The IRA, they argued, violated past treaty agreements and threatened their hard-won sovereignty. Although the reservations in New York petitioned overwhelmingly in protest against Congress's passage of the IRA, it passed over their objections because most other Native American governments stood behind it. Despite that loss, the Six Nations would continue to argue in court they were an exception to the IRA's rules.[72]

In addition to national issues like the IRA, local concerns—not to mention the economic devastation wrought by the Great Depression—gave the Haudenosaunee even more reason to distrust state and federal authorities. The same year that Congress passed the IRA, the New York state legislature advanced a Syracuse dam project over Onondaga protests. This effectively granted the city the authority to take "unused" Onondaga reservation land by condemnation. It did not help matters when Parker clashed on this issue with Joseph Bruner, the president of a Native American rights group the American Indian Federation, who had openly criticized the IRA and attempted to start a national movement to secure its repeal. This was a position embraced by the Six Nations, but Parker had made it clear to Secretary of State Harold Ickes that he supported Collier—and by extension the IRA—and believed him to generally be "good for the Indians."[73]

Despite his unpopular position on the IRA, over the next two years Parker proposed the creation of a new and broadly popular state-funded Community House on the Tonawanda Reservation and applied for federal Works Progress Administration (WPA) funds to build it. The Community House proposal was massive. It would create a new medical facility, library, public space, and museum all on the Tonawanda Reservation. The project had a powerful ally in the indefatigable Nameé Hendricks, a friend of Parker's who was later adopted by the Senecas. For Parker, the Community House would provide critical infrastructure for the reservation while also "lay[ing] the foundation of understanding of native culture in this area for generations." This project also attracted a local anthropologist, William Fenton, who worked under Parker's direction for two years and would become his successor as the foremost anthropologist studying the Haudenosaunee. The Community House also captured the attention of First Lady Eleanor Roosevelt who, along with Hendricks, "smoothed the project's way" through numerous state and federal bureaucratic hurdles.[74]

But the Tonawanda Senecas, with the Syracuse dam project fresh in their minds, were concerned that the "temptation and destruction" of the nearby city of Akron would similarly prevent them from choosing their own economic fate once the Community House opened. They wanted to ensure that "surrounding friends and local Indian organizations were in control of the situation," not Akron. Added to the fear of the loss of control, the Community House project would be funded primarily by WPA funds which, by law, required an official sponsor. None of the reservations, however, were recognized as official sponsors by state or federal agencies. The Tonawanda, to the anger of many, had no authority to sponsor their own project and were forced to cede control of it to the federal government. But Hendricks had a solution to this, albeit a compromising one. After self-funding eleven trips to the offices of the governor, the state commissioner of Indian affairs, and the Washington WPA, she convinced the New York State Department of Social Welfare to sponsor the project. It did, but on the condition that it was the state, not the Tonawandas, who would own the lease of the reservation land in question for ninety-five years before passing ownership to the Senecas.[75] For the Tonawandas, it was a short-term compromise that solved a long-term problem.

While Parker oversaw the development of the Community House project, he also worked to secure federal funding for his proposed Seneca Indian Arts Project (SIAP). This program would hire local Seneca artisans to both "restore the ancient cultural arts of the Indian of Western New York" and "produce a better type of New York Indian souvenir" to sell to white Americans. These "souvenirs," Parker explained, were authentically Iroquois because they were "based on the best in the old art" and "eliminated the crudeness of the denigrated art of recent times." The SIAP was on one hand a natural extension of his dedication to museum education and public outreach, and on the other it was intended to replenish the ethnographic collections lost during the 1911 Albany fire. Much like his dioramas at the State Museum which relied on the local knowledge of Seneca craftswomen and models, the SIAP promised to revive authentic Haudenosaunee art forms by relying solely on Seneca talent to make them. Parker did not think much about dedicating resources to support or champion contemporary Seneca art, but he insisted that only Senecas could and should create or replicate their material culture. The SIAP thus became a factory that produced "duplicates of ancient patterns" for scientific study and sale under the direct supervision and guidance of Parker's Municipal Museum.[76]

As expected, however, the SIAP encountered some resistance among the Haudenosaunee. A. H. Poody, a Tonawanda Seneca chief, rejected outright what he saw as Parker's attempts to submit the reservation's cultural authority and the Senecas' local artistic voice to the Municipal Museum. Parker was a capable coalition builder, however, and over Poody's objections succeeded in bringing the state legislature, the Tonawanda Council, and John Collier on board. By the end of 1935, the SIAP was fully funded by the WPA and was overseen locally by the Municipal Museum, which began construction on the workshop in an abandoned warehouse nearby. As early as 1936, Seneca artists were sourced, hired, and began to produce historically accurate "etchings, water colors . . . and examples of ceremonial masks" that decorated the new Council House. They also made hundreds of historic artifact reproductions that greatly expanded the archives and public exhibitions of the Municipal Museum. Despite the protestations of some Haudenosaunee leaders, the program proved generally popular among the Tonawanda Senecas. Its success even inspired Collier to "recommended a country-wide adoption of the plan." This became the famed Indian Arts Project, a project of the Indian Arts and Crafts Board of the BIA.[77]

Despite the success and relative popularity of the SIAP, critics have leveled some criticism at Parker's efforts to bend artistic labor toward the exclusive manufacture of reproductions. This, they argue, ignored the value of contemporary Haudenosaunee cultural productions. That is all true, but to Parker, the SIAP was "an opportunity to test the reverse application of [an] old practice of enforced deculturation." He saw little wrong with the exclusive production of historic and distinctly Haudenosaunee cultural forms, even if he never articulated why he thought contemporary Seneca art might have been any less culturally or historically relevant than the reproductions. To Parker, the SIAP was a project that served the Senecas and employed people in a museum and was therefore "in social service to people." Despite the criticisms, it culturally and economically empowered Seneca craftspeople. In addition, the project would, in the long term, remain under Tonawanda cultural control, stay local, and provide Senecas on other reservations and in Canada with the raw materials to create "articles of their old culture-things." As Parker made clear, the SIAP cultivated among his people and the public "a new respect" for Haudenosaunee culture and history. Crucially, this project was original in that it produced "nothing broadly 'just Indian,'" but objects and artwork that were distinctly Haudenosaunee.[78] For Parker, the success of the SIAP meant that the Municipal Museum would become the site of a revival of the culture of the Senecas and of the public's interest and investment in Iroquois exceptionalism.

Following his success with the SIAP, Parker brought his culturally specific educational mission to the airwaves. In 1937–1938 he wrote, directed, and produced the radio program "Romance of Old Indian Days," which aired in upstate New York and Iroquois country every Sunday at 7:15 PM. Each installment was a historical drama written and narrated by Parker about an important aspect of the culture and history of the Haudenosaunee. The stories covered a range of topics such as the ancient origins of the Haudenosaunee Confederacy, the life of Red Jacket, the relationship of Sir William Johnson and Molly Brant, the life of Handsome Lake and the creation of the Longhouse religion after the War of 1812, and the public service of his Uncle Ely.[79] These stories humanized famous Iroquois of the past while rejecting out of hand the Wild Western–style stereotypes that were so familiar to its audience.

In these programs, Parker took care to use exclusively Haudenosaunee names in popular productions like the "Epic of Hiawatha." This was an important production because, as he explained, "Its special interest lies in the fact that it is an attempt of the Iroquois themselves to explain their own civic and social system." In other words, he began to subtly decolonize a popular story by retelling it on Iroquoian terms, in contrast to the wildly inaccurate Wild West Show versions of the same epic. On the air, Parker touted the educational value of these stories and, critically, reminded the listening audience that his were a people "you can't beat . . . for Patriotism." By telling these pseudo-decolonized stories in a way that connected with his white listeners through those vague appeals to Iroquoian patriotism, Parker invited

New Yorkers to first listen and then to think critically about what they truly knew of "the Indians" in their state. When asked by the host: didn't the world already know all there was to know about the Iroquois? Parker countered that he "scarcely believe[d] that any writer has even commenced to tell anything" at all.[80] These radio stories, told in part on the Haudenosaunees' own terms, were proof of that.

By the end of the 1930s, Parker had enjoyed professional and social successes and supported the Tonawanda economy in ways that seemed to defy the economic conditions that devestated much of the rest of the country. The Chicago Indian Council Fire agreed and named him the "most famous person of Indian ancestry in the United States." The Municipal Museum also secured private funding for a brand-new and massive 7,500 square foot facility in the center of Rochester. In addition, his museum was chosen by the 1938 World's Fair Commission to "assist in creating a display to represent the Rochester area." Parker, at this point in his career, had ample reason to think that he had "created one of the most advanced museum systems in the world." Others, like Herbert Gambrell, the director of the Dallas Historical Society, agreed and declared that "just as truly as the modern high school is a monument to Horace Mann, so the modern history museum is the creation of Arthur C. Parker." But Parker's work didn't stop there. During World War II, he created a Peabody Award-winning wartime "civilian protection" radio program designed to cultivate patriotism and encourage wartime volunteerism. Hosted by the Municipal Museum, this series, titled "Rochester on Guard," produced over six hundred broadcasts and harnessed the talents of "nearly 100" guest speakers. Parker saw it as proof that museums were valuable because they offered a "harried people . . . solace and inspiration" even in their own homes and provided the public a glimpse into their own local history in the context of a global war. Collectively, museums performed an important wartime public service because they inspired a "revived interest" in one's own national pride.[81]

Soon after the war's end in 1945, Parker retired from the Municipal Museum, though he remained an active public figure. That same year he was elected president of the New York State Historical Association and received other accolades. Parker continued to give lectures on Haudenosaunee history and culture and on the their "Science of Government," reinforcing his longtime emphasis of the wisdom of the Six Nations Confederated government and why it set an admirable example for the postwar world of international fellowship, patience, and "brotherhood." The Six Nations, his theory explained, "settled [conflict] amicably by federation, a federation that leaves each nation autonomous, but tied to all others by a great purpose." This was the "'one world' that Dekanawida envisioned." Other than a thinly veiled commentary on how the Haudenosaunee's Tree of Peace predicted the United Nations, these were reminders that, for the Iroquois, "adherence to old tradition . . . made survival possible in the face of an accelerated accultur- ation." This message fit neatly with the early years of the Cold War. Parker's description of the Tree of Peace was a powerful symbol of Native American resistance, but it also aligned with a patriotic narrative wherein the United States once again borrowed a uniquely American diplomatic model to better combat the spread of foreign communism across the globe.[82]

Parker thrived in an atmosphere in which he could contribute to the cultivation of American patriotism on his own terms. In 1947, the City of Rochester's history curriculum was investigated by a self-organized committee of a local chapter of the Sons of the American Revolution, which had taken it upon itself to find "evidence" of "subversive teachers"—or communists—in the school district. Parker, although he was an active member of the SAR, defended the school's intellectual freedom. He argued that the search was il- legitimate because academic freedom was a cornerstone of the educational system, but if groups like the SAR insisted that learning different perspectives on government equaled wrongdoing, then the American people would fall into a morass of ignorance. He illustrated this point with two dark-humored examples from the SAR's findings. One was of an Albany mother who complained to the state that local teachers "tried to give my child an unbiased viewpoint instead of teaching him real Americanism." The other complaint was from another mother who rejected objectivity altogether and professed that "I don't want my boy to know the truth; I want him to be patriotic."[83] With these examples, Parker made light of the absurdity of their perspectives and, in the process, revealed the ignorance inherent in the conspiracy-theory thinking that accompanied the lack of a good historical education. As a re- sult, the SAR backed off. As Parker shamed the SAR into acknowledging, more knowledge, not less, would better prepare Americans to resist Soviet influences.

In retirement, Parker also made the decision to write a magisterial history of the Iroquois, a project he would eventually title "The Amazing Iroquois." It was his *magnum opus*, even if this huge undertaking took a decade to write and remains unfinished.[84] In its final 1955 draft, the incomplete series was already ten volumes long. If it ever got published, Parker's epic would have had to compete with condensed single-volume ethnographies like Paul A. W. Wallace's popular *The White Roots of Peace* (1946). Still Parker persisted, and after nearly a decade of writing, in 1944 he was awarded a five-thousand-dollar fellowship from the Guggenheim Foundation to finish his work by the end of December. Unfortunately, Parker died on January 1, 1955.

———

Unlike what some historians suggest, "The Amazing Iroquois," by far Parker's greatest written project, is more than a lay account of Haudenosaunee history written by "an educated twentieth-century Iroquois rather than that of a scholar or anthropologist."[85] Its pages reveal a pioneering scholarly voice that had long been influential in public history. The manuscript was written from the perspective of a Seneca, as historians acknowledge, but also of a museologist and scholar of the Haudenosaunee, one who understood that scholarship must exist at the intersection of the academy and the public. This was an idea that would not resonate until the 1960s when figures such as Staughton Lynd, Howard Zinn, and Richard Hofstadter modeled to the academy that scholarship should be public and in service to social and civil rights activism.

In that vein, Parker in the 1940s and 1950s sought to do something new with "The Amazing Iroquois." In its pages, he made clear that the process of colonization was not only a vestige of the past, it was an active force that still impacted the Haudenosaunee today. Parker sought a new scholarly trajectory that would not simply copy the "many books [that] have been written about the Iroquois and what they now are," but would root itself in a historical process that would "tell what became of them." He sought to answer why, despite popular interest in everything from the Six Nations Confederacy to Thanksgiving stories, "the pattern idea of the Iroquois as irreclaimable savages sticks." Parker found the answer in the long legacy of colonialism. Colonialism drove and perpetuated these stereotypes and, despite his best efforts in his museums and his politics, the Haudenosaunee were still "known" to the public when they "have feathers growing from their scalps," "brandish tomahawks," and "still live in bark huts and ride pinto ponies!" He expressed shock at how many people still "wrinkle their brows" when they see or hear stories of Haudenosaunee men and women working as New York "clerks, teachers, laborers, physicians, engineers, steelworkers, technicians in hospitals and ~~farmers~~ college professors."[86] His books would remedy that oversight.

These stereotypes were reinforced by contemporary Americans who held limited views about Indigenous racial capacities and generally understood the history of Euro-America in parallel, but never intersecting with, that of Native America. To Parker, this was the critical problem that reinforced damaging stereotypes. Thinking about Indigenous history that way led to only one conclusion: that they were a "disintegrating race . . . wallowing in the sludge made by our own inept social chemists" who refused to adopt white ways. Parker therefore proposed in his study of the Haudenosaunee a "unique study of race transformation and rebirth" that was only visible when these two histories are intertwined. His was a story of a unique people who, in the face of Euro-American colonization, were beaten, rose again "transfigured as one of us [Americans]," and yet who resisted and still retained those original Haudenosaunee "qualities that are peculiarly native." In that respect, "The Amazing Iroquois" sought to introduce Americans to the Haudenosaunee who "are with us as a living force today, and we need them in our future." Just as he had demonstrated countless times in his museums, Parker hoped that the world would finally acknowledge that the Haudenosaunee defy stereotypes as exceptional "Americans of the older stock [and] champions of racial ideals that humanity cannot ignore if it is to survive."[87]

Despite never being published, "The Amazing Iroquois" succeeded in condensing Parker's lifelong public scholarship into a single ethnohistory.[88] It marked the culmination of a dynamic and prolific body of public historical work that hinged on the idea of Iroquois exceptionalism and sought once again to use that narrative to shape how New Yorkers remembered the history of the Haudenosaunee.

Conclusion

THE PEACE MEDAL COMES HOME

IT WAS A bright day on May 17, 2021, on the Senecas' Allegheny Territory. In the city of Salamanca, New York, in front of the backdrop erected by the Seneca-Iroquois National Museum's grand rear entrance, a large audience faced a podium adorned with a representation of the Western Door of the Longhouse. The podium was flanked by two tables draped in red and purple cloth, one the color of the Seneca Nation's flag and the other the traditional color of the shell wampum belts that recorded the Six Nations' national history. Seated at those tables were dignitaries from the Senecas as well as New York State. From the Seneca Nation sat President Matthew Pagels, Director of the Seneca-Iroquois National Museum Dr. Joe Stahlman, and Councilor Robert Jones. From the Buffalo History Museum were Executive Director Melissa Brown and Senior Director of Museum Collections Walter Mayer. From the State of New York were State Senators George Borello and Sean Ryan, and the Chief of Staff for State Senator Tim Kennedy, Adam Fogel.

The speakers and the audience had gathered that day in person and virtually to celebrate an auspicious occasion: after 125 years under the care of the Buffalo History Museum, the Red Jacket Peace Medal was returning home to the Seneca Nation.[1] The Seneca-Iroquois National Museum, the "safe keepers" of the history and legacy of the Senecas and the Haudenosaunee, was the perfect site for such a homecoming.[2] Stahlman, the master of ceremonies, explained that the Seneca Nation and the museum have "been at the forefront" of such efforts to bring their history home by "pushing repatriation, creating relationships, and beginning conversations that should have been taking place thirty, forty, fifty years ago."[3] Part of that shift to this moment, from Stahlman's perspective, is rooted in those "museum and cultural

FIGURE C.1 Photograph of the Red Jacket Peace Medal on display at the Seneca-Iroquois National Museum. Photograph by Hayden Haynes. Seneca-Iroquois National Museum and Onöhsagwë:de' Cultural Center.

resource specialists" who "have been trained with NAGPRA (the Native American Graves Protection and Repatriation Act of 1990) as a permanent fixture in our lives." These professionals "don't know what it was like before NAGPRA," when an older "pro-science perspective . . . [of] study[ing] the past" prevailed, and thus could change the conversation about who and where these objects should and can be studied. Although repatriations in general "do not see much press," perhaps that will shift as these new museum professionals become more dominant and as the country reflects on race after the Black Lives Matter movement called into question "how we celebrate/honor the past."[4] Stahlman thus invoked a host of pressing scholarly and public issues when he said that this repatriation, in particular, marked "a great moment."[5]

As for the actual process of repatriation and transfer that led to that day, it all happened quickly. The Seneca Nation had issued its formal repatriation claim to the Buffalo History Museum on November 16, 2020, and just six months later, the process was complete. The initial request was addressed to Melissa Brown, the Executive Director of the Buffalo History Museum, and cited § 3005(a)(5) of NAGPRA, which details the conditions in which "Upon request . . . sacred objects and objects of cultural patrimony shall be expeditiously returned." Of primary relevance to the Senecas in making that claim was the Seneca Nation's well-documented national ownership of the object. Similarly well-documented was the personal ownership of the Peace Medal by Ely S. Parker which, after his death, was inherited by his wife Minnie Parker who sold the Peace Medal to the Buffalo Historical Society.[6] For the Senecas, the nation's collective ownership of the Peace Medal was not in question. Interestingly, however, the sale of it by Minnie to the Buffalo Historical Society was. "As an individual cannot own an object of cultural patrimony," the repatriation claim explained, "this sale from an individual to a museum should not have taken place." The claim recognized the financial "duress" Minnie was under that necessitated the sale, but as her husband Ely proved when he stopped the sale of the Medal to a museum in 1851 and bore it for the rest of his life on behalf of the Senecas, the Peace Medal "cannot belong to any individual or museum; it is inalienable and belongs to the Seneca people as a collective."[7] The Buffalo History Museum, for their part, agreed. It was announced that the Peace Medal would be officially repatriated and, weeks later, this symbol of Seneca nationhood went on its last trip home.[8]

Overall, the repatriation process seemed to be a mutually collaborative one. Conversation between the two parties began in February 2020, when then-State Assembly Member Ryan introduced Stahlman and Brown to one another. As Brown explained, after "several other meetings," tours, and other events, her museum and the Senecas' museum began "learning more about the other." This, as she put it, was particularly important to her as a steward of New York history. When she began her career at the museum twenty years earlier, Brown had a chance to see and handle the Peace Medal in the museum's collection. She of course marveled at the fact that George Washington himself had "touched this medal," but then admitted that she did not "know about the Seneca orator for whom the Medal is named." But after years of exposure to Museum events and historical programming about Native America and the Haudenosaunee in particular, her understanding of the Peace Medal's history expanded.[9]

Much like Brown's own intellectual evolution over those years, the relationship between the two museums was also changing. For Brown, her conversations with the Senecas had changed what it meant for the Buffalo History Museum to be a "steward of local history." She explained that it was one thing to reassess a collection every so often to consider new information—this is a normal part of museum development—but mere "reassessment" in cases like these are "not enough. Action is imperative to ensure that any artifacts of cultural patrimony are returned." There was, clearly, much at stake. In a sentiment that echoed throughout the speeches on May 17, Brown explained that the museum's "relationship with the Seneca Nation does not end here. In fact, this is a new beginning. Much like what the Peace Medal represents, this is a sign of friendship and connection between us and the Seneca Nation."[10]

Stahlman's response following Brown's also referenced these early interinstitutional meetings, but his perspective was slightly different. He agreed that repatriation started "much needed conversations if we are going to travel together into the future," but he also revealed that "the first time I saw you [Brown], I didn't know what to expect." For those Indigenous museums and cultural centers who seek to repatriate objects from state and private museums, they "don't know how these things are going to play out. You don't know if they are going to get angry, or what kind of answer you will receive," and they are generally not "an easy moment" to work through. Complicating the interpersonal realities of these moments is the "sterile" language that, Stahlman explained, defines repatriation as "the return of culturally important objects to the communities of origin." This is inadequate because the "objects [in question] mean much, much more" than that language suggests. The seemingly straightforward act of returning an object not only undersells the cultural importance of the objects in question, but it also hides the fact that the conversations that make it happen can create new building blocks for future collaborations. For Stahlman, these conversations meant that "the Buffalo Museum and the Seneca Nation" are on "good footing at this point, and we do have a future together." He saw "a lot of opportunity created in this moment" and used that example to encourage other Indigenous organizations to begin talking to their own neighbors. To truly "talk about" and achieve "reconciliation and decolonization," Stahlman explained, "we have to have those hard, difficult conversations." And for the Buffalo History Museum's part, "they never turned me away."[11]

The speed and success of this outcome contrasts with many other tension-filled examples of repatriation and reclamation. Published how-to guides on repatriation reinforce Stahlman's speech and explain that even talking about repatriation can be problematic for some institutions. Beyond the legal battles, the issues with how the federal government defines indigeneity and belonging, as well as the general reluctance of institutions to part with their collections, can lead to conflict. Even in academic settings, those supposedly neutral and fact-based arenas, repatriation "stirs heated debate before the presentations begin."[12] As the life of Harriet M. Converse shows, this tension, indeed the fierce resistance to repatriation without knowing all the facts, is not all that surprising. After all, museum ownership of Indigenous material culture is big business.

Stahlman's concerns and the current realities of repatriation serve as a reminder of the history of how Native American culture became the property of predatory collectors and museums. Throughout the nineteenth and twentieth centuries, people like Converse created an international industry out of selling Indigenous material culture to the highest bidder. Even Arthur C. Parker's development of his own museum collections involved excavating, collecting, and storing his peoples' history for the edification of those who sought to bury that culture in the first place. Still, as his dioramas and the Seneca Arts Project at the Tonawanda Cultural Center revealed, Parker also made a point of hiring Haudenosaunee women and men to create these objects. Even if the artisans themselves had no say over what they created, it was nevertheless important to him that only Senecas make Seneca culture. In that sense, he clearly saw the cultural, institutional, and economic value of forming a mutually beneficial relationship between the Haudenosaunee, New Yorkers, and their respective museums. Those gathered at the Seneca-Iroquois National Museum on May 17 were witnesses to a part of that complex legacy.

Today, the Red Jacket Peace Medal sits on display at the Seneca-Iroquois National Museum. As the repatriation request explained, "like the Canandaigua Treaty . . . [the Peace Medal] is a representation of the on-going sovereign relationship between the Federal Government and the Seneca Nation." The request echoed what Red Jacket and Ely S. Parker had long made clear, that for the Senecas, "it has always maintained an inviolable place in our cultural memory."[13] As Seneca Nation President Pagels explained, the Peace Medal

represents far more than the respect George Washington had for Red Jacket. It's more than a physical artifact from our shared history. This medal represents what lives inside each and every Seneca person: the

heart of a sovereign and our rightful recognition as such. This is part
of our identity as a nation. It cannot be owned, it cannot be bought or
sold. It belongs to us all. It is passed on from generation to generation
and it lives forever.

The Peace Medal and its long history, in this sense, are a fundamental part of
Seneca national identity. From its new institutional home, it will forever more
be "shared with others" so that they "know and understand their history, our
culture, and our identity."[14]

That legacy was precisely what Red Jacket, the Parkers, and Converse revealed to New York. The Peace Medal, despite its name, was not an object
of friendship or even peace. It was transformed by Red Jacket from a colonial emblem into an Indigenous symbol of sovereignty, imperial might, and
national identity. It was—and remains—a physical reminder to the United
States of their treaty obligations to the Haudenosaunee, their violation of the
Covenant Chain, and the Six Nations' historic political, cultural, and social
influence on New Yorkers. And while Red Jacket's reputation among white
Americans changed over time, the memory and symbolism of the medal itself remained consistent because of the broader institutional and public
memory-work of the Parkers. It was even strong enough to survive Converse's
salvage and her attempts to bring Haudenosaunee history under the control
of New York State. That memory of the Haudenosaunee remains intact just as
the physical object of the Peace Medal lives on.

The medal is a reminder of a long and complex history. First and foremost, as President Pagels explained, it is an object that represents Seneca national identity, history, and culture for the nation and "each and every Seneca
person." It was precisely that for Red Jacket, the architect of that symbolism.
Even Ely Parker, the assimilationist, understood and leveraged the power of
that symbol among the Haudenosaunee and his various white audiences. It is
fitting that the Peace Medal is back in its rightful home.

Second, for white Americans, the Peace Medal is a reminder of the complex legacy of the Iroquois exceptionalism created by Red Jacket, the Parkers,
and Converse. It is and was a symbol of how "The Amazing Iroquois" shaped
aspects of the Empire State's history and its conception of self, even as the
Haudenosaunee elements of that story were constantly in tension with the
very stereotypes, pressures, and mythologies that they were designed to,
or by their very existence did, reject. The legacy of that is etched into the
Peace Medal's face. On one hand it was transformed by Red Jacket into an
emblem of Seneca identity, but the pastoral imagery still bears the imprint

of Anglo-America's unyielding efforts to assimilate Indigenous peoples by eliminating their culture and society. The Peace Medal is thus a living symbol of the complex, and often competing, memories that white New Yorkers have of "The Amazing Iroquois" and their place in the history and culture of the Empire State.

Last, the Peace Medal is a museum object. Once it left the care of the Senecas after Ely's death, it became a public example of the colonial influence of museums on Native American objects. It was first decolonized by Red Jacket who transformed it into a reminder of Haudenosaunee imperial power and American obligations to the Six Nations, a legacy that Ely Parker harnessed for his own ends. But the medal was then recolonized after it came into the possession of the Buffalo Historical Society in the 1850s. Once that happened, the Peace Medal gained a new meaning. Like the objects Converse collected, it was still a living part of Seneca culture and history but, more importantly for the public, they saw it as a piece of their own history once it entered the public domain of the museum. This had the very literal effect of transforming public understanding of who owned that history.

That movement of an idea or an object by a museum into the public realm, as Converse and Arthur Parker made abundantly clear, opens an object to reinterpretation, even cooptation. This is why museums were (and in some cases still are) major contributors to the colonization of Indigenous cultures.[15] Yet museums also had the capacity to be redemptive institutions that, with careful institutional self-reflection and a great deal of effort, reformed their own relationship to Indigenous communities. As aspects of Arthur Parker's career suggest, museums—with the right leadership and mission—were capable of breaking older interpretations of Indigenous loss by privileging Indigenous voices. This, of course, may not have happened in ways that were entirely satisfying, nor does Parker's work deserve the accolade of being "decolonized" in that way. But his experiments in presenting a Haudenosaunee history told on its own peoples' terms was a radical notion at the time. It showed that museums had the capacity, and sometimes the will, to use the very same tools that first colonized Indigenous history to start breaking that predatory and often one-sided legacy. In that respect, just as Parker wanted museums to use their unique collections and energies to "bring to citizens of every age, all those things of earth and man which shed light upon life's values and which inspire both mind and spirit," the Peace Medal's homecoming to the Seneca-Iroquois National Museum will do exactly that. But this time, it will be on the Senecas' own terms.[16]

Notes

INTRODUCTION

1. Notable work on the history and cultural aspects of the supposed tension between Indians and modernity are Jean M. O'Brien, *Firsting and Lasting: Writing Indians out of Existence in New England* (Minneapolis: University of Minnesota Press, 2010); Paige Raibmon, *Authentic Indians: Episodes of Encounter from the Late Nineteenth-Century Northwest Coast* (Durham, NC: Duke University Press, 2005); Philip Deloria, *Playing Indian* (New Haven, CT: Yale University Press, 1998).

2. "Mohawk Iroquois Longhouse," New York State Museum website, http://www.nysm.nysed.gov/exhibitions/ongoing/native-peoples-new-york/mohawk-longhouse (accessed Sept 2020); "About the Museum," Iroquois Museum, https://www.iroquoismuseum.org/copy-of-about-the-museum (accessed Sept 2020); "Bark Longhouse," Ganondagan Historic Site and Seneca Art & Culture Center, https://ganondagan.org/Visit/Bark-Longhouse (accessed Sept 2020).

3. There have been many public history exhibitions and documentaries on this topic. This includes a long-term exhibition at the Iroquois Indian Museum in Howes Cave, New York, which the author visited in 2017 titled "Walking the Steel: From Girder to Ground Zero," https://www.iroquoismuseum.org/2017-feature-exhibition (accessed May 2020); see also a 2018 exhibition on view through January 2020 at the 9/11 Memorial and Museum called "Skywalkers: A Portrait of Mohawk Ironworkers at the World Trade Center," https://www.911memorial.org/visit/museum/exhibitions/past-exhibitions/skywalkers-portrait-mohawk-ironworkers-world-trade-center (accessed December 2019); Lucy Levine, "Men of Steel: How Brooklyn's Native American Ironworkers Built New York," *6sqft*, July 25, 2018, https://www.6sqft.com/men-of-steel-how-brooklyns-native-american-ironworkers-built-new-york/ (accessed May 2020); Reaghan Tarbell, *Little Caughnawaga: To Brooklyn and Back* (National Film Board of Canada, 2015). On land and placenames, see Chad L. Anderson, *The*

      Storied Landscape of Iroquoia: History, Conquest, and Memory in the Native Northeast (Lincoln, NE: University of Nebraska Press, 2020).

4. Oneida Indian Nation, "Haudenosaunee Women and Equality," https://www. oneidaindiannation.com/haudenosaunee-women-and-equality/ (accessed 11/ 2020). See also Sally Roesch Wagner, *Sisters in Spirit: Haudenosaunee (Iroquois) Influences on Early American Feminists* (Summertown, TN: Native Voices, 2001) and Wagner's YA book, *We Want Equal Rights: How Suffragists Were Influence by Native American Women* (Summertown, TN: Native Voices, 2020); Gail H. Landsman, "The 'Other' as Political Symbol: Images of Indians in the Women Suffrage Movement," *Ethnohistory* 36, no. 3 (Summer 1992): 246–284.

5. Donald A. Grinde, Jr. and Bruce E. Johansen, *Exemplar of Liberty: Native America and the Evolution of Democracy* (Los Angeles: University of California Press, 1991), xx, xxv. Bruce E. Johansen, *Forgotten Founders: Benjamin Franklin, the Iroquois, and the Rationale for the American Revolution* (Ipswich, MI: Gambit, 1982), xiii. The Iroquois Influence Thesis is also proposed in Bruce E. Johansen, "Native American Societies and the Evolution of Democracy in America, 1600–1800," *Ethnohistory* 37, no. 3 (1990): 279–290; Donald A. Grinde, Jr., *The Iroquois and the Founding of the American Nation* (San Francisco: The Indian Historian Press, 1977). See the most recent scholarly rejection of the Iroquois Influence Thesis in "Forum: The 'Iroquois Influence' Thesis—Con and Pro," *The William and Mary Quarterly* 53, no. 3 (July 1996): 587–636; for a reference to other scholarly rejections of the Thesis, see Philip Levy's article in the roundtable "Exemplars of Taking Liberties," fn. 10. See also Elisabeth Tooker, "The United States Constitution and the Iroquois League," *Ethnohistory* 35, no. 4 (1988): 305–336; "Rejoinder to Johansen," *Ethnohistory* 37, no. 3 (1990): 291–297. Responses to the roundtable's critiques in Donald A. Grinde, Jr. and Bruce E. Johansen, "Sauce for the Goose: Demand and Definitions for "Proof" Regarding the Iroquois and Democracy," *William and Mary Quarterly* 53, no. 3 (July 1996): 621–636. The Smithsonian Institution has also compiled a reference guide for educators that compares/contrasts the Six Nations government to that of the United States. Smithsonian Institution, "Haudenosaunee Guide for Educators, National Museum of the American Indian," https://americanindian.si.edu/sites/1/ files/pdf/education/HaudenosauneeGuide.pdf (accessed November 2017).

6. Arthur C. Parker, "The Amazing Iroquois," 1954 typescript, Arthur Caswell Parker Papers, 1915–1953, Boxes 4–7, New York State Library Manuscripts and Special Collections, Albany, New York, microfilm (hereafter cited as ACPA).

7. These centuries have long been overlooked by historians who simply "omit the presence of the Iroquois over the past two hundred years of the state's history." Laurence Hauptman, *Seven Generations of Iroquois Leadership: The Six Nations Since 1800* (Syracuse, NY: Syracuse University Press, 2008), xi. Even authors who write about the nineteenth century often end their periodization by the 1830s, the era of so-called Indian Removal. See a description of these histories in Edward Countryman,

"Toward a Different Iroquois History," *The William and Mary Quarterly* 69, no. 2 (April 2012): 347–360.

8. Grinde and Johansen, *Exemplar*, xx.

9. Scholar Maureen Konkle defines "Iroquois supremacy" as how the Iroquois understand themselves as having an exceptional and superior political history based on their organization under the metaphorical Great Tree of Peace (discussed below). Maureen Konkle, *Writing Indian Nations: Native Intellectuals and the Politics of Historiography, 1827–1863* (Chapel Hill, NC: The University of North Carolina Press, 2004), 209–210. The Great Tree of Peace was an important part of this notion of supremacy because it framed the Iroquois' theoretically infinite capacity to absorb foreign peoples through kinship and affinity. The result would be a war-less and collaborative society in which the Iroquois would provide for its members who found "shelter, security, and strength under the branches of the Great Tree of Peace." Matthew Dennis, *Cultivating a Landscape of Peace: Iroquois-European Encounters in Seventeenth-Century America* (Ithaca, NY: Cornell University Press, 1993), 8.

10. Hauptman, *Seven Generations*, xiii

11. Deloria, *Playing Indian*, 135–142.

12. Audra Simpson, *Mohawk Interruptus: Political Life Across the Borders of Settler States* (Durham, NC: Duke University Press, 2014), 47. See more discussions of kinship and its relationship to politics in Brian Rice, *The Rotinonshonni: A Traditional Iroquoian History Through the Eyes of Teharonhia:wako and Sawiskera* (Syracuse, NY: Syracuse University Press, 2013), chapter 2; Parmenter, *The Edge of the Woods*, xi–xv, xxxvi, 9, 48–54; Dennis, *Cultivating*, 8–9; Kurt Jordan, "Enacting Gender and Kinship Around a Large Outdoor Fire Pit at the Seneca Iroquois Townley-Read Site," *Historical Archeology* 48, no. 2 (2014): 61–90.

13. Francis Jennings, *The Ambiguous Iroquois Empire: The Covenant Chain Confederation of Indian Tribes with English Colonies* (New York: W.W. Norton, 1984), xvii, xix, 15–18; Lewis Henry Morgan, *League of the Iroquois*, ed. William Fenton (New York: Corinth Books, 1962), 15. For the first utterance of "Romans of the Woods," see Cadwallader Colden, *The History of the Five Indian Nations: Depending on the Province of New-York in America* (Ithaca, NY: Cornell University Press, 2016), xlv, xxxii, xxxiii, 19, 202, 203, 206; the allusion to "Romans" is further contextualized by historians as part of a British effort to understand Iroquois power in William Howard Carter, "Anglicizing the League: The Writing of Cadwallader Colden's History of the Five Indian Nations," in *Anglicizing America: Empire, Revolution, Republic*, eds. Ignacio Gallup-Diaz, Andrew Shankman, and David J. Silverman (Philadelphia: University of Pennsylvania Press, 2015), 84. The history of the real and potent seventeenth and eighteenth century military power of the Iroquois, the realities of "empire" notwithstanding, is explored in Jon Parmenter, *The Edge of the Woods: Iroquoia, 1534–1701* (East Lansing, MI: Michigan State University Press, 2010); and Jon Parmenter, "'L'Arbre

de Paix': Eighteenth Century Franco-Iroquois Relations," *French Colonial History* 4 (2003): 63–80.

14. Morgan, *League*, 15. Comparisons to the Aztecs also appear in 1877 when historian David Gray argued that the League, without European intervention, "ultimately would at least have divided with the Aztecs the dominion of the continent." David Gray, "The Last Indian Council on the Genesee," *Scribner's Monthly* 14, no. 3 (July 1877): 338–348.

15. On the "crusader mentality" see John Demos, *The Heathen School: A Story of Hope and Betrayal in the Age of the Early Republic* (New York: Vintage Books, 2014), 1–5. On national myths, see Sara L. Spurgeon, *Exploding the Western: Myths of Empire on the Postmodern Frontier* (College Station, TX: Texas A&M University Press, 2005), 3. On New York land seizure, see Alan Taylor, *The Divided Ground: Indians, Settlers, and the Northern Borderland of the American Revolution* (New York: Alfred A. Knopf, 2006), 391.

16. Eric Foner describes mini-biographies as "intended to be both less and more than another biography" in the sense that while they fill biographical gaps for each individual, their stories are supported and reinforced by a well-established scholarly literature. Eric Foner, *The Fiery Trial: Abraham Lincoln and American Slavery* (New York: W.W. Norton, 2011), xvi. There are a few important and recent biographies of each of these four. For Red Jacket: introduction to Granville Ganter, *The Collected Speeches of Sagoyewatha, or Red Jacket* (Syracuse, NY: Syracuse University Press, 2006); Christopher Densmore, *Red Jacket: Iroquois Diplomat and Orator* (Syracuse, NY: Syracuse University Press, 1999). For Ely S. Parker: William H. Armstrong, *Warrior in Two Camps: Ely S. Parker, Union General and Seneca Chief* (Syracuse, NY: Syracuse University Press, 1978); Arthur C. Parker, *The Life of General Ely S. Parker: Last Grand Sachem of the Iroquois and General Grant's Military Secretary* (Buffalo: Buffalo Historical Society, 1919). For Harriet M. Converse: Laurence Hauptman, "Chief Publicist," *New York Archives* 18, no. 2 (2018): 21–24; Harriet Maxwell Converse, Arthur C. Parker ed., *Myths and Legends of the New York State Iroquois* (Albany, NY: University of the State of New York, 1908), introduction. For Arthur C. Parker: Chip Colwell-Chanthaphonh, *Inheriting the Past: The Making of Arthur C. Parker and Indigenous Archaeology* (Tucson: University of Arizona Press, 2009); Joy Porter, *To Be Indian: The Life of Iroquois-Seneca Arthur Caswell Parker* (Norman, OK: University of Oklahoma Press, 2001).

17. Quotation in Camilla Townsend, *Malintzin's Choices: An Indian Woman in the Conquest of Mexico* (Albuquerque: University of New Mexico Press, 2006), 8.

18. Hauptman, "Chief Publicist," 23.

19. Deloria, *Playing Indian*, 124.

20. These people appear in various places throughout the book. They include Cornplanter, Joseph Brant, Governor Blacksnake, Ely Parker's siblings Nicholson and Caroline, Jesse Lyons, and others.

21. These categories dominate the first scholarly works about white-made Indian stereotypes in Robert F. Berkhofer, Jr., *The White Man's Indian: Images of the American Indian from Columbus to the Present* (New York: Vintage Books, 1978), xv. For Indigenous peoples as antimodern, see Deloria, *Playing Indian*; Thomas King, *The Inconvenient Indian: A Curious Account of Native People in North America* (Canada: Anchor Canada Publishing, 2010); Alan Trachtenberg, *Shades of Hiawatha: Staging Indians, Making Americans, 1880–1930* (New York: Hill and Wang, 2004). Critical readings on Indigenous resistance and adaptation include: Camilla Townsend, *Fifth Sun: A New History of the Aztecs* (New York: Oxford University Press, 2019); Roxanne Dunbar-Ortiz, *An Indigenous Peoples' History of the United States* (Boston: Beacon Press, 2014); Rice, *The Rotinonshonni*; King, *Inconvenient Indian*; Trachtenberg, *Shades of Hiawatha*; Stephen Conn, *History's Shadow: Native Americans and Historical Consciousness in the Nineteenth Century* (Chicago: University of Chicago Press, 2004); Deloria, *Playing Indian*. See also decolonized studies where scholars apply a theoretical approach to scholarship for the purpose of seeking self-determination and historical justice for silenced Indigenous peoples. Select readings on the method in theory and practice include: Linda Tuhiwai Smith, *Decolonizing Methodologies: Research and Indigenous Peoples* (London: Zed Books, 2012); Patricia Galloway, *Practicing Ethnohistory: Mining Archives, Hearing Testimony, Constructing Narrative* (Lincoln, NE: University of Nebraska Press, 2006); Angela Cavender Wilson, *Remember This!: Dakota Decolonization and the Eli Taylor Narratives* (Lincoln, NE: University of Nebraska Press, 2005); Wilson, *For Indigenous Eyes Only: A Decolonization Handbook* (Santa Fe, NM: School of American Research Press, 2005).

22. Simpson, *Mohawk Interruptus,* 67–85.

CHAPTER 1

1. Prucha, *Indian Peace Medals*, xiv.

2. These speeches and letters, sixty-seven in total, are collected and edited in Ganter, *Collected Speeches*.

3. William L. Stone, *The Life and Times of Red-Jacket, or Sa-Go-Ye-Wat-Ha; Being the Sequel to the History of the Six Nations* (New York and London: Wiley and Putnam, 1841), ii.

4. See these images in Jadviga da Costa Nunes, "Red Jacket: The Man and His Portraits," *The American Art Journal* 12, no. 3 (Summer 1980): 4–20. Other images not included in Nunes' work are found in Densmore, *Red Jacket*, cover image (painting), 30 (silhouette) and 97–100 (paintings). See also fn102.

5. On America's relatively weak position in continental North America, see Leonard J. Sadosky, *Revolutionary Negotiations: Indians, Empires, and Diplomats in the Founding of America* (Charlottesville, VA: University of Virginia Press, 2009); David Andrew Nichols, *Red Gentlemen and White Savages: Indians, Federalists,*

and the Search for Order on the American Frontier (Charlottesville, VA: University of Virginia Press, 2008). On Native and border histories of the Revolution, see Kathleen Duval, *Independence Lost: Lives on the Edge of the American Revolution* (New York: Random House, 2015); Taylor, *The Divided Ground*; Gail MacLeitch, *Imperial Entanglements: Iroquois Change and Persistence on the Frontiers of Empire* (Philadelphia: University of Pennsylvania Press, 2011). For broader continental and relevant perspectives around the Revolution, see Michael A. McDonnell, *Masters of Empire: Great Lakes Indians and the Making of America* (New York: Hill and Wang, 2015); Gregory Ablavsky, "Species of Sovereignty: Native Nationhood, the United States, and International Law, 1783–1795," *Journal of American History* 106, no. 3 (December 2019): 591–613; Pekka Hämäläinen, "The Politics of Grass: European Expansion, Ecological Change, and Indigenous Power in the Southwest Borderlands," *The William and Mary Quarterly* 67, no. 2 (April 2010): 173–208.

6. For a broader look at the United States' complex Indian policy, see Colin Calloway, *The Indian World of George Washington: The First President, the First Americans, and the Birth of the Nation* (New York: Oxford University Press, 2019), 12–13. On the fear of Iroquois power and of Indian violence and war, see MacLeitch, *Imperial Entanglements*; Peter Silver, *Our Savage Neighbors: How Indian War Shaped Early America* (New York: W.W. Norton and Company, 2009); Rob Harper, *Unsettling the West: Violence and State Building in the Ohio Valley* (Philadelphia: University of Pennsylvania Press, 2018), chapters 5–6. For commentary on the state of early American anxiety, see David W. Thomas, "The Anxious Atlantic: War, Murder, and a 'Monster of a Man' in Revolutionary New England" (PhD diss, Temple University, 2018).

7. For Washington as a contemporary nationalist icon, see David Waldstreicher, *In the Midst of Perpetual Fetes: The Making of American Nationalism, 1776–1820* (Chapel Hill, NC: University of North Carolina Press, 1997), 119–120; Alan Taylor, *American Revolutions: A Continental History, 1750–1804* (New York: W.W. Norton and Company, 2016), 396.

8. Taiaiake Alfred, *Peace, Power, Righteousness: An Indigenous Manifesto* (Ontario: Oxford Press Canada, 1999), xvi–xxiii. For the meaning of the Two Rows belt in scholarship, see Jon Parmenter, "The Meaning of *Kaswentha* and the Two Rows Wampum Belt in Haudenosaunee (Iroquois) History: Can Indigenous Oral Tradition be Reconciled with the Documentary Record?" *Journal of Early American History* 3 (2013): 82–109. See also Onondaga Nation, "Two Row Wampum – Guswẽta," Onondaga Nation Official Website, https://www.ono ndaganation.org/culture/wampum/two-row-wampum-belt-guswenta/ (accessed August 2018).

9. Jennings, *Ambiguous Iroquois Empire*, xvii; Taylor, *Divided Ground*, 22–23.

10. Carolyn Eastman, "The Indian Censures the White Man: 'Indian Eloquence' and American Reading Audiences in the Early Republic," *The William and Mary Quarterly* 65:3 (July 2008): 535–564. See also Helen Carr, *Inventing the American*

Primitive: Politics, Gender, and the Representation of Native American Literary Traditions 1789-7936 (New York: New York University Press, 1999).

11. Deloria, *Playing Indian*, 22.

12. Densmore, *Red Jacket*, xviii, 3–5.

13. Parker, *Red Jacket*, 82.

14. Densmore, *Red Jacket*, 11–18, xvii.

15. Densmore, *Red Jacket*, xiii; Orasmus Turner, *History of the Pioneer Settlement of Phelps & Gorham's Purchase, and Morris' Reserve* (Rochester: William Alling, 1852), 487. Also cited in Densmore, *Red Jacket*, 8.

16. Stone, *Red Jacket*, xviii; Ganter, "'Make Your Minds,'" 121.

17. Taylor, *American Revolutions*, 80–81; Barbara Graymont, *The Iroquois in the American Revolution* (Syracuse, NY: Syracuse University Press, 1975), 49.

18. Calloway, *Indian World*, 207–211; Taylor, *American Revolutions*, 80. See also Glenn F. Williams, *Dunmore's War: The Last Conflict of the American Colonial Era* (Chicago: Westholme Publishing, 2017). The violence from the war and other events caused a general "fear and horror" that, for white Americans, threatened to "remake whole societies and their political landscapes." Silver, *Our Savage Neighbors*, xviii.

19. Logan's Lament, for most Americans, became known to the public after Thomas Jefferson published it in his 1781 *Notes on the State of Virginia*. He infamously spun the speech as an example of a racially-specific indigenous oratorical ability, a sign that the "primitive" Natives of North America were not, in fact, irredeemable. Thomas Jefferson, *Notes on the State of Virginia,* ed. David Waldstreicher (New York: Bedford St. Martins, 2002), 27, 39. See also Calloway, *The Indian World*, 208; Wallace, *Jefferson and the Indians*, ix; Onuf, *Jefferson's Empire*, 23.

20. Transcript of Logan's Lament, "Ohio History Central," Ohio History Center https://ohiohistorycentral.org/w/Logan%27s_Lament_(Transcript) (accessed October 2019).

21. Calloway, *Indian World*, 211; Graymont, *Iroquois*, 55.

22. Densmore, *Red Jacket*, 11–12.

23. Oneida Declaration of Neutrality, June 19, 1775, in Peter Force, *American Archives* (Washington, DC: Matthew St. Claire, 1837), 1116–1117.

24. Graymont, *Iroquois*, 95–100.

25. Michael K. Foster, "Another Look at the Function of Wampum in Iroquois-White Councils," in *History and Culture of Iroquois Diplomacy: An Interdisciplinary Guide to the Treaties of the Six Nations and their League.* ed. Francis Jennings, et al (Syracuse: Syracuse University Press, 1995), 99–114.

26. Graymont, *Iroquois*, 105–111; Calloway, *Indian World*, 257–259.

27. Densmore, *Red Jacket*, 11–12.

28. Karim Tiro, *The People of Standing Stone: The Oneida Nation from the Revolution through the Era of Removal* (Amherst, MA: University of Massachusetts Press, 2011), 54–56.

29. Taylor, *Divided Ground*, 97–99.
30. Tiro, *The People of Standing Stone*, 54–56; Konkle, *Writing Indian Nations*, 207. I also found (in 2018) the name "Town Destroyer" explained in the permanent museum exhibition of the Iroquois Indian Museum in Howes Cave, New York.
31. Graymont, *Iroquois*, 215–216; Densmore, *Red Jacket*, 13–14.
32. Densmore, *Red Jacket*, 13–14; Ganter, *Red Jacket*, 14.
33. Morgan, *League*, 90; Ganter, *Collected Speeches*, xxvi; Densmore, *Red Jacket*, 18–19. Stone, *Life and Times*, 27. Densmore, *Red Jacket*, 14; Graymont, *The Iroquois*, 185. This story of the portrait is not retold in Blacksnake's memoirs. See Governor Blacksnake, *Chainbreaker: The Revolutionary War Memoirs of Governor Blacksnake as told to Benjamin Williams,* Thomas S. Abler ed. (Lincoln, NE: University of Nebraska Press, 2005).
34. Virginia Delegates to Benjamin Harrison, October 1, 1782, James Madison Papers, Volume 5, The Papers of James Madison Digital Edition, (Charlottesville, VA: University of Virginia Press, Rotunda, 2010), 176–177.
35. Graymont, *Iroquois*, 277; Taylor, *American Revolutions*, 334–336.
36. Nichols, *Red Gentlemen*, 5; Anthony F. C. Wallace, *The Death and Rebirth of the Seneca* (New York: Alfred A. Knopf, 1970), 152; Sadusky, *Revolutionary Negotiations*, 137.
37. The Six Nations of the Grand River reservation near Brantford, Ontario, is on a portion of the Haldimand Grant.
38. Laurence Hauptman, *Conspiracy of Interests: Iroquois Dispossession and the Rise of New York State* (Syracuse, NY: Syracuse University Press, 1999), 108; Tiro, *People of Standing Stone*, 62–63.
39. Densmore, *Red Jacket*, 102; Tiro, *People of Standing Stone*, 63.
40. Sadosky, *Revolutionary Negotiations*, 137–138.
41. Taylor, *American Revolutions*, 315.
42. Waldstreicher, *In the Midst*, 9.
43. Harper, *Unsettling the West*, 146–147. See also Taylor, *American Revolutions,* chapter 9. On the "maddening" state of war, see Silver, *Our Savage Neighbors*, 263. See also Hinderaker, *Elusive Empires*, 258–259. On the southwest, see DuVal, *Independence Lost*, 256–258.
44. Smith-Rosenberg, *Violent Empire*, 219.
45. Gregory Evans Dowd, *War Under Heaven: Pontiac, The Indian Nations & The British Empire* (Baltimore, MD: Johns Hopkins University Press, 2002), 1 and 116; Calloway, *Indian World*, 176–181.
46. Smith-Rosenberg, *This Violent Empire*, 219–220; Taylor, *American Revolutions*, 340–342. On the UIN, see Lisa Brooks, *The Common Pot: The Recovery of Native Space in the Northeast* (Minneapolis: University of Minnesota Press, 2008) map 10, 136–139; Calloway, *Indian World*, 317–318; Tiro, *People of Standing Stone*, 62, 95.
47. Turner, *Pioneer Settlements*, 288–289, quoted in Calloway, *Indian World*, 327; Taylor, *American Revolutions*, 334–336.

48. John Sugden, *Tecumseh: A Life* (New York: Holt Publishers, 1999); Sugden, "Early Pan-Indianism: Tecumseh's Tour of the Indian Country, 1811–1812," *American Indian Quarterly* 10, no. 4 (1986): 273–304; Colin Calloway, *The Shawnees and the War for America* (New York: Viking Press, 2007).

49. Waldstreicher, *In the Midst*, 108; see also Pauline Meyer, *Ratification: The People Debate the Constitution, 1787–1788* (New York: Simon and Schuster, 2011). On Indigenous diplomacy, see Calloway, *Indian World*, 325–329, 483; Nichols, *Red Gentleman*, 10.

50. This sparked what some historians have called a "decade of dispossession." Tiro, *People of Standing Stone*, 65; Hauptman, *Conspiracy*, 108; Sadusky, *Revolutionary Negotiations*, 169–202. Calloway, *Indian World*, 283. Hamilton is cited in Calloway, *Indian World*, 398.

51. The summit was held in present-day Athens, Pennsylvania, on the north branch of the Susquehanna River. Ganter, *Collected Speeches*, 2–4.

52. Ganter, *Collected Speeches*, 1–15. Densmore, *Red Jacket*, 24–25. Hauptman, *Conspiracy*, 68–71. Harper, *Unsettling the West*, 167–169; Calloway, *Indian World*, 380–381. On the Phelps-Gorham Purchase, see Hauptman, *Conspiracy*, 68–71; see also Jack Campisi and William A. Starna, "On the Road to Canandaigua: The Treaty of 1794," *American Indian Quarterly* 19, no. 4 (1995): 467–490; Barbara Ann Chernow, "Robert Morris: Genesee Land Speculator," *New York History* 58 (April 1977): 198–202.

53. Chernow, "Robert Morris," 201; Densmore, *Red Jacket*, 24–25; Stone, *Life and Times*, 41–42. On the land returned, see Ganter, *Collected Speeches*, 61–67; Harper, *Unsettling the West*, 170–171.

54. Densmore, *Red Jacket*, 32; Turner, *History of the Pioneer*, 289–90; Calloway, *Indian World*, 401; Ganter, *Collected Speeches*, 42. On gender in Native American and Euro-American diplomacy, see MacLeitch, *Imperial Entanglements*, chapter 4. For the women who spoke with Pickering at the Tioga Point council, see Ganter, *Collected Speeches*, 4. Quotation in Dennis, *Cultivating*, 7.

55. St. Claire's defeat is discussed in Densmore, *Red Jacket*, 34–35. On Kirkland's involvement, see Ganter, *Collected Speeches*, 33. It is unclear if Red Jacket was actually invited to Philadelphia, and it is also not clear who else came with him. Colin Calloway finds that he arrived with Farmer's Brother, Good Peter, "and many other chiefs," but not Cornplanter or Joseph Brant. Calloway, *Indian World*, 406. Christopher Densmore claims that Red Jacket came with Cornplanter, New Arrow, and (maybe) Governor Blacksnake, although Blacksnake was not invited. Densmore, *Red Jacket*, 36. Red Jacket offered to come to Philadelphia again at the end of the year, but did not arrive as promised. Instead, "Farmers Brother, the Young King, the Infant, the Shining Breast plate, and two inferiors" arrived in January 1793. Tobias Lear to Henry Knox, December 11, 1792, The Papers of George Washington Digital Edition v.11 (Charlottesville, VA: University of Virginia Press, Rotunda, 2008–2019), 499–501 (hereafter cited as GW Papers).

In Philadelphia, there were also several side negotiations between the new federally appointed Commissioner of Iroquoian Affairs Timothy Pickering, Cornplanter, Red Jacket, Farmer's Brother, and others to secure Iroquois nonintervention in the Ohio wars. On these side negotiations, see Calloway, *Indian World*, 598–405. On Joseph Brant's attendance, Henry Knox to GW, September 15, 1792, GW Papers v.11, 501; Henry Knox to GW, December 6, 1792, and Henry Knox to Anthony Wayne, January 26, 1793, GW Papers v.11, 478.

56. They were only two of seven who died on the trip. Ganter, *Collected Speeches*, 33fn1. On Washington's silence, see Calloway, *Indian World*, 406–408. Quotations in Ganter, *Collected Speeches*, 33–34.

57. April 2, 1792, "The Speech of Red Jacket, transmitted From Henry Knox to George Washington," GW Papers v.10, 191–194; Ganter, *Collected Speeches*, 36–37.

58. Italics are in the printed speeches. Ganter, *Collected Speeches*, 34–42.

59. Italics are Red Jacket's. Ganter, *Collected Speeches*, 38–44; Calloway, *Indian World*, 405–407. On the projection of power, see Calloway, *Indian World*, 326–327.

60. Shannon, *Iroquois Diplomacy*, 43–44.

61. The "cult of Washington" is discussed in Waldstreicher, *In the Midst*, 118–120. See more on Washington's carefully cultivated persona in Taylor, *American Revolutions*, 395–398.

62. Thatcher, *Indian Biography*, 277. Henry Knox to Anthony Wayne, January 4–5, 1793, GW Papers, Volume 11.

63. The Haudenosaunee were mass-scale farmers and had been for centuries. Jane Mt. Pleasant, "A New Paradigm for Pre-Columbian Agriculture in North America," *Early American Studies* 13, no. 2 (2015): 374–412. On the annuities, see Ganter, *Collected Speeches*, 41. Stone, *Red Jacket*, 181–182; Ganter, *Collected Speeches*, 135–137. The accusation of witchcraft became the subject of intense fascination by the painter John Mix Stanley who painted the event in 1869. Densmore, *Red Jacket*, 56–58. The only reference to this "assassination" is a letter from Peregrine Fitzhugh to Thomas Jefferson, December 2, 1807, The American Founding Era Collection. The Papers of Thomas Jefferson Digital Edition, eds. James P. McClure and J. Jefferson Looney (Charlottesville, VA: University of Virginia Press, Rotunda, 2008–2019).

64. Densmore, *Red Jacket*, 34–35. On the pan-Indian council, see Stone, *Life and Times*, 107; Calloway, *Indian World*, 436–437; Densmore, *Red Jacket*, 34–35. Washington's failure to raise southern Indian troops is explored in Calloway, *Indian World*, 422–431. On the Whiskey Rebellion, see Taylor, *American Revolutions*, 413–414.

65. Harper, *Unsettling the West*, 170–171; Ganter, *Collected Speeches*, 61–67.

66. Ganter, *Collected Speeches*, 45–118. On "rebirth" and the new political strategy, see Wallace, *Death and Rebirth*, 270–272; Densmore, *Red Jacket*, 58–59.

67. On the long-lived perception that there is a racial basis for oratorical ability, see Reverend John Heckewelder's *History, Manners, and Customs of The Indian Nations who once Inhabited Pennsylvania and the Neighbouring States with an Introduction and Notes by the Rev. William C. Reichel* (Bethlehem, PA: The Historical Society

of Pennsylvania, 1881), 132–137. The topics of indigenous speeches that became objects of American interest are discussed in Eastman, "Indian Censures," 536.

68. Ganter, *Collected Speeches*, xxii–xxiv; Turner, *History*, 487–488. Jasper and Parish were "go-betweens," people who like "Hermes" bore messages of diplomatic protocol, kept track of the international "vocabulary," and had an intimate knowledge of the "pace and rhythm" of intercultural exchange. James Merrell, *Into the American Woods: Negotiators on the Pennsylvania Frontier* (New York: W.W. Norton, 2000), 19. On the issue of captivity, see Ian Steele, *Setting all the Captives Free*, 210–211; Richter, *Ordeal of the Longhouse*, 66–71.

69. Alan Taylor, "The 'Art of Hook and Snivey':Political Culture in Upstate New York During the 1790s," *Journal of American History* 80 (March 1993): 1371–1396. Also cited in Hauptman, *Conspiracy*, 94–95. On the land cessions, see Taylor, *American Revolutions*, 427–431.

70. "Defense of Stiff Armed George," *Albany Centinel*, September 3, 1802. See also Densmore, *Red Jacket*, 60.

71. Names are capitalized in the original translated text. Ganter, *Collected Speeches*, 119–122; *American Citizen and General Advertiser*, September 10, 1802; "Defense of Stiff Armed George," *Albany Centinel*, September 3, 1802.

72. See the role of newspapers in "strenuous electioneering" in Waldstreicher, *In the Midst*, 185. On the history of the *Bee*, see Jeffrey L. Pasley, *The Tyranny of Printers: Newspaper Politics in the Early American Republic* (Charlottesville, VA: University of Virginia Press, 2001), 141–148. Italics are the *Bee*'s. "Distortions," *The Hudson Bee* (New York), September 28, 1802. This racially inspired suspicion of political eloquence was akin to what David Waldstreicher has called "literary blackface," the "aggregated dialects and malapropisms" often used in print by white authors to politicize race while simultaneously reinforcing racial exclusion. Waldstreicher, *In the Midst*, 337. See also the "hybrid" language used by indigenous writers themselves in Philip H. Round, *Removeable Type: Histories of the Book in Indian Country, 1663-1880* (Chapel Hill, NC: University of North Carolina Press, 2010), 210.

73. Italics are the *American Citizen's*. *American Citizen and General Advertiser*, September 10, 1802; Ganter, *Collected Speeches*, 119.

74. *The Albany Centinel*, Sept 28, 1802.

75. "Albany, March 4, 1803," *Chronicle Express*, March 17, 1803; *Albany Gazette*, March 14, 1803; *Albany Centinel*, March 15, 1803; *New-York Morning Chronicle*, March 15, 1803; *Chronicle Express*, March 17, 1803; *American Citizen*, March 23, 1803; *The Albany Register*, March 11, 1803; *Morning Chronicle*, March 14, 1803; *Chronicle Express*, March 17, 1803; *The Evening Post*, March 15, 1803; *Morning Chronicle*, March 15, 1803; *Mercantile Advertiser*, March 16, 1803.

76. Ganter, *Collected Speeches*, 138–143. Reprinted in Stone, *Life and Times*, 188–193. See also Densmore, *Red Jacket*, 140–145. There has been some debate over the speech's authenticity, though that has little bearing on how it is indicative of Red Jacket's

growing reputation. Ganter and Densmore are convinced that this is Red Jacket's speech, but Harry Robie is less sure. Harry Robie, "Red Jacket's Reply: Problems in the Verification of A Native American Speech Text," *New York Folklore* 12, no. 3 (Jan 1986): 99–117.

77. Nathan Hatch, *The Democratization of American Christianity* (New Haven, CT: Yale University Press, 1991), 9–10. Waldstreicher, *In the Midst*, 257.

78. Ganter, *Collected Speeches*, 163–164. "Native Eloquence," *The Albany Balance and State Journal*, August 6, 1811; "Native Eloquence," *Long-Island Star* August 21, 1811; *Chenango Weekly Advertiser,* November 7, 1811; *New-York Spectator,* August 17, 1811.

79. Ganter, *Collected Speeches*, 164–165. On the Ogden Land Company broadly, see Laurence Hauptman, *The Tonawanda Senecas' Heroic Battle Against Removal: Conservative Activist Indians* (Albany, NY: State University of New York Press, 2011), chapter 1; Tiro, *The People of Standing Stone*, chapter 5; Konkle, *Writing Indian Nations*, 236–237.

   Native Eloquence appeared at the same time as rumors of Red Jacket's abusive drinking. William Stone believed these rumors, but that impression may be attributable to his favoritism of Joseph Brant. Stone, *Life and Times*, 152. Christopher Densmore reveals the many contradictory stories of Red Jacket's alcoholism, all of which cast doubt on the veracity of the rumors. Densmore, *Red Jacket,* 101.

   Origin stories are regarded by some scholars as the "*ur* genre of American literary history." They were already deeply popular in this era, so this may have accounted for the interest generated by the arrival of Ogden, the Iroquois' new enemy. Rivett, *Unscripted America*, 7.

80. "Native Eloquence," *The Balance and State Journal,* August 6, 1811; *New-York Spectator,* August 17, 1811; *Long-Island Star,* August 21, 1811; *Cenango Weekly Advertiser,* November 7, 1811.

81. On Tecumseh, see Nichols, *Red Gentlemen*, 198–199.

82. His speeches are in Ganter, *Collected Speeches*, 149–183. See also Densmore, *Red Jacket,* 78–81; Stone, *Life and* Times, 217–219; Mathew Dennis, "Red Jacket's Rhetoric: Postcolonial Persuasions on the Native Frontiers of the Early American Republic" in Earnest Stromberg, ed., *American Indian Rhetorics of Survivance: Word Medicine, Word Magic,* (Pittsburg: University of Pittsburg Press, 2006), 15–33. On neutrality, see Nichols, *Red Gentlemen*, 198–199. On the war, see Carl Benn, *The Iroquois in the War of 1812* (Toronto: The University of Toronto Press, 1998).

83. The Erie Canal, in particular, was a "spectacle of progress," Waldstreicher, *In the Midst*, 292; *What Hath God Wrought*, 117. Edward Countryman explained that the construction of the canal "marked as momentous a change in New York's material, economic, and social life as the Revolution had marked in its political life half a century earlier." Edward Countryman, "A New Empire" in Klein, *The Empire State*, 70. The "illustrious" institutions in David I. Spanagel, *Dewitt Clinton and Amos Eaton: Geology and Power in Early New York* (Baltimore: Johns Hopkins University Press, 2014), 2. Clinton supported an embargo over war. Evan Cornog,

The Birth of Empire: DeWitt Clinton and the American Experience, 1769–1828 (New York: Oxford University Press, 1998), 121. James Renwick wrote in 1840, "Few men have been more the object of virulent animosity or of more exalted praise" James Renwick, *Life of DeWitt Clinton* (New York: Harper & Brothers, 1840), 13.

84. Cornog, *The Birth of Empire*, 8; Daniel Walker Howe, *What Hath God Wrought: The Transformation of America, 1815–1848* (New York: Oxford University Press, 2007), 19. Clinton's thoughts are echoed by the Tuscarora scholar David Cusick who conceived of a "revived Iroquois empire [defined] on Tuscarora terms" more than a decade later in 1828, Anderson, *Storied Landscapes*, 13, 133–141. The two speeches are Dewitt Clinton, *Discourse Delivered Before the New-York Historical Society* (New York: New-York Historical Society, 1812), https://archive.org/details/discou rsedelive01socigoog/page/n9/mode/2up (accessed September 2019); DeWitt Clinton, *Introductory Discourse Delivered Before the Literary and Philosophical Society of New York* (New York: David Longworth, 1815) https://archive.org/deta ils/introductorydiscooclinrich/page/n8/mode/2up (accessed September 2019).

85. Clinton, *Discourse*, 6.

86. Clinton, *Discourse*, 40–45.

87. Clinton, *Discourse*, 40–41. For more on Red Jacket's trial, see Densmore, *Red Jacket*, 56–57; Stone, *Life and Times*, 447–450.

88. Clinton, *Discourse*, 86–91. This followed the contemporary fascination with mounds, *castles*, and other examples of indigenous architecture among archaeologists and amateurs. Conn, *History's Shadow*, 127–129; Gordon M. Sayre, "The Mound Builders and the Imagination of American Antiquity in Jefferson, Bartram, and Chateaubriand," *Early American Literature* 33, no. 3 (1998): 225–249. Clinton's interpretation of indigenous history was wrong on many counts. Clinton, *Speech*, 92–93. The Haudenosaunees' retelling of their own history is borne out by documentary and ecological evidence. See Mt. Pleasant, "A New Paradigm," 374–412; Arthur C. Parker, "Forever the Five Nations: A Survey of the Amazing Iroquois and Their Way of Life," ACPA 4, no. 6: 169–171.

89. Clinton, *Speech*, 97–98. See also Anderson, *Storied Landscapes*, 126–128.

90. Howe, *What Hath God Wrought*, 117. On the "admired" speech, see Cornog, *The Birth of Empire*, 6. The indigenous sources are referenced in Clinton, *Introductory Discourse*, 126–127, 94, 37–38, 25. The subject of indigenous knowledge shaping Euro-American science is discussed in Susan Scott Parrish, *American Curiosity: Cultures of Natural History in the Colonial British Atlantic World* (Chapel Hill, NC: University of North Carolina Press, 2006). "The literati" are found in Clinton, *Introductory Discourse*, 3.

91. Milton M. Klein ed., *The Empire State: A History of New York* (Ithaca, NY: Cornell University Press, 2001), xix. Some push the timeline back decades earlier with a 1785 letter from George Washington to the New York Common Council who described the state as "the Seat of the Empire," owing perhaps to the fact that

New York City was the first American capital city. New-York Historical Society, "How Did New York Get Its Famous Nickname: The Empire State?," https://www.nyhistory.org/community/empire-state-nickname (accessed March 2020); Daniel Hulsebosch, "Tracing the Origins of 'Empire State,'" letter to the editor, *The New York Times*, March 28, 1990.

92. In order, the pillars of the "Empire State" are discussed in the following works. Craig and Mary Hanyan, *DeWitt Clinton and the Rise of the People's Men* (Montreal: McGill-Queens University Press, 1996), 229; DeWitt Clinton, *Memoir of DeWitt Clinton: With an appendix, containing numerous documents, illustrative of the principle events of his life* (New York: J. Seymour, 1829), 420 https://archive.org/details/memoirofdewittcloohosa (accessed 2018); also cited in Cornog, *The Birth of Empire*, 123; James Renwick, *Life of DeWitt Clinton* (New York: Harper and Brothers, 1840), 223. That the origins of the term Empire State "remain unknown" is explored in Klein, *The Empire State*, xix. An interesting addition to this core set of qualities, perhaps a fourth pillar, is that by 1850 New York City was the seat of America's publications distribution network, which facilitated the growth of a local and national print culture. Steven Carl Smith, *An Empire of Print: The New York Publishing Trade in the Early American Republic* (Philadelphia: University of Pennsylvania Press, 2018).

93. Some Haudenosaunee men also participated in the construction of the canal. Hauptman, *Conspiracy*, 101, 212. From the 1810s to 1840, the population of these areas and cities exploded from a population less than 1,500 to more than 40,000. Hauptman, *Conspiracy*, 162–163. "On the defensive" in Hauptman, *Conspiracy*, 213. "Nationalizing" in John Seeyle, "'Rational Exultation': The Erie Canal Celebration," *Proceedings of the American Antiquarian Society* 94, no. 2 (January 1985): 247; *Seneca Chief* is mentioned in 256–263.

94. "Indian Letter," *Orange County Patriot*, March 20, 1818; *Albany Gazette*, March 11, 1818; *New-York Columbian*, April 3, 1818; *Palmyra Register*, March 24, 1818; *Commercial Advertiser*, March 7, 1818. The "Red Jacket legacy" is in Ganter, "Red Jacket," 561. On his travels, see Hauptman, *Conspiracy*, 139–157.

95. Densmore, *Red Jacket*, 116–118; Stone, *Life and Times*, 389; Thatcher, *Indian Biography*, 298–300. His public events were catalogued in "Seneca Chiefs," *Saratoga Sentinal*, April 8, 1823; *The Watch-Tower*, April 14, 1823. "Sons of the Forest," *The New York Statesman*, February 28, 1823; *Liverpool Mercury*, March 28, 1823. "Seneca Indians," *The Watch-Tower*, August 19, 1822. Originally Reprinted in the *Palmyra Gazette*.

96. "Liverpool Music Festival," *New-York Evening Post*, November 17, 1823. "Popular Oratory and Poetry in the New World," *Freeman's Journal and Daily Commercial Advertiser* (Dublin), July 23–25, 1849.

97. Densmore, *Red Jacket*, 124; Ganter, *Collected Speeches*, 233–238; Hauptman, *Conspiracy*, 148–149. The religious aspects of this were publicized in: "Married," *New York Mercantile Advertiser*, December 28, 1820; *The American*, Dec 28, 1820;

Orange County Patriot, January 1, 1821; *New-York Daily Advertiser,* December 28, 1820. It was originally reported in *The Twenty-Second Annual Report of the Directors of the New-York Missionary Society, Presented at the Annual Meeting, on Tuesday, April 6, 1819* (New York: New-York Missionary Society, 1819). On the separation, see Stone, *Red Jacket,* 356.

98. "Red Jacket and the Seneca Indians," *The Western Star,* October 26, 1827; *The Troy Sentinel,* November 6, 1827; "Red Jacket Deposed," *The Standard* (London), October 24, 1827; "Foreign intelligence," *Examiner* (London), October 28, 1827; *North Wales Chronicle,* November 1, 1827. See also Hauptman, *Conspiracy,* 156–159; Densmore, *Red Jacket,* 117–119.

99. The meeting with Jackson was ultimately a failed enterprise considering Jackson's brutal Indian Removal policies. Densmore, *Red Jacket,* 117–119; Stone, *Life and Times,* 389–390.

100. Camilla Townsend offers a telling example of the conscious image-making of indigenous people that shaped how white observers saw them. Red Jacket cultivated his own public image in a similar manner. Camilla Townsend, *Pocahontas and the Powhattan Dilemma* (New York: Hill and Wang, 2004), chapter 2. Taken together, Jadviga da Costa Nunes and Christopher Densmore have done the important work of compiling nearly all original portrayals of Red Jacket and offer us an opportunity to view these images side-by-side. Nunes, "Red Jacket," 4–20; Densmore, *Red Jacket,* cover image (painting), 30 (silhouette) and 97–100 (paintings). The silhouette that Densmore mentions in located in the Joseph Downs Collection at the Winterthur Library. Laura Parish, "'Chief Speaker of the Five Nations' in the Downs Collection," *Winterthur Library News* (Summer 2019): 1–8. Another possible addition to this list is a painting mentioned by Arthur C. Parker who suggests that a J. L. D. Mathies from Canandaigua was the first to paint Red Jacket in the early nineteenth century. Parker cites Orasmus Turner's 1855 *History of the Holland Purchase* as where he found the reference to the painting. I cannot, however, find this reference in Turner's work or any evidence of the painting elsewhere. Parker, *Red Jacket,* 214. http://pressroom. winterthur.org/pdfs/Winterthur-Library-News-2019-Summer.pdf   (accessed December 2019).

     The one exception to the Peace Medal rule is an 1807 watercolor and graphite drawing by the Baroness Hyde de Neuville, or Anne Marguerite Henriette de Marigny. The portrait is, according to the artist, of a young Red Jacket "busy making foot-gear of deer skin called mocassins (sic)." If this is truly him, it is likely the first image of Red Jacket ever recorded. Baroness Anne-Marguerite-Henriette Hyde de Neuville, *Portrait of an Indian Chief, Red Jacket,* Luce Center, New-York Historical Society.   https://www.nyhistory.org/exhibit/portrait-indian-chief-red-jacket-c1758-1830. For her biography, see "Baroness Hyde de Neuville (Anne Marguerite Henriette de Marigny)," *New Jersey Women's History,* a project of the Alice Paul Institute, http://www.njwomenshistory.org/discover/biographies/baroness-hyde-de-neuville-anne-marguerite-henriette-de-marigny/ (accessed December

2019). See also "Artist in Exile: The Visual Diary of Baroness Hyde de Neuville," November 1, 2019–January 26, 2020, *New-York Historical Society*: https://www. nyhistory.org/exhibitions/artist-exile-visual-diary-baroness-hyde-de-neuville (accessed December 2019). Hyde de Neuville, Jean Guillaume ed., *Memoires et souvenirs du Baron Hyde de Neuville* 2nd edition, 3 vols (Paris: Librarie Plon, 1892), 1: 458–459. See also William Fenton, "The Hyde de Neuville Portraits of New York Savages in 1807-1808," *New-York Historical Society Quarterly* 38:2 (1954): 119–137; Anthony F. C. Wallace *The Death and Rebirth of the Seneca* (New York: Alfred A. Knopf, 1970), 142.

101. William Dunlap, *A History of the Rise and Progress of the Arts of Design in the United States* (Boston: C.E. Goodspeed, 1918), 193.

102. "The Red Jacket Medal," 324. James Fenimore Cooper, *The Leatherstocking Tales* (New York: Penguin Random House, 2012). See also Burrows and Wallace, *Gotham*, 469–470; Thomas Bender, *New York Intellect: A History of Intellectual Life in New York City from 1750 to the Beginnings of Our Own Time* (New York: Alfred A. Knopf, 1987), chapter 4.

103. Fitz-Greene Halleck, *Alnwick Castle: With Other Poems* (Ann Arbor, MI: University of Michigan Humanities Text Initiative, 1995), 56–61, https:// quod.lib.umich.edu/a/amverse/BAC5662.0001.001/1:11?cite1=halleck;cite1r estrict=author;rgn=div1;view=toc;q1=red+jacket (accessed December 2019). Original: Fitz-Greene Halleck, *Alnwick Castle: With Other Poems* (New York: George Dearborn Publishers, 1836).

104. On Darley's work, see the exhibition catalogue of Nancy Finlay, *Inventing the American Past: The Art of F.O.C. Darley* (New York: New York Public Library, 1999). A small collection of Darley's art and letters is held by the Winterthur Library in *The Joseph Downs Collection of Manuscripts and Printed Ephemera*. For the *Harper's* critique, see "The Red Jacket Medal," *Harper's New Monthly Magazine* 32, 1865–66, 324.

105. "Most familiar" quotation in Stone, *Life and Times*, v. This marks an early moment in scholarly ethnohistory that anticipated the first formal meetings of ethnohistorians in 1953 which, by 1966, became the American Society of Ethnohistorians. "About," American Society for Ethnohistory, https://ethnohist ory.org/about/ (accessed November 2020). Stone's son, William Leete Stone, Jr., would write the two-volume biography of Johnson in 1865 that his father never finished. William L. Stone, Jr., *The Life and Times of Sir William Johnson* 2 vols. (Albany: J. Munsel, 1865). The origins of Red Jacket's memory were settled in the nineteenth century, but the orator and his Peace Medal continue to be the subject of new interpretation. See "But What About the Indians?" *Ask A Slave,* Season 2, Episode 3, November 24, 2013, http://www.askaslave.com/ (accessed January 2017).

106. *Rochester Times Union,* June 4, 1953. Ely S. Parker to William Cullen Bryant, May 8, 1884, Harriet M. Converse Scrapbook, William M. Beauchamp Collection,

SC17369: Box 45 Scrapbook 2, New York State Library and Archives, page 4 (Hereafter cites as HMCSB).

107. Ely S. Parker to William Cullen Bryant, May 8, 1884, HMCSB, 4-5. "The Great Iroquois Chief," *The Buffalo Courier,* October 1884. "Sa-go-ye-wa-tha," HMCSB, 2.

CHAPTER 2

1. Armstrong, *Warrior,* 109–110. C. Joseph Genetin-Pilawa, *Crooked Paths to Allotment: The Fight over Federal Indian Policy After the Civil War* (Chapel Hill, NC: University of North Carolina Press, 2012), 1. "Real American" appears in multiple places: Joseph Bruchac's poem "Appomattox" in Joseph Bruchac, *The White Man's War: Ely S. Parker: Iroquois General* (New York: Bowman Books, 2011), 27–28; mentioned but unattributed in Burke Davis, *To Appomattox: Nine April Days, 1865* (New York: Rinehart Publishers, 1959), 386; James M. McPherson, *Battle Cry of Freedom: The Civil War Era* (New York: Oxford University Press, 1988), 849; Parker, *The Life,* 133; Elizabeth R. Varon, *Appomattox: Victory, Defeat, and Freedom at the End of the Civil War* (New York: Oxford University Press, 2014), 64. The phrase "We Are All Americans" is also mentioned in Ari Kelman, "We Are All Americans": Native People in the National Narrative," *Reviews in American History* 42:4 (December 2014): 661–669.

2. Horace Porter, *Battles and Leaders of the Civil War* volume 4 (New York: The Century Company, 1888), 741. See also Adam Badeau, *Military History of Ulysses S. Grant* volume 3 (Bedford: Applewood Books, 1885), 602–608; Genetin-Pilawa, *Crooked Paths,* 1; Armstrong, *Warrior,* 110. It is also notable that Horace Porter, a friend of Parker's and Colonel in the US Army, recognized the importance of Lee's mistaking "Parker for a negro" rather than the "full blooded Indian" he was and chose to comment on it. Horace Porter, *Campaigning With Grant* (New York: The Century Company, 1897), 481; "By an Ex-Editor," *The Philadelphia Inquirer,* September 2, 1895. As it relates to the war over slavery, see McPherson, *Battle Cry of Freedom,* 849; Heather Cox Richardson, "We Are All Americans: Ely Parker at Appomattox," We're History blog, April 9, 2015, http://werehistory.org/ely-parker/ (accessed January 2020). On the Indian dimensions, see Mariam Touba, "'We Are All Americans:' Grant, Lee, and Ely Parker at Appomattox Court House," From the Stacks blog, entry posted April 2, 2015 http://blog.nyhistory.org/we-are-all-americans-grant-lee-and-ely-parker-at-appomattox-court-house-2/ (accessed February 2020); Parker, *Life,* 133–134; Genetin-Pilawa, *Crooked Paths,* 1; Appomattox Court House, "Ely Parker: Chief, Lawyer, Engineer, and Brigadier General," blog post for the National Park Service https://www.nps.gov/apco/parker.htm (accessed March 2020).

3. The suspicion that the story is apocryphal is in Genetin-Pilawa, *Crooked Paths,* 1. It is not included in the stories told after Porter, *Battles and Leaders,* 741; or even in Ely Parker's unfinished autobiography in Autobiography, *Publications of the Buffalo*

Historical Society 8 (1908): 534–535. Arthur discussed where he heard this story in Parker, *Life*, 134.

4. Karen Cox, *Dreaming of Dixie: How the South was Created in American Popular Culture* (Chapel Hill, NC: University of North Carolina Press, 2011), chapter 5. Keith D. Dickson, *Sustaining Southern Identity* (Baton Rouge, LA: Louisiana State University, 2011), 10; Davis, *To Appomattox*, 386; McPherson, *Battle Cry*, 849.

5. Conn, *History's Shadow*, 32.

6. The western "Indian problem" was part of what historians have broadly termed the era of Greater Reconstruction; Elliot West, *The Last Indian War: The Nez Perce Story* (New York: Oxford University Press, 2009), xvii–xix. Parker's reputation echoes Philip Deloria's Indian "anomalies" at the turn of the twentieth century. Deloria, *Indians in Unexpected Places*, 14, quote from 188.

7. I acknowledge the importance of those jobs and they are certainly relevant to this chapter, but I add only little to what has already been said by Laurence Hauptman and others. Hauptman, *Tonawanda Senecas'*; Hauptman, *Seven Generations*, chapters 1–4; Hauptman, *Conspiracy*, chapters 10–13; Genetin-Pilawa, *Crooked Paths,* chapters 1–4.

8. Craig Miner, *Seeding Civil War: Kansas in the National News, 1854–1858*, (Lawrence, KS: University Press of Kansas, 2008), ix.

9. Parker, *Life*, 41–51; quote from Armstrong, *Warrior in Two Camps*, 7–8.

10. Armstrong, *Warrior*, 1–2. A living descendant of Ely Parker offers another corrective. See Special Report, *The Life of Ely Parker* on WRRZ-TV Buffalo, November 23, 2017, https://www.youtube.com/watch?v=Q5dgv-ScQGw (accessed January 2020); Jane Kwiatkowski, "Recalling the historic role of a Tonawanda Seneca," *The Buffalo News*, April 8, 2015, https://buffalonews.com/2015/04/08/recalling-the-historic-role-of-a-tonawanda-seneca/ (accessed January 2020); Michael Wilson, "A Seneca Indian Connects With His New York Roots," *The New York Times: City Room Blog*, September 19, 2010, https://cityroom.blogs.nytimes.com/2010/09/19/wilson-indian-post-for-sunday/ (accessed January 2020). Parker remembered Stone from his childhood. Letter from ESP to Mrs. Edith L. Wilner, May 28, 1895; quoted also in Parker, *Life*, 321. On his selection of familial names, see Parker, *Life*, 50, 204.

11. Reginald Horsman, "The Indian Policy of an 'Empire for Liberty'," *Native Americans and the Early Republic*, Frederick F. Hoxie, Ronald Hoffman, Peter Alberts, eds. (Charlottesville, VA: University of Virginia Press, 1999), 55. The brutal policies of Indian removal are further discussed in Saunt, *Unworthy Republic*, xv–xvi; Horsman, "The Indian Policy," 54. "Ethnically cleanse" in Dunbar-Ortiz, *An Indigenous Peoples' History*, 96. On Manifest Destiny, see Howe, *What Hath God Wrought*, 365; Theda Perdue, "The Legacy of Indian Removal," *Journal of Southern History* 78:1 (2012): 3–36. On the presidents, see Michael Paul Rogin, *Fathers and Children: Andrew Jackson and the Subjugation of the American Indian* (New York: Alfred Knopf, 1979), 3–4, cited in Ortiz, *An Indigenous Peoples'*

History, 109. On "expulsion" and a new language for Indian Removal, see Saunt, *Unworthy Republic,* xiii-xiv.

12. Hauptman, *Tonawanda Senecas',* 38–43.

13. Hauptman, *Tonawanda Senecas',* 31–43. Who the "81" chiefs were is unclear, and it does not match the number of Seneca leaders that would have existed at any one time, Armstrong, *Warrior,* 10–13. See also Hauptman, *Tonawanda Senecas',* 31–75.

14. On Richard M. Johnson and his complex legacy, see Christina Snyder, *Great Crossings: Indians, Settlers, and Slaves in the Age of Jackson* (New York: Oxford University Press, 2017). On Ogden, see Armstrong, *Warrior,* 11. On Kansas, see Tiro, *People of Standing Stone,* 135–141.

15. Hauptman, *Tonawanda Senecas',* 43–46.

16. Armstrong, *Warrior,* 16–17. Parker, *Life,* 69.

17. Parker, *Life,* 72–73; Autobiography of Ely S. Parker, *Publications of the Buffalo Historical Society* Volume 8 (Buffalo, 1908), 530–531. See a similar moment in Armstrong, *Warrior,* 17–18. Parker, *Life,* 74; Elizabeth Tooker, "Ely S. Parker: Seneca, ca. 1828-1895," *American Indian Intellectuals,* ed. Margot Liberty (St. Paul, MN: West Publishing Company, 1978), 17.

18. *The Buffalo Express,* March 24, 1915, printed in Parker, *Life,* 262. *Newark Daily Advertiser,* November 12, 1844; *New York True Sun,* November 12, 1844; *New York True Sun,* November 15, 1844; *The Sun* (Philadelphia), November 16, 1844; *The New York Herald,* November 18, 1844; "A Five-Mile Foot Race Against Time," *Evening Post,* August 4, 1847; *Long Island Farmer, and Queens County Advertiser,* August 10, 1847; *The National Eagle,* August 27, 1847. His transfer is described in Tooker, "Ely S. Parker," 18.

19. Hauptman, *Tonawanda Senecas',* 76. On Blacksmith and politics, see Armstrong, *Warrior,* 21

20. Armstrong, *Warrior,* 20. Hauptman, *Tonawanda Senecas',* 73

21. Quoted in Hauptman, *Tonawanda Senecas',* 79–80. On Indian delegates in DC, see Herman Viola, *Diplomats in Buckskins: A History of Indian Delegations in Washington City* (Washington, DC: Smithsonian Institution Press, 1981).

22. Thomas R. Trautmann, *Lewis Henry Morgan and the Invention of Kinship* (Lincoln, NE: University of Nebraska Press, 2008), 31–86; Armstrong, *Warrior,* chapters 2–4. Lewis Henry Morgan, *League of the Iroquois* (New York: Corinth Press and Carol Publishing, 1993). Morgan's *League* was originally published as *League of the Ho-de-no-sau-nee, Iroquois* (Rochester: Sage and Brothers, Inc., 1851). On religion, see Hauptman, *Tonawanda Senecas',* 31–33; Wallace, *Death and Rebirth of the Seneca,* 335–336.

23. Tooker, "Ely S. Parker," 19; Morgan, *League,* 4–5.

24. Parker, *Life,* 75; Tooker, "Ely S. Parker," 16. On publications, see Tooker, "Ely S. Parker," 19; Parker, *Life,* 81; Trautmann, *Lewis Henry Morgan,* 47. On Morgan's connection to the family, see Armstrong, *Warrior,* 10, 48; Laurence M. Hauptman, "On Our Terms: The Tonawanda Seneca Indians, Lewis Henry Morgan, and Henry

Rowe Schoolcraft, 1844-1851," *New York History* 91, no. 4 (2010): 314–335. The collection of about five hundred items were given piecemeal to the museum over the years 1848–1851. Many objects, however, did not survive the Albany capitol fire of 1911. For more on the history and provenance of the collection, see the finding aid and collection summary of "The Lewis Henry Morgan Collection of Mid-Nineteenth Century Iroquois Objects" at the New York State Museum, http://www.nysm.nysed.gov/native-american-ethnography/collections/lewis-henry-mor gan-collection-mid-nineteenth-century (accessed November 2019). See Caroline's role in Trautmann, *Lewis Henry Morgan*, 38, 44–45. "Regents of the University," *Weekly Argus* (Albany), February 22, 1851. See also "Cornplanter's pipe tomahawk officially repatriated to Seneca Nation by New York State Museum," *Indian Country Today*, January 13, 2020, https://newsmaven.io/indiancountrytoday/the-press-pool/cornplanter-s-pipe-tomahawk-officially-repatriated-to-seneca-nation-by-new-york-state-museum-HUu-IPcRoEa-tcosN9guoA (accessed January 2020).

25. Tooker, "Ely S. Parker," 19–20; Robert Bieder, "Grand Order of the Iroquois," *Ethnohistory* 27:4 (1980): 349–350. See also Tooker, "Lewis H. Morgan and the Senecas," in *Strangers to Relatives*, 31–36. On the dress code of the Grand Order, see Trautmann, *Lewis Henry Morgan*, 43–48; Parker, *Life*, 80.

26. Tooker, "Ely S. Parker," 19–20; Bieder, "Grand Order," 350–352. "Crooked schemes" in Parker, *Life*, 81. On the Batavia Lodge, see Armstrong, *Warrior*, 37.

27. "League of the Ho-De-No-Sau-Nee, or Iroquois. By Lewis H. Morgan, Rochester: Sago & Brother; New York: Mark H. Newman and Co. 1851," *The New York Evening Post*, March 19, 1851. The comments of the editors were printed in "Indian Council of the Six Nations at Tonawanda, *The New York Evening Post*, October 23, 1847.

28. Tooker, "Ely S. Parker," 18; Parker, *Life*, 79. Armstrong, *Warrior*, 41–42.

29. Armstrong, *Warrior*, 43; Parker, *Life*, 89–92.

30. "Indian Council of the Six Nations," *Albany Journal*, September 24, 1851. Reprinted in *Weekly Argus*, September 27, 1851; *The Daily Union* (DC), September 28, 1851; *Daily Evening Transcript* (Boston), October 1, 1851; *New-York Observer*, October 2, 1851; *The Christian Times* (Boston), October 3, 1851; *The Weekly Union* (DC), October 18, 1851; *Daily Alta California*, November 5, 1851. See also Armstrong, *Warrior*, 1 and 49. For Parker's engineering career, see Armstrong, *Warrior*, 50; "Indian Council of the Six Nations," *Albany Journal*, September 24, 1851.

31. Hauptman, *Tonawanda Senecas'*, 94. Parker's correspondence is described in Hauptman, *Tonawanda Senecas'*, 106. Newspapers also tracked Parker's whereabouts and his dual roles as engineer and chief: "An Indian Chief in the Nineteenth Century," *Newark Daily Advertiser*, July 27, 1855; *Salem Register* (MA), July 30, 1855; *The Sentinel of Freedom* (Newark), July 31, 1855; *New-York Observer*, August 2, 1855; *The Puritan Recorder* (Boston), August 9, 1855; *Daily Picayune* (New Orleans), August 9, 1855; *The Zion's Advocate* (Portland, Maine), August 10, 1855; *The Catholic Herald* (Philadelphia), August 16, 1855. Parker was also notably connected

to Tonawanda politics from Philadelphia while attending the "dedication of the Masonic Hall." "An Indian Visitor," *The Mining Register* (Pottsville, PA), October 6, 1855.

32. For a summary of Martindale's court battles, see Hauptman, *Tonawanda Senecas,* chapter 5–7. Quote in Armstrong, *Warrior,* 44–58. See also *Rochester Daily Union,* January 24, 1852.

33. The Treaty is described in Armstrong, *Warrior,* 64–65; "The Tonawanda Indians," *Albany Journal,* June 10, 1857. Nicholson and Ely's participation: *The Washington Union* (DC), April 5, 1859; *The Washington Union* (DC), April 6, 1859; *The Press* (Philadelphia), April 23, 1860; "A Creditable Indian Treaty," *Boston Daily Advertiser,* April 27, 1860. The many attempts by New York to dismantle Tonawanda sovereignty and force them to accept "the long arm of the state" is detailed in Hauptman, *Tonawanda Senecas,* 107–108, chapter 9.

34. Parker, *Life,* 96. See his appointment as engineer covered in newspapers in "News Article," *Evening Star* (DC), March 14, 1857; *Alexandria Gazette,* March 16, 1857; *Philadelphia Inquirer,* March 17, 1857; *Wisconsin Patriot,* March 28, 1857; *The Louisville Daily Journal,* April 2, 1857; *The Daily Pioneer and Democrat* (St Paul), April 21, 23, 1857; *Boston Evening Transcript,* April 27, 1857. Armstrong, *Warrior,* chapter 6. For his promotion to "Grand Orator," see Parker, *Life,* 97–98. On "respect," see Armstrong, *Warrior,* 61–72.

35. *Lowell Daily Journal and Courier,* October 29, 1859. For another similar episode, see Armstrong, *Warrior,* 64–65.

36. "Masonic Speech of an Indian," *The Napa County Reporter,* May 5, 1860; *Daily True American,* May 31, 1860; *Memphis Daily Avalanche,* June 12, 1860; *The Constitution* (DC), June 13, 1860; *Salem Register,* December 8, 1862; *Exeter News-Letter, and Rockingham County Advertiser,* January 19, 1863. See also reprints in Armstrong, *Warrior,* 69–70; Parker, *Life,* 97–98. In addition to being a member, Parker had a historic connection to the Tonawanda local Batavia Lodge through a rumor. William Morgan, the anti-Mason who was famously murdered in 1826 for threatening to reveal the secrets of the Lodge and the structures of American party power, had supposedly hidden out on the Tonawanda reservation while he was being hunted. Armstrong, *Warrior,* 37; for more on the murder and its influence on the development of regional political parties, see Lee S. Tillotson, *Anti-Masonry and the Murder of Morgan: Lee S. Tillotson's Ancient Craft Masonry in Vermont,* ed. Guillermo De Los Reyes (Washington, DC: Westphalia Press, 2013).

37. "Masonic Speech of an Indian," *The Napa County Reporter,* May 5, 1860; *Daily True American,* May 31, 1860; *Memphis Daily Avalanche,* June 12, 1860; *The Constitution* (DC), June 13, 1860; *Salem Register,* December 8, 1862; *Exeter News-Letter, and Rockingham County Advertiser,* January 19, 1863. See also reprints in Armstrong, *Warrior,* 69–70; Parker, *Life,* 97–98.

38. For Haudenosaunee service in the Civil War, see Laurence Hauptman, *The Iroquois in the Civil War: From Battlefield to Reservation* (Syracuse: Syracuse University

Press, 1993), 90. Answering this question also points to Parker's role in the "long Civil War," see Aaron Sheehan-Dean, "The Long Civil War," *Virginia Magazine of History & Biography* 119:2 (2011): 106–153.

39. Genetin-Pilawa, *Crooked Paths*, 11. On antislavery, see James Oakes, *Freedom National: The Destruction of Slavery in the United States, 1861-1865* (New York: W.W. Norton and Company, 2013), 30. See also Oakes, *The Scorpion's Sting: Antislavery and the Coming of the Civil War* (New York: W.W. Norton and Company, 2015).

40. Waldstreicher, *In the Midst*, 328–330. On the *Freedman's Journal*, see Shane White, "'It Was A Proud Day': African Americans, Festivals, and Parades in the North, 1741–1834," *Journal of American History* 81, no. 1 (June 1994): 38.On the association, see Edwin G. Burrows and Mike Wallace, *Gotham: A History of New York City to 1898* (New York: Oxford University Press, 1999), 548–549; Armstrong, *Warrior*, 54–55.

41. Howe, *What Hath God Wrought*, 414–423; Krauthamer, *Black Slaves, Indian Masters*, 8. On Manypenny's report, see Hauptman, *Tonawanda Senecas'*, 103.

42. Parker, *Life*, 96; Armstrong, *Warrior*, 73–77.

43. Parker, *Life*, 309–310.

44. Hauptman, *Iroquois in the Civil War*, 13–16; Letter from Parker to Harriet Maxwell Converse, *Publications of the Buffalo Historical Society* 8 (1908): 525. On "naturalization," see Parker, *Life*, 309–310.

45. On Isaac, see "Indians Refused for the Service," *Missouri Republican*, October 14, 1861; *Daily Missouri Republican*, October 15, 1861; *Daily Louisville Democrat*, October 17, 1861; *New-York Weekly Day Book*, October 19, 1861; *The Dubuque Herald*, October 23, 1861. "Petitions, etc." *The Daily Globe* (DC), February 15, 1862. On the numbers of Haudenosaunee in the war, see Hauptman, *Iroquois in the Civil War*, 11–22.

46. Armstrong, *Warrior*, 83–88; "Personal Items," *Boston Evening Transcript*, July 7, 1863; *Alexandria Gazette*, July 8, 1863; *New Haven Daily Palladium*, July 8, 1863; *The Sun* (Baltimore), July 8, 1863. See the details of Parker's wartime exploits in Armstrong, *Warrior*, chapters 8 and 9; Parker, *Life*, chapter 11 and 12. Parker's wartime service is also noted, albeit in less detail, in Robert U. Johnson and Clarence C. Buel, eds., *Battle and Leaders of the Civil War* 4 (New York: The Century Company, 1887–1888), 810.

47. ESP to Caroline Parker, November 21, 1863, transcribed in Parker, *Life*, 292–295. On federal emancipation and the Civil War, see Scott Ackerman, "'We Are Abolitionizing the West': The Union Army and the Implementation of Federal Emancipation Policy, 1861–1865" (PhD diss, City University of New York, 2019).

48. "Letter From General Grant's Indian Aid," *The Press* (Philadelphia), January 15, 1864; *Cleveland Morning Leader*, January 21, 1864; *Sacramento Daily Union*, February 23, 1864; *Cleveland Morning Leader*, January 21, 1864; *Daily Morning Chronicle* (DC), March 21, 1864. For "purest blood," see "New of the Day the War," *New-York Daily Tribune*, April 18, 1865.

49. "One of General Grant's Aids," *The New-Orleans Times*, May 5, 1865. Reprinted from *N.Y. Daily Advertiser*. Parker on military parade in Armstrong, *Warrior*, 113. On the complex history of the memories of the war, see Michael Kammen, *Mystic Chords of Memory: The Transformation of Tradition in American Culture* (New York: Vintage Press, 1993), 101.

50. *Baltimore Clipper*, August 12, 1865. Genetin-Pilawa, *Crooked Paths*, 51–56. C. Joseph Genetin Pilawa, "Ely S. Parker and the Paradox of Reconstruction Politics in Indian Country," *The World the Civil War Made*, Gregory P. Downs and Kate Masur, eds. (Chapel Hill, NC: University of North Carolina Press, 2015), 200.

51. Robert M. Utley, *The Indian Frontier of the American West, 1846-1890* (Albuquerque: New Mexico University Press, 1984), 117; Armstrong, *Warrior*, 113–116; Genetin-Pilawa, *Crooked Paths*, 60; see the contemporary summary in "Abstract of the Report of the Commissioner of Indian Affairs," *Daily National Intelligencer* (DC), December 29, 1865. See also Genetin-Pilawa, *Crooked Paths*, 56.

52. The *Inquirer's* report also noted that some of these "freedmen, or slaves," had come to the meeting as "delegates from the colored population of the Territory" to petition the Americans for freedom. The population of "colored" Indians was estimated to be around "10,500" people. "The Indians." *The Philadelphia Inquirer*, October 6, 1865; Armstrong, *Warrior*, 115.

53. "Washington," *New York Herald*, June 6, 1867; Genetin-Pilawa, *Crooked Paths*, 61–63.

54. *The Buffalo Express*, September 8, 1866; "Indians of New-York State," *The World* (NY), September 27, 1867; "The Green Corn Festival," *Cleveland Daily Leader*, September 29, 1866; *Weekly Alta California*, October 27, 1866; "Indians, Tonawanda," *San Francisco Bulletin*, November 1, 1866. The speech and its reception was recorded in "The Green Corn Festival," *Cleveland Daily Leader*, September 29, 1866; *The Buffalo Express*, September 8, 1866.

55. Henry G. Waltman, "Ely Samuel Parker, 1869-1871," *The Commissioners of Indian Affairs, 1824–1977*, eds. Robert M. Kvasnicka and Herman J. Viola (Lincoln, NE: University of Nebraska Press, 1979): 123-133. On Parker's politics, see Genetin-Pilawa, *Crooked Paths*, 73. "Sympathized" in Richardson, *West from Appomattox*, 114. On the "reformers," see Waltman, "Ely Samuel Parker," 123.

56. "Reminiscences of Red Jacket," *Pomeroy's Democrat* (NY), January 27, 1869; *Buffalo Commercial Advertiser*, January 27, 1869; *Frank Leslie's Illustrated Newspaper*, February 6, 1869; "Appointments," *The New York Journal of Commerce*, March 12, 1869. On the corruption of the "Indian ring," see Francis Paul Prucha, *The Great Father: The United States Government and the American Indians* 2 vols (Lincoln, NE: University of Nebraska Press, 1984). See also Prucha, *American Indian Policy in Crisis: Christian Reformers and the Indian, 1865–1900* (Norman, OK: University of Oklahoma, 1976). The "Indian ring" is succinctly described in Armstrong, *Warrior*, 140; Genetin-Pilawa, *Crooked Paths*, 76. Parker was also, for some, an obvious choice for the position: "Reminiscences of Red Jacket," *Pomeroy's*

Democrat (NY), January 27, 1869; *Buffalo Commercial Advertiser,* January 27, 1869; *Frank Leslie's Illustrated Newspaper,* February 6, 1869. On Parker's "beloved" reputation: "The Reported New Indian Commissioner," *New York Herald,* March 17, 1869; *The Independent Democrat* (Concord, NH), March 18, 1869; *The Cincinnati Daily Gazette.* March 23, 1869. On post-war Indian policy, see Richardson, *West From Appomattox,* 36. Parker's approval by the Senate: *Cleveland Daily Leader,* March 23, 1869; *Daily Evening Traveler,* March 29, 1869.

57. Waltman, "Ely Samuel Parker," 125; Genetin-Pilawa, *Crooked* Paths, 73; Armstrong, *Warrior,* 139 and 143. "Collect the Indians" in *The Evening Star* (DC), June 8, 1869.

58. Genetin-Pilawa, *Crooked Paths,* 96–97; Armstrong, *Warrior,* 140–152. Quotation in "Reply to Charges of Fraud," *The Missouri Democrat,* January 13, 1871.

59. "Reply to Charges of Fraud," *The Missouri Democrat,* January 13, 1871; "The Bureau of Indian Affairs. Commissioner Parker's Defense of his Administration.," *New York Herald,* January 13, 1871; "Indian Commissioner Parker," *Sacramento Daily Union,* January 26, 1871.

60. "Washington," *The Cincinnati Gazette,* July 18, 1871. "News of the Week: Weekly Gossip and Review," *Springfield Weekly Republican,* July 21, 1871; Parker, *Life,* 304–309. *The Daily Milwaukee News,* July 18, 1871; *National Republican* (DC), July 18, 1871; *The New York Herald,* July 18, 1871. The internal letters and memos of this accusation and investigation are detailed in Armstrong, *Warrior,* chapter 13.

61. Armstrong, *Warrior,* 162–169.

62. On his clerkship and relationship to Converse, see Armstrong, *Warrior,* 166–177. Some letters between them were reprinted in Parker, *Life,* chapter 14.

63. "How the American Indian Remains a Savage." *Idaho Daily Statesman,* January 13, 1893. "General Parker," *The San Diego Weekly Union,* July 27, 1893; "A Famous Telegram," *The Macon Telegraph,* July 14, 1886.

64. Ely S. Parker to William Cullen Bryant, May 8, 1884, HMCSB, 4; "Red Jacket's Bones," undated, HMCSB, 4. "The Great Iroquois Chief," *The Buffalo Courier,* October 1884, HMSCB, 9.

65. "The Last of the Senecas," November 1884, HMCSB, 5–6; Armstrong, *Warrior,* 178; *The Thirty-Sixth Annual Report of the Buffalo Historical Society* (Buffalo, NY: Mathews-Northrup Printing Company, 1898), 35; "The Last of the Senecas," undated, HMCSB, 5 6; "Red Jacket's Burial," October 9, 1884, HMCSB, 7; "Sa-go-ye-wa-tha", HMCSB, 2.

66. The bust currently resides in the registrar's office of the Rochester Museum and Science Center. The statue was described in "Monuments to the Indian," *New York World,* March 12, 1892, found in the Ely S. Parker Scrapbook in the William M. Beauchamp Papers, New York State Museum, Albany, NY (hereafter cited as WMBP EPS); "The Red Jacket Plans," *The Buffalo Express,* March 30, 1890, WMBP EPS; "Persons Worth Knowing About," *Morning Oregonian,* October 2, 1890; Armstrong, *Warrior,* 181.

67. "Monuments to the Indian," *New York World*, March 12, 1892, WMBP EPS; "Statue of Red Jacket," *Bay City Times-Press* (MI), January 19, 1892. Quotations from "Monuments to the Indian," *New York World*, March 12, 1892, WMBP EPS; Ganter, *Collected Speeches*, 34. The bronze turtles were reminiscent of the bronze sea crabs that held up the Metropolitan Museum of Art's most famous contemporary 1881 acquisition, the ancient Egyptian obelisk Cleopatra's Needle. See "Crab from Cleopatra's Needle," *The Metropolitan Museum of Art*, https://www.metmuseum.org/art/collection/search/551893 (accessed March 2020); Martina D'Alton, *The New York Obelisk, or, How Cleopatra's Needle Came to New York and What Happened When It Got Here* (New York: The Metropolitan Museum of Art, 1993) https://www.metmuseum.org/art/metpublications/The_New_York_Obelisk_or_How_Cleopatras_Needle_came_to_New_York_and_what_happened_when_it_got_here (accessed March 2020).

68. Parker, Life, 212–213.

69. Armstrong, *Warrior*, 179–180. Hamilton and the new statue were described in "Red Jacket: Two Monuments to the Indian Chiefs Memory," *The Buffalo Telegram*, June 7, 1884, HMCSB, 3.

70. "Red Jacket: Two Monuments," HMCSB, 3. The inscription in the original design did not make it into the final design of the memorial. The original description is as follows: "Red Jacket (Sa-yo-ge-wa-tha), The Resolute Champion of a Wronged and Hapless People, The Inspired Orator, 'The Rienzi of the Iroquois.'" The first paragraph of the quotation made it on the final version of the memorial. "Sa-go-yeh-wa-tha", 1884, HMCSB, 2. Another reference to Red Jacket as the "Rienzi of the Iroquois" in "Red Jacket, *Buffalo Telegram*, September 30, 1884, HMCSB, 22. See the history of Cola di Rienzo in Anthony DiRenzo, "Sortilegio: Cola Di Rienzo and the Blasphemy of Documentation," Ithaca College Faculty Publications, https://faculty.ithaca.edu/direnzo/docs/scholarship/sortilegio/ (accessed September 2018).

71. "The Last of the Senecas," November 1884, HMCSB, 5–6.

72. Waterloo Library and Historical Society. *Unveiling of the monument erected by the Waterloo Library and Historical Society: As a Memorial of Red Jacket, At Canoga, N.Y., the Place of His Birth, October 14, 1891* (Waterloo: Waterloo Library and Historical Society Observer Printing Company, 1892), 14–54, https://archive.org/details/unveilingofmonumoowate/page/n9/mode/2up (accessed May 2020). See more images of the memorial in "Red Jacket," *The Historical Marker Database*, https://www.hmdb.org/m.asp?m=8179 (accessed December 2020).

73. On his expertise, see "The Iroquois," *The Albany Argus*, June 13, 1874; Excerpt from the "Annual report of the Board of Regents of the Smithsonian Institution, showing the operations, expenditures, and condition of the Institution to July, 1885," January 1, 1886; "New York's Indians." *New York Herald*, February 2, 1890; ESP to CW Hutchinson, February 26, 1890, Joseph Keppler Jr. Iroquois Papers, 1882–1944, Microform Collection, Cornell University Library Division of Rare

and Manuscript Collections, Roll 5 Part 2.2 Folder 1 (hereafter cited as JKP); ESP to CW Hutchinson, Nov 25, 1889, JKP R5 P2.2:5; Parker continued to speak at Masonic meetings in his role as the "renowned Seneca Indian, Chief of the Six Nations," and "equal of Red Jacket in silvery eloquence" in "Finis Coronat Opus." *The Sunday Inter Ocean* (Chicago), October 3, 1889. Parker was also called on to use his engineering experience to advise the Edison Electric Light Company on how to lay the NYPD's "electric wires" underground. "To Bury the Police Wires," *New York Herald*, May 30, 1885.The story of the Indian Colony is told partly in chapter three and more completely in the forthcoming article John C. Winters, "'The Great White Mother': Harriet Maxwell Converse, the Indian Colony of New York City, and the Media, 1885-1903," *The Journal of the Gilded Age and Progressive Era* (forthcoming October 2022).

74. The Chamber of Commerce building was marked in the Fifth Ward of the City of Philadelphia. Map Collection of the Digitized Free Library of Philadelphia, *Atlas of the City of Philadelphia by Wards, 1892* (Philadelphia: J.E. Shiedt, draughtsman, 1892), https://www.philageohistory.org/rdic-images/view-image.cfm/JES1892. Phila.007.Ward_5 (accessed March 2020). The description of the "plot of ground" is in "Summary of the News" *The Sun* (Baltimore), May 25, 1892; *Boston Daily Journal*, May 31, 1892. The story of Penn hoping to "Cement" an alliance is in "An Indian Reservation in the Heart of Philadelphia," *The Philadelphia Inquirer*, January 29, 1899.

75. "An Indian Reservation in the Heart of Philadelphia," The Philadelphia Inquirer, January 29, 1899. "After Valuable Land," The Sunday Star (DC), January 28, 1906. On Penn's "peaceable" legacy, see Dawn Marsh, "Penn's Peaceable Kingdom: Shangri-la Revisited," *Ethnohistory* 56, no. 4 (2009): 651–667. See also a 2020 visit of Haudenosaunee women to the Wampum lot. Charles Fox, "These Native American women came to Philadelphia to see their ancestral land. They found apartments and a parking garage," *The Philadelphia Inquirer*, March 25, 2020 https://fusion. inquirer.com/news/philadelphia/welcome-park-philadelphia-native-americans-stolen-land-iroquois-haudenosaunee-20200325.html (accessed November 2020). Public historian Harry Kyriakodis also gives a brief account of the "Wampum Lot" in Kyriakodis, "Before Even Old Original Bookbinder's: An Official Indian Reservation," Hidden City: Exploring Philadelphia's Urban Landscapes blog, October 24, 2013, https://hiddencityphila.org/2013/10/before-even-bookbind ers-an-official-indian-reservation/ (accessed March 2021).

76. Kammen, *Mystic Chords,* 101. On Memorial Days and the GAR see Kammen, *Mystic Chords*, 102–104. Memorial Day also called to mind "memories of the war" and was "a festival of our dead." Stuart McConnell, *Glorious Contentment: The Grand Army of the Republic, 1865–1900* (Boulder, CO: University of Colorado Press, 1999), 184. On Parker in the GAR, the Legion, and in musters, see: "General Curtis's Staff," *New-York Tribune*, April 16, 1888; on the dinners and the Legion, see Armstrong, *Warrior*, 189, 169. "A Great Grant Number," *The*

Morning Olympian (Olympia, WA), April 17, 1894; "A Great Grant Number,"
The New Haven Evening Register, April 16, 1894; "Notes Among the Periodicals,"
Springfield Daily Republican, April 13, 1894. On Parker in Thomas Nast's
painting "Peace in Union," see: "Peace in Union," *Worcester Daily Spy*, December
8, 1894; "Art and Artists." *Plain Dealer* (Cleveland, OH), December 23, 1894;
At Galena Today: Talk with Thomas Nast, Who Painted the Historic Picture to
be Unveiled." *Daily Inter Ocean* (Chicago, IL), April 27, 1895; "Peace in Union,"
Worcester Daily Spy, December 8, 1894. Today, the painting hangs at the Galena
and U.S. Grant Museum.

77. "A Famous Telegram," *The Macon Telegraph*, July 14, 1886; "The Birthday of Gen.
Grant," *The Boston Herald*, April 28, 1893; *Publications of the Buffalo Historical
Society* volume 8 (1908), 534. "Tributes to the Memory of U.S. Grant," *New York
Herald*, April 28, 1893; "In Memory of Gen. Grant," *New-York Tribune,* April 28,
1893; Grant Memorial Association, "Burial, Construction, and Early History,"
Official Website of the Grant Memorial Association, https://grantstomb.org/bur
ial-construction-early-history/ (accessed March 2020).

78. "Its Monument Dedicated," *The New York Times*, September 25, 1891; "Dedicated
by Tammany," *The Evening Star*, September 24, 1891; "Tammany Braves Celebrate,"
The New Haven Evening Register, September 24, 1891; "To Dedicate the Tammany
Monument," *New-York Tribune*, September 24, 1891; "The Patriotic Dead.
Dedication of Another Monument on the Gettysburg Battlefield," *The Duluth
Tribune*, September 25, 1891; "Observed and Heard," *Patriot* (Harrisburg),
September 25, 1891. See also a more recent scholarly treatment of federal use of
Indian symbolism in Cécile R. Ganteaume, *Officially Indian: Symbols That
Define the United States* (Minneapolis: The University of Minnesota Press and
the Smithsonian Institution, 2017), 90–93. "Memory of your comrades" in "The
Gettysburg Speech of Grant's Military Secretary," September 26, 1891, JKP R5
P2.2:3.

79. "The Gettysburg Speech of Grant's Military Secretary," September 26, 1891, JKP R5
P2.2:3.

80. "The Gettysburg Speech of Grant's Military Secretary," September 26, 1891, JKP R5
P2.2:3.

81. On the origins of the language of the Delawares as "women," see Jennings, *The
Ambiguous Iroquois Empire,* 301–303. The Delawares were not alone in being
diplomatically—if not in reality—subsumed by the Iroquois. Shannon, *Iroquois
Diplomacy*, 152–157. For more on the Delawares and Iroquois in the Seven Years'
War, see William N. Fenton, *The Great Law and the Longhouse: A Political History
of the Iroquois Confederacy* (Norman, OK: University of Oklahoma Press, 1998),
485–489; Francis Jennings, *Empire of Fortune: Crowns, Colonies, and Tribes in
the Seven Years' War in America* (New York: W.W. Norton and Company, 1988),
371–372; Jay Miller, "The Delaware as Women: A Symbolic Solution," *American
Ethnologist* 1:3 (1974): 507–514; Matthew C. Ward, *Breaking the Backcountry: The*

Seven Years' War in Virginia and Pennsylvania, 1754-1765 (Pittsburgh: University of Pittsburgh Press, 2004), 137–141.

82. "Gen. Ely S. Parker Dead" *The Evening Star* (DC), August 31, 1895; "Was Chief of Six Nations," *St. Albens Daily Messenger* (VT), August 31, 1895; *The New York Herald*, September 1, 1895; "One of Grant's Staff. Gen. Ely S. Parker, a Full Blooded Indian," *Plain Dealer* (Cleveland), September 1, 1895; "General Parker Dead," *Trenton Evening Times*, September 1, 1895; "Donehowaga is Dead," *The Daily Inter Ocean*, September 3, 1895; "Death of General Ely S. Parker," *The Sunday Herald* (Boston); "Donehowaga is Dead," *The New York Herald*, September 1, 1895; "Heap Big Injun," *The State* (Columbia, SC), September 1, 1895; "Donehowaga is Dead," *The New York Herald*, September 1, 1895; "By an Ex-Editor," *The Philadelphia Inquirer*, Sept 2, 1895; "Gen. Parker and the Senecas," *Plain Dealer* (Cleveland), September 15, 1895; "Parker and the Senecas," *Kalamazoo Gazette*, October 2, 1895. The wake was described in "Wampum on His Coffin," *New York World*, September 5, 1895,WMBP EPS; Armstrong, *Warrior*, 192.

83. "Wampum on His Coffin," *New York World*, September 5, 1895, WMBP EPS. On "succession," see "Gen. Parker and the Senecas," *Plain Dealer* (Cleveland), September 15, 1895. The next "Grand Sachem" in "Personal," *New-York Tribune*, June 27, 1896.

84. The pension is described in Armstrong, *Warrior*, 194. Grant's letter is listed in "Grant's Famous Letter," *The Sunday Herald* (Boston), April 26, 1896; "Original of General Grant's Famous 'Unconditional Surrender' Letter," *New York Herald*, April 26, 1896. As discussed in the next chapter, most of these Haudenosaunee items, along with his sister Caroline's collection, ended up at the Albany State Museum. His library, as Arthur Parker explains, mostly "perished during the process of clearing up his estate." Parker, *Life*, 231. On the family collections, see Parker, *Life*, 238; "Red Jacket's Noted Medal," *The New York Tribune*, December 27, 1895; "Red Jacket's Noted Medal," *Plain Dealer* (Cleveland), December 27, 1896; "The Red Jacket Medal." *The Morning Oregonian*, December 29, 1896. "Part of the history of this country" from "Red Jacket's Famous Medal," *Springfield Daily Republican*, January 11, 1897. The Peace Medal: "Buried in the Land of his People," *New-York Tribune*, January 21, 1897; "Body of Gen. Ely S. Parker" *The Boston Herald*, January 21, 1897; *New-York Tribune*, February 1, 1897; "Interesting People," *Northern Christian Advocate* (Syracuse), February 3, 1897.

85. Armstrong, *Warrior*, 192. "By an Ex-Editor," *The Philadelphia Inquirer,* Sept 2, 1895.

86. Bureau of Indian Affairs, "Ely S. Parker Building Officially Opens: Dedication Ceremony Honors First Indian Commissioner," December 21, 2000, https://www.bia.gov/as-ia/opa/online-press-release/ely-s-parker-building-officially-opens (accessed October 2019).

87. "Ely S. Parker Building."

CHAPTER 3

1. Her reputation as a writer is detailed in Frances Elizabeth Willard, *A Woman of the Century: Fourteen Hundred-seventy Biographical Sketches Accompanied by Portraits of Leading American Women in All Walks of Life*, Mary A. Livermore and Frances Elizabeth Willard, eds., (New York: Moulton, 1893), 200–201.

2. Harriet Maxwell Converse, "The Ho-De'-No-Sau-Nee: The Confederacy of the Iroquois," (New York: G.P. Putnam and Sons, 1884), 13, https://qspace.library.quee nsu.ca/bitstream/handle/1974/11588/hodenosauneeconfooconv.pdf?sequence= 1&isAllowed=y (accessed August 2018). Reprinted in "The Six Nations," *The Buffalo Courier*, October 8, 1884, HMCSB, 11; "Historical Society Donations," paper unknown, 1884, HMCSB, 1.

3. Jacob W. Gruber, "Ethnographic Salvage and the Shaping of Anthropology," *American Anthropologist* 72, no. 6 (1970): 1290; Margaret Bruchac, "Broken Chains of Custody: Possessing, Dispossessing, and Repossessing Lost Wampum Belts." *Proceedings of the American Philosophical Society* 162, no. 1 (March 2018): 66; Linda Tuhiwai Smith, *Decolonizing Methodologies*, x. See also Colwell, *Plundered Skulls*.

4. R. H. Pratt, "The Advantage of Mingling Indians With Whites," in *Official Report of the Nineteenth Annual Conference of Charities and Correction* (National Conference on Social Welfare, 1892): 48–49, https://quod.lib.umich.edu/n/ncosw/ach8 650.1892.001/68?page=root;size=100;view=image (accessed October 2018). See more about the Dawes Act in White, *The Republic*, 606; Anthony F. C. Wallace, *Tuscarora: A History* (Albany, NY: State University of New York Press, 2012), 126.

5. Sergei Kan, ed., *Strangers to Relatives: The Adoption and Naming of Anthropologists in Native North America* (Lincoln, NE: University of Nebraska Press, 2001), 5–7.

6. Her membership and various titles are detailed in Laurence Hauptman, "Chief Publicist," *New York Archives* 18, no. 2 (2018): 23. The use of outsiders, particularly women, in various levels of Iroquoian politics is explored in Barbara Alice Mann, *Iroquoian Women: The Gantowisas* (New York: Peter Lang, 2000), 175–177; Bruce E. Johansen and Barbara Alice Mann eds., *Encyclopedia of the Haudenosaunee (Iroquois Confederacy)* (Westport, CT: Greenwood Press, 2000), 3–7.

7. Hauptman, "Chief Publicist," 23. Parker's biography of Converse is located in his introduction to Converse, *Myths*, 14–30. Other small biographical treatments of Converse are found in Armstrong, *Warrior*, 174–177; William Fenton, "Harriet Maxwell Converse," *Notable American Women, 1607–1950: A Biographical Dictionary* Vol. 1 (Cambridge, MA: Harvard University Press, 1971), 375–377; C. Joseph Genetin-Pilawa, "Confining Indians: Power, Authority, and the Colonialist Ideologies of Nineteenth-Century Reformers: Volume One," (PhD Diss, Michigan State University, 2008); Mary A. Livermore and Frances Elizabeth Willard, eds., *A Woman of the Century: Fourteen Hundred-Seventy Biographical Sketches Accompanied by Portraits of Leading American Women in All Walks of Life* (Buffalo: Charles Wells Moulton, 1893), 200–201.

8. Trachtenberg, *Shades*, 98; Richard White, *The Republic for Which It Stands: The United States During Reconstruction and the Gilded Age, 1865-1896* (New York: Oxford University Press, 2017), chapter 11; Alfred W. McCoy and Francisco A. Scarano eds., *Colonial Crucible: Empire in the Making of the Modern American State* (Madison, WI: University of Wisconsin Press, 2009). For descriptions of the specific immigrant racial and ethnic groups who flocked to New York City, see Wallace and Burrows, *Gotham*, chapter 63.

9. Henry Adams cited in Thomas Kessner, *Capitol City: New York City and the Men Behind America's Rise to Economic Dominance, 1860–1900* (New York: Simon and Schuster, 2003), xii–xiii, xv.

10. On New Women: Charlotte J. Rich, *Transcending the New Woman: Multiethnic Narratives in the Progressive Era* (Columbia, MO: University of Missouri Press, 2009); Caroll Smith-Rosenberg, *Disorderly Conduct: Visions of Gender in Victorian America* (New York: Oxford University Press, 1986). Women were also at the forefront of the maternalistic efforts to "save" Indigenous people from their own cultures and religions through boarding schools. Margaret D. Jacobs traces the incredible damage done to those Native children at those boarding schools in *White Mother to a Dark Race: Settler Colonialism, Maternalism, and the Removal of Indigenous Children in the American West and Australia, 1880-1940* (Lincoln, NE: University of Nebraska Press, 2009). On the role of women in the preservation of Americana, see Barbara J. Howe, "Women in Historic Preservation: The Legacy of Ann Pamela Cunningham," *The Public Historian* 12 (1990): 31–61; Barbara J. Howe, "Women in the Nineteenth-Century Preservation Movement," in *Restoring Women's History through Historic Preservation*, Gail Lee Dubrow and Jennifer B. Goodman eds. (Baltimore: Johns Hopkins University Press, 2003), 17–36. On Americana and memory more broadly, see Kammen, *Mystic Chords*, 254.

11. Sherry L. Smith, *Hippies, Indians, and the Fight for Red Power* (New York: Oxford University Press, 2012), 15.

12. Converse, *Myths and Legends*, 14. David Hackett Fischer, *Albion's Seed: Four British Folkways in America* (New York: Oxford University Press, 1986), 626–627. Historic Environment Scotland, *Caerlaverock Castle*, https://www.historicenvironment. scot/visit-a-place/places/caerlaverock-castle/history/ (accessed August 2018).

13. Buffalo Historical Society, *Annual Report of the Buffalo Historical Society* (Buffalo: The Buffalo Historical Society, 1885), 4.

14. Converse, *Myths*, 14–17. Her poetry culminated in the publication of *Sheaves: A Collection of Poems* (New York: G.P. Putnam and Sons, 1882). Her marriage to Frank is in "Marriage of the Great Banjoist to a Lady of Wealth," *Hartford Daily Courant,* January 30, 1860. Descriptions of Frank are also in Armstrong, *Warrior,* 176. Frank's book is Frank B. Converse, *Frank B. Converse's Analytical Banjo Method* (New York: Hamilton S. Gordon Publishers, 1887). On the location of Converse's home as well as the various locations of boarding houses and Indian Colony offices, as well as the Colony's role in shaping perspectives on the relationship between

the "immigrant and the Indian," see Winters, " 'The Great White Mother.' " There is not much clarity on the precise location of Converse's townhouse. Converse's 20th Street address is cited in "Live False-Face as a Gift," *The Sun*, August 16, 1903; "Death of Mrs. Converse," *The Evening Post*, November 19, 1903; "The Indians' Friend Dead," *The Sun*, November 20, 1903; " 'The Great White Mother,'" *The Sun*, November 21, 1903. Converse's home was also reported as being at 155 West 46th in: "New York's Indian Colony," *Daily People*, April 10, 1904; "Indians of New York," *The Cleveland Leader*, May 8, 1904; Armstrong, *Warrior*, 176.

15. Armstrong, *Warrior*, 166–181; Converse, *Myths*, 17.

16. Shortly thereafter, that conception of Indians as violent "savages" took a brutal postwar turn in the 1890 Massacre at Wounded Knee. Deloria, *Indians in Unexpected Places*, 47.

17. White, *The Republic for Which It Stands*, 155–156; Trachtenberg, *Shades*, 39; Louis S. Warren, *Buffalo Bill's America: William Cody and the Wild West Show* (New York: Vintage Books, 2005), 215–217; Kammen, *Mystic Chords*, 273; Hall, *Performing*, 233.

18. Hall, *Performing*, 2–8; Warren, *Buffalo Bill's America*, 248–250, 481.

19. "Introduction," McCoy and Scarano, *Colonial Crucible*, 198; the notion of a "cacophony" in Trachtenberg, *Shades*, 98. See descriptions of racial and ethnic groups flocking to New York city in Wallace and Burrows, *Gotham*, chapter 63. On the world's fairs, see Robert W. Rydell, *World of Fairs: The Century-of-Progress Expositions* (Chicago: University of Chicago Press, 1993), 40; Robert W. Rydell, *All the World's a Fair: Visions of Empire at American International Expositions, 1876-1916* (Chicago: University of Chicago Press, 1984), 2; Robert W. Rydell, John E. Findling, and Kimberly D. Pelle, *Fair America: World's Fairs in the United States* (Washington, DC: The Smithsonian Institution Press, 2000), 38; White, *Republic*, 758–759. On the Wild West in World's Fairs, see Warren, *Buffalo Bill's America*, 419. See also a visual depiction of the races listed in "progressive order of development from primitive . . . to the highest level of civilization" in James W. Buel, *Louisiana and the Fair: An Exposition of the World, Its People, and Their Achievements* vol. 5 (St. Louis: World's Progress Publishing Company, 1904), frontispiece and printed glassine.

20. "Clinging To Their Lands," "Sitting Bull's Pernicious Presence," "Found in Sweet Grass," 1885–1886. HMCSB, 42; "Will they go . . . : Commissioner Atkins Favors the Removal of All Extreme Western Indians", Nov 24, 1886, HMCSB, 42.

21. G.S. Uncle to Harriet Maxwell Converse, December 4, 1900, Arthur Caswell Parker Papers, A.P23, River Campus Libraries, University of Rochester, Rochester, NY, Box 2 Folder 8 (hereafter cited as ACPR); Edward Cornplanter to Harriet Maxwell Converse, December 26, 1900, 1:12 JKP. Edward Cornplanter's career in Edward Cornplanter and Delos B. Kittle to Joseph Keppler, August 25, 1899, JKP R1F3. Cornplanter joined the Flaming Arrow Company with the famous Mohawk Actress, Gowango Mohawk, as described in untitled article, October 8, 1900, JKP

R1F10. Cornplanter also expressed to Converse his interest in performing with the 1901 Pan-American Exposition in Buffalo, NY, in EC to HMC, December 26, 1900, JKP R1F12.

22. Converse, *Myths*, 19, 171.

23. "Red Jacket's Burial," unknown paper, before Oct 9, 1884, HMCSB, 7; "The Six Nations," *Buffalo Courier*, Oct 8, 1884, HMCSB, 11. Flowers preserved in HMCSB, 28.

24. Converse, "How I Became," 64–67. Converse, *Myths*, 26.

25. "The Last of the Senecas," November 1884, HMCSB, 5–6.

26. "Converse, *Myths*, 18. Harriet Maxwell Converse, "The Historic Iroquois Indians: A Series of Lectures by Ga-ie-wa-noh (Harriet Maxwell Converse), An Adopted Member and Honorary Chief of the New York State Iroquois Indians," undated (after 1892), 2:8 ACPR. See also Armstrong, *Warrior*, 176–177.

27. Kammen, *Mystic Chords*, 268–269.

28. Hoganson, *Consumers' Imperium*, 14–15. The masculinity of collection in Kammen, *Mystic Chords*, 269. Her *salon* is briefly described in Porter, *To Be Indian*, 22–23.

29. "Indians of New York City: A Colony With Two Interesting People at Its Head," undated, HMCSB, 92; "Some Indian Treasures," paper unknown, undated, WMBP EPS.

30. "Onondaga Indians," *Buffalo Union and Advertiser*, October 18, 1886, HMCSB, 42. "Conceivable aliens" described in White, *Republic*, 697; Trachtenberg, *Shades of Hiawatha*, 98–101.

31. White, *The Republic*, 603–604.

32. An Act to Provide for the Allotment of Lands in Severalty to Indians on the Various Reservations (General Allotment Act or Dawes Act), Statutes at Large 24, 388–391, NADP Document A1887 https://www.ourdocuments. gov/doc.php?flash=false&doc=50&page=transcript (accessed May 2019). For the Dawes Act in context, see White, *Republic*, 636–640; Utley, *The Indian Frontier*, 213–269.

33. Wallace, *Tuscarora*, 126. See more on the broad impact of policy-driven cultural genocide in Hoxie, *A Final Promise*, chapter 2. The millions of acres are described in White, *The Republic*, 606.

34. Wallace, *Tuscarora*, 126. New York Assembly Document No. 51, J.S. Whipple, *The Report of Special Committee to Investigate the Indian Problem* (1889), part 1 and 3. On the report's inaccuracies, see Hauptman, *Seven Generations*, 62–64.

35. "Copy of Agreement between the Tonawanda Senecas and the New York West Shore & Buffalo Railway Company," March 2, 1882, JKP R5FW3N1. Untitled article, unknown paper, February 1901, JKP R1F1. Edward Cornplanter to Harriet M. Converse, December 7, 1899, JKP R1F6. Keppler would also serve as a formal representative of the Senecas as early as 1900. Edward Cornplanter to Harriet M. Converse, April 21, 1900, JKP R1F6; Harriet M. Converse to Joseph Keppler, November 27, 1902, JKP R1F1.

36. Parker, *Ely S. Parker*, 323. John Buck and Josiah Hill to HMC, June 9, 1891, ACPR B2F8; Wallace, Tuscarora, 126. On Converse's election, see Parker, *Ely S. Parker*, 324.

37. Delos Kittle broaches the subject with Converse while she is in Washington. Delos Kittle to HMC, May 13, 1903, JKP R1F8. Chauncy Abrams announces a Six Nations meeting to talk about the same thing. Chauncy Abrams to JK, Sept 12, 1902, JKP R1F9; HMC to JK, September 8, 1902, JKP R1F10.

38. Harriet Maxwell Converse, "Induction of Women into Iroquois Tribes," *Journal of American Folklore* 6, no. 21 (April-June 1893): 147–148; "Negro Superstitions concerning the Violin" reprinted in a clip from the *Evening Telegraph,* October 28, 1892; "Friday not an Unlucky Day according to Columbus," *Journal of American Folklore* 5, no. 19 (October–December 1892): 329–330. Converse's retelling of her adoption in Harriet Maxwell Converse, "A Woman Elected a Chief of the Six Nations," *Journal of American Folklore* 5, no. 17 (April-June 1892): 146–147. Lee's letter in Sara L. Lee, "To the Editor of the Journal of American Folklore," *Journal of American Folklore* 5, no. 19 (October-December 1892): 337.

39. Italics are Lee's. Lee, "To the Editor," 338.

40. Italics are Converse's. Converse, "Induction of Women," 147–148.

41. Annette Kolodny, *In Search of First Contact: The Viking of Vineland, The Peoples of the Dawnland, and the Anglo-American Anxiety of Discovery* (Durham, NC: Duke University Press, 2012), 17. "Firsts" have also been identified as the "*ur* genre" in American literature. Rivett, *Unscripted America*, 7. Her "induction" in Converse, *Myths*, 19. Mary Jemison in Susan Scheckel, *The Insistence of the Indian: Race and Nationalism in Nineteenth-Century Culture* (Princeton, NJ: Princeton University Press, 1998), 70. For the numbers of copies sold, Scheckel cites June Namias' 1992 edition of *Narrative* which was the 21st edition published. June Namias ed., James Seaver, *Narrative of the Life of Mary Jemison* (Norman, OK: University of Oklahoma Press, 1992), appendix. See Jemison's story also in John Demos, *The Unredeemed Captive: A Family Story from Early America* (New York: Alfred Knopf, 1994), 254.

42. Steele, *Setting all the Captives Free*, 7.

43. Armstrong, *Warrior*, chapter 12; Genetin-Pilawa, "Confining Indians," chapter 2. Her affiliations are listed in "The Historic Iroquois Indians: A Series of Lectures by Ga-ie-wa-noh (Harriet Maxwell Converse), An Adopted Member and Honorary Chief of the New York State Iroquois Indians," ACPR 2:8. See the use of Converse's Seneca life as a foil for the women's suffrage movement in Gail H. Landsman, "The 'Other' as Political Symbol: Images of Indians in the Women Suffrage Movement," *Ethnohistory* 36 no. 3 (Summer 1992): 246-284.

44. Harriet Maxwell Converse, "How I Became a Seneca Indian," B1F19, page 65–66, ACPA.

45. Converse, "How I Became," 65, 61–62.

46. As historians explain, other women of Converse's background decorated the interiors of their houses in ways that reflected how America connected to the

world through its expanding empire. She chose, in that sense, to recognize those same design choices in Iroquoian homes. Hoganson, *Consumers' Imperium*, 8–9, 13. For the quotations, see Deloria, *Playing Indian*, 94; Genetin-Pilawa, "Confining Indians," 108.

47. Converse, *Myths and Legends*, 135–138. On the cultural role of Haudenosaunee women, see Hauptman, *Seven Generations*, 45; Rice, *Rontinonshonni*, 22–23; Nancy Shoemaker, "The Rise and Fall of Iroquois Women," *Journal of Women's History* 2 (Winter 1991): 39–57; Elisabeth Tooker, "Women in Iroquois Society," in *Extending the Rafters: Interdisciplinary Approaches to Iroquoian Studies*, ed. Michal Foster, *et al* (Albany: State University of New York Press, 1984), 109–123.

48. Historians find "prehistoric" to be an inherently flawed term because it presupposes that people had no history before the written word. See Julianna Barr, "There's No Such Thing as "Prehistory": What the Longue Durée of Caddo and Pueblo History Tells Us about Colonial America," *William and Mary Quarterly* 74, no. 2 (April 2017): 204.

49. Margaret Bruchac, "Broken Chains of Custody: Possessing, Dispossessing, and Repossessing Lost Wampum Belts," *Proceedings of the American Philosophical Society* 162:1 (March 2018): 66. See also Bruchac, *Savage Kin: Indigenous Informants and American Anthropologists* (Tucson: University of Arizona Press, 2018). See Haudenosaunee perspectives on present day and historical wampum in Darren Bonaparte's website, *The Wampum Chronicles*, http://www.wampumchr onicles.com/ (accessed 2017). Reproductions of wampum and learning materials are provided to the public by the Jake Thomas Learning Centre in Wilsonville, Ontario, Canada. See also Marc Shell, *Wampum and the Origins of American Money* (Champaign-Urbana, IL: University of Illinois Press, 2013). Converse's wampum trades included items of high value and political importance: Chapman Shanandoah to Joseph Keppler, June 4, 1899, JKP R1F1; Fellow amateur anthro- pologist William Beauchamp mentions Converse is in possession of an extremely rare "women's belt," William M. Beauchamp to Harriet M. Converse, October 30, 1899, ACPR B2F8; John Buck "or Ska-na-wah-deh, Speaker of the Fire Keepers" and Josiah Hill, Secretary of the Six Nations Council at the Ohsweken Council House in Oneida Country, sent HMC a belt that was used by chief John Buck at a Six Nations meeting to represent "peace throughout eternity" among all of the nations, in letter, June 9, 1891, ACPR B2F8; A belt, owned by Converse and sold to the AMNH, is mentioned in Harriet M. Converse to Frederick W. Putnam, August 10, 1902, ACPR B2F8; Harriet M. Converse to Frederick Ward Putnam, August 10, 1902, ACPR B2F8; Arthur C. Parker to Joseph Keppler, December 1, 1903, JKP R4P2. The quotations on masks is from Jesse Cornplanter to Joseph Keppler, February 14 and March 11, 1936, JKP R2P64–65. For more on *hadu:wi*, see Bruchac, *Broken Chains*, 58; William N. Fenton, *False Faces of the Iroquois* (Norman, OK: University of Oklahoma Press, 1987), 5–7. Outsiders seeking to ac- quire these masks came to Converse for contacts to buy masks that ranged from

50¢ to $3: Frederick Starr to Harriet M. Converse, September 22 and October 11, 1901, ACPR B2F8. For other instances of mask trades from Converse's papers, see Edward Cornplanter to Joseph Keppler, Undated 1899 letter and November 22, 1899, JKP R1F4 and R1F5; Harriet M. Converse to Joseph Keppler, November 5, 1899, JKP R1F4.

How William Fenton arrives at the "100" number of masks that survived the fire is not clear, but it does give an indication of how popular the market for masks—whether culturally significant or created specifically for trade—was at the time. Fenton does provide some context for the significance of that 100 number when he includes in his book *False Faces of the Iroquois* an exhaustive list of masks he encountered in his research from 1935 to 1973 in which he finds a grand total of 1,509 Iroquois masks of different construction materials that are in the collections and archives of museums all over the world. The 100 masks that survived the fire, in that case, reveals Converse's significant influence on the worldwide trade of one of the most sensitive aspects of Haudenosaunee material culture. Fenton, *False Faces of the Iroquois*, 10, 20–21.

Today, "False Faces" have mostly been removed from public view to protect their sensitive cultural use and history, which is why no images of any masks appear in this chapter. In addition, Fenton's *False Faces* itself is now long out of print, Haudenosaunee museums have blacked out pictures of masks from historic photographs, and even the modern photographs of masks in Arthur C. Parker's famous dioramas that are on display at the Oneida Shako:wi Cultural Center in Oneida, New York, are blacked out, and visitors are prohibited from taking their own pictures of those censored images.

50. Her collection is described in "A Chief of Six Nations," *New York Recorder*, December 1892, WMBP EPS. *Thirty-Fifth Annual Report of the Buffalo Historical Society*, (Buffalo, NY: Buffalo Historical Society, 1897), 28; Harriet Maxwell Converse to Frederick Ward Putnam, August 10, 1902, ACPR B2F8; Arthur C. Parker to Joseph Keppler, April 15, 1904, JKP R4P2; Arthur C. Parker to Joseph Keppler, December 1, 1903, JKP R4P2. On the state buying her collections, see Arthur C. Parker to Joseph Keppler, February 25, 1905, JKP R4P2; Arthur C. Parker to Joseph Keppler, October 31, 1905, JKP R4P2. On the brooches and the Freemasons, she may have meant it belonged to Joseph Brant who was inducted into the masons. William M. Beauchamp to Harriet M. Converse, November 17, December 5, December 18, 1896, April 1, 1898, ACPR B2F8; Harriet M. Converse to Joseph Keppler, November 27, 1902, JKP R1F1; Harriet Maxwell Converse, "The Iroquois Silver Brooches," *Annual Report of the Regents of the New York State Museum*, 54:1 (Albany, 1900), 1232–1233, https://archive.org/stream/annualreportof5411900newy#page/n373/search/converse (accessed September 2018). Dewey's title is found in "The Woman Who Works for the Indians" in Converse, *Myths and Legends*, 27–28. On the new ethnography department, see Arthur C. Parker, "Excavations in an Erie Village," *New York State Museum Bulletin* 117 (December 1907): 462.

51. She was part of the "Neh Ho-noh-tei-noh-gah, the Guardians of the Little Waters, a Seneca Medicine Society," a group tasked with preserving and administering medicinal treatments and rituals. "No Seneca" society, claimed Arthur C. Parker, is "more exclusive, more secret." Converse, *Myths*, 149–183. See also Harriet Maxwell Converse, "The Secret Medicine Society of the North American Indians," unnamed newspaper, Fairfield, Connecticut, January 18, 1895, ACPR B2F8; "Indian Medicine Man," *The Republic* (St. Louis), October 16, 1892, WMBP EPS. More recently, William Fenton published a comprehensive study of the Little Water Medicine Society that acknowledges while "such matters [of the Society] are sacred to believers, who may be disturbed to see them in print," the "materials" nevertheless "cry out for release, explanation and synthesis." That is unlike Converse who, despite the cultural damage she wrought, showed a modicum of restraint in keeping those secrets secret. William N. Fenton, *The Little Water Medicine Society of the Senecas* (Norman, OK: University of Oklahoma Press, 2002), 4.

52. "Six Nations Wampum Belts," *The Sun* (New York), June 12, 1898. Her public call to action was published in Harriet Maxwell Converse, "Keeper of the Wampum," *The Buffalo Examiner*, July 11, 1897, HMCSB, 14.

53. William N. Fenton, "The New York State Wampum Collection: The Case for the Integrity of Cultural Treasures," *Proceedings of the American Philosophical Society* 115, no. 6 (December 1971): 437. To this day, Fenton's paternalistic efforts to prevent the transfer of these wampum belts back to the Onondaga is a case study in why some Haudenosaunee today refer to those who claim to be *"Iroquoianists"* (a term Fenton used widely) as *"Fentonites"* or *"trolls."* Gail Landsman and Sara Ciborski, "Representation and Politics: Contesting Histories of the Iroquois," *Cultural Anthropology* 7:4 (November 1992): 428.

54. The creation of open public spaces was a relatively new venture that had begun with the preservation of Yellowstone National Park in 1871. On the changing role of government in the preservation of that history and memory, see Kammen, *Mystic Chords of Memory*, chapter 14; Mark David Spence, *Dispossessing the Wilderness: Indian Removal and the Making of the National Parks* (New York: Oxford University Press, 1999), 55. On the federal government's first real efforts to preserve and protect Indigenous knowledge in NAGPRA and the Smithsonian, see Susan Sleeper-Smith, *Contesting Knowledge: Museums and Indigenous Perspectives* (Lincoln, NE: University of Nebraska Press, 2009); Amy Lonetree and Amanda J. Cobb, eds., *The National Museum of the American Indian: Critical Conversations* (Lincoln, NE: University of Nebraska Press, 2008).

55. "Indian Wampum Case," *The Daily News*, December 23, 1898; *The Evening Post*, December 23, 1898; *Norwood News*, December 27, 1898; "Local News," *The Naples News*, December 29, 1898. The advertisements for this event were publicized in Parker, "Excavations," 465; "Rates for Indian Day at Albany," *The Daily Leader* (NY), June 20, 1898; *The Chateaugay Journal*, June 23, 1898; *The Adirondack News*, June 25, 1898.

56. JK to HMC, February 1, 1901, JKP R1F1; G.S. Uncle(sic) to HMC and JK, December 4, 1900, ACPR B2F8.

57. William G. Hoag to HMC, December 22, 1902, ACPR B2F8.

58. E. D. Lannon to HMC, December 17, 1900, ACPR B2F8.

59. E. D. Lannon to HMC, December 17, 1900, ACPR B2F8. C. H. Abrams to HMC, November 26, 1901, ACPR B2F8.

60. Andrew John to HMC, February 4, 1902, ACPR B2F8. The Ogden settlement is described in Parker, *Life,* 324. "Swindle" in Andrew John to HMC, February 28, 1902, ACPR B2F8. The Vreeland "scheme" in Andrew John to HMC, March 5, 1902, ACPR B2F8.

61. Edward Cornplanter to JK, February 3, 1902, JKP R1F2. Parker and Harrington mobilized in HMC to JK, June 22, 1902, JKP R1F1. John's letter in Andrew John to HMC, February 28, 1902, ACPR B2F8.

62. Converse updated Keppler regularly on the Vreeland fight. HMC to JK, March 18, 1902, JKP R1F4; parliamentary tricks were defeated, HMC to JK, March 15, 1902, JKP R1F3. Her aggressive media presence in AJ to HMC, February 28, 1902, ACPR B2F8. Parker, *Life,* 324. See more on Converse's interactions with the media in New York City in Winters, "The Great White Mother."

63. On liquor, see Hauptman, *Conspiracy,* 210. "Statement of the General Meeting of the Seneca Indians in their 'Long Homes,' in Newtown, New York, July 19, 1903," July 20, 1903, ACPR B2F8. On the association between temperance societies and Indigenous communities, see Thomas J. Lappas, *In League Against King Alcohol: Native American Women and the Women's Christian Temperance Union, 1874-1933* (Norman, OK: University of Oklahoma Press, 2020). Converse died in New York City and was buried in her birthplace of Elmira, New York. Find A Grave Database, *Harriet Arnot Maxwell Converse,* https://www.findagrave.com/memorial/40668716/harriet-arnot-converse (accessed January 2021). See more on her funeral in Winters, "The Great White Mother."

64. "Joseph Brant Statue," paper unknown, October 22, 1886, B3 SB23 WMBP. The overt patriotism displayed in Brant's memorial was not uncommon and was reflected in other reburials as well. See Michael Kammen, *Digging Up the Dead: A History of Notable American Reburials* (Chicago: University of Chicago Press, 2010), chapter 2.

65. HMC to JK, June 3, 1899, JKP R1F1.

CHAPTER 4

1. David Hurst Thomas, "Afterword: Who Is Arthur C. Parker, Anyway?," in *Working Together: Native Americans and Archaeologists,* eds. Kurt E. Dongoske, Mark S. Aldenderfer, and Karen Doehner (New York: Society for American Archaeology, 2000), 222.

2. Arthur C. Parker, *Parker on the Iroquois: Iroquois Uses of Maize and Other Food Plants, The Code of Handsome Lake, the Seneca Prophet, The Constitution of the Five Nations* (Syracuse: Syracuse University Press, 1968), 10.

3. Dorothy Lippert, "Building a Bridge to Cross a Thousand Years," *American Indian Quarterly* 30, no. 3/4 (2009): 433–434. Also cited in Colwell-Chanthaphonh, *Inheriting the Past*, 19.

4. Other scholars have acknowledged his archaeology and anthropology in fragments; see Thomas, "Afterward: Who Was Arthur C. Parker, Anyway?," in Dongoske, *Working Together*; Deloria, *Playing Indian*, 124; Hazel Whitman Hertzberg, "Nationalist, Anthropology, and Pan-Indianism in the Life of Arthur C. Parker (Seneca)," *Proceedings of the American Philosophical Society* 123, no. 1 (February 1979): 47–72; W. Stephen Thomas, "Arthur C. Parker: Master of Hobbies," *Museum Service* 32, no. 8 (October 1959): 134–135; Thomas, "Arthur Caswell Parker: 1881–1955: Anthropologist, Historian, and Museum Pioneer," *Rochester History* 17:3 (July 1955): 1–20; David Hurst Thomas, "Arthur Caswell Parker: Leader and Prophet of the Museum World," *Museum Service* 28, no. 2 (February 1955): 18–28. This professional list is taken from one of Parker's late-life resumes. The Professional Record of Arthur C. Parker, 5:9 ACPR. Parker's foremost biographer, Joy Porter, touches and contextualizes many of these aspects of his life in *To Be Indian*; see also Joy Porter, "Arthur Caswell Parker, 1881–1955: Indian American Museum Professional," *New York History* 81, no. 2 (April 2000): 211–236.

5. Porter, *To Be Indian,* xvi–xvii. Porter, "Arthur Caswell Parker," 212. For more perspective on Parker as a public figure and not just an archaeologist, see Deloria, *Playing Indian*, 125; Terry Zeller, "Arthur C. Parker: A Pioneer in American Museums," *Curator: The Museum Journal* 30, no. 1 (1987): 41–62; Zeller, "Arthur Parker and the Educational Mission of American Museums," *Curator: The Museum Journal* 32, no. 2 (1989): 104–122.

6. Porter, *To Be Indian*, 165–166.

7. Porter, *To Be Indian*, chapters 5 and 6. Quotes from Deloria, *Playing Indian*, 146–147.

8. Porter, *To Be Indian*, 51–53.

9. Porter, *To Be Indian*, 17–23.

10. Colwell-Chanthaphonh, *Inheriting*, 65–75. On his adoption, see Porter, *To Be Indian*, 53. On the digs, see ACP to FWP, April 8, 1904 and July 17, 1904, 1:1, ACPR.

11. Conn, *History's Shadow*, 194–195; see also Porter, *To Be Indian*, 53. His connection to Boas is detailed in Thomas, "Who Is," 215. For more on Putnam's efforts to formalize anthropological education, see David Browman, "The Peabody Museum, Frederic W. Putnam, and the Rise of U.S. Anthropology, 1866–1903," *American Anthropologist* 102, no. 2 (2002): 510.

12. Parker was awarded an Honorary Doctorate of Science by Union College and an Honorary Doctorate of Humane Letters by the women of Keuka College for his "long work in assisting women to find better places in the world of education and

administration." Dixon Ryan Fox to ACP, March 7, 1940, B1F8 ACPR; Henry Allen to ACP, May 12, 1943, B1F8 ACPR. On Parker's PhD choice, see Hertzberg, "Nationality," 54; Porter, *To Be Indian*, 54.

13. Porter, *To Be Indian*, 55.

14. Many scholars overlook this aspect of his life, which signals a broader dismissal of his professional and academic contributions to museology. The exception is Joy Porter, who spends much of Parker's biography *To Be Indian* investigating his museum career.

15. This "first" moves his museological timeline backward a few months before the start of his tenure at the State Museum which historians usually see as his "first" exposure to museum work. Porter, *To Be Indian*, xvi. The offer is described in ACP to FWP, April 8, 1904, 1:1, ACP MS.

16. "Seven Millions Built This Huge Hotel Pile," *The New York Times*, July 10, 1904; Hotel Astor, *Hotel Astor, Indian Hall* (New York: Malcolm & Hayes, c. 190?), https://iiif.lib.harvard.edu/manifests/drs:34288811 (accessed April 2021). This pamphlet is also in the author's collection; "Hotel Astor Builder Anticipated Growth," *New York Times*, January 12, 1930. See more about the Hotel Astor in Charles W. Clinton and William H. Russell, "The Hotel Astor," *Architects' and Builders' Magazine* 6, no. 2 (New York: William T. Comstock, 1904), 49–71. See also Diane Boucher, "'Under the Pavement of Broadway': The Indian Hall in the Hotel Astor," *American Indian Art Magazine* 35, no. 4 (2010): 70–77. Descriptions of the hotel and the Indian Hall in "Indian Room His Fad," *The Washington Post Special Sunday Edition*, January 29, 1905. Harriet Converse provided the bulk of the materials for the Iroquois section, and others came mostly from George Hubbard Pepper of the AMNH. Boucher, "Under the Pavement," 73–75. Much of the Grill Room's collection was donated in 1937 by Nancy Astor to the University of Virginia, and it remains part of the Astor Collection, though mostly in storage. The University of Virginia Art Museum, "Welcome to the Hall of the American Indian," from the Astor Collection, https://xroads. virginia.edu/~MA04/ranger/astor_collection/introduction.html (accessed April 2021).

17. "Retail ethnography" is a term of art in the advertising world. Michael J. Healy, et al., "Understanding Retail Experiences: The Case for Ethnography," *International Journal of Market Research* 49, no. 6 (2007): 751–778. For an historical perspective on the power and ubiquity of retail ethnography in this era, see Trachtenberg, *Shades*, 219–220. The Camp Grant massacre is described in Karl Jacoby, *Shadows at Dawn: A Borderlands Massacre and the Violence of History* (New York: Penguin Books, 2008), 4, 206; White, *Republic*, 154. Crawford's claim that he gave the war bonnet to Converse "twenty-five years ago" may be slightly overstated. Converse was not then a well-known salvage ethnographer, nor did she begin collecting indigenous material culture in earnest until she met Ely Parker in 1884, just over twenty years before Crawford's claim. "Indian Room His Fad," January 29, 1905.

18. ACP to FWP, April 8, 1904, 1:1 ACPR. On Draper and Parker, see Parker, *Parker on the Iroquois,* 11. Parker also invited Iroquois informants to the museum to help build his museum, in "Indians in Albany on Peaceful Errand," paper unknown, February 1910, 44:SB2.

19. On Clarke's tense relationship with Parker, see Porter, *To Be Indian*, 61. Quotations from ACP to FWP, July 17, 1904, 1:1, ACPR. Arthur C. Parker, *A Manual for History Museums* (New York: Columbia University Press, 1935), 105.

20. ACP to FWP, June 20, 1906, 1:1, ACPR. Andrew S. Draper to ACP, October 14, 1904, 1:1, ACPR. He expresses this desire to protect New York collections in ACP to FWP, October 22, 1904, 1:1, ACPR.

21. *The Republican*, September 8, 1911, 44:SB2 WMBP.

22. ACP to FWP, April 20, 1906, 1:1 ACPR. Arthur C. Parker, "An Erie Indian Village and Burial Site at Ripley, Chautauqua Co., N.Y.," *New York State Museum Bulletin* 117 (1907): 455–508. See the Erie woman's hand in " 'The Copper Woman' of the Erie Tribe," paper unknown, date unknown, WMBP 44:SB2. Opening to future study in ACP to FWP, June 20, 1906, 1:1, ACPR. William Fenton is quoted in Joy Porter, *To Be Indian*, 62.

23. Porter, *To Be Indian*, 63. His connections are detailed in Parker, *Parker on the Iroquois*, 13; Melville Dewey to ACP, February 22, 1905, 1:1 ACPR. Albert was a descendent of the famed David Cusick, nineteenth century author of *Sketches of Ancient History of the Six Nations* (Lewiston, Niagara Co: Tuscarora Village, 1828). On Cusick's wax cylinders and Parker's work as viewed by other anthropologists, see William M. Beauchamp to Melville Dewey, March 30, 1905, 1:1: ACPR. "Museum of standing" quotes and Parker's perspective on institutional growth in ACP to FWP, June 20, 1906, 1:1, ACPR; ACP to FWP, November 2, 1906, 1:1, ACPR.

24. Converse, *Myths and Legends*, Part III and Appendices A–D; Porter, *To Be Indian*, 70–71. Local publications in "Christians Among Indians: How the Pagan Iroquois Observe the Holiday: Seneca at Home," *Ontario County Times*, December 25, 1907, 44:SB2 WMBP. William Henry Holmes to ACP, March 14, 1908, 1:1, ACPR. On supporting his uncles legacy, see Parker, *Life*, 3–4.

25. Today, one part of these famous dioramas is on display—albeit in pieces—at the Oneida Nation's Shako:wi Cultural Center in Oneida, New York. Visitors are prohibited from taking their own photographs of the dioramas or of the historic photographs on display because some show sensitive cultural images and political events that were supposed to have remained closed to the public. To respect that request, and because these images were published elsewhere, I did not include any image of the sensitive political or cultural dioramas in this book. "New Indian Exhibit in the State Museum," *The Sunday Press*, June 6, 1909, 44:SB2 WMBP. On the financial gift, see "Immortalizing the American Indians," *The Sunday Press*, September 5, 1909, 44:SB2 WMBP.

26. "New Indian Exhibit," June 6, 1909. On Crouse and the other women, see February 13, 1910, "Indian Dressmaker in State Museum," *The Sunday Press*, 44:SB2

WMBP; "Habitat Groups in Wax and Plaster," *Museum Work* 8, no. 19 (December 19), ACPR.

27. On the dioramas more broadly, Noémie Etienne includes a brief description and some photographs (some from the Shako:wi Cultural Center that visitors are no longer allowed to photograph) that explore the varied production methods Parker used to create these "authentic" Haudenosaunee experiences for museum-goers. Noémie Etienne, "Memory in Action: Clothing, Art, and Authenticity in Anthropological Dioramas (New York, 1900)," *Material Culture Review* 79 (March 2014): 46–59. The legacy of the dioramas stretches well into the twentieth century. I have in my personal collection a full slate of images of these dioramas from a 1960 exhibition catalogue, *The People of the Longhouse: A Guide to the Iroquois Indian Groups in the New York State Museum,* (Albany, NY: The New York State Museum, 1960). "Hunter's Group is True to History," June 9, 1918, 37:SB12 WMBP. On the construction of the dioramas, see "Habitat Groups," December 1916. The largest diorama is described in "The Seneca Indians," *Geneva Times*, December 22, 1911, 44:SB2 WMBP. Comparisons to Wild West stereotypes in "Life and Customs of New York Indians Vividly Depicted at State Museum," *Kuick-Press Albany*, May 14, 1916, 37:SB12 WMBP. Protection of unique Seneca history in "The Seneca Indians," December 22, 1911.

28. "Habitat Groups," December 1916. See also how meaning is "performed" in more recent dioramic exhibitions in Barbara Kirshenblatt-Gimblett, *Destination Culture: Tourism, Museums, and Heritage* (Berkeley, CA: University of California Press, 1998). Italics are Parker's. "Habitat Groups," December 1916.

29. "The Seneca Indians," December 22, 1911. Women's "significant" power in "Life and Customs," May 14, 1916; "Habitat Groups," December 1916. Commentary on women's comparative rights in "Christians Among Indians," December 25, 1907.

30. "Women's Rights in America Five Hundred Years Ago: Five Points of Savagery to Civilization," *The Albany Press*, April 11, 1909, 44:SB2 WMBP. Honorary degrees in Henry Allen to ACP, May 12, 1943, 1:8 ACPR.

31. "Indian Dressmaker," February 13, 1911, 44:SB2 WMBP. Converse, *Myths*, 138.

32. "New Indian Exhibit," June 6, 1909, 44:SB2 WMBP. The Albert Cusick quotation is mentioned by Parker in September 28, 1937, "Romance of the Old Indian Days," Radio Broadcast, 13: Radio Scripts 1937, ACPR.

33. "Canadian Indians at War," *The Sun*, June 5, 1910, 44:SB2 WMBP. His perspectives on Canadian Haudenosaunee in "Where Hiawatha's Laws Still Govern," *The Argus: Sunday Morning*, May 26, 1910, 44:SB2 WMBP.

34. Cited in Porter, *To Be Indian*, 76–77. Clarke's comments in "Archaeologist Writes of the Fire," paper unknown, 1912, 44:SB2 WMBP. Parker's illness is mentioned in New York State Museum, "The 1911 Capitol Fire," http://exhibitions.nysm. nysed.gov/capitolfire/ (accessed October 2018). See more images of the fire in Paul Mercer and Vicki Weiss, *The New York State Capitol and the Great Fire of 1911* (Mount Pleasant, NY: Arcadia Publishing, 2011).

35. Italics are his. Arthur C. Parker, "The American Indian, the Government and the Country," *American Indian Quarterly* IV, no. 1 (January–March, 1916): 38–49, in Roll 10 Papers of the Society of the American Indian (hereafter referred to as SAI). See also Porter, *To Be Indian*, chapter 5. On Du Bois, see Conn, *History's Shadow*, 1–2.

36. Arthur C. Parker, "Speech," *First Annual Conference of the Society of American Indians*, October 12–15, 1911, 8:10 ACPR.

37. "Speech," October 12–15. On the Ghost Dance, see White, *Republic*, 642–647; Deloria, *Indians in Unexpected Places*, chapter 1.

38. Porter, *To Be Indian*, 97. "Speech," October 12–15. William H. Taft to ACP, September 17, 1912, 1:1 ACPR.

39. ACP to Henry Roe Cloud, February 15, 1912, Roll 6 SAI. *Constitution and Laws of The Society of American Indians*, 1912, Roll 9 SAI. "American Indian Day" publication, *Society of American Indians Magazine*, February 17, 1913, Roll 9 SAI. New York Governor Charles W. Whitman officially designated AID day in NY on May 13, 1916, 2:1 ACPR. Other letters related to AID can be found in 2:1 ACPR. The dedication of AID passed the Senate on June 14, 1946, but did not pass the House. "American Indian Day," 79th Cong., 1st sess., Reported in Senate May 3, 1945, Passed in Senate June 14, 1946, S. 1074, 217; "Aid Program of the American Indian Council," pamphlet, September 23, 1944, 2:3 ACPR.

40. On "limiting membership," see Porter, *To Be Indian*, 91. Fayette A. McKenzie to ACP, June 14, 1913, 1:1 ACPR. The inconvenience of SAI conference locations is described in Letter to ACP, September 27, 1915, Roll 9 SAI.

41. ACP to Rosa B. LaFlesche, November 27, 1911, ACPA; cited also in Porter, To Be Indian, 102. Montezuma mentioned in Porter, *To Be Indian*, 127; "Making Democracy Safe for the Indian," *The American Indian Magazine* 6:1 (Spring 1918): 25–30, 9:3 ACPR. The SAI papers reveal the years-long and varied efforts Parker put into connecting Native Americans to the appropriate legal aid forces in state and federal governments. SAI Papers, Roll 8. "Intertribal consensus" in Porter, *To Be Indian*, 93.

42. Porter, *To Be Indian*, pages 126–133. His perspectives on the Haudenosaunee in "State Museum is Rich in Handiwork of Aborigines," *The Albany Argus*, May 21, 1916, 37:SB12 WMBP.

43. Arthur C. Parker "The Civic and Governmental Ideals of the Iroquois Confederacy," *Case and Comment: The Lawyer's Magazine* XXIII, no. 9 (February 1917): 717–720, 8:23: ACPR. "War Machine of Iroquois Indians Very Efficient," *Rochester Democrat*, May 30, 1916, 37:SB12 WMBP.

44. "Adoptions' All an Indian Joke," *Albany Herald*, September 21, 1916, 37:SB12 WMBP.

45. Arthur C. Parker, "The Constitution of the Five Nations: A Reply," 1916, 9:2 ACPR. The original publication in question is Arthur C. Parker, *The Constitution of the Five Nations* (Albany, NY: The State University of New York Press, 1916).

46. Parker, "A Reply."

47. Parker, "A Reply."

48. Helen M. Upton, *The Everett Report in Historical Perspective: The Indians of New York* (Albany, NY: New York State American Revolution Bicentennial Commission, 1980), 77. State draft commission appointment in "Indians Are Serving the U.S. Colors," *Albany Tribune*, 1918, 37:SB12 WMBP. Indigenous wartime contributions detailed in "Illustrated Lecture on the American Indian's Part in the World War," January 25, 1918, 1:2 ACPR.

49. Underlined word is Parker's embellishment. Report of ACP to Major F.S. Hutchinson, June 25, 1918, 3:15 ACPR. This "alien" problem would continue when Parker served on a committee to draft the Everett Report, an attempt in 1919–1922 to, once again, figure out how to solve the Indian problem in New York State through allotment, education, healthcare, and the dissolution of tribal governments. Upton, *The Everett Report*, chapter 4. "Indians Object to Term 'Alien,'" *Albany Argus*, June 28, 1918, 37:SB12 WMBP.

50. Open Letter from President Parker to SAI Membership, July 15, 1918, 1:2 ACPR. "Non-citizen" and "protect yourself" cited from ACP to "Sir", July 17, 1918, 3:15 ACPR. Arthur H. Dretader to ACP, July 22, 1918, 3:15 ACPR. Onondaga report in George Van Every Sr. (Secretary to the Chiefs of the Onondaga) to ACP, July 23, 1918, 3:15 ACPR.

51. Upton, *Everett Report*, 79. Haudenosaunee patriotism in "Report," May 17, 1919, 1:2 ACPR; "Indians Are Serving," 1918.

52. Upton, *The Everett Report*, 79. Parker's pro-citizenship appeal in "Big 'Pow-Wow' Is Expected to Help Red Men," *Albany Argus*, July 4, 1920, 37:SB12 WMBP. Seneca rejection of citizenship in "Majority Chooses Old Ways at New York State Indian Welfare Association Indications Show," paper unknown, May 1920, 37:SB12 WMPB; "Chiefs of the Six Nations to Reject Citizenship," *Syracuse Post Standard*, May 9, 1920, 37:SB12 WMBP. IWS in "Expect Indian Chiefs to Show Old Traditions," *Rochester Democrat and Chronicle*, November 10, 1920, 37:SB12 WMBP; "Wampum Belts will be Shown as Proof," *Rochester Democrat and Chronicle*, November 11, 1920, 37:SB12 WMBP.

53. "Address Before Indian Welfare Society," paper unknown, November 13, 1920, 37:SB12 WMBP.

54. Porter, *To Be Indian*, 141–142. Lyon's photograph in "Wampum Belts Will be Shown as Proof," November 11, 1920.

55. Letter of Congratulations, April 1, 1922, 1:4 ACPR. Dodge introduction in ACP to WHC, September 1, 1922, 1:4 ACPR; Nathan Miller to ACP, November 27, 1922, 1:4 ACPR. Hubert Work to ACP, May 21, 1923, 1:4 ACPR

56. ACP to Robert Moses, September 10, 1923, 4:16 ACPR; Fred B. Parker to ACP, September 11, 1923, 4:16 ACPR; Albert Moot to ACP, September 14, 1923, 4:16 ACPR. Ely Parker's homestead in "Project to Make Beautiful Indian Falls State Park," September 16, 1923, 4:16 ACPR. See also Porter, *To Be Indian*, 184.

57. "Great Capitol Area Empire Seen by Arthur C. Parker in Voicing Indian's Vision," *The Albany Knickerbocker Press*, December 2, 1923, 7:3 ACPR. Park failure is described in Porter, *To Be Indian*, 183–184.

58. Frederick B. Richards to ACP, October 9, 1925, 1:4 ACPR. Institutional partnerships described in ACP and Charles Adams, "Special Report on an Educational Program for the Letchworth State Park," July 22, 1926, 4:14 ACPR.

59. Arthur C. Parker, "An Approach to a Plan for Historical Society Museums," *Museum Work* VIII, no. 2 (1925): 50, 10:4 ACPR.

60. This philosophy anticipated public historians of today who find that most people, whether interested in a topic or not, learn best when they can personally experience the thing they are meant to learn, or at least when they are given the opportunity to relate that thing to a personal experience that has meaning to them. Catherine M. Cameron and John B. Gatewood, "Excursions into the Un-Remembered Past: What People Want from Visits to Historical Sites," *The Public Historian* 22, no. 3 (Summer 2000): 107–127.

61. "Special Report," July 22, 1926. NPS standards are described in Spence, *Dispossessing the Wilderness*, 115–118. Parker's emphasis on local history in ACP to Charles C. Adams, September 16, 1926, 4:14 ACPR.

62. "Proposed Stockade Located in Allegany State Park," paper unknown, 1926, 4:12 ACPR. Critiques of Countryman's plan in Charles C. Adams to ACP, September 29, 1926, 4:14 ACPR.

63. Underlines are Parker's. Charles C. Adams to ACP, September 14, 1926, 4:12 ACPR. The Letchworth plan also included plans to erect a statue of local hero, Mary Jemison. Arthur C. Parker and Charles Adams, "An Educational and Museum Program for Letchworth State Park," *New York State Museum Bulletin* 23 (1929): 73–80, 10:17 ACPR; Arthur C. Parker, "Indian Episodes of New York: A Drama Story of the Empire State," (Rochester, NY: Rochester Municipal Museum, July 2, 1935), 13, 1:13 ACPA.

64. Porter, *To Be Indian*, 165–166. See also Porter, chapter 7.

65. Porter, *To Be Indian*, 110. "Parker Says Municipal Museum has Outgrown Quarters," *Rochester Democrat and Chronicle* and *Rochester Herald*, April 11, 1926, 7:5 ACPR.

66. "Museist[s]" quote from Arthur C. Parker speech to the American Association of Museums, "The Place of the Small History Museum," June 1, 1934, 12:4 ACPR. All others from Arthur C. Parker, "An Approach to a Plan"; see also Arthur C. Parker Speech to the American Association of Museums, May 17, 1928, reprinted in *Museum Services* (June 15, 1928), 10:14 ACPR.

67. Porter, *To Be Indian*, 187–189.

68. "Modern Museum Stand for Commerce," *Rochester Commerce*, June 24, 1929, 10:19 ACPR. "'Collecting' an Old Country Store," *Rochester Commerce*, September 23, 1929, 10:16 ACPR. The social and cultural importance of museums is in "Modern Museum," June 24, 1929.

69. "Mr. Parker Designed the Bronze Tablet," paper unknown, October 12, 1933, 4:9 ACPR; "Red Jacket's Old Home," *Rochester Democrat and Chronicle*, December 11, 1933, 4:9 ACPR. Unveiling of the memorial in "Honor Red Jacket Mother in Unveiling of Memorial," *The Rochester Democrat*, October 22, 1933, 4:9 ACPR. Commentary on the danger of poor interpretation in Irving Adler and ACP to Frank Decker, January 11, 21, 23, 1935, 1:6 ACPR.

70. Frank Decker to ACP, January 25, 1935, 1:6 ACPR.

71. The three monographs, now out of print, are republished with an introduction by William Fenton in Fenton, *Parker on the Iroquois*. A comprehensive collection of the dozens of Parker's published papers are contained in boxes 8 to 11, ACPR. His service on committees and membership in "Service on Committee," 1934–1935, 1:5 ACPR; "Membership Notice," 1935, 1:7 ACPR. Groundhog day research in John White Johnston to ACP; March 18, 1935, and ACP to Donald Cadzow, March 4, 1935, 1:6 ACPR. USSR report in "Note on the SAR Report," 1947, 4:12 ACPR; I.N. Vinikov to ACP, December 28, 1934, 4:4 ACPR; "Iroquois Studies Since Morgan's Investigations," Report for the Russian Academy of Science, September 1935, 12:5 ACPR.

72. For that correspondence, see 1:6, ACPR. See the IRA, Haudenosaunee complaints, and the program's structural problems in Laurence Hauptman, *The Iroquois and the New Deal* (Syracuse, NY: Syracuse University Press, 1988).

73. Six Nations Association Membership Notice, October 15, 1934, 1:5 ACPR. Parker's support of Collier in Joseph Bruner Harold Ickes to Joseph Bruner, January 16, 1935, 1:6 ACPR.

74. *WPA Announcement of Tonawanda Community House*, August 17, 1936, 4:17 ACPR; Porter, *To Be Indian*, 199. "Smoothed" cited in William Newell to ACP, January 3, 1936, 1:8 ACPR; Porter, *To Be Indian*, 197–198.

75. ACP to Harry H. Kirsch, May 27, 1936, 4:17 ACPR. On official sponsors, see ACP to George W. Kellogg, August 4, 1936, 4:17 ACPR; Porter, *To Be Indian*, 198.

76. ACP to John C. Brennan, January 11, 1935, 1:6 ACPR. The Rochester Museum and Science Center has compiled some of these in an online database of photographs of early twentieth century Iroquoian material culture and history. The collections include photographs taken by Chief Freeman C. Johnson from the 1920–1960s, and it includes photographs taken by Arthur C. Parker and others during the Indian Arts Project. "Ögweʼöweʼka:ʼ Native Things," http://collections.rmsc.org/LibCat/Ogweoweka.html, accessed September 2019. Parker's insistence on only Senecas creating Seneca cultural things in ACP to President Jones, November 21, 1935, 1:6 ACPR; also cited in Porter, *To Be Indian*, 197–202.

77. A. H. Poody to ACP, November 26, 1935, 1:7 ACPR; Porter, *To Be Indian*, 198. Production begins in General Release on the Council House, September 20, 1936, 4:17 ACPR; Porter, *To Be Indian*, 204. Influence on the nationwide Indian Arts Project in Arthur C. Parker, "A Museum Sponsors an Indian Arts Project," *Social Welfare Bulletin* (January and February 1936): 12–14.

78. Parker, "A Museum Sponsors," 12-14.

79. These radio programs, in their entirety, can be found in Box 13, Radio Script 1937–38 in ACPR. The reach and scope of radio programs like these is analyzed in Lawrence W. Levine, "The Folklore of Industrial Society: Popular Culture and Its Audiences," *The American Historical Review* 97, no. 5 (1992): 1369–1399.

80. "The Epic of Hiawatha Part I," 13:RS 1937–1938 ACPR. "Red Jacket," *Romance of Old Indian Days*, 13:RS 1937, ACPR.

81. Porter, *To Be Indian*, 205–206. Gambrell was only one of many well-wishers. Herbert Gambrell to ACP, Jan 1, 1945, B1F8, ACPR. The "Rochester on Guard" series in "Annual Report of Rochester War Council, Speaker's Bureau," February 24, 4:11 ACPR. The "harried people" quotation in Arthur C. Parker, "The Local History Museum and the War Program," *Bulletin of the American Association for State and Local History* 1:4 (October 1942): 75–98, 11:13 ACPR.

82. "Parker Named By Historical Unit of State," *Rochester Democrat and Chronicle*, July 1, 1945, 4:6 ACPR; Rochester Museum to ACP, March 20, 1946, 1:9 ACPR. The accolades he received came from across the country. See Box 1 Folder 9 ACPR. Quotations from "The Role of the Iroquois In the Science of Government," speech to Sigma XI at the University of Rochester, November 22, 1946, 12:15 ACPR. On the many cultural efforts to combat Soviet influence during the Cold War, see John Lewis Gaddis, *The Cold War* (New York: Penguin Press, 2005), chapter 1.

83. "Notes on SAR Report," 1948, 4:12 ACPR.

84. Parker, "The Amazing Iroquois," unpublished typescript, boxes 4–7, ACPA.

85. Porter, *To Be Indian*, 226–227.

86. Parker, "The Amazing Iroquois: Red Embers," 4, Box 6 Volume 1 ACPA. The "pattern idea" quotation and those that follow, including the strikethrough and correction in the last quotation, are in Parker, "The Amazing Iroquois: Red Embers," 5, Box 6 Volume 1 ACPA.

87. Parker, "The Amazing Iroquois: Red Embers," 5–8, Box 6 ACPA.

88. For a brief historiography of ethnohistory, see Merrell, "American Nations," 334; James Axtell, *Natives and Newcomers*, prologue.

CONCLUSION

1. "Red Jacket Peace Medal returned to Seneca Nation after more than a century," *Niagara Frontier Publications*, May 7, 2021 https://www.wnypapers.com/news/article/current/2021/05/07/146540/red-jacket-peace-medal-returned-to-seneca-nation-after-more-than-a-century (accessed May 2021); "Red Jacket Peace Medal is Returned to its rightful owner: The Seneca Nation," *Buffalo Rising*, May 9, 2021 https://www.buffalorising.com/2021/05/red-jacket-peace-medal-is-bestowed-upon-its-rightful-owner-the-seneca-nation/ (accessed May 2021); "Red Jacket Peace Medal Returned to Seneca Nation by Buffalo Museum," *New York Almanac*,

May 9, 2021 https://www.newyorkalmanack.com/2021/05/red-jacket-peace-medal-returned-to-seneca-nation-by-buffalo-museum/ (accessed May 2021); "Seneca Nation welcomes return of Red Jacket Peace Medal," *WIVB4.com*, May 17, 2021 https://www.wivb.com/news/local-news/buffalo/seneca-nation-welcomes-return-of-red-jacket-peace-medal/ (accessed May 2021); "Red Jacket Peace Medal welcomed back to rightful home with Seneca Nation," *Indian Country Today*, May 18, 2021 https://indiancountrytoday.com/the-press-pool/red-jacket-peace-medal-welcomed-back-to-rightful-home-with-seneca-nation (accessed May 2021).

2. About Us, Seneca-Iroquois National Museum website, https://www.senecamuseum.org/about/ (accessed March 2020).
3. Recording of live public Repatriation Ceremony, Seneca Media and Communications Center, Facebook video link, https://www.facebook.com/senecamedia/videos/835151430692404 (accessed May 2021).
4. Email correspondence with Dr. Joe Stahlman. My thanks go out to Joe Stahlman for his time, perspective, and insight into the state of the museum field. Also, special thanks to him and the Seneca leadership for facilitating and approving my request for access to the Seneca Nation of Indian's original repatriation request.
5. Recording of live public Repatriation Ceremony.
6. *Native American Graves Protection and Repatriation Act of 1990*, H.R. 5237, Public Law 101–601, *U.S. Statutes at Large* 104 [November 16, 1990]: 3048–3058.
7. President Matthew B. Pagels, *Repatriation Claim for the Red Jacket Peace Medal*, November 16, 2020. Courtesy of The Seneca Nation of Indians.
8. "Red Jacket Peace Medal Returned to Seneca Nation After More Than A Century," SNI Official Newsletter: Community News, May 6, 2021 https://sninews.org/2021/05/14/red-jacket-peace-medal-returned-to-seneca-nation-after-more-than-a-century/ (accessed May 17, 2021). See also President Pagel's video announcement of the repatriation alongside COVID-19 news in Presidential Update Video, SNI Official Newsletter: Feature, May 13, 2021 https://sninews.org/2021/05/13/presidential-update-05-13-21/ (accessed May, 17, 2021).
9. Melissa Brown Speech, Repatriation Ceremony.
10. Melissa Brown Speech, Repatriation Ceremony.
11. Joe Stahlman, Repatriation Ceremony.
12. Devon A. Mihesuah, ed., *Repatriation Reader: Who Owns American Indian Remains?* (Lincoln, NE: University of Nebraska Press, 2000), 1, 6. See also Colwell, *Plundered Skulls*; Susan Sleeper-Smith ed., *Contesting Knowledge*.
13. Pagels, *Repatriation Claim*.
14. Matthew Pagels Speech, Repatriation Ceremony.
15. An important contribution to this conversation is Dan Hick's *The Brutish Museums: The Benin Bronzes, Colonial Violence and Cultural Restitution* (London: Pluto Press, 2020). See also Colwell, *Plundered Skulls and Stolen Spirits*.
16. Parker, *Manual for History Museums*, 156.

Bibliography

NOTE ON LANGUAGE

Throughout this book I alternate between "Haudenosaunee" and "Iroquois." While it is needed in certain areas to avoid literary redundancy, it is also intentional. Conceptually, I deploy Haudenosaunee predominately and broadly when Indigenous peoples are talking about their own histories and experiences—or scholars are offering nuanced accounts of those topics—and Iroquois when referring broadly to the warped memories and the popular conceptions of that history. As literary framing devices, these terms help provide a clearer picture of the complex interactivity between history and memory-making. Individual tribal, clan, band, and national names are also used where appropriate.

ARCHIVAL COLLECTIONS

The American Founding Era Collection. Charlottesville, VA: University of Virginia Press, Rotunda, 2010.

The Papers of Thomas Jefferson Digital Edition. Edited by James P. McClure and J. Jefferson Looney. Charlottesville, VA: University of Virginia Press, 2008–2019.

The Papers of George Washington Digital Edition. Charlottesville, VA: University of Virginia Press, 2008.

The Papers of James Madison Digital Edition, J. C. A. Stagg, editor. Charlottesville, VA: University of Virginia Press, 2010.

Beauchamp, William M. Papers. New York State Museum, Albany, New York.

Ganter, Granville. *The Collected Speeches of Sagoyewatha, or Red Jacket.* Syracuse, NY: Syracuse University Press, 2006.

The Historical Marker Database. "Public history cast in metal, carved on stone, or embedded in resin." Digital Database. http://hmdb.com, founded 2006.

Keppler Jr., Joseph. *Iroquois Papers.* Microform. Bronx, NY: Huntington Free Library, 1994.

Larner, John W. *The Papers of the Society of American Indians.* Microform. Wilmington, DE: Scholarly Resources, 1987.

Morgan, Lewis Henry. Papers. River Campus Libraries, University of Rochester, Rochester, New York.

Parker, Arthur Caswell. Papers. River Campus Libraries, University of Rochester, Rochester, New York.

Parker, Arthur Caswell. Papers, 1915–1953. New York State Library, Albany, New York.

Parker, Ely Samuel. Papers. River Campus Libraries, University of Rochester, Rochester, New York.

SELECTED HISTORICAL MANUSCRIPTS AND PUBLICATIONS

Abel, Annie H. *The American Indian and the End of the Confederacy, 1863–1866.* Edited by Theda Purdue. Lincoln, NE: University of Nebraska Press, 1993.

Abel, Annie H. "History of Events Resulting in Indian Consolidation West of the Mississippi River." *American Historical Association Annual Report for 1906.* Edited by A. Howard Clark. Washington, DC: American Historical Association, 1906: 235–450.

Badeau, Adam. *Military History of Ulysses S. Grant.* 3 vols. New York: Applewood Books, 1881–1885.

Blacksnake, Governor. *Chainbreaker: The Revolutionary War Memoirs of Governor Blacksnake as told to Benjamin Williams.* Edited by Thomas S. Abler. Lincoln, NE: University of Nebraska Press, 2005.

Bryant, William Cullen. *A Popular History of the United States.* 4 vols. New York: Scribner and Sons, 1876–1881.

Buel, James W. *Louisiana and the Fair: An Exposition of the World, Its People, and Their Achievements.* Vol. 5. St. Louis: World's Progress Publishing Company, 1904.

Buffalo Historical Society. *Annual Reports of the Buffalo Historical Society.* Buffalo, NY: The Buffalo Historical Society, 1884–1928.

Charles W. Clinton and William H. Russell, "The Hotel Astor." *Architects' and Builders' Magazine* 6, no. 2. New York: William T. Comstock, 1904, 49–71.

Clinton, DeWitt. "Introductory Discourse Delivered Before the Literary and Philosophical Society of New York." New York: David Longworth, 1815.

Clinton, DeWitt. "Discourse Delivered Before the New-York Historical Society." New York: New-York Historical Society, 1812.

Clinton, DeWitt. *Memoir of DeWitt Clinton: With an Appendix, Containing Numerous Documents, Illustrative of the Principle Events of His Life.* New York: J. Seymour, 1829.

Colden, Cadwallader. *The History of the Five Indian Nations: Depending on the Province of New-York in America.* Ithaca, NY: Cornell University Press, 2016.

Cooper, James Fenimore. *Last of the Mohicans: A Narrative of 1757*. New York: W.A. Townsend and Company, 1859.

Cooper, James Fenimore. *Notions of the Americans: Picked Up By A Travelling Bachelor*. Philadelphia: Carey, Lea and Carey, 1828.

Converse, Harriet Maxwell. *Myths and Legends of the New York State Iroquois*. Edited by Arthur C. Parker. Albany, NY: University of the State of New York, 1908.

Converse, Harriet Maxwell. *Sheaves: A Collection of Poems*. New York: G.P. Putnam and Sons, 1882.

Dunlap, William. *A History of the Rise and Progress of the Arts of Design in the United States*. Boston: C.E. Goodspeed & Co., 1918.

Eggleson, Edward and Lillie Eggleston Seelye. *Brant and Red Jacket Including an Account of the Early Wars of the Six Nations, and the Border Warfare of the Revolution*. New York: Dodd, Mead & Company, 1879.

Exhibition Catalogue. *The People of the Longhouse: A Guide to the Iroquois Indian Groups in the New York State Museum*. Albany, NY: The New York State Museum, 1960. From the author's collection.

Halleck, Fitz-Greene. *Alnwick Castle: With Other Poems*. Reprint. Ann Arbor, MI: University of Michigan Humanities Text Initiative, 1995.

Heckewelder, Reverend John. *History, Manners, and Customs of The Indian Nations who once Inhabited Pennsylvania and the Neighbouring States with an Introduction and Notes by the Rev. William C. Reichel*. Bethlehem, PA: The Historical Society of Pennsylvania, 1881.

Hotel Astor. *Hotel Astor, Indian Hall*. New York: Malcolm & Hayes, 190?. In the author's collection.

Hubbard, J. Niles. *An Account of Sa-Go-Ye-Wat-Ha or Red Jacket and His People, 1750–1880*. Albany, NY: Joel Munsell's Sons, 1886.

Jefferson, Thomas. *Notes on the State of Virginia*. Edited by David Waldstreicher. New York: Bedford St. Martins, 2002.

Johnson, Robert U. and Clarence C. Buel editors. *Battle and Leaders of the Civil War*. 4 vols. New York: The Century Company, 1887–1888.

Livermore, Mary A. and Frances Elizabeth Willard, eds. *A Woman of the Century: Fourteen Hundred-seventy Biographical Sketches Accompanied by Portraits of Leading American Women in All Walks of Life*. Buffalo, NY: Charles Wells Moulton, 1893.

New York State Museum. New York State Museum Bulletins. Albany, NY: 1887– http://www.nysm.nysed.gov/publications/bulletins (accessed 2018).

Parker, Arthur Caswell. "The American Indian, the Government and the Country." *American Indian Quarterly* 4, no. 1 (January-March, 1916): 38–49.

Parker, Arthur Caswell. *American Indian Freemasonry*. Buffalo, NY: Buffalo Consistory, 1919.

Parker, Arthur Caswell. *The Constitution of the Five Nations*. Albany, NY: The State University of New York Press, 1916.

Parker, Arthur Caswell. "An Erie Indian Village and Burial Site at Ripley, Chautauqua Co., N.Y." *New York State Museum Bulletin* 117 (1907): 455–508.

Parker, Arthur Caswell. *The Life of General Ely S. Parker: Last Grand Sachem of the Iroquois and General Grant's Military Secretary.* Buffalo, NY: Buffalo Historical Society, 1919.

Parker, Arthur Caswell. *A Manual for History Museums.* New York: Columbia University Press, 1935.

Parker, Arthur Caswell. "A Museum Sponsors an Indian Arts Project." *Social Welfare Bulletin* 7, no. 1-2 (January and February, 1936): 12–14.

Parker, Arthur Caswell. *Parker on the Iroquois: Iroquois Uses of Maize and Other Food Plants, The Code of Handsome Lake, the Seneca Prophet, The Constitution of the Five Nations.* Edited by William Fenton. Syracuse, NY: Syracuse University Press, 1968.

Parker, Arthur Caswell. *Red Jacket: Last of the Seneca.* New York: McGraw Hill Books, 1952.

Parker, Arthur Caswell. *Red Jacket: Seneca Chief.* Edited by Thomas Abler. Lincoln, NE: Bison Books and the University of Nebraska Press, 1998.

Porter, Horace. *Campaigning With Grant.* New York: The Century Company, 1897.

Seaver, James. *Narrative of the Life of Mary Jemison.* Edited by June Namias. Norman, OK: University of Oklahoma Press, 1992.

Shiedt, J. E. *Atlas of the City of Philadelphia by Wards, 1892.* Philadelphia: 1892. Digitized Free Library of Philadelphia. Map Collection. https://www.philageohistory.org/rdic-images/view-image.cfm/JES1892.Phila.007.Ward_5 (accessed March 2020).

Stone, William L. *The Life and Times of Red-Jacket, or Sa-Go-Ye-Wat-Ha; Being the Sequel to the History of the Six Nations.* New York and London: Wiley and Putnam, 1841.

Stone, William L. *Life of Joseph Brant-Thayendanegea: Including the Border Wars of the American Revolution and Sketches of the Indian Campaigns of Generals Harmar, St. Clair, and Wayne, and Other Matters.* 2 Vols. New York: Alexander V. Blake, 1838.

Thatcher, Benjamin Bussey. *Indian biography, or, An historical account of those individuals who have been distinguished among the North American natives as orators.* 2 Vols. New York: Harper and Brothers, 1842.

Turner, Orasmus. *History of the Pioneer Settlement of Phelps & Gorham's Purchase, and Morris' Reserve. To which is added, a Supplement or Continuation of the Pioneer History of Ontario, Wayne, Livingston, Yates and Allegany.* Rochester, NY: William Alling, 1852.

Waterloo Library and Historical Society. "Unveiling of the Monument Erected by the Waterloo Library and Historical Society: As a Memorial of Red Jacket, At Canoga, N.Y., the Place of His Birth, October 14, 1891." Waterloo, NY: Waterloo Library and Historical Society Observer Printing Company, 1892.

SECONDARY SOURCES

Ablavsky, Gregory. "Species of Sovereignty: Native Nationhood, the United States, and International Law, 1783–1795." *Journal of American History* 106, no. 3 (December 2019): 591–613.

Ackerman, Scott. "'We Are Abolitionizing the West': The Union Army and the Implementation of Federal Emancipation Policy, 1861–1865." PhD diss., City University of New York, 2019.

Alfred, Taiaiake. *Peace, Power, Righteousness: An Indigenous Manifesto.* Toronto: Oxford University Press Canada, 1999.

Anderson, Chad. "Rediscovering Native North America: Settlements, Maps, and Empires in the Eastern Woodlands." *Early American Studies: An Interdisciplinary Journal* 14, no. 3 (Summer, 2016): 478–505.

Anderson, Chad. *The Storied Landscape of Iroquoia: History, Conquest, and Memory in the Native Northeast.* Lincoln, NE: University of Nebraska Press, 2020.

Anderson, Fred. *The Crucible of War: The Seven Years War and the Fate of British North America, 1754–1766.* New York: Vintage Books, 2007.

Armstrong, William H. *Warrior in Two Camps: Ely S. Parker, Union General and Seneca Chief.* Syracuse, NY: Syracuse University Press, 1989.

Axtell, James. *Natives and Newcomers: The Cultural Origins of North America.* New York: Oxford University Press, 2000.

Barbour, Chad A. *From Daniel Boone to Captain America: Playing Indian in American Popular Culture.* Jackson, MS: University of Mississippi Press, 2016.

Barr, Julianna. "There's No Such Thing as 'Prehistory': What the Longue Durée of Caddo and Pueblo History Tells Us about Colonial America." *William and Mary Quarterly* 74, no. 2 (April 2017): 203–240.

Beckert, Sven. *The Monied Metropolis: New York City and the Consolidation of the American Bourgeoisie, 1850–1896.* Cambridge, MA: Harvard University Press, 1993.

Bender, Thomas. *New York Intellect: A History of Intellectual Life in New York City from 1750 to the Beginnings of Our Own Time.* New York: Alfred A. Knopf, 1987

Benn, Carl. *The Iroquois in the War of 1812.* Toronto: University of Toronto Press, 1998.

Berkhofer, Jr. Robert F. "The Political Context of a New Indian History." *Pacific Historical Review* 40, no. 3 (August 1971): 357–382.

Berkhofer, Jr. Robert F. *The White Man's Indian: Images of the American Indian from Columbus to the Present.* New York: Vintage Books, 1978.

Bieder, Robert. "Grand Order of the Iroquois." *Ethnohistory* 27, no. 4 (1980): 349–361.

Blackhawk, Ned. *Violence over the Land: Indians and Empires in the Early American West.* Cambridge, MA: Harvard University Press, 2008.

Blight, David W. *Race and Reunion: The Civil War in American Memory.* Cambridge, MA: Harvard University Press, 2001.

Bonaparte, Darren. *The Wampum Chronicles.* http://www.wampumchronicles.com/ (accessed 2017).

Boucher, Diane. "'Under the pavement of Broadway': The Indian Hall in the Hotel Astor." *American Indian Art Magazine* 35, no. 4 (2010): 70–71.

Bowes, John P. *This Land Is Too Good for Indians: Histories of Northern Indian Removal.* Norman, OK: University of Oklahoma Press, 2015.

Bowes, John P. "American Indian Removal Beyond the Removal Act." *Journal of the Native American and Indigenous Studies Association* 1, no. 1 (Spring, 2014): 65–87.

Brooks, Lisa. *The Common Pot: The Recovery of Native Space in the Northeast.* Minneapolis: University of Minnesota Press, 2008.

Brown, Dee. *Bury My Heart at Wounded Knee: An Indian History of the American West.* New York: Henry Holt and Company, 1970.

Browman, David. "The Peabody Museum, Frederic W. Putnam, and the Rise of U.S. Anthropology, 1866–1903." *American Anthropologist* 102, no. 2 (2002): 508–519.

Bruchac, Joseph. *The White Man's War: Ely S. Parker: Iroquois General.* New York: Bowman Books, 2011.

Bruchac, Joseph and Diana Magnuson. *The Trail of Tears.* New York: Random House, 2003.

Bruchac, Margaret. "Broken Chains of Custody: Possessing, Dispossessing, and Repossessing Lost Wampum Belts." *Proceedings of the American Philosophical Society* 162, no. 1 (March 2018): 56–105.

Bruchac, Margaret. *Savage Kin: Indigenous Informants and American Anthropologists.* Tucson: University of Arizona Press, 2018.

Burrows, Edwin G. and Mike Wallace. *Gotham: A History of New York City to 1898.* New York: Oxford University Press, 1999.

Calloway, Colin. *The Indian World of George Washington: The First President, the First Americans, and the Birth of the Nation.* New York: Oxford University Press, 2019.

Calloway, Colin. *The Shawnees and the War for America.* New York: Viking Press, 2007.

Cameron, Catherine M. and John B. Gatewood. "Excursions into the Un-Remembered Past: What People Want from Visits to Historical Sites." *The Public Historian* 22, no. 3 (Summer 2000): 107–127.

Campisi, Jack and William A. Starna. "On the Road to Canandaigua: The Treaty of 1794." *American Indian Quarterly* 19, no. 4 (1995): 467–490.

Carr, Helen. *Inventing the American Primitive: Politics, Gender, and the Representation of Native American Literary Traditions 1789–7936.* New York: New York University Press, 1999.

Charleyboy, Lisa and Mary Beth Leatherdale. *Urban Tribes: Native Americans in the City.* New York: Annick Press, 2015.

Chernow, Barbara Ann. "Robert Morris: Genesee Land Speculator." *New York History* 58 (April 1977): 194–220.

Chernow, Barbara Ann. "Robert Morris: Genesee Land Speculator." PhD diss., Columbia University, 1978.

Colwell-Chanthaphonh, Chip. *Inheriting the Past: The Making of Arthur C. Parker and Indigenous Archaeology.* Tucson: University of Arizona Press, 2009.

Colwell-Chanthaphonh, Chip. *Plundered Skulls and Stolen Spirits: Inside the Fight to Reclaim Native America's Culture*. Chicago: University of Chicago Press, 2017.

Confer, Clarissa. *The Cherokee Nation in the Civil War*. Norman, OK: University of Oklahoma Press, 2007.

Conn, Stephen. *History's Shadow: Native Americans and the Historical Consciousness in the Nineteenth Century*. Chicago: University of Chicago Press, 2004.

Cornog, Evan. *The Birth of Empire: DeWitt Clinton and the American Experience, 1769–1828*. New York: Oxford University Press, 1998.

daCosta Nunes, Jadviga. "Red Jacket: The Man and His Portraits." *The American Art Journal* 12, no. 3 (Summer 1980): 4–20.

Countryman, Edward. "Toward a Different Iroquois History." *The William and Mary Quarterly* 69, no. 2 (April 2012): 347–360.

Cox, Karen L. *Dreaming of Dixie: How the South Was Created in American Popular Culture*. Chapel Hill, NC: University of North Carolina Press, 2011.

Crosby, Sara L. *Poisonous Muse: The Female Poisoner and the Framing of Popular Authorship in Jacksonian America*. Cedar Rapids, IA: University of Iowa Press, 2016.

Cutrer, Thomas W. *Theater of a Separate War: The Civil War West of the Mississippi River, 1861–1865*. Chapel Hill, NC: University of North Carolina Press, 2017.

D'Alton, Martina. *The New York Obelisk, or, How Cleopatra's Needle Came to New York and What Happened When It Got Here*. New York: Metropolitan Museum of Art, 1993. https://www.metmuseum.org/art/metpublications/The_New_York_Obelisk_or_How_Cleopatras_Needle_came_to_New_York_and_what_happened_ed_when_it_got_here (accessed March 2020).

Davis, Burke. *To Appomattox: Nine April Days, 1865*. New York: Rinehart Publishers, 1959.

Deloria, Philip J. *Indians in Unexpected Places*. Lawrence, KS: University Press of Kansas, 2004.

Deloria, Philip J. *Playing Indian*. New Haven, CT: Yale University Press, 1999.

Deloria Jr., Vine. *Custer Died for Your Sins: An Indian Manifesto*. New York: The Macmillan Company, 1967.

Demos, John. *The Unredeemed Captive: A Family Story from Early America*. New York: Knopf Publishers, 1994.

Demos, John. *The Heathen School: A Story of Hope and Betrayal in the Age of the Early Republic*. New York: Vintage Books, 2014.

Dennis, Matthew. *Cultivating a Landscape of Peace: Iroquois-European Encounters in Seventeenth-Century America*. Ithaca, NY: Cornell University Press, 1993.

Dennis, Matthew. "Red Jacket's Rhetoric: Postcolonial Persuasions on the Native Frontiers of the Early American Republic" in *American Indian Rhetorics of Survivance: Word Medicine, Word Magic*, edited by Earnest Stromberg, 15–33. Pittsburg: University of Pittsburg Press, 2006.

Densmore, Christopher. *Red Jacket: Iroquois Diplomat and Orator*. Syracuse, NY: Syracuse University Press, 1999.

Dickson, Keith D. *Sustaining Southern Identity*. Baton Rouge: Louisiana State University, 2011.

DiRenzo, Anthony. "Sortilegio: Cola Di Rienzo and the Blasphemy of Documentation." Ithaca College Faculty Publications, 1997. https://faculty.ithaca.edu/direnzo/docs/scholarship/sortilegio/ (accessed September 2018).

Dongoske, Kurt E., Mark S. Aldenderfer, and Karen Doehner, eds. *Working Together: Native Americans and Archaeologists* New York: Society for American Archaeology, 2000.

Dowd, Gregory Evans. *War Under Heaven: Pontiac, The Indian Nations & The British Empire*. Baltimore: Johns Hopkins University Press, 2002.

Downs, Gregory P. and Kate Masur, editors. *The World the Civil War Made*. Chapel Hill, NC: University of North Carolina Press, 2015.

Dubrow, Gail Lee, and Jennifer B. Goodman, eds. *Restoring Women's History through Historic Preservation*. Baltimore: Johns Hopkins University Press, 2003.

Dunbar-Ortiz, Roxanne. *An Indigenous Peoples' History of the United States*. Boston: Beacon Press, 2014.

Dusinberre, William. *Strategies for Survival: Recollections of Bondage in Antebellum Virginia*. Charlottesville, VA: University of Virginia Press, 2009.

Duval, Kathleen. *Independence Lost: Lives on the Edge of the American Revolution*. New York: Random House, 2015.

Earle, Jonathan and Diane Matti Burke, eds. *Bleeding Kansas, Bleeding Missouri: The Long Civil War on the Border*. Lawrence, KS: University Press of Kansas, 2013.

Eastman, Carolyn. "The Indian Censures the White Man: 'Indian Eloquence' and American Reading Audiences in the Early Republic." *The William and Mary Quarterly* 65, no. 3 (July 2008): 535–564.

Etcheson, Nicole. *Bleeding Kansas: Contested Liberty in the Civil War Era*. Lawrence, KS: University Press of Kansas, 2006.

Etienne, Noémie. "Memory in Action: Clothing, Art, and Authenticity in Anthropological Dioramas (New York, 1900)." *Material Culture Review* 79 (March 2014): 46–59.

Fahs, Alice and Joan Waugh, eds. *The Memory of the Civil War in American Culture*. Chapel Hill, NC: University of North Carolina Press, 2004.

Faragher, Mack. *Eternity Street: Violence and Justice in Frontier Los Angeles*. New York: Norton and Company, 2015.

Fenton, William N. *False Faces of the Iroquois*. Norman, OK: University of Oklahoma Press, 1987.

Fenton, William N. *The Great Law and the Longhouse: A Political History of the Iroquois Confederacy*. Norman, OK: University of Oklahoma Press, 1998.

Fenton, William N. "Harriet Maxwell Converse." *Notable American Women, 1607-1950: A Biographical Dictionary*, Edward T. James, Janet Wilson James, and Paul S. Boyer, eds. Vol. 1. Cambridge, MA: Harvard University Press, 1971, 375–377.

Fenton, William N. "The Hyde de Neuville Portraits of New York Savages in 1807-1808." *New-York Historical Society Quarterly* 38, no. 2 (1954): 119–137 .

Fenton, William N. *The Little Water Medicine Society of the Senecas*. Norman, OK: University of Oklahoma Press, 2002.

Fenton, William N. "The New York State Wampum Collection: The Case for the Integrity of Cultural Treasures." *Proceedings of the American Philosophical Society* 115, no. 6 (December 1971): 437–461.

Finlay, Nancy. *Inventing the American Past: the Art of F.O.C. Darley*. New York: New York Public Library, 1999.

Fischer, David Hackett. *Albion's Seed: Four British Folkways in America*. New York: Oxford University Press, 1986.

Foner, Eric. *The Fiery Trial: Abraham Lincoln and American Slavery*. New York: W.W. Norton and Company, 2011.

Foreman, Grant. *Indian Removal*. Norman, OK: University of Oklahoma Press, 1972.

"Forum: The 'Iroquois Influence' Thesis—Con and Pro." *The William and Mary Quarterly* 53, no. 3 (July 1996): 587–636.

Donald A. Grinde, Jr. and Bruce E. Johansen, "Sauce for the Goose: Demand and Definitions for "Proof" Regarding the Iroquois and Democracy." *The William and Mary Quarterly* 53, no 3 (July 1996): 621-636.

Philip A. Levy, "Exemplars of taking Liberties: The Iroquois Influence Thesis and the Problem of Evidence." *The William and Mary Quarterly* 53, no 3 (July 1996): 588–604.

Samuel B. Payne, Jr., "The Iroquois League, the Articles of Confederation, and the Constitution." *The William and Mary Quarterly* 53, no 3 (July 1996): 605–620.

Foster, Michael K., Jack Campisi, and Marianne Mithun, eds. *Extending the Rafters: Interdisciplinary Approaches to Iroquoian Studies*. Albany, NY: State University of New York Press, 1984.

Freeman, Douglas Southall. *R. E. Lee: A Biography*. Volume 4. New York: Scribner's and Sons, 1935.

Freeman, Joanne B. *Affairs of Honor*. New Haven, CT: Yale University Press, 2001.

Gaddis, John Lewis. *The Cold War*. New York: Penguin Press, 2005.

Galloway, Patricia. *Practicing Ethnohistory: Mining Archives, Hearing Testimony, Constructing Narrative*. Lincoln, NE: University of Nebraska Press, 2006.

Gallup-Diaz, Ignacio, Andrew Shankman, and David J. Silverman, eds. *Anglicizing America: Empire, Revolution, Republic*. Philadelphia: University of Pennsylvania Press, 2015.

Ganteaume, Cécile R. *Officially Indian: Symbols That Define the United States*. Minneapolis: University of Minnesota Press for the Smithsonian National Museum of the American Indian, 2017.

Ganter, Granville. "'Make Your Minds Perfectly Easy': Sagoyewatha and the Great Law of the Haudenosaunee." *Early American Literature* 44, no. 1 (2009): 121–146.

Ganter, Granville. "Red Jacket and the Decolonization of Republican Virtue." *American Indian Quarterly* 31, no. 4 (Fall 2007): 559–581.

Genetin-Pilawa, Joseph. *Crooked Paths to Allotment: The Fight over Federal Indian Policy After the Civil War.* Chapel Hill, NC: University of North Carolina Press, 2012.

Ganter, Granville. "Confining Indians: Power, Authority, and the Colonialist Ideologies of Nineteenth-Century Reformers: Volume One." PhD diss., Michigan State University, 2008.

Ganter, Granville. "Ely S. Parker and the Paradox of Reconstruction Politics in Indian Country." In *The World the Civil War Made,* edited by Gregory P. Downs and Kate Masur, 183–205. Chapel Hill: University of North Carolina Press, 2015.

Graymont, Barbara. *The Iroquois in the American Revolution.* Syracuse, NY: Syracuse University Press, 1975.

Grimes, Richard S. "The Early Years of the Delaware Indian Experience in Kansas Territory, 1830–1845." *Journal of the West* 41 (Winter 2002): 73–82.

Grinde, Jr., Donald A. *The Iroquois and the Founding of the American Nation.* San Francisco: The Indian Historian Press, 1977.

Grinde, Jr. Donald A. and Bruce E. Johansen. *Exemplar of Liberty: Native America and the Evolution of Democracy.* Los Angeles: University of California Los Angeles Press, 1991.

Gruber, Jacob W. "Ethnographic Salvage and the Shaping of Anthropology." *American Anthropologist* 72, no. 6. (1970): 1290.

Hall, Roger A. *Performing the American Frontier, 1870–1906.* Cambridge: Cambridge University Press, 2001.

Hall, Ryan. *Beneath the Backbone of the World: Blackfoot People and the North American Borderlands, 1720–1877.* Chapel Hill, NC: University of North Carolina Press, 2020.

Hämäläinen, Pekka. *The Comanche Empire.* New Haven, CT: Yale University Press, 2008.

Hämäläinen, Pekka. *Lakota America: A New History of Indigenous Power.* New Haven, CT: Yale University Press, 2019.

Hämäläinen, Pekka. "The Politics of Grass: European Expansion, Ecological Change, and Indigenous Power in the Southwest Borderlands." *The William and Mary Quarterly* 67, no. 2 (April 2010): 173–208.

Harmon, Alexandra. *Rich Indians: Native People and the Problem of Wealth in American History.* Chapel Hill, NC: University of North Carolina Press, 2010.

Harper, Rob. *Unsettling the West: Violence and State Building in the Ohio Valley.* Philadelphia: University of Pennsylvania Press, 2018.

Harrold, Stanley. *Subversives: Antislavery Community in Washington, D.C., 1828–1865.* Baton Rouge: Louisiana State University, 2003.

Hatch, Nathan. *The Democratization of American Christianity.* New Haven, CT: Yale University Press, 1991.

Hauptman, Laurence. *Between Two Fires: American Indians in the Civil War.* New York: The Free Press, 1995.

Hauptman, Laurence. "Chief Publicist." *New York Archives* 18, no. 2 (2018): 21–24.

Hauptman, Laurence. *Conspiracy of Interests: Iroquois Dispossession and the Rise of New York State.* Syracuse, NY: Syracuse University Press, 1999.

Hauptman, Laurence. "On Our Terms: The Tonawanda Seneca Indians, Lewis Henry Morgan, and Henry Rowe Schoolcraft, 1844–1851." *New York History* 91, no. 4 (2010): 314–335.

Hauptman, Laurence. *The Iroquois and the New Deal.* Syracuse, NY: Syracuse University Press, 1988.

Hauptman, Laurence. *The Iroquois in the Civil War: From Battlefield to Reservation.* Syracuse, NY: Syracuse University Press, 1993.

Hauptman, Laurence. *The Tonawanda Senecas' Heroic Battle Against Removal: Conservative Activist Indians.* Albany, NY: State University of New York Press, 2011.

Healy, Michael J., Michael B. Beverland, Harmen Oppewal, and Sean Sands. "Understanding Retail Experiences: The Case for Ethnography." *International Journal of Market Research* 49, no. 6 (2007): 751–778.

Hertzberg, Hazel Whitman. "Nationalist, Anthropology, and Pan-Indianism in the Life of Arthur C. Parker (Seneca)." *Proceedings of the American Philosophical Society* 123, no. 1 (February 1979): 47–72.

Hertzberg, Hazel Whitman. *The Search for an American Indian Identity: Modern Pan-Indian Movements.* Syracuse, NY: Syracuse University Press, 1971.

Hinderaker, Eric. *The Two Hendricks: Unraveling a Mohawk Mystery.* Cambridge, MA: Harvard University Press, 2010.

Hoganson, Kristin L. *Consumers' Imperium: The Global Production of American Domesticity, 1865-1920.* Chapel Hill, NY: University of North Carolina Press, 2010.

Holton, Woody. *Forced Founders: Indians, Debtors, Slaves & the Making of the American Revolution in Virginia.* Chapel Hill, NC: University of North Carolina Press, 1999.

Howe, Barbara J. "Women in Historic Preservation: The Legacy of Ann Pamela Cunningham." *The Public Historian* 12 (1990): 31–61.

Howe, Daniel Walker. *What Hath God Wrought: The Transformation of America 1815–1848.* New York: Oxford University Press, 2007.

Hoxie, Frederick E. *A Final Promise: The Campaign to Assimilate the Indians, 1880–1920.* Lincoln, NE: University of Nebraska Press, 2001.

Hoxie, Frederick E., Ronald Hoffman, and Peter J. Albert, eds. *Native Americans and the Early Republic.* Charlottesville, VA: University of Virginia Press, 1999.

Isenberg, Nancy. *White Trash: The 400-Year Untold History of Class in America.* New York: Penguin Press, 2017.

Isaac, Rhys. "The First Monticello." In *Jeffersonian Legacies*, edited by Peter Onuf, 77–108. Charlottesville, VA: University of Virginia Press, 1993.

Jacobs, Margaret D. *White Mother to a Dark Race: Settler Colonialism, Maternalism, and the Removal of Indigenous Children in the American West and Australia, 1880–1940.* Lincoln, NE: University of Nebraska Press, 2009.

Jacobson, Matthew Frye. *Barbarian Virtues: The United States Encounters Foreign Peoples at Home and Abroad*. New York: Hill and Wang, 2000.

Jacoby, Karl. *Shadows at Dawn: A Borderlands Massacre and the Violence of History*. New York: Penguin Books, 2008.

Jennings, Francis. *The Ambiguous Iroquois Empire: The Covenant Chain Confederation of the Indian Tribes with English Colonies*. New York: Norton and Sons, 1984.

Jennings, Francis. *Empire of Fortune: Crowns, Colonies, and Tribes in the Seven Years' War in America*. New York: W.W. Norton and Company, 1988.

Jennings, Francis, ed. *History and Culture of Iroquois Diplomacy: An Interdisciplinary Guide to the Treaties of the Six Nations and Their League*. Syracuse, NY: Syracuse University Press, 1995.

Johansen, Bruce E. *Forgotten Founders: Benjamin Franklin, the Iroquois, and the Rationale for the American Revolution*. Ipswich: Gambit Incorporated, 1982.

Johansen, Bruce E. "Native American Societies and the Evolution of Democracy in America, 1600–1800." *Ethnohistory* 37, no. 3 (1990): 279–290.

Johansen, Bruce E. and Barbara Alice Mann, eds. *Encyclopedia of the Haudenosaunee (Iroquois Confederacy)*. Westport: Greenwood Press, 2000.

Jones, David E. *Poison Arrows: North American Indian Hunting and Warfare*. Austin: University of Texas Press, 2007.

Jones, Dorothy V. *License for Empire: Colonialism by Treaty in Early America*. Chicago: University of Chicago Press, 1982.

Jordan, Kurt. "Enacting Gender and Kinship Around a Large Outdoor Fire Pit at the Seneca Iroquois Townley-Read Site." *Historical Archeology* 48, no. 2 (2014): 61–90.

Kagan, Richard L. "Prescott's Paradigm: American Historical Scholarship and the Decline of Spain." *The American Historical Review* 101, no. 2 (April 1992): 423–446.

Kammen, Michael. *Digging Up the Dead: A History of Notable American Reburials*. Chicago: University of Chicago Press, 2010.

Kammen, Michael. *Mystic Chords of Memory: The Transformation of Tradition in American Culture*. New York: Vintage Press, 1993.

Kan, Sergei, ed. *Strangers to Relatives: The Adoption and Naming of Anthropologists in Native North America*. Lincoln, NE: University of Nebraska Press, 2001.

Kelman, Ari. *A Misplaced Massacre: Struggling Over the Memory of Sand Creek*. Cambridge, MA: Harvard University Press, 2013.

Kelman, Ari. "We Are All Americans" Native People in the National Narrative." *Reviews in American History* 42, no. 4 (December 2014): 661–669.

Kelsay, Isabel Thompson. *Joseph Brant 1743–1807, Man of Two Worlds*. Syracuse, NY: Syracuse University Press, 1984.

Kessner, Thomas. *Capitol City: New York City and the Men Behind America's Rise to Economic Dominance, 1860–1900*. New York: Simon and Schuster, 2003.

King, Thomas. *The Inconvenient Indian: A Curious Account of Native People in North America*. Minneapolis: University of Minnesota Press, 2018.

Kirshenblatt-Gimblett, Barbara. *Destination Culture: Tourism, Museums, and Heritage*. Berkeley: University of California Press, 1998.

Klein, Milton M., ed. *The Empire State: A History of New York*. Ithaca, NY: Cornell University Press, 2001.

Kolodny, Annette. *In Search of First Contact: The Viking of Vineland, The Peoples of the Dawnland, and the Anglo-American Anxiety of Discovery*. Durham, NC: Duke University Press, 2012.

Konkle, Maureen. *Writing Indian Nations: Native Intellectuals and the Politics of Historiography, 1827-1863*. Chapel Hill, NC: University of North Carolina Press, 2004.

Krauthamer, Barbara. *Black Slaves, Indian Masters*. Chapel Hill, NC: University of North Carolina Press, 2013.

Kvasnicka, Robert M. and Herman J. Viola, eds. *The Commissioners of Indian Affairs, 1824–1977*. Lincoln, NE: University of Nebraska Press, 1979.

Lahti, Janne. *Cultural Construction of Empire: The U.S. Army in Arizona and New Mexico*. Lincoln, NE: University of Nebraska Press, 2012.

Landsman, Gail H. "The 'Other' as Political Symbol: Images of Indians in the Women Suffrage Movement." *Ethnohistory* 36, no. 3 (Summer 1992): 246–284.

- Landsman and Sara Ciborski, "Representation and Politics: Contesting Histories of the Iroquois," *Cultural Anthropology* 7, no. 4 (November 1992): 425–447.

Lappas, Thomas J. *In League Against King Alcohol: Native American Women and the Women's Christian Temperance Union, 1874–1933*. Norman, OK: University of Oklahoma Press, 2020.

Lepore, Jill. "Historians Who Love Too Much: Reflections on Microhistory and Biography." *The Journal of American History* 88, no. 1 (June 2001): 129–144.

Levine, Lawrence W. "The Folklore of Industrial Society: Popular Culture and Its Audiences." *The American Historical Review* 97, no. 5 (1992): 1369–1399.

Liberty, Margot, ed. *American Indian Intellectuals*. St. Paul: West Publishing Company, 1978.

Lippert, Dorothy. "Building a Bridge to Cross a Thousand Years." *American Indian Quarterly* 30, no. 3/4 (2009): 431–440.

Littlefield, Daniel F. and James W. Parins, eds. *Encyclopedia of American Indian Removal* 2 volumes. Santa Barbara, CA: Greenwood Press, 2011.

Lonetree, Amy and Amanda J. Cobb, eds. *The National Museum of the American Indian: Critical Conversations*. Lincoln, NE: University of Nebraska Press, 2008.

Lyons, Oren. *Exiled in the Land of the Free: Democracy, Indian Nations, and the U.S. Constitution*. Sante Fe, NM: Clear Light Publishers, 1992.

MacLeitch, Gail. *Imperial Entanglements: Iroquois Change and Persistence on the Frontiers of Empire*. Philadelphia: University of Pennsylvania Press, 2011.

Malone, Patrick. *The Skulking Way of War: Technology and Tactics among the New England Indians*. Lanham, MA: Madison Books, 1993.

Mann, Barbara Alice. *Iroquoian Women: The Gantowisas*. New York: Peter Lang, 2000.

Mark, Joan. *Four Anthropologists: An American Science in its Early Years*. New York: Science History Publications, 1980.

Marsh, Dawn. "Penn's Peaceable Kingdom: Shangri-la Revisited." *Ethnohistory* 56, no. 4 (2009): 651–667.

McConnell, Stuart. *Glorious Contentment: The Grand Army of the Republic, 1865–1900*. Boulder, CO: University of Colorado Press, 1999.

McCoy, Alfred W. and Francisco A. Scarano, eds. *Colonial Crucible: Empire in the Making of the Modern American State*. Madison, WI: University of Wisconsin Press, 2009.

McPherson, James M. *Battle Cry of Freedom: The Civil War Era*. New York: Oxford University Press, 1988.

Mercer, Paul and Vicki Weiss. *The New York State Capitol and the Great Fire of 1911*. Mount Pleasant, NY: Arcadia Publishing, 2011.

Merrell, James. *Into the American Woods: Negotiators on the Pennsylvania Frontier*. New York: W.W. Norton and Company, 2000.

Mihesuah, Devon A., ed. *Repatriation Reader: Who Owns American Indian Remains?* Lincoln, NE: University of Nebraska Press, 2000.

Miller, Douglas K. *Indians on the Move: Native American Mobility and Urbanization in the Twentieth Century*. Chapel Hill, NC: University of North Carolina Press, 2019.

Miller, Jay. "The Delaware as Women: A Symbolic Solution." *American Ethnologist* 1, no. 3 (1974): 507–514.

Miner, Craig. *Seeding Civil War: Kansas in the National News, 1854–1858*. Lawrence, KS: University Press of Kansas, 2008.

Morgan, Lewis Henry. *League of the Iroquois*. Edited by William N. Fenton. New York: Citadel Press, 1993.

Moulton, Gary E. "Chief John Ross During the Civil War." *Civil War History* 19, no. 4 (December 1973): 314–333.

Moulton, Gary E. *John Ross: Cherokee Chief*. Athens, GA: University of Georgia Press, 1978.

Mt. Pleasant, Jane. "A New Paradigm for Pre-Columbian Agriculture in North America." *Early American Studies* 13, no. 2 (2015): 374–412.

McDonnell, Michael A. *Masters of Empire: Great Lakes Indians and the Making of America*. New York: Hill and Wang, 2015.

Nelson, Megan Kate. "The Civil War from Apache Pass." *Journal of the Civil War Era* 6, no. 4 (December 2016): 510–535.

Nelson, Megan Kate. *The Three-Cornered War: The Union, the Confederacy, and Native Peoples in the Fight for the West*. New York: Scribners, 2020.

Nichols, David Andrew. *Red Gentlemen and White Savages: Indians, Federalists, and the Search for Order on the American Frontier*. Charlottesville, VA: University of Virginia Press, 2008.

Oakes, James. *Freedom National: The Destruction of Slavery in the United States, 1861–1865*. New York: W.W. Norton and Company, 2013.

Oakes, James. *The Scorpion's Sting: Antislavery and the Coming of the Civil War*. New York: W.W. Norton and Company, 2015.

O'Brien, Jean M. *Firsting and Lasting: Writing Indians out of Existence in New England*. Minneapolis: University of Minnesota Press, 2010.

Onuf, Peter. *Jefferson's Empire: The Language of American Nationhood*. Charlottesville, VA: University of Virginia Press, 2000.

Ortiz, Roxanne Dunbar. *An Indigenous Peoples' History of the United States*. Boston: Beacon Press, 2014.

Otis, D.S., ed. *The Dawes Act and the Allotment of Indian Lands*. Norman, OK: University of Oklahoma Press, 1973.

Parish, Laura. "'Chief Speaker of the Five Nations' in the Downs Collection." *Winterthur Library News* Summer Edition (Summer 2019): 3. http://pressroom.winterthur. org/pdfs/Winterthur-Library-News-2019-Summer.pdf (accessed December 2019).

Parish, Susan Scott. *American Curiosity: Cultures of Natural History in the Colonial British Atlantic World*. Chapel Hill, NC: University of North Carolina Press, 2006.

Parks, Ronald D. *The Darkest Period: The Kanza Indians and Their Last Homestead, 1846–1873*. Norman, OK: University of Oklahoma Press, 2014.

Parmenter, Jon. "After the Mourning Wars: The Iroquois as Allies in Colonial North American Campaigns, 1676-1760." *The William and Mary Quarterly* 64, no. 1 (January 2007): 39–76.

Parmenter, Jon. *The Edge of the Woods: Iroquoia, 1534–1701*. East Lansing, MI: Michigan State University Press, 2010.

Parmenter, Jon. "'L'Arbre de Paix': Eighteenth Century Franco-Iroquois Relations." *French Colonial History* 4 (2003): 63–80.

Parmenter, Jon. "The Meaning of *Kaswentha* and the Two Rows Wampum Belt in Haudenosaunee (Iroquois) History: Can Indigenous Oral Tradition be Reconciled with the Documentary Record?." *Journal of Early American History* 3 (2013): 82–109.

Pasley, Jeffrey L. *The Tyranny of Printers: Newspaper Politics in the Early American Republic*. Charlottesville, VA: University of Virginia Press, 2001.

Paxton, James W. *Joseph Brant and His World: 18th Century Mohawk Warrior and Statesman*. Ontario: James Lorimor & Company, 2008.

Perdue, Theda. "The Legacy of Indian Removal." *Journal of Southern History* 78, no. 1 (2012): 3–36.

Perdue, Theda. *Slavery and the Evolution of Cherokee Society, 1540–1866*. Knoxville, TN: University of Tennessee Press, 1979.

Perdue, Theda, and Michael D. Green. *The Cherokee Nation and the Trail of Tears*. New York: Penguin Books, 2007.

Pewewardy, Cornel D. "Playing Indian at Halftime: The Controversy over American Indian Mascots, Logos, and Nicknames in School-Related Events." *The Clearing House* 77, no. 5 (May-June 2004): 180–185.

Pickering, Robert B., ed. *Peace Medals: Negotiating Power in Early America*. Tulsa: Gilcrease Museum, 2011.

Piker, Joshua. *The Four Deaths of Acorn Whistler*. Cambridge, MA: Harvard University Press, 2013.

Porter, Joy. "Arthur Caswell Parker, 1881-1955: Indian American Museum Professional." *New York History* 81, no. 2 (April 2000): 211–236.

Porter, Joy. *To Be Indian: The Life of Iroquois-Seneca Arthur C. Parker*. Norman, OK: University of Oklahoma Press, 2001.

Prucha, Francis Paul. *American Indian Policy in Crisis: Christian Reformers and the Indian, 1865–1900*. Norman, OK: University of Oklahoma, 1976.

Prucha, Francis Paul. *The Great Father: The United States Government and the American Indians* 2 volumes. Lincoln, NE: University of Nebraska Press, 1984.

Prucha, Francis Paul. *Indian Peace Medals in American History*. Norman, OK: University of Oklahoma Press, 1971.

Raibmon, Paige. *Authentic Indians: Episodes of Encounter from the Late Nineteenth-Century Northwest Coast*. Durham, NC: Duke University Press, 2005.

Remini, Robert. *Andrew Jackson and His Indian Wars*. New York: Viking Press, 2001.

Rice, Brian. *The Rotinonshonni: A Traditional Iroquoian History Through the Eyes of Teharonhia:wako and Sawiskera*. Syracuse, NY: Syracuse University Press, 2013.

Rich, Charlotte J. *Transcending the New Woman: Multiethnic Narratives in the Progressive Era*. Columbia, MO: University of Missouri Press, 2009.

Richardson, Heather Cox. *West From Appomattox: The Reconstruction of America After the Civil War*. New Haven, CT: Yale University Press, 2007.

Richardson, Heather Cox. *Wounded Knee: Party Politics and the Road to an American Massacre*. New York: Basic Books, 2010.

Richter, Daniel. *Before the Revolution: America's Ancient Pasts*. Cambridge, MA: Belknap Press of Harvard University Press, 2011.

Richter, Daniel. *Facing East from Indian Country: A Native History of Early America*. Cambridge, MA: Harvard University Press, 2001.

Richter, Daniel and James Merrell, eds. *Beyond the Covenant Chain: The Iroquois and their Neighbors in Indian North America, 1600–1800*. Syracuse, NY: Syracuse University Press, 1987.

Robie, Harry. "Red Jacket's Reply: Problems in the Verification of A Native American Speech Text." *New York Folklore* 12, no. 3 (Jan 1986): 99–117.

Rogin, Michael Paul. *Fathers and Children: Andrew Jackson and the Subjugation of the American Indian*. New York: Alfred Knopf, 1979.

Ross, Joann M. and John R. Wunder, eds. *The Nebraska-Kansas Act of 1854*. Lincoln, NE: University of Nebraska Press, 2008.

Round, Phillip. *Removeable Type: Histories of the Book in Indian Country*. Chapel Hill, NC: University of North Carolina Press, 2010.

Rydell, Robert W. *All the World's a Fair: Visions of Empire at American International Expositions, 1876–1916*. Chicago: University of Chicago Press, 1984.

Rydell, Robert W. *World Of Fairs: The Century-of-Progress Exhibitions*. Chicago: University of Chicago Press, 1993.

Rydell, Robert W., John E. Findling, and Kimberly D. Pelle. *Fair America: World's Fairs in the United States*. Washington, DC: The Smithsonian Institution Press, 2000.

Sadosky, Leonard J. *Revolutionary Negotiations: Indians, Empires, and Diplomats in the Founding of America*. Charlottesville, VA: University of Virginia Press, 2009.

Sarris, Greg. *Keeping Slug Woman Alive: A Holistic Approach to American Indian Texts*. Berkeley: University of California Press, 1993.

Savage, John. "'Black Magic' and White Terror: Slave Poisoning and Colonial Society in Early 19th Century Martinique." *Journal of Social History* 40, no. 3 (Spring 2007): 635–662.

Saunt, Claudio. "Mapping Early American Historiography." *The William and Mary Quarterly* 65, no. 4 (October 2008): 745–778.

Saunt, Claudio. *Unworthy Republic: The Dispossession of Native Americans and the Road to Indian Territory*. New York: Norton and Company, 2020.

Sayre, Gordon M. "The Mound Builders and the Imagination of American Antiquity in Jefferson, Bartram, and Chateaubriand." *Early American Literature* 33, no. 3 (1998): 225–249.

Scheckel, Susan. *The Insistence of the Indian: Race and Nationalism in Nineteenth-Century Culture*. Princeton, NJ: Princeton University Press, 1998.

Seeyle, John. "'Rational Exultation': The Erie Canal Celebration." *Proceedings of the American Antiquarian Society* 94, no. 2 (January 1985): 241–267.

SenGupta, Gunja. *For God and Mammon: Evangelicals and Entrepreneurs, Masters and Slaves in Territorial Kansas, 1854–1860*. Athens, GA: University of Georgia Press, 1996.

Sheehan-Dean, Aaron. "The Long Civil War." *Virginia Magazine of History & Biography* 119, no. 2 (2011): 106–153.

Shell, Marc. *Wampum and the Origins of American Money*. Champaign-Urbana, IL: University of Illinois Press, 2013.

Shoemaker, Nancy. "The Rise and Fall of Iroquois Women." *Journal of Women's History* 2 (Winter 1991): 39–57.

Silver, Peter. *Our Savage Neighbors: How Indian War Shaped Early America*. New York: W.W. Norton and Company, 2009.

Simpson, Audra. *Mohawk Interruptus: Political Life Across the Borders of Settler States*. Durham, NC: Duke University Press, 2014.

Sleeper-Smith, Susan. *Contesting Knowledge: Museums and Indigenous Perspectives*. Lincoln, NE: University of Nebraska Press, 2009.

Slotkin, Richard. *Regeneration Through Violence: The Mythology of the American Frontier, 1600–1860*. Hanover, CT: Wesleyan University Press, 1973.

Smith-Rosenberg, Caroll. *Disorderly Conduct: Visions of Gender in Victorian America*. New York: Oxford University Press, 1986.

Smith, Sherry L. *Hippies, Indians, and the Fight for Red Power*. New York: Oxford University Press, 2012.

Spanagel, David I. *Dewitt Clinton and Amos Eaton: Geology and Power in Early New York*. Baltimore: Johns Hopkins University Press, 2014.

Spence, Mark David. *Dispossessing the Wilderness: Indian Removal and the Making of the National Parks*. New York: Oxford University Press, 1999.

Spurgeon, Sara L. *Exploding the Western: Myths of Empire on the Postmodern Frontier*. College Station, TX: Texas A&M University Press, 2005.

Stanley, Harrold. *Border War: Fighting over Slavery before the Civil War*. Chapel Hill, NC: University of North Carolina Press, 2010.

Steele, Ian K. *Setting all the Captives Free: Capture, Adjustment, and Recollection in Allegheny Country*. Quebec: McGill-Queens University Press, 2013.

Steele, Ian K. *Warpaths: Invasions of North America*. New York: Oxford University Press, 1995.

Steward, Dick. *Duels and the Roots of Violence in Missouri*. Columbia, MO: University of Missouri Press, 2000.

Sturtevant, William C. "Patagonian Giants and Baroness Hyde de Neuville's Iroquois Drawings." *Ethnohistory* 27, no. 4 (Autumn, 1980): 331–348.

Sugden, John. "Early Pan-Indianism: Tecumseh's Tour of the Indian Country, 1811–1812." *American Indian Quarterly* 10, no. 4 (1986): 273–304.

Sugden, John. *Tecumseh: A Life*. New York: Holt Publishers, 1999.

Tarbell, Reaghan. *Little Caughnawaga: To Brooklyn and Back*. DVD. National Film Board of Canada. 2015.

Taylor, Alan. *American Revolutions: A Continental History, 1750–1804*. New York: W.W. Norton and Company, 2016.

Taylor, Alan. "The 'Art of Hook and Snivey':Political Culture in Upstate New York During the 1790s." *Journal of American History* 80 (March 1993): 1371–1396.

Taylor, Alan. *The Divided Ground: Indians, Settlers, and the Northern Borderland of the American Revolution*. New York: Alfred A., Knopf, 2006.

Thomas, David W. "The Anxious Atlantic: War, Murder, and a "Monster of a Man" in Revolutionary New England." PhD diss., Temple University, 2018.

Thomas, W. Stephen. "Arthur Caswell Parker: 1881–1955: Anthropologist, Historian, and Museum Pioneer." *Rochester History* 17, no. 3 (July 1955): 1–20.

Thomas, W. Stephen. "Arthur Caswell Parker: Leader and Prophet of the Museum World." *Museum Service* 28, no. 2 (February 1955): 18–28.

Thomas, W. Stephen. "Arthur C. Parker: Master of Hobbies." *Museum Service* 32, no. 8 (October 1959): 134–135.

Tillotson, Lee S. *Anti-Masonry and the Murder of Morgan: Lee S. Tillotson's Ancient Craft Masonry in Vermont*. Edited by Guillermo De Los Reyes. Washington, DC: Westphalia Press, 2013.

Tiro, Karim. *The People of Standing Stone: The Oneida Nation from the Revolution through the Era of Removal*. Amherst, MA: University of Massachusetts Press, 2011.

Tooker, Elizabeth. *Lewis H. Morgan on Iroquois Material Culture*. Tucson: University of Arizona Press, 1994.

Tooker, Elizabeth. "Rejoinder to Johansen." *Ethnohistory* 37, no. 3 (1990): 291–297.

Tooker, Elizabeth. "The United States Constitution and the Iroquois League." *Ethnohistory* 35, no. 4 (1988): 305–336.

Townsend, Camilla. *Fifth Sun: A New History of the Aztecs*. New York: Oxford University Press, 2019.

Townsend, Camilla. *Malintzin's Choices: An Indian Woman in the Conquest of Mexico*. Albuquerque: University of New Mexico Press, 2006.

Townsend, Camilla. *Pocahontas and the Powhattan Dilemma*. New York: Hill and Wang, 2004.

Trachtenberg, Alan. *Shades of Hiawatha: Staging Indians, Making Americans, 1880–1930*. New York: Hill and Wang, 2005.

Trautmann, Thomas R. *Lewis Henry Morgan and the Invention of Kinship*. Lincoln, NE: University of Nebraska Press, 2008.

Truer, Anton. *The Assassination of Hole in the Day*. St. Paul: Borealis Books, 2011.

Tuhiwai Smith, Linda. *Decolonizing Methodologies: Research and Indigenous Peoples*, 2nd ed. London: Zed Books, 2012.

Upton, Helen M. *The Everett Report in Historical Perspective: The Indians of New York*. Albany, NY: New York State American Revolution Bicentennial Commission, 1980.

Utley, Robert M. *The Indian Frontier of the American West, 1846-1890*. Albuquerque: New Mexico University Press, 1984.

Varon, Elizabeth R. *Appomattox: Victory, Defeat, and Freedom at the End of the Civil War*. New York: Oxford University Press, 2014.

Viola, Herman. *Diplomats in Buckskins: A History of Indian Delegations in Washington City*. Washington, DC: Smithsonian Institution Press, 1981.

Waite, Kevin. "Jefferson Davis and Proslavery Visions of Empire in the Far West." *Journal of the Civil War Era* 6, no. 4 (December 2016): 536–565.

Waldstreicher, David. *In the Midst of Perpetual Fetes: The Making of American Nationalism, 1776–1820*. Chapel Hill, NC: University of North Carolina Press, 1997.

Wallace, Anthony F. C. *The Death and Rebirth of the Seneca*. New York: Alfred A. Knopf, 1970.

Wallace, Anthony F. C. *Jefferson and the Indians: The Tragic Fate of the First Americans*. New York: Belknap Press, 2001.

Wallace, Anthony F. C. *The Long, Bitter Trail: Andrew Jackson and the Indians*. New York: Hill and Wang, 1993.

Wallace, Anthony F. C. *Tuscarora: A History*. Albany, NY: State University of New York Press, 2012.

Ward, Matthew C. *Breaking the Backcountry: The Seven Years' War in Virginia and Pennsylvania, 1754–1765*. Pittsburgh: University of Pittsburgh Press, 2004.

Warren, Louis S. *Buffalo Bill's America: William Cody and the Wild West Show.* New York: Vintage Books, 2005.

Washburn, Wilcomb E. *The Assault on Indian Tribalism: The General Allotment Law (Dawes Act) of 1887.* Edited by Harold M. Hyman. Malabar: Krieger Publishing Company, 1986.

West, Elliot. *The Last Indian War: The Nez Perce Story.* New York: Oxford University Press, 2009.

White, Richard. *The Republic for Which It Stands: The United States during Reconstruction and the Gilded Age, 1865-1896.* New York: Oxford University Press, 2017.

Willard, Shirley and Susan Campbell, eds. *Potawatomi Trail of Death: 1838 Removal from Indiana to Kansas.* Rochester, IN: Fulton County Historical Society, 2003.

Williams, Glenn F. *Dunmore's War: The Last Conflict of the American Colonial Era.* Chicago: Westholme Publishing, 2017.

Williams, Jack K. *Dueling in the Old South: Vignettes of Social History.* College Station, TX: Texas A & M University Press, 1980.

Wilson, Angela Cavender. *For Indigenous Eyes Only: A Decolonization Handbook.* Santa Fe, NM: School of American Research Press, 2005.

Wilson, Angela Cavender. *Remember This!: Dakota Decolonization and the Eli Taylor Narratives.* Lincoln, NE: University of Nebraska Press, 2005.

Winkle, Kenneth. *Lincoln's Citadel: The Civil War in Washington, D.C.* New York: W.W. Norton and Company, 2014.

Winters, John C. "'The Great White Mother': Harriet Maxwell Converse, the Indian Colony of New York City, and the Media, 1885–1903." *The Journal of the Gilded Age and Progressive Era* 21, no.4 (2022): 279–300.

White, Shane. "'It Was A Proud Day': African Americans, Festivals, and Parades in the North, 1741–1834." *The Journal of American History* 81, no. 1 (June 1994): 13–50.

Yokota, Kariann Akemi. *Unbecoming British: How Revolutionary America Became a Postcolonial Nation.* New York: Oxford University Press, 2011.

Zeller, Terry. "Arthur C. Parker: A Pioneer in American Museums." *Curator: The Museum Journal* 30, no. 1 (1987): 41–62.

Zeller, Terry. "Arthur Parker and the Educational Mission of American Museums." *Curator: The Museum Journal* 32, no. 2 (1989): 104–122.

MUSEUMS

Albany Institute of History and Art. Albany, New York.

Forest Lawn Cemetery. Buffalo, New York.

Iroquois Museum. Howes Cave, New York.

Jake Thomas Learning Centre. Six Nations of the Grand River. Wilsonville, Ontario, Canada

Galena and U. S. Grant Museum. Galena, Illinois.

The New-York Historical Society. New York, New York.

New York State Museum. Albany, New York.

Shako:wi Cultural Center. Oneida Indian Nation. Oneida, New York.

Rochester Museum of Arts and Sciences. Rochester, New York.

Seneca-Iroquois National Museum and Onöhsagwë:De' Cultural Center. Allegany Territory. Salamanca, New York.

The University of Virginia Art Museum. Charlottesville, Virginia.

Index

For the benefit of digital users, indexed terms that span two pages (e.g., 52–53) may, on occasion, appear on only one of those pages.

Figures are indicated by *f* following the page numbers.